KT-388-253

A GUIDE TO EEC LAW
in
NORTHERN IRELAND

The Servicing The Legal System Programme

The Programme was inaugurated in August 1980 in the Faculty of Law of the Queen's University, Belfast, to promote the dissemination of information about the law and legal system of Northern Ireland. Generous financial and other support for the Programme has been provided by the Northern Ireland Court Service, the Inn of Court of Northern Ireland, the Bar Council of Northern Ireland, the Law Society of Northern Ireland, the Northern Ireland Bankers' Association, the Nuffield Foundation and the Queen's University. Details of other SLS publications may be obtained from SLS Legal Publications (NI), Faculty of Law, Queen's University, Belfast BT7 1NN.

A GUIDE TO EEC LAW in NORTHERN IRELAND

by

Sylvia E. Paisley LLB
(Lecturer in Law, The Queen's University of Belfast)

SLS Legal Publications (NI)
Faculty of Law
Queen's University, Belfast
1986

First published in 1986 by SLS Legal Publications (NI), Faculty of Law, Queen's University, Belfast BT7 1NN.

ISBN 0 85389 262 8

Printed in Northern Ireland for SLS

by

W. & S. Magowan Ltd.

CONTENTS

PAGE

Preface x
Table of United Kingdom Legislation xi
Table of Northern Ireland Legislation xi
Table of Community Treaties xii
Table of European Convention on Human Rights xiv
Table of Rules and Protocol of the European Court of Justice xiv
Table of Commission Regulations, Notices and Communications xiv
Table of Measures of the Council of Ministers xv
Table of Cases xvii
Table of Abbreviations xxii

SCOPE AND PURPOSE OF THIS GUIDE 1

CHAPTER 1

HISTORICAL DEVELOPMENT OF THE EUROPEAN COMMUNITIES 2

CHAPTER 2

WHAT IS THE EUROPEAN ECONOMIC COMMUNITY ABOUT? 8

CHAPTER 3

INSTITUTIONS OF THE EEC 11

1. Council of Ministers 12
2. The Commission 15
3. The European Parliament 19
4. The European Court of Justice 25
5. Other Advisory Bodies 29

CHAPTER 4

PAGE

THE SOURCES OF COMMUNITY LAW AND HOW TO FIND THEM 32

1. Treaties 32
2. Measures Taken by the Community Institutions 33
3. Decisions of the European Court of Justice 41
4. General Principles of Law 42

CHAPTER 5

NATURE OF COMMUNITY LAW 44

1. Autonomy 44
2. Supremacy 45
3. Direct Applicability and Direct Effect 46
4. General Application in All Member States 50

CHAPTER 6

RELATIONSHIP BETWEEN COMMUNITY LAW AND UK DOMESTIC LEGISLATION 52

1. Direct Application of Community Law 53
2. Implementation of Community Obligations 54
3. Supremacy of Community Law 55
4. Decisions on, and Proof of, Community Law 57
5. Charge on the Consolidated Fund 58

CHAPTER 7

REFERENCES FOR PRELIMINARY RULINGS FROM THE EUROPEAN COURT OF JUSTICE 60

1. Questions Which May be Referred 63
2. Courts and Tribunals That May Make References 64
3. When to Make a Reference 65
4. Duty or Discretion to Make a Reference 67
5. Procedures For Making References 70
6. Effect of Preliminary Rulings 71

PAGE

CHAPTER 8

PROCEEDINGS AGAINST COMMUNITY INSTITUTIONS 74

A—Legality of Community Action 75
1. Appeal Against Fines 75
2. Action For Annulment 75
3. Action For Inactivity 80
4. The Plea of Illegality 82

B—Liability of the Community 83
1. Contractual Liability of the EEC 84
2. Non-Contractual Liability of the EEC 85

CHAPTER 9

FREE MOVEMENT OF GOODS WITHIN THE EEC 90

Problems Involving the Free Movement of Goods 90
The Main Provisions on the Free Movement of Goods 91
Internal Taxation 100

CHAPTER 10

FREE MOVEMENT OF CAPITAL AND PAYMENTS WITHIN THE EEC 101

The Main Provisions on the Free Movement of Capital 101
The Main Provisions on the Free Movement of Payments 104

CHAPTER 11

FREEDOM OF MOVEMENT FOR WORKERS WITHIN THE EEC 106

Problems Involving Freedom of Movement of Workers 107
The Main Provisions on the Free Movement of Workers 108
Entry and Residence in Another Member State 110
Equality of Treatment For Migrant Community Workers 113
Residence After Retirement or Incapacity to Work 116
Limitations on the Free Movement of Workers 117

CHAPTER 12 PAGE

FREE MOVEMENT OF SELF-EMPLOYED PERSONS WITHIN THE EEC 122

Problems Involving Freedom of Movement of Self-employed Persons 122
The Main Provisions Concerning Free Movement of Self-employed Persons 123
The Right of Establishment of Self-employed Persons 124
Freedom of Self-employed Persons to Provide Services 128
Provisions Common to Both the Right of Establishment and the Freedom to Provide Services 131
Companies 137

CHAPTER 13

SOCIAL SECURITY FOR PERSONS MOVING WITHIN THE EUROPEAN COMMUNITY 140

Problems Involving the EEC Provisions on Social Security 140
The Main EEC Provisions on Social Security 141
Problems Concerning EEC Social Security Legislation 145

CHAPTER 14

THE INFLUENCE OF EUROPEAN COMMUNITY LAW UPON THE UNITED KINGDOM'S CRIMINAL PROCESS 151

1. EEC Law as a Complete Defence to a Criminal Charge 152
2. EEC Law as a Mitigating Factor in Sentencing 154
3. EEC Law as a Source of New Criminal Offences 157

CHAPTER 15

THE EEC COMPETITION RULES: PROHIBITION OF RESTRICTIVE TRADE PRACTICES 159

Problems Involving the EEC Competition Rules 160
The Main EEC Competition Rules 161
Restrictive Trade Practices 162
Consequences of Infringing Article 85(1) 167

CHAPTER 16 PAGE

THE EEC COMPETITION RULES: PROHIBITION OF ABUSES BY DOMINANT UNDERTAKINGS 177

Consequences of Infringing Article 86 186
EEC Commission's Powers in Competition Cases 187

CHAPTER 17

AGRICULTURE 189

Problems Involving the Common Agricultural Policy 189
Main EEC Rules on Agriculture 191

CHAPTER 18

PROTECTION OF HUMAN RIGHTS BY COMMUNITY LAW 203

APPENDICES

APPENDIX I (Order 114, RSC (NI) 1980) 211
APPENDIX II (Order 23, CCR (NI) 1981) 212
APPENDIX III (Art 85 of EEC Treaty) 213
APPENDIX IV (Art 86 of EEC Treaty) 213
APPENDIX V (Council Regulation 17/62) 214
APPENDIX VI (Exclusive Distribution Regulations 1983/83) 223
APPENDIX VII (Exclusive Purchasing Regulations 1984/83) 228

BIBLIOGRAPHY 237

INDEX 238

PREFACE

"Community law is now part of our law; and, whenever there is any inconsistency, Community law has priority. It is not supplanting [United Kingdom] law. It is part of our law which overrides any other part which is inconsistent with it." *(per* Lord Denning MR, *Macarthy's Ltd* v *Wendy Smith)*

It was with this assessment of the impact of European Community law in the back of my mind that I embarked upon the project of writing a brief and very general Guide about Community law. However, I soon discovered that where the EEC is concerned brevity and generality are not only rare but, worse still, misleading. Therefore, the end product covers a greater number of topics in more detail than was originally intended. Nevertheless, even at the end, it remains an introductory work about Community law for legal practitioners in Northern Ireland and law students alike. Readers are referred throughout the text to more detailed books about Community law in the hope that the Guide will serve both as a siren for practitioners, warning them about those areas where Community law may be relevant, and a springboard for students, assisting them in further research. The case-law and legislation cited in the Guide are correct as of 31st August 1985.

In the preparation of this Guide there are several people to whom I owe a debt of gratitude for without them this book would not have seen the light of day. In particular, I wish to thank my colleague, Herbert Wallace, for his unflagging assistance and constant encouragement throughout the past months. I would also like to express my sincere gratitude to Mrs Anne Brown, Miss Elizabeth McCaffrey and Miss Brigid Hadfield for the time and effort they devoted to checking the proofs of this book. Errors which remain are my own. Thanks are also due to the staff of the SLS office for their patience in deciphering my original manuscript and their speed in typing it. Last, but certainly not least, I must mention my father and Flo, who like certain well-known chocolate bars, kept me going to the end and so it is to them that I dedicate this book.

SYLVIA PAISLEY

November 1985

AUTHOR'S NOTE: Spain and Portugal joined the European Communities on 1 January 1986, bringing the total membership to twelve. Moreover, at the Luxembourg summit meeting of the European Council in December 1985 it was agreed that certain reforms needed to be made to the EEC Treaty. Amendments to the Treaty require the unanimous agreement of all member states. (See *The Times,* 5 December 1985).

TABLE OF UNITED KINGDOM LEGISLATION

Page

Companies Act 1980 138
Companies Act 1981 138
Competition Act 1980 159
Criminal Law Act 1977 55
s 32(3) 55,158
Customs and Consolidation Act 1876
s 42 94
Equal Pay Act 1970 51
European Communities Act 1972 52, 53, 54, 55, 56, 57, 58, 60, 110, 204
s 1 . . . . 53, 58
(2)(d) 53, 58
(3) 53
2 . . . . 53, 58
(1) 54, 55, 56, 59, 113, 142, 158, 161, 177
(2) 54, 55, 59, 130, 158
(3) 59
(4) 55, 56, 57, 59
3 . . . . 53, 59
(1) 57, 59, 72, 162
(2) 57, 59
9(1) 138
Sch 2 . . . . . . 54, 55, 59, 158
(2)(1)(d) 158
European Communities (Definition of Treaties) (Undertaking on Supplementary Finance for the Community) Order 1984 . . . 53

Page

European Communities (Services of Lawyers) Order 1978 (SI 1978 No. 1910) 131
Art 5 131
6 131
9 131
11 131
Immigration Act 1971 120
Misuse of Drugs Act 1971
s 5(2) 154
National Insurance Act 1965
s 49(1) 143
Northern Ireland Constitution 1973
s 13 58
Prevention of Terrorism (Temporary Provisions) Act 1984 156
Radio-Telephonic Transmitters (Control of Manufacture and Importation) Order 1968 . . . . . 96, 153
Restrictive Trade Practices Act 1976 159
Restrictive Trade Practices Act 1977 159
Social Security Act 1975 143
s 85(5) 143
Suckler Cow Premium Regulations 1981 (SI 1981/1700)
Art 6 158
Wireless Telegraphy Act 1967
s 7 . . . . 96, 153

TABLE OF NORTHERN IRELAND LEGISLATION

Page

Companies (Northern Ireland) Order 1981 138
Companies (Northern Ireland) Order 1982 138
County Court Rules (Northern Ireland) 1981 (SR 1981 No. 225)
Order 23 . . . . . 70, Appendix II
Employment Miscellaneous Provisions (Northern Ireland) Order 1981 110
Fines and Penalties (Northern Ireland) Order 1984
Art 4(6)(a) 55, 158
8 . . . . 55, 158
17 . . . . 55, 158
Homosexual Offences (Northern Ireland) Order 1982 204

Page

Movement of Pigs Regulations (Northern Ireland) 1972 . . . 50, 51, 152, 190
Passenger and Goods Vehicles (Recording Equipment) Regulations (Northern Ireland) 1979 . 47, 152, 190
Rules of Supreme Court (Northern Ireland) 1980 Order 114 . 70, Appendix I
Safeguarding of Employment Act (NI) 1947 110
Supplementary Benefit (Resources) Regulations (Northern Ireland) 1984 146

TABLE OF COMMUNITY TREATIES

Page

Budgetary Treaty 1970 32
Budgetary Treaty 1975 32
Convention on Certain Institutions Common to the European Communities 1957 . . . . 11, 32
Convention on the Mutual Recognition of Companies and Legal Persons 1968 138
Merger Treaty 1965 . . . 11, 12, 15, 16, 19, 28, 32
Art 4 15
10 16
13 28
16 16
Treaty Amending the Treaties Establishing the European Communities 1985 33
Treaty of Accession 1972 . 7, 12, 15, 19, 25, 32, 63
Treaty of Accession 1979 . 12, 15, 19, 25 32, 63
Treaty of Accession (Third) . . . 33
Treaty of Paris (ECSC Treaty) 1951 1, 4, 11, 32
Art 4 5
Treaty of Rome (Euratom Treaty) 1957 . . . . 1, 11, 32

Treaty of Rome (EEC Treaty) 1957
Art 2 8
3 . . . . 89, 191
3(d) 9
3(f) 9, 161, 185
5 46
(2) 45
7 . . . . 38, 48, 205
9 . . . . 91, 92, 93
10 92
12 . . . . 47, 48, 49, 92, 93
13 48
14 38
16 48
17 93
29 92
30 . . . . 94, 95, 97, 99, 104, 152, 153, 191, 199
31 48
32 48
33 48

Page

Treaty of Rome (EEC Treaty) 1957—*contd.*
34 . . . . 48, 94, 95, 99, 152, 191, 199
36 . . . 94, 95, 96, 97, 98, 99, 104, 153, 154, 159
37 91
38 191
(1) 191, 192
(3) 192
39 196
(1) 192, 196
(a)—(e) 192, 193
40 198
(1) 196
(3) 87, 196
43 . . . . 22, 38, 78
(2) 37
47 191
48 . . 48, 108, 109, 110, 111, 112, 113, 117, 119, 136, 144, 154, 205
(1) 108
(2) 108, 113
(3) 108, 112, 118, 135, 149, 154, 156, 157, 159
(a)—(d) . . 108, 110, 116
(4) 117, 118
51 . . 134, 140, 141, 142, 144
52 . . 124, 125, 126, 137, 205
(2) 123
54 38
(1) 124
(3)(g) 138
55 . . . . 130, 136
56 . . . . 135, 136, 154, 159
(1) 135
57 . . . . . . 124, 130, 133
(1) 125
58 . . . . . . 130, 137, 138
59 . . . . . . 124, 128, 129
60 . . . . 128, 129
63 38
66 . . . . 128, 130, 135, 136, 137, 154, 159
67 . . . . 101, 102
(1) 101, 102
69 . . . . 101, 102
73 101
75 38

Page

Treaty of Rome (EEC Treaty) 1957—*contd.*

Art 84(2) 13
85 . . . 48, 161, 162 166, 167, 170, 174, 177, 182, 186, 187, Appendix III
(1) . 48, 161, 162, 163, 164, 165, 166, 167, 169, 170, 171, 172, 173, 174, 182, 188
(a—e) 162, 166
(2) . . 48, 161, 169, 170, 171
(3) . . . 169, 171, 172, 173, 174, 176, 178, 184
86 . . 48, 161, 162, 167, 174, 177, 178, 179, 180, 181, 182, 183, 184, 185, 186, 187, Appendix IV
(a)—(d) 181-182, 184
87 38
89 167
90 . . . . 161, 163
91 161
92 161
94 161
95 . . . . 66, 100
100 . . . . 38, 96
106 . . . . 104, 105
(1) 104
119 . . . . 51, 205
126 38
127 38
136 13
137 . . . . 19, 22
138 19
(1) 20
144 . . . . 19, 24
145 . . . . 12, 13
148(1) 13
(2) 14
149 13
(2) 39
155 . . . . 15, 17, 18
164 . . . . 25, 27
166 26
167 25
169 . . . . . 17, 28, 34, 81, 99, 157
170 . . . . 17, 28
172 . . . . . . 75, 170, 186
173 . . . . 28, 37, 40, 63, 64, 72, 75, 76, 77, 78, 79,

Page

Treaty of Rome (EEC Treaty) 1957—*contd.*

Art 80, 82, 83, 85, 206
(1) 75, 76, 78, 82
(3) 76, 78, 82
174 79
(2) 79
175 . . . . 28, 40, 64, 75, 79, 80, 81, 82
(1) 80
(2) 81
(3) 80, 81
176 . . . . 79, 82
177 . . . 27, 28, 45, 49, 51, 57, 61, 62, 63, 64, 65, 66, 67, 68, 69, 70, 71, 72, 74, 86, 87, 93, 94. 109, 111, 119, 120, 121, 125, 126, 129, 133, 143, 144, 147, 152, 154, 155, 157, 190, 198, 200, 205, 209
(1) 61, 63
(a) 61, 63
(b) 61, 63
(c) 61, 63
(2) 65, 67
(3) 68, 69, 70
178 . . . . 85, 86
179 . . . . 28, 84
184 . . . . . 28, 75, 82, 83
188 25
189 . . . . 33, 35, 47, 49, 77, 79, 99, 125, 167, 190
190 . . . . 36, 37
191 39
193 30
201 38
203 . . . . 23, 38
(a) 38
205 23
210 208
215 . . . . 29, 83
(1) 84
(2) . . . 79, 85, 86, 87, 88
228 13
235 . . . . 36, 37, 38
236 38
238 38
Annex II 191, 196

TABLE OF EUROPEAN CONVENTION ON HUMAN RIGHTS

	Page
European Convention on Human Rights	3-4, 203, 204, 206, 207, 208, 209
Art 8	168, 207
9	207
11	206
53	204
Protocol, First	
1	207, 209

TABLE OF RULES AND PROTOCOL OF THE EUROPEAN COURT OF JUSTICE

	Page
Rules of Procedure	71
Art 72	71
Art 104	71
Protocol on the Statute of ECJ (of the EEC)	
Art 43	85-86
Art 41	26

TABLE OF COMMISSION REGULATIONS, NOTICES AND COMMUNICATIONS

	Page
Regulations	
67/67 (OJ Sp Ed, 1967, 10)	175
1251/70 (OJ Sp Ed, 1970 (II) 402)	107, 112, 116, 117, 134
Art 2(1)(a)	117
(1)(b)	117
3(1)	117
(2)	117
2779/72 (OJ 1972 L 292/23)	175
1983/83 (OJ 1983 L 173/1)	175, Appendix VI
1984/83 (OJ 1983 L 173/5)	175, Appendix VII
2349/84 (OJ 1984 L 219/15)	175
123/85 (OJ 1985 L 15/16)	175
417/85 (OJ 1985 L 53/5)	175
418/85 (OJ 1985 L 53/1)	175
2526/85 (OJ 1985 L 240/1)	176
Notices	
(JO 1962, 2921/62)	164
(JO 1970, C/84/1)	166, 167
(OJ 1977, C 313/3)	167
[1980] 2 CMLR 369	174, 188
(OJ 1983, C 355/7)	175
[1984] 1 CMLR 38	176
[1984] 1 CMLR 128	176
17/03 (OJ 1985, C 17/3)	175
Communication	
(OJ 1980 C 256/2); [1981] 1 CMLR 177	99
Memorandum	
Accession to ECHR	208

TABLE OF MEASURES OF THE COUNCIL OF MINISTERS

Page

Act Concerning the election of the Representatives of the Assembly by Direct Universal Suffrage . . 19
General Programme on Right of Establishment (OJ Sp Ed, 1960 II, 7) 124, 125
General Programme on Freedom to Provide Services (OJ Sp Ed, 1960) 128, 129

Regulations

Regulation 3/58 (JO 1958, 561) . . 141
Regulation 4/58 (JO 1958, 597) . . 141
Regulation 7a/59 (JO 1961, 71) . 192, 196
Regulation 17/62 (OJ Sp Ed, 1959-62, 87) . . . . 75, 168, 169, 174, 187, Appendix V
Art 2 167
3(1) 174, 187, 188
4 172
4(2) 172
7 . . . . 172, 174
8(1) 173
8(3) 173
9(1) 171
14 . . . . 168, 169
15 178
(1)(a) 167
(2) 170, 186
(5) 172
(6) 172
16 170
17 . . . . 75, 170
Regulation 950/68 (OJ Sp Ed, 1968 (1), 275) 93
Regulation 1612/68 (OJ Sp Ed, 1968 (II), 475) 113, 116
Art 1 109
3(1) 113
7(1) 114
(2) 107, 114, 147, 148
(3) 114, 115
8 107
9 . . . . 107, 115
(1) and (2) 115
10 116
(1) 110
11 116
12 116

Regulations—*contd.* Page

Regulation 1463/70 (OJ Sp Ed, 1970, 482) 47, 151, 157
Art 21 . . . . 47, 49
(1) 157, 158
Regulation 1408/71 (OJ Sp Ed, 1971,416) 141, 142, 143, 144, 145, 146, 147, 148
Art 1(f) 145
2 144
4 148
(1) 146
(2) 146
(4) 146
5 147
22(1) 144
67 . . . . 141, 148
(1) 148
(2) 149
(3) 149
69 . . . . 141, 149
(1) 149
(2) 149
71 148
Regulation 574/72 (OJ Sp Ed, 1972 (1), 160) 141, 142, 145
Regulation 2988/74 (OJ 1974 L 319/1)
Art 1 170
2 170
Regulation 2759/75 (OJ 1975) L 282/1) 152, 190, 191, 199
Regulation 1357/80 (OJ 1980 L 140/1) 158
Regulation 1056/81 (OJ 1981 L 142/6) 158
Regulation 1390/81 (OJ 1981 L 143/1) 134, 145, 148
Art 2(c) 145
Regulation 3795/81 (OJ 1981 L 378/1) 145

Decisions

Decision 70/234 (JO 1970 L 94) "own resources" 32
Decision 76/787 (OJ 1976 L 278/1) direct elections to E. Parliament 32

Directives

Directive 921/60 (OJ Sp Ed, 1959/62, 49) 102

Page

Directives—*contd.*

Directive 62/63 (OJ Sp Ed, 1963/64, 5) 102
Directive 64/221 (OJ Sp Ed, 1963-64, 117) 118, 135, 154
Art 3(1) 118, 119
(2) 119, 154
9 . . . . 120, 121, 155
Annex 121
Directive 64/427 (OJ Sp Ed, 1963-63, 155) 126
Directive 68/151 (OJ 1968 L 65/8) 138
Directive 68/360 (OJ Sp Ed, 1968 (II), 485) 110, 112, 132
Art 1 109
4 111
6(2) 111
6(3) 113
7(2) 112
8 113
10 112
Directive 73/148 (OJ 1973 L 172/14) 132
Art 1 132
(a)—(d) 132
4 133
(1) 132, 133
Directive 75/34 (OJ 1975 L 14/10) 134

Page

Directives—*contd.*

Directive 76/207 (OJ 1976 L 39/40) 36, 49
Art 1(2) 36
Directive 77/91 (OJ 1977 L 26/1) . . 138
Directive 77/452 (OJ 1977 L 176/1) . 127
Directive 78/1026 (OJ 1978 L 362/1) . 127
Directive 77/249 (OJ 1977 L 78/17) 127, 130, 131
Art 1 131
3 131
4(1) 131
5 131
Directive 78/660 (OJ 1978 L, 222/11) 138
Directive 78/855 (OJ 1978 L 295/36) 138
Directive 79/7 (OJ 1979 L 6/24) . . 36, 40
Directive 82/891 (OJ 1982 L 378/47) 138
Directive 83/349 (OJ 1983 L 193/1) 139
Directive 84/253 (OJ 1984 L 126/20) 139

TABLE OF CASES

Page

Adams *v* Commission, *The Times,* 8 November 1985 . . . . 86, 87, 184
Adoui and Cornuaille *v* Belgian State [1982] ECR 1665, [1982] 3 CMLR 631 . 123, 135, 156
Alfons Lutticke *v* Commission [1966] ECR 19, [1966] CMLR 378 . . . . 81, 82
Ahmad *v* ILEA [1978] 1 All ER 574 204
Amministrazione delle Finanze dello Stato *v* Simmenthal (No. 2) [1978] ECR 629, [1978] 3 CMLR 263 . . . . 45, 56, 57, 91
AM & S Europe Ltd *v* Commission [1983] 1 All ER 705, [1982] ECR 1575, [1982] 2 CMLR 264 168
Amsterdam Bulb BV *v* Produkschap voor Siergewassen [1977] ECR 137, [1977] 2 CMLR 218 . . . . 158, 198, 199
Auer *v* Ministère Public [1985] 1 CMLR 123 123
Beguelin Import Co *v* Import-Export SA [1971] ECR 949, [1972] CMLR 81 . . . 159, 165
Bela-Mühle Josef Bergmann *v* Grows-Farm [1977] ECR 1211, [1979] 2 CMLR 83 . . 156
Bertholet [1966] CMLR 191 48
Beus *v* Hauptzollamt Munchen [1968] ECR 83, [1968] CMLR 131 193
Biason [1974] ECR 999, [1975] 1 CMLR 59 147
Bock *v* Commission [1971] ECR 897, [1972] CMLR 160 77
Boyle *v* An Taoiseach [1981] ECR 735, [1981] 2 CMLR 455 200
Brack *v* Insurance Officer [1976] ECR 1429, [1976] 2 CMLR 592 . . . 65, 122, 143, 144
Brasserie de Haecht *v* Wilkin (No. 2) [1973] ECR 77, [1973] CMLR 287 . . . 42, 171, 174
British Beef Co Ltd *v* Intervention Board for Agricultural Produce [1978] ECR 1347, [1978] 3 CMLR 47 189
Broekmeulen *v* Huisarts Registratie Commissie [1981] ECR 2311, [1982] 1 CMLR 91 64
Bulmer Ltd *v* Bollinger SA [1974] 2 All ER 1226, [1974] 2 CMLR 91, [1974] 3 WLR 202; [1974] Ch 401 . . . . 67, 68
Callemeyn *v* Belgian State [1974] ECR 553 147
Camera Care Ltd *v* Commission [1980] ECR 119, [1980] 1 CMLR 334 . . . . 160, 174, 177, 184, 187
Casati, Criminal Proceedings Against [1981] ECR 2595, [1982] 1 CMLR 365 . . 102, 103, 105, 153
Cassis de Dijon (Rewe-Zentrale AG *v* Bundesmonopolverwaltung fur Branntwein) [1979] ECR 649, [1979] 3 CMLR 494 . . . . 98, 99, 100
CFDT *v* The European Communities [1979] 2 CMLR 229 208
Charmasson *v* Minister for Economic Affairs (for France) [1975] ECR 1383, [1975] 2 CMLR 208 . . . . 190, 202
Chemial Faemaceutici *v* DAF [1981] ECR 1, [1981] 3 CMLR 350 67
CILFIT *v* Italian Minister of Health [1983] 1 CMLR 472 [1982] ECR 3415 . . . 69, 70
Commission *v* The Belgian State (Re: Public Employees) (No 1) [1980] ECR 3881, [1981] 2 CMLR 413 118
Commission *v* The Belgian State (Re: Public Employees) (No 2) [1982] ECR 1845, [1982] 2 CMLR 539 118
Commission *v* Council (Re: Civil Service Salaries) [1973] ECR 575, [1973] CMLR 639 79
Commission *v* Council (Re: ERTA) [1971] ECR 263, [1971] CMLR 335 76
Commission *v* France (Re: Lamb Imports) (No 1) [1979] ECR 2729, [1980] 1 CMLR 418 202
Commission *v* France (Re: Lamb Imports) (No 2) [1981] 3 CMLR 25, [1980] ECR 1319 202
Commission *v* Great Britain and N Ireland (Re: Import Licences for Poultry) [1984] 1 ECR 283 . . . . 95, 97

Page

Commission *v* Italy (Re: Export Tax on Art Treasures) (No 1) [1968] ECR 423, [1969] CMLR 1 . . . . 91, 92,96
Commission *v* Italy (Re: Export Tax on Art Treasures) (No 2) [1972] ECR 527, [1972] CMLR 699 91
Commission *v* Italy (Re: Premium for Slaughtering Cows) [1973] ECR 101, [1973] CMLR 439 194
Commission *v* UK (Re: Equal Pay) [1982] ECR 2601, [1982] 3 CMLR 284 35
Commission *v* UK (Re: Import of Poultry) [1982] ECR 2793, [1982] 3 CMLR 497 . . 95
Commission *v* UK (Re: Tachographs) [1979] ECR 419, [1979] 2 CMLR 45 . . . 34, 157
Commission *v* UK (Re: UHT Milk) [1983] 2 CMLR 1 . . . . 42, 91
Consten and Grundig *v* Commission [1966] ECR 299, [1966] CMLR 418 . . 79, 160, 164, 165, 173
Costa *v* ENEL [1964] ECR 585, [1964] CMLR 425 . . . . 41, 44, 45, 62, 208
Dannenberg *v* Secretary of State for Home Affairs [1984] 2 CMLR 456 155
Defrenne *v* SABENA [1976] ECR 455, [1976] 2 CMLR 98 51
Diatta *v* Land-Berlin *The Times,* 12 March 1985 . . . . 110, 116
Donà *v* Mantero [1976] ECR 1333, [1976] 2 CMLR 578 127
Dudgeon *v* United Kingdom [1982] 4 EHRR 149 . . . . 203, 204
European Parliament *v* Council (Re: Common Transport Policy) *The Times,* 27 May 1985 80
Europemballage Corporation and Continental Can Co *v* Commission [1973] ECR 215, [1973] CMLR 199 . . . . 160, 180, 182, 185
Foglia *v* Novello (No 1) [1980] ECR 745, [1981] 1 CMLR 45 . . . . 66, 67
Foglia *v* Novello (No 2) [1981] ECR 3045, [1982] 1 CMLR 585 . . . . 66, 67
Frilli *v* The Belgian State [1972] ECR 457, [1973] CMLR 386 147
Galli, Criminal Proceedings Against [1975] ECR 47, [1975] 1 CMLR 211 201
Garden Cottage Foods Ltd *v* Milk Marketing Board [1983] 3 CMLR 43, [1983] 2 All ER 770 . . . . 161, 177, 184
Garland *v* British Railway Engineering Ltd [1982] ECR 359, [1982] 1 CMLR 696 51
Geddo *v* Ente Nazionale Risi [1973] ECR 865, [1974] 1 CMLR 13 94
Gema *v* Commission [1979] ECR 3173, [1980] 2 CMLR 177 82
General Motors Continental *v* Commission [1975] ECR 1367, [1976] 1 CMLR 95 160, 184, 186
Grad *v* Finanzamt Traunstein [1970] ECR 825, [1971] CMLR 1 48
Grand Duchy of Luxembourg *v* European Parliament (No 1) [1983] ECR 283, [1983] 2 CMLR 726 . . . . 21, 76
Grand Duchy of Luxembourg *v* European Parliament (No 2) [1984] ECR 1945 . . . 21
Haegeman *v* Commission [1972] ECR 1005, [1973] CMLR 365 86
Haegeman *v* The Belgian State [1974] ECR 449, [1975] 1 CMLR 515 63
Hagan *v* Fratelli D & G Moretti SNC [1980] 3 CMLR 253 68
Hasselblad GB Ltd *v* Commission [1982] ECR 1555, [1984] 1 CMLR 559 188
Hauer *v* Land Rheinland-Pfalz [1979] ECR 3727, [1980] 3 CMLR 42 207
Hauptzollamt Bielefeld *v* König [1974] ECR 607 192
Hauptzollamt Hamburg *v* Bollman (The Turkey Tail case) [1970] ECR 69, [1970] CMLR 141 197
Hessische Knappschaft *v* Maison Singer [1966] CMLR 82 144
Hoeckx *v* Openbarr Centrum voor Maatschappelijk, *The Times,* 11 April 1985 . . 146, 148
Hoekstra (nee Unger) *v* Bestuur [1964] ECR 177 . . . . 107, 144
Hoffmann-La Roche *v* Commission [1979] ECR 461, [1979] 3 CMLR 211 . 42, 160, 184, 186
ICI *v* Commission [1972] ECR 619, [1972] CMLR 557 . . . . 160, 163
International Fruit Co *v* Commission [1971] ECR 411 . . . . 36, 76
Internationale Handelsgesellschaft *v* EVST [1970] ECR 1125, [1972] CMLR 255 (ECJ); [1974] 2 CMLR 540 (Gm Constit Ct.) 42, 60, 156, 205, 206, 207

Page

Inzirillo *v* Caisse d'Allocations Familiales de L'Arrondissement de Lyon [1976] ECR 2057, [1978] 3 CMLR 596 148
Ireks-Arkady GmbH *v* Council and Commission (Quellmehl Case) [1979] ECR 2955 87
Istituto and Commercial Solvents Corp *v* Commission [1974] ECR 223, [1974] 1 CMLR 309 . . . . 160, 178, 182, 186
Johnston *v* Chief Constable of the Royal Ulster Constabulary. NI unreported judgment, 17 May 1982 . . . . 49, 60
Kampffmeyer *v* Commission [1967] ECR 245 . . . . 86, 88
Kenny *v* Insurance Officer [1978] ECR 1489, [1978] 3 CMLR 651 . . . . 141, 143
Knoors *v* Secretary of State for Economic Affairs [1979] ECR 399, [1979] 2 CMLR 357 126
La Technique Minière *v* Maschinenbau Ulm [1966] ECR 235, [1966] CMLR 357 163, 166, 171
Lee *v* Minister of Agriculture [1980] ECR 1495, [1980] 2 CMLR 682 71
Lipton's Cash Registers Ltd *v* Hugin Kassaregister AB and Hugin Cash Registers Ltd [1978] 1 CMLR D 19; [1979] ECR 1869 (ECJ) 179
Lord Bethell *v* Commission [1982] ECR 2277, [1982] 3 CMLR 300 81
Lutticke (Alfons) *v* Commission [1971] ECR 325 85
Macarthy's Ltd *v* Wendy Smith [1979] 3 CMLR 44 (CA); [1980] 2 CMLR 205 (ECJ); [1980] 2 CMLR 217 (CA) 51, 56
MacMahon *v* Department of Education and Science [1982] 3 WLR 1129, [1982] 3 CMLR 91 . . . . 107, 114
McAfee *v* Smyth and Quigley [1981] 1 CMLR 410 . . . . 91, 96, 152, 153
McWhirter *v* Attorney-General [1972] CMLR 882 52
Merkur *v* Commission [1973] ECR 1055 86
Metro *v* Commission [1977] ECR 1875, [1978] 2 CMLR 1 77
Miliangos *v* George Frank Textiles Ltd [1975] 2 CMLR 585, [1975] 3 All ER 801 105
Ministère Public *v* Auer [1979] ECR 437, [1979] 2 CMLR 373 and [1985] 1 CMLR 123 . . . . 123, 127
Morson and Jhanjan *v* The Netherlands [1982] ECR 3723, [1983] 2 CMLR 221 116
Moser *v* Land-Baden Württemberg [1984] 3 CMLR 720 . . . . 109, 156
Moulins et Huileries de Pont-à-Mousson *v* ONIC (Gritz case) [1977] ECR 1795, [1979] 2 CMLR 445 87
National Panasonic (UK) Ltd *v* Commission [1980] ECR 2033, [1980] 3 CMLR 169, [1981] 2 All ER 1 . . . . 168, 207
Nold *v* Commission [1974] ECR 491, [1974] 2 CMLR 338 . . . . 79, 206
Nordsee *v* Nordstern A G [1982] ECR 1095 64
Officier van Justitie *v* Van Haaster [1974] ECR 1123, [1974] 2 CMLR 521 . 190, 197, 198, 199
Paola Piscitello *v* Istituto Nazionalle della Previdenza, [1984] 1 CMLR 108 147
Paris Bar *v* Klopp [1985] 1 CMLR 99 . . . . 125, 127
Pellegrini *v* Commission [1976] ECR 1807, [1977] 2 CMLR 77 84
Pigs Marketing Board (Northern Ireland) *v* Redmond [1978] ECR 2347, [1979] 1 CMLR 177 . . . . 50, 60, 63, 91, 151, 152, 189, 190, 199
Plaumann *v* Commission [1963] ECR 95, [1964] CMLR 29 77
Prais *v* Council [1975] ECR 1589, [1976] 2 CMLR 708 207
Procureur du Roi *v* Dassonville [1974] ECR 837, [1974] 2 CMLR 436 95
Procureur du Roi *v* Royer [1976] ECR 497, [1976] 2 CMLR 619 . . . . 112, 113, 133, 156
Pubblico Ministero *v* Ratti [1979] ECR 1629, [1980] 1 CMLR 96 48
Quellmehl (Ireks Arkady *v* Council and Commission) [1979] ECR 2955 87
R *v* Bouchereau [1977] ECR 1999, [1977] 2 CMLR 800 . . 48, 71, 107, 119, 151, 154, 155
R *v* Deery [1977] NI 164 204
R *v* Goldstein (HL) [1983] 1 All ER 434, [1983] 1 CMLR 244; [1983] 1 WLR 151 153

Page
R *v* Henn & Darby [1978] 3 All ER 1190 (CA); [1979] 2 CMLR 495 (HL); [1979] ECR 3795, [1980] 1 CMLR 246 (ECJ); [1980] 2 CMLR 229 (HL) . 65, 91, 94, 96, 97, 154
R *v* HM Treasury, ex parte Smedley [1985] All ER 589 53
R *v* Inner London Education Authority, ex parte Hinde and ex parte Duverley, (QBD), *The Times,* 19 November 1984 . . . . 107, 115
R *v* Kent Kirk [1984] 3 CMLR 522 . . . . 60, 153
R *v* Knowsley Metropolitan Borough Council, ex parte Phillips, (QBD), *The Times,* 19 November 1984 . . . . 107, 115
R *v* National Insurance Commissioner, ex parte Warry, *The Times,* 26 July 1980 141
R *v* Pieck [1980] ECR 2171, [1980] 3 CMLR 220, [1981] 3 All ER 46 . . . 111, 113, 155
R *v* Saunders [1979] ECR 1129, [1979] 2 CMLR 216 . . . . 107, 109, 156
R *v* Secchi [1975] 1 CMLR 383 111
R *v* Secretary of State for Home Affairs, ex parte Santillo [1980] ECR 1585, [1980] 2 CMLR 308 (ECJ); [1981] 2 All ER 897 (H Ct); [1981] 1 CMLR 569 (CA) . 120, 155
R *v* Thompson, Johnston and Woodiwiss [1978] ECR 2247, [1979] 1 CMLR 47 . 91, 104, 154
Re Agreement of Ford Werke AG [1982] 3 CMLR 267 188
Re Borker [1980] ECR 1975, [1980] 3 CMLR 638 64
Re Christiani and Neilsen NV [1969] CMLR D 36 164
Re ERTA (Commission *v* Council) [1971] ECR 263, [1971] CMLR 335 63
Re Kodak [1970] CMLR D 19 164
Re Omega Watches [1970] CMLR D 49 173
Re Transocean Marine Paint [1967] CMLR D 9 173
Rewe-Zentral AG *v* Bundesmonopolverwaltung fur Branntwein (Cassis de Dijon case) [1979] ECR 649, [1979] 3 CMLR 494 98
Reyners *v* The Belgian State [1974] ECR 631, [1974] 2 CMLR 305 . 123, 125, 126, 129, 136
Rheinmühlen-Düsseldorf *v* EVST (No 1), [1974] ECR 33, [1974] 1 CMLR 523 and (No 2) [1974] ECR 139 . . . . 62, 67
Roquette Frères *v* Council (Isoglucose Case) [1980] ECR 3333 . . . . . . 22, 37, 78
Russo *v* Aima [1976] ECR 45 190
Rutili *v* Minister for the Interior for France [1975] ECR 1219, [1976] 1 CMLR 140 206
Sadam [1976] ECR 323, [1977] 2 CMLR 183 190
Schorsch Meier GmbH *v* Hennin [1975] 1 CMLR 20, [1975] 1 All ER 152; [1975] QB 416 105
Simmenthal *v* Commission [1979] ECR 777, [1980] 1 CMLR 25 83
Şotgiu *v* Deutsche Bundespost [1974] ECR 153 118
SpA International Chemical Corporation *v* Amministrazione delle Finanze dello Stato [1981] ECR 1191 72
Stauder *v* City of Ulm [1969] ECR 419, [1970] CMLR 112 . . . . . . 27, 41, 42, 62, 205
Stork *v* High Authority [1959] ECR 17 27
Surjit Kaur *v* The Lord Advocate [1981] SLT 322, [1980] 3 CMLR 79 204
Tasca [1976] ECR 291, [1977] 2 CMLR 183 190
The Irish Creamery Milk Suppliers' Association *v* Government of Ireland [1981] ECR 735, [1981] 2 CMLR 455 . . . . 190, 200, 201
The Italian State *v* Watson and Belmann [1976] ECR 1185, [1976] 2 CMLR 552 . . . . 124, 133
Toepfer and Getreide Import *v* Commission [1965] ECR 405, [1966] CMLR 111 77
Transocean Marine Paint *v* Commission [1974] ECR 1063, [1974] 2 CMLR 459 42
United Brands Co *v* Commission [1978] ECR 207, [1978] 1 CMLR 429 . 160, 178, 179, 181, 183, 184
Van Binsbergen *v* Bestuur van- de Bedrijfsvereniging voor de Metaalnijverheid [1974] ECR 1299, [1975] 1 CMLR 298 . . . . 123, 129, 130, 131
Van Duyn *v* Home Office [1974] ECR 1337, [1975] 1 CMLR 1 . . 48, 107, 108, 119, 136

Page

Van Gend en Loos *v* Nederlandse Belastingadministratie [1963] ECR 1, [1963] CMLR 105 . . . . 41, 44, 46, 47, 48, 49, 62, 92
Variola *v* Amministrazione Italiana delle Finanze [1973] ECR 981 . . . . 34, 47, 93, 196
Vaassen-Göbbels *v* Beambtenfonds voor het Mijnbedrijf [1966] ECR 261, [1966] CMLR 508 64
Vereeniging van Cementhandelaren *v* Commission (Dutch Cement Dealers Case) [1972] ECR 977, [1973] CMLR 7 . . . . 159, 163, 165
Volk *v* Verwaecke [1969] ECR 295, [1969] CMLR 273 166
Walrave and Koch *v* Association Union Cycliste Internationale [1974] ECR 1405, [1975] 1 CMLR 320 127
Wohrmann and Lütticke GmbH *v* Commission [1962] ECR 501, [1963] CMLR 152 83

ABBREVIATIONS

A–G	Advocate-General
Bull EC	Bulletin of the European Communities
CAP	Common Agricultural Policy
CCBE	Committee of European Bar and Law Societies
CEEC	Committee of European Economic Co-operation
CMLR	Common Market Law Reports
CML Rev	Common Market Law Review
COM	Common Organisation of the Market
COREPER	Committee of Permanent Representatives of the Member States
D-G	Directorate-General of the Commission
DHSS	Department of Health and Social Services
ECHR	European Convention for the Protection of Human Rights and Fundamental Freedoms
ECJ	European Court of Justice
ECLR	European Competition Law Review
ECR	European Court Reports
ECSC	European Coal and Steel Community
ECU	European Currency Unit
EDC	European Documentation Centre
EEC	European Economic Community
EL Rev	European Law Review
EMS	European Monetary System
EMU	European Monetary Union
ESC	Economic and Social Committee
EURATOM	European Atomic Energy Community
FEOGA	European Agricultural Guidance and Guarantee Fund
ICLQ	International and Comparative Legal Quarterly
JO	Journal Officiel (French version of OJ)
LIEI	Legal Issues of European Integration
LQR	Law Quarterly Review
MCA	Monetary Compensatory Amount
MEP	Member of the European Parliament
MLR	Modern Law Review
NATO	North Atlantic Treaty Organisation
OECD	Organisation for European Co-operation and Development
OEEC	Organisation of European Economic Co-operation
OJ	Official Journal of the European Communities

SCOPE AND PURPOSE OF THIS GUIDE

Ever since the United Kingdom joined the European Communities in January 1973, the very mention of European Community law has been enough to strike fear into the hearts of some Northern Ireland lawyers. The fear stems for the most part from ignorance of Community law which in turn has been brought about by the absence of a comprehensive guide geared towards the needs of Northern Ireland's legal practitioners. This is most unfortunate since there are various problems involving EEC law that are peculiar to Northern Ireland when compared to the rest of the United Kingdom because of differences in Northern Ireland domestic legislation and the fact that the Province shares a land frontier with another EEC country, the Republic of Ireland. This Guide is intended to fill the gap by introducing local practitioners to Community law, explaining how it can be relevant to many of the problems with which they have to deal and pointing them towards the material which they should consult. It is not intended to rival the many detailed textbooks on Community law, which are now available.

It is often forgotten that the United Kingdom by acceding to the European Community Treaties in 1973, joined not one, but three Communities, namely:

— the European Coal and Steel Community (ECSC);
— the European Atomic Energy Community (EURATOM); and
— the European Economic Community (the EEC or, as it is better known, "the Common Market").

As their names would suggest the ECSC and EURATOM are highly specialised Communities concerned with coal and steel and with atomic energy, respectively. The EEC, on the other hand, is much more diverse in nature affecting a very wide range of economic and social activities including agriculture, trade, employment, corporate enterprizes, social security, transport, and regional development. Because of its greater importance, it is upon the EEC that this Guide will concentrate and reference to the ECSC and EURATOM will only be made where such references are relevant for the three Communities as a whole.

To understand the nature and effect of EEC law it is necessary to have some knowledge of its origins, and, therefore, the historical development of the Communities will be considered first. This will be followed by an examination of the institutions of the EEC and an analysis of the sources and nature of Community law and how it relates to the domestic law of the United Kingdom. Thereafter the various procedures for judical review by the European Court of Justice will be discussed. Finally various areas of the substantive law of the EEC will be examined in more detail. In this way it is hoped to touch upon all the major areas of EEC law, highlighting the kinds of problems involving Community law that might arise in Northern Ireland and explaining how to set about resolving them.

CHAPTER 1

HISTORICAL DEVELOPMENT OF THE EUROPEAN COMMUNITIES

As explained, the European Communities comprise not just one but three separate Communities: the European Coal and Steel Community, the European Atomic Energy Community and the European Economic Community. Some knowledge of their historical development is necessary for a better appreciation of the aims and activities of these Communities. The year 1945 is taken as the starting point for this purpose since most of the practical steps taken to achieve unity in political, defence and economic matters in Western Europe are post 1945 in origin.

1 CHURCHILL'S SPEECH

After the Second World War, the Allies felt that action had to be taken to prevent another war in Europe; they hoped that by bringing the European countries closer together such an eventuality would be regarded as unthinkable. At this time the eastern part of Europe was being brought under the Soviet sphere of influence and the fear of Soviet expansion into the then divided and war-ravaged Western European countries spurred statesmen to consider ways of rebuilding and unifying Western Europe. In particular Winston Churchill, in a speech at Zurich University on 19 September 1946, called for the creation of "a kind of United States of Europe" and dared to suggest that a partnership between France and Germany should be the first step towards this unity even though these two countries had so recently waged a bitter and bloody war against each other. It was, therefore, the desire for lasting peace in Europe that constituted the principal motivating factor behind the moves for unity. The war had devastated Europe and the harsh winter of 1946-47 only deepened its troubles. By then Europe urgently needed finance to begin to rebuild from the ashes.

2 MARSHALL'S SPEECH

On 5 June 1947 at Harvard University, American statesman, General Marshall, proposed a new experiment in financial aid to help the economic recovery of the countries of Europe. In the so-called "Marshall Plan" he proposed that the European countries should get together and decide on a joint-aid programme which America would finance. Eastern European countries would have nothing to do with this American offer but some sixteen Western European States accepted it. They called a conference where the Committee of European Economic Co-operation (the CEEC) was established to provide America with a list of their needs. This Committee later created the Organisation for European Economic Co-operation (OEEC) in Paris. The OEEC drew up a programme for distribution of the American financial aid and also tried to liberalise trade between its member states. The OEEC operated as an inter-governmental organisation rather than a supra-national body, that is one whose institutions have power to dictate policies to the governments of its member states. The OEEC was in fact transformed in 1961 into the Organisation for Economic Co-operation and Development (OECD) and still operates in Paris.

3 NORTH ATLANTIC TREATY ORGANISATION

As well as this burgeoning economic co-operation, the fear that Germany might rise again to threaten peace in Europe led to military co-operation between several European countries. For instance, in 1947 France and the United Kingdom signed the Dunkirk Treaty, pledging mutual support in time of attack. The following year the Benelux countries—Belgium, Luxembourg and the Netherlands—joined them in signing the Brussels Treaty from which emerged the Brussels Treaty Organisation, again designed to give mutual assistance in time of attack in Europe. It was this Brussels Treaty Organisation that was formally extended in April 1949 to include the United States of America and Canada, thus forming the North Atlantic Treaty Organisation. Many other Western European countries have since joined NATO, with notable exceptions like the Republic of Ireland, Sweden and Switzerland.

4 COUNCIL OF EUROPE

While these military agreements were being made, Churchill's rallying speech of 1946 had encouraged other European statesmen to work together for closer political co-operation. Thus at the Congress of Europe, convened in The Hague in 1948 with Churchill as its President, it was agreed to establish an international organisation called the Council of Europe. The Statute of the Council of Europe, signed in London on 5 May 1949 by ten countries, states that its aim is to bring about greater unity between its members by discussion and by agreements in "economic, social, cultural, scientific, legal and administrative matters and in the maintenance and further realisation of human rights and fundamental freedoms". Under the auspices of the Council of Europe many important treaties, or conventions as they are normally called, have been agreed such as the recent ones on the suppression of terrorism and data protection. Undoubtedly though, the Council of Europe's greatest achievement has been the European

Convention on the Protection of Human Rights and Fundamental Freedoms, which was drafted in 1950 and entered into force in 1953. The United Kingdom participated in its drafting, signed it and later ratified it in 1951. The Convention has now been signed and ratified by all twenty-one members of the Council of Europe, including all of the EEC member states and also countries like Cyprus, Iceland and Liechtenstein. The Convention is enforced by the European Commission of Human Rights and European Court of Human Rights and by the Committee of Ministers, all of which are based in Strasbourg.

One should always be very careful indeed not to confuse the European Convention on Human Rights of 1950 and its enforcement agencies with the EEC, set up some years later in 1957 and its institutions; the Convention and the EEC Treaty are quite distinct. (For further details, see Chapter 18 *post.*)

5 EUROPEAN COAL AND STEEL COMMUNITY

Shortly after the Congress of Europe, in May 1950, Robert Schuman, then French Foreign Minister, declared that a united Europe was essential for world peace and that such unity required an end to the long animosity between France and Germany. It was his plan to make war between the two countries not only "unthinkable but materially impossible". The "Schuman Plan" was to create a common market in coal and steel, the basic materials of a war effort, and to place a supra-national body, a so-called "High Authority", in charge of this market. The Schuman Plan was welcomed by six European states, namely The Federal Republic of Germany, France, Italy and the three Benelux countries. These six states are commonly referred to as "the Original Six". The United Kingdom was invited to join but refused. As Clement Attlee, the British Prime Minister at the time, explained:

> We on this side are not prepared to accept the principle that the most vital economic forces of this country should be handed over to an authority that is utterly undemocratic and is responsible to nobody.[1]

The United Kingdom remained sceptical about any supra-national body which might threaten its sovereignty. However, "The Original Six" persevered and in April 1951 the Treaty of Paris was signed, setting up the European Coal and Steel Community.[2] The importance of the ECSC lies in the fact that it was not merely an inter-governmental body but a supra-national organisation with its own institutions to manage the common market in coal and steel. The ECSC's institutions included a High Authority, a Court of Justice, a Special Council of Ministers and a Common Assembly. The following were regarded as incompatible with the common market for coal and steel and were prohibited by the Treaty of Paris: import

[1] Quoted from Palmer, Lambert, Forsyth, Morris and Wohlgemuth, *European Unity: A Survey of the European Organisations,* (1968) 258.

[2] The ECSC Treaty is set out in Rudden & Wyatt, *Basic Community Laws,* (1980) p 3 *et seq.*

and export duties, or charges having equivalent effect, and quantitative restrictions on the movement of products; measures or practices that discriminated between producers, purchasers or consumers; subsidies or aids granted by government; and restrictive practices that shared or exploited markets (Article 4).

6 EUROPEAN DEFENCE COMMUNITY

At that time, the early 1950s, tension was mounting throughout the world. With the outbreak of the Korean War came America's suggestion that Germany be rearmed. France strongly opposed this suggestion and instead the French Defence Minister, Pleven, put forward a plan for a joint European army to which European states, including Germany, would contribute troops. Again "The Original Six" were enthusiastic about forming this European Defence Community and in fact they signed a treaty in May 1952 to establish the EDC. However, for a variety of reasons, the French Parliament refused to ratify the EDC Treaty and consequently it failed to come into existence.

7 WESTERN EUROPEAN UNION

The failure of the EDC was followed by a British initiative also aimed at achieving the rearmament of Germany in a way acceptable to France. This was done by extending the Brussels Treaty Organisation, formed in 1948, to include Italy and the Federal Republic of Germany and consequently a new organisation, the Western European Union, was established. The response of Eastern Europe was to form the Warsaw Pact. The WEU still functions and, like NATO, works towards Western European integration in defence matters.

8 EEC and EURATOM

By 1955 international tension had eased somewhat with the end of the Korean War and so less emphasis was placed upon closing military ranks in Western Europe and instead more attention was given to further economic integration. The Benelux countries in particular wanted more than the European Coal and Steel Community; they wanted an economic community covering matters like agriculture, trade and industry and also an atomic energy community. In response to their initiative, the Foreign Ministers of "The Original Six" met at Messina in June 1955. There an intergovernmental committee, headed by Paul-Henri Spaak, the Belgian Foreign Minister, was set up to study the feasibility of establishing an economic and an atomic energy community in Europe. When invited to attend the Spaak Committee meetings, the United Kingdom sent a Board of Trade representative but, after only a few months, he was withdrawn. After intensive work by the Spaak Committee, two treaties were signed in Rome on 25 March 1957. Both treaties were duly ratified by the national parliaments of "The Original Six" and thus it was that on 1 January 1958 the European Economic Community and EURATOM came into being.

Various reasons may be put forward to explain the United Kingdom's lukewarm response throughout the 1950s towards economic integration with other European countries through joining the ECSC, EEC and EURATOM. First, the United Kingdom had not been ravaged as much by the Second World War as the continental countries and therefore did not feel the same need to surrender its independence and become instead economically interdependent on other European countries. Secondly, the United Kingdom was always suspicious of any supra-national body which might erode the sovereignty of the country. Thirdly, for a time it still had its colonial Empire to trade with instead of turning to Europe.

9 EUROPEAN FREE TRADE ASSOCIATION

By the late 1950s, however, circumstances had changed. The United Kingdom needed a larger and different trading market for its industrial goods because the colonial markets were closing as colonies gained independence. Rather than join a highly-structured organisation like the EEC, the United Kingdom preferred some kind of loosely-connected European trading group, and so it was upon the United Kingdom's initiative that the European Free Trade Association (EFTA) was formed in 1960. It provided a free-trade area for industrial goods produced by its members. The Association did not encroach upon United Kingdom sovereignty as it was not a supra-national organisation and so at the beginning it suited the United Kingdom admirably. Other countries that joined EFTA included Norway, Denmark, Austria and Sweden.

10 FIRST ACCESSION

Hardly had the ink dried on the agreement setting up EFTA, when Harold MacMillan, then British Prime Minister, announced that the United Kingdom intended to apply for membership of the European Communities. Apparently the United Kingdom Government felt that trade with EFTA countries in industrial goods was insufficient as the United Kingdom needed wider markets for these and for its agricultural produce too. The United Kingdom's first attempt to join in 1961 failed, however, because the French President, de Gaulle, exercised his veto in the Council of Ministers. As unanimity amongst Council members is required for the admission of a new member state to the European Communities, the 1961 application of United Kingdom as well as those of Norway, Denmark and the Republic of Ireland, which had also applied for membership in 1961, could not proceed. A second attempt by these four countries to join in 1967, this time with the United Kingdom under a Labour Government led by Harold Wilson, also failed. Again it was because of the French veto. It was only after de Gaulle resigned in 1968 and was replaced by President Pompidou, that the Council of Ministers finally unanimously agreed that negotiations should begin on the accession of the four applicant states to the Communities. The first Accession Treaty between "The Original Six" and the four new member states was signed in 1972. While the parliaments of the United Kingdom, Denmark and the Republic of Ireland ratified this treaty, that of Norway did not, following an adverse result in a national referendum on that country's proposed membership. Since Norway then withdrew, only the United Kingdom, Denmark and the Republic of Ireland actually acceded to the three European Communities on 1 January 1973. In 1974 the Labour Government "renegotiated" the United Kingdom's terms of membership and in June 1975 a referendum throughout the country confirmed a wish to continue membership of the Communities by a large overall majority of 67.2 per cent. of those voting. In Northern Ireland, however, only 52.1 per cent voted in favour of membership.[3]

11 SECOND ACCESSION

In the same month as the United Kingdom's referendum took place, Greece applied for membership of the European Communities and, after several years of negotiations, became a full member as of 1 January 1981.

12 THIRD ACCESSION

The Communities are expected to be enlarged again by the accession of Portugal and Spain at the beginning of 1986. At the moment the EEC constitutes the largest trading block in the world, has an overall population of more than 270 million and member states of varying sizes, wealth and cultural and political views.

[3] See Irving, "The United Kingdom Referendum June 1975" (1975) *EL Rev* 3.

CHAPTER 2

WHAT IS THE EUROPEAN ECONOMIC COMMUNITY ABOUT?

In the previous chapter it was noted that the EEC was established by the Treaty of Rome in 1957 (hereafter referred to as the EEC Treaty) and that the United Kingdom eventually joined it on 1 January 1973. The questions which must now be asked are what is the EEC really about and how does it affect our daily lives in Northern Ireland? Moreover legal practitioners here should be asking if they need to consider aspects of EEC law when advising their clients. Since the ordinary man or woman on the City Hall omnibus increasingly wants to know his or her legal rights and since no solicitor or barrister wishes to, let alone can afford to, be negligent in giving professional advice, it is of the utmost importance for all lawyers and other law enforcement agencies to be fully aware of the implications of EEC law for the Province.

The best starting point for an understanding of what the EEC is about is to look at Articles 2 and 3 of the EEC Treaty for they outline the main task and activities of the Community. It is worth setting out these two Articles in full because not only do they give a clear idea of the extent of the EEC's activities but they also form a very important aid for the European Court of Justice, the court of the EEC, when interpreting Community law.

According to Article 2 of the EEC Treaty, the Community has as its task:

> by establishing a common market and progressively approximating the economic policies of Member States, to promote throughout the Community a harmonious development of economic activities, a continuous and balanced expansion, an increase in stability, an accelerated raising of the standard of living and closer relations between the States belonging to it.

From Article 2 one can understand immediately why the European Economic Community is more familiarly known as "the Common Market". However, this Article does not spell out exactly what the EEC is involved in. For this purpose Article 3 of the Treaty is much more useful as it lists the activities which the Community will engage in to fulfil its task.

Article 3 of the EEC Treaty states that the activities of the Community shall include the following:

(a) the elimination, as between Member States, of customs duties and of quantitative restrictions on the import and export of goods, and of all other measures having equivalent effect;

(b) the establishment of a common customs tariff and of a common commercial policy towards third countries;

(c) the abolition, as between Member States, of obstacles to freedom of movement for persons, services and capital;
(d) the adoption of a common policy in the sphere of agriculture;
(e) the adoption of a common policy in the sphere of transport;
(f) the institution of a system ensuring that competition in the common market is not distorted;
(g) the application of procedures by which the economic policies of Member States can be co-ordinated and disequilibria in their balances of payments remedied;
(h) the approximation of the laws of Member States to the extent required for the proper functioning of the common market;
(i) the creation of a European Social Fund in order to improve employment opportunities for workers and to contribute to the raising of their standard of living;
(j) the establishment of a European Investment Bank to facilitate the economic expansion of the Community by opening up fresh resources;
(k) the association of the overseas countries and territories in order to increase trade and to promote jointly economic and social development.

Subsequent Articles in the EEC Treaty provide further details about these activities and timetables for the implementation of some of them. These details will be examined in due course. For the moment it is sufficient to note that the EEC affects a whole variety of activities, including trade between member states, agriculture, transport, competition between companies, finance, the mobility of people within Europe and the living and working conditions of workers, as well as trade with and the development of the so-called "Third World" countries. Given that the EEC affects all these activities, it is indisputable that there is scarcely anyone in Northern Ireland who is not affected by the Community. For example, it will affect farmers who want to claim EEC subsidies; businessmen who trade with the Republic of Ireland, or any other member state of the EEC; consumers purchasing eggs now labelled to a uniform Community standard; haulage firms which must install tachographs in their lorries; bankers concerned with the difference between the "Snake", an "EMU" and the EMS; people claiming social security payments; men and women seeking equal pay or equal access to job opportunities; company officials puzzled by the EEC competition rules on mergers and monopolies; and last but not least, the legal adviser, Citizens' Advice Bureau, Law Centre or court asked to deal with an EEC problem. All of these, and this list is far from exhaustive, are affected by the EEC's activities.

This raises the question of the method by which the EEC affects our lives here? Basically, the answer is that the EEC Treaty established certain bodies, or institutions, of its own to carry out the Community's tasks by making laws which apply throughout all the member states and which may thus affect us directly in Northern Ireland.

In subsequent chapters consideration is given to the main areas influenced by Community law. The types of problems, and indeed benefits, that might arise in these areas will be suggested and readers directed to materials for solving the problems and exploiting the benefits. Before that, however, further information is needed about the Community's institutions, in particular how they make laws, and about where to find EEC legislation and about its nature and its effect on the United Kingdom's domestic legislation.

CHAPTER 3

INSTITUTIONS OF THE EEC

Each of the three treaties establishing a European Community made provision for certain bodies, or institutions as they are more commonly known, to carry out the tasks of the particular Community. Under the Treaty of Paris of 1951 the ECSC had a High Authority, a Common Assembly, a Special Council of Ministers and a Court of Justice. As for the two Treaties of Rome of 1957, they provided for a Commission, a Council of Ministers, an Assembly and a Court of Justice for the EEC and also for EURATOM. It was quickly realised, however, that such a proliferation of bodies was unnecessary and so these institutions were subsequently amalgamated in two stages. Firstly, under the Convention on Certain Institutions Common to the European Communities of 25 March 1957 it was agreed that the same Assembly and the same Court of Justice should serve all three Communities. Secondly, by the Merger Treaty of 8 April 1965 a single Council of Ministers and a single Commission were to serve the three Communities. Therefore, since then the same four institutions have served the EEC, EURATOM and the ECSC but the institutions still have different powers and functions depending upon which of the three treaties they are acting under. As this Guide concentrates upon the EEC, the following examination of the composition and powers of the institutions will be of those provided for under the EEC Treaty.

The four main institutions of the EEC—the Council of Ministers, the Commission, the Assembly (or the European Parliament as it is normally called), and the European Court of Justice—share legislative, executive and judicial functions.[1] In comparison with the United Kingdom's constitutional framework one could regard the Council of Ministers as the legislative body, the Commission as the executive, the European Parliament as an advisory body and the Court of Justice as the judicial organ of the EEC. However, such a comparison only provides a rough guide to the powers of each institution as there are certain overlaps between them. Consequently a more detailed examination of the composition and functions of each institution is necessary in order to reveal the extent of these overlaps. Although there is no definite hierarchy amongst the four institutions, it seems logical, from the point of view of how EEC law is made, to examine them in the following order: first, the Council of Ministers as it passes most EEC legislation; second, the Commission as it initiates much of that legislation; third, the European Parliament as it is consulted on most legislative proposals; and finally the Court of Justice as it must uphold EEC law.

[1] For details see Lasok and Bridge, *An Introduction to the Law and Institutions of the European Communities* (3rd ed, 1982).

1 COUNCIL OF MINISTERS

The Council of Ministers is governed by Articles 145 to 154 of the EEC Treaty as amended by the Merger and Accession Treaties. The Council combines the role of the legislature of the EEC with that of its decision-maker. It is based in Brussels, right beside the Commission building in the Rue de la Loi.

(a) COMPOSITION

The Council consists of one representative of each of the governments of the member states. While at present it consists of ten members,[2] it will increase to twelve when Spain and Portugal join the EEC at the beginning of 1986. However the Council is not a fixed body of the same ten members. Normally the Council comprises the Foreign Ministers from each of the ten member states and as such it is referred to as the "General Council of Ministers". Frequently, though, the composition of the Council changes depending on the subject matter for discussion at the particular Council meeting. For example, if agriculture is to be discussed the Council will be comprised of the Agriculture Ministers of each member state whereas if transport is on the agenda, the Transport Ministers will meet; these are known as meetings of the "Specialised Councils". It is possible, therefore, to have various Council meetings going on simultaneously in different places. The office of President of the Council rotates every six months amongst the member states in strict alphabetic order. Whenever a country has the presidency, its ministers are responsible for chairing meetings of the General and Specialised Council, representing the EEC at international forums such as the United Nations, reporting to and answering questions from members of the European Parliament and also organising meetings of the European Council (*post* p 29). Therefore, although the Presidency of the EEC is a prestigious role it can also place an onerous burden upon a member state, especially a smaller one.

The Council meets in private but it is normal practice for the member of the EEC Commission with the appropriate portfolio to attend Council meetings to represent the general Community interest but without a vote at such meetings. As representatives of their own governments, members of the Council of Ministers represent their national interests and yet in Council they have to strive to reach agreement to further the policies of the European Community as a whole. It is important therefore that a Commissioner attends Council meetings to remind Ministers of the best interests of the entire Community.

[2] Belgium, Denmark, West Germany, Greece, France, Republic of Ireland, Italy, Luxembourg, Netherlands and the UK.

(b) FUNCTIONS

Article 145 of the EEC Treaty boldly states that the Council of Ministers must "ensure the co-ordination of the general economic policies of the member states" and has "power to take decisions." As Article 145 is written in such general terms it is difficult to enumerate the precise duties and powers of the Council. Instead, the wide range of Council powers can be gathered under the two broad headings of "decision-maker" and "legislature".

(i) DECISION-MAKER: The Council of Ministers is the main decision-maker of the EEC, taking all the most important decisions concerning its development, for example the enlargement of the Community by the accession of other European countries, association of the Community with non-EEC countries, any amendments of the EEC Treaty itself and the compulsory expenditure element of the Community budget. The Council clearly has an enormously influential role in the overall expansion and development of the EEC. Thus, for instance, it was the power of veto in the Council of Ministers of one member state, namely France, that prevented the United Kingdom from acceding to the EEC for several years for unless Council members are unanimous, there can be no accession of other European countries to the EEC.

(ii) LEGISLATURE: The Council of Ministers is also the primary legislative organ of the EEC. It acts almost entirely upon legislative proposals put before it by the Commission because there is in fact only a limited number of Treaty provisions enabling the Council to act upon its own initiative.[3] Consequently the EEC would ultimately grind to a halt if the Commission ceased to send proposals through for enactment by the Council and so one should appreciate the considerable influence the Commission has upon the workload of the Council. The adage, "the Commission proposes and the Council disposes" is a useful reminder of the respective roles of the two institutions in relation to EEC legislation. The Commission's influence over the precise content of the legislation enacted by the Council is further enhanced by the fact that in accordance with Article 149 of the EEC Treaty the Council can only amend Commission proposals by a unanimous vote. Failing that, the Council may accept the Commission proposal, reject it outright or send it back to the Commission for alteration.

On the matter of voting, the EEC Treaty does stipulate specific voting procedures to be followed by the Council when enacting EEC legislation or taking decisions. Under Article 148 (1) of the Treaty the general rule is that the Council acts by a simple majority of its members unless the Treaty provides otherwise. In fact the Treaty does frequently provide otherwise,

[3] *Eg* Arts 84 (2), 136 and 217 EEC Treaty 1957 which deal with a sea and air transport policy for the EEC, association agreements with non-EEC countries and the languages to be used by each institution.

sometimes requiring unanimity and at other times requiring what is called a "qualified majority." A qualified majority is where the votes of each member state are weighted, basically to ensure that the "Big Four" member states together cannot dictate policies to the smaller member states. The various weights given to the votes of the member states are specified in Article 148 (2) of the Treaty so that each of the "Big Four"—the United Kingdom, France, West Germany and Italy—has ten votes; Greece, Netherlands and Belgium have five votes each; Denmark and the Republic of Ireland have three votes each; and Luxembourg has two, totalling sixty-three votes in all. Where the Council of Ministers is required to act on a Commission proposal by a qualified majority, then any forty-five votes out of the sixty-three must be cast in favour. In other cases, where the Council can act on its own initiative by a qualified majority, then forty-five votes out of the sixty-three must be cast in favour *by at least six of the member states.* Thus the EEC Treaty had checks written into it to ensure the Community was not dominated by the few most powerful of its members. After their accession Spain will have eight votes and Portugal five, bringing the total to seventy-six instead of the present sixty-three. The qualified majority will be fifty-four votes.

One must, however, add a rider to the formal voting procedures of the Council of Ministers as laid down in the EEC Treaty because of the so-called "Luxembourg Accords".[4] These Accords represent a gentlemen's agreement, entered into, quite outside the EEC Treaty, by "the Original Six" member states in 1966 in order to resolve a constitutional crisis within the Community. At that time France had refused to attend any Council meetings for several months, thereby allowing EEC business to stagnate. By these Accords the Council of Ministers agreed that where the EEC Treaty allowed it to reach a decision by a majority vote on a proposal from the Commission, the Council should instead try, within a reasonable time, to reach a unanimous decision where "very important interests" of one or more member states were at stake. In other words, these Accords represent a veto mechanism, or a blocking power, in the Council for any member state which claims that its vital national interests would be imperilled if a particular decision was taken by the Council of Ministers. When other countries, the United Kingdom, Republic of Ireland, Denmark and latterly Greece, joined the EEC, they did so on the understanding that each of them might in the Council rely upon the veto contained in the Luxembourg Accords. As a result of frequent reliance upon the Accords, Council business has been slowed down because unanimity between ten countries is certainly harder to achieve than between the six who originally agreed upon the Accords. The situation is expected to become even worse when the European Community is enlarged to twelve members. Consequently there

[4] See Rudden and Wyatt, *Basic Community Laws* (1980) 71.

are now proposals to move away from the Accords and revert to the majority voting provided for by the EEC Treaty itself.[5]

In order to smooth and speed up the progress of Council meetings a Committee of Permanent Representatives of the Member States was established by Article 4 of the Merger Treaty of 1965. This committee is called COREPER, an acronym derived from its French title, the Comite des Representants Permanents. It is composed of the ambassadors and their deputies, who are accredited to the EEC by each member state. Just as the United Kingdom has an ambassador to many countries around the world, so too it has an ambassador to the Community as a separate legal entity. COREPER is based in Brussels and is responsible for preparing the work of the Council of Ministers by liaising between their own national governments and the Commission in order to solve as many disagreements as possible about proposed EEC legislation before it goes on the agenda for the Council meetings. Proposals on which agreement has been reached are placed on the Council agenda by COREPER at "Point A" stage and matters which are still unresolved go to "Point B". It is important to note though that COREPER has itself no power of decision-making and so, even if matters are listed at "Point A", it is still up to the Council of Ministers to say yeah or nay to the proposals. Therefore lengthy Council meetings still occur despite the efforts of COREPER.

As most of the Council's workload is generated by the Commission it is now appropriate to consider the composition and functions of this latter institution.

2 THE COMMISSION

The composition and powers of the Commission are governed by Articles 155 to 163 of the EEC Treaty as amended by the Accession Treaties and the Merger Treaty.

(a) COMPOSITION

The Commission presently consists of fourteen members but the Accession Treaty for Spain and Portugal provides that the membership will increase to seventeen with the inclusion of two Spaniards and one Portuguese. Commissioners must be nationals of member states and no member state may appoint more than two Commissioners. The practice has been for each of the "Big Four"—the United Kingdom, France, Italy and West Germany—to have two Commissioners while the six smaller member states have one each. The two Commissioners from the United Kingdom are Lord Cockfield, formerly a Conservative junior minister and Mr Stanley Clinton Davis, formerly a Labour MP at Westminster. They replaced Commissioner

[5] *Eg* Art 23 Draft Treaty on European Union, adopted by the European Parliament, 14 February 1984, Bull EC2 1984.

Tugendhat and Commissioner Richard at the beginning of 1985. Mr Peter Sutherland, formerly Irish Attorney-General, is the newly-appointed Commissioner from the Republic of Ireland. Commissioners must be appointed by "the common accord", or unanimous agreement, of the governments of all the member states. In accordance with Article 10 of the Merger Treaty they are chosen on grounds of their general competence and their independence must be beyond doubt. This is because the Commission is expected to represent the general interest of the whole European Community rather than national or sectional interests. Member states' governments are therefore urged by Article 10 of the Merger Treaty not to try to influence the members of the Commission in the exercise of their functions.

A Commissioner's term of office is four years and is renewable. His term of office ends if he is replaced, dies, resigns or is compulsorily retired. A Commissioner can only be compulsorily retired if he no longer fulfils the conditions required for the performance of his duties or if he is guilty of serious misconduct and even then only the European Court of Justice may, on application from the Council of Ministers or the Commission, require him to retire. The Commissioners elect their own President and five Vice-Presidents from amongst their number for a term of two years. Monsieur Delors, formerly the French Finance Minister, was appointed President of the Commission in January 1985. Various portfolios, corresponding to the EEC's main areas of activity, are shared out amongst the Commissioners at the beginning of the Commission's term of office and it is believed that there is considerable rivalry between them for the more prestigious portfolios like agriculture or budgetary affairs.[6] The Commission acts by a majority of its members and has adopted its own rules of procedure as required by Article 16 of the Merger Treaty.

The Commission, which is based in the Berlaymont Building in Brussels, just across the road from the Council of Ministers' building, employs over 9,500 staff in its various departments or "directorates-general" (D-Gs) as

[6] The full list of new Commissioners appointed in January 1985 and their respective portfolios is as follows:

Mr Andriessen (NL) (Vice-President)—Agriculture and Fisheries. Mr Cheysson (F)—Mediterranean policy; North-South relations. Mr Christophersen (Den) (Vice-President)—Budget; Financial Control; Personnel. Mr Clinton Davis (UK)—Environment; Consumer Protection; Nuclear Safety; Forests; Transport. Lord Cockfield (UK) (Vice-President)—Internal Market; Customs; Tax and Financial Institutions. Mr de Clerq (B)—External Affairs. Mr Delors (F) (President)—Monetary Affairs; Co-ordination of the Community's structural funds; General administration. Mr Ripa di Meana (I)—Institutional questions; Information; Culture; Tourism. Mr Mosar (Lux)—Energy; the Euratom Supply Agency; Publications. Mr Narjes (WG) (Vice-President)—Industrial Affairs; Information technology; Scientific Research. Mr Natali (I)—Development, including overseeing Spain and Portugal's accession. Mr Pfeiffer (WG)—Economic Affairs; Employment; Credit and Investment; the Statistical Office. Mr Sutherland (IR)—Competition; Social Affairs; Education. Mr Varfis (GK)—Regional Policy; relations with the European Parliament.

they are more properly called. These are headed by a Director-General, who is in turn responsible to the Commissioner with the portfolio for the subject matter handled by that particular D-G. There are some 20 Directorates-General, operating in the Berlaymont Building, Rue de La Loi 200, Brussels.

(b) FUNCTIONS

The functions of the Commission are listed in Article 155 of the EEC Treaty. In order to ensure "the proper functioning and development of the common market" the Commission is required by Article 155 to undertake four specific tasks.

(i) SUPERVISION: The Commission must ensure that the EEC Treaty and its implementing measures are applied. Thus the Commission has a supervisory watch-dog role to see that EEC law is obeyed by member states and where appropriate by business enterprises. If a member state breaches EEC law the main onus is upon the Commission to see that the state complies either by skilful persuasion and negotiations or ultimately by bringing that member state before the European Court of Justice under Article 169 of the EEC Treaty. Since the Commission is an independent body representing the general interests of the Community as a whole it is well-suited for the task of investigating possible breaches of EEC law by a member state and taking a case before the Court of Justice if necessary. If the Commission considers that a member state has breached EEC law, it will first try informally to persuade that state to comply. Failing that, the Commission will issue a "reasoned opinion" giving the reasons for believing that the country in question has failed to fulfil its Community obligations, setting out the steps needed to be taken by that country and stipulating a time-limit, normally two months, for compliance. If the country fails to comply with the "reasoned opinion", or does so late, the Commission *may* bring it before the Court of Justice for a declaration that it has failed to fulfil its Community obligations. This is certainly preferable to the alternative procedure under Article 170 of the EEC Treaty, whereby a member state may take another member state before the Court of Justice for a breach of EEC law, for this latter procedure creates much political embarrassment and tension between the partners in the EEC. Since 1958 the Commission has brought before the European Court of Justice more than two hundred actions against member states under Article 169 whereas only one inter-state case has been decided by the Court, thus demonstrating the important role of the Commission in this area.[7] The Commission also has the primary responsibility for ensuring that individual traders and companies obey the EEC's competition rules and this topic will be considered later (See Chapters 15 and 16 *post*).

[7] For details see Brown and Jacobs, *The Court of Justice of the European Communities* (2nd ed, 1983) Ch 5.

(ii) MAKING RECOMMENDATIONS AND OPINIONS: The Commission must make Recommendations or deliver Opinions whenever the EEC Treaty expressly so provides or whenever the Commission itself considers it necessary. Although neither Recommendations nor Opinions are legally binding measures, the making of them allows the Commission to prepare the ground for legislation. This provision in Article 155(b) is a particularly important source of residual power where the EEC Treaty is otherwise silent about giving the Commission power to initiate legislation. The Commission also quite often issues Notices or Communications. Again although neither of these is legally binding, they provide general information and occasionally guidance about the interpretation of other binding EEC legislation. Thus, for example, the Commission has recently issued a Notice giving further guidance on the new Commission Regulation granting a block exemption from the EEC's competition rules to certain categories of motor vehicle distribution and servicing agreements.

(iii) DECISION-MAKING: The Commission has its own power of decision and power to participate in the shaping of measures taken by the Council of Ministers and by the European Parliament as provided by the EEC Treaty. Herein lies the Commission's major function in that it is the initiator of the bulk of Community legislation. It is the Commission which, after consulting a wide range of interested parties makes proposals for enactment by the Council of Ministers. Again the adage, "the Commission proposes and the Council disposes" may be repeated as a reminder of the overlap in the legislative functions of these two bodies. As the Commission is an independent institution, representing the best interests of the EEC as a whole, it is appropriate that it should have primary responsibility for proposing Community legislation leaving the Council of Ministers with little power of its own to initiate EEC legislation. The Commission's proposals for legislation may be found in the "C" section of the Official Journal of the European Communities. Although media reports may give a contrary impression it is important to remember that Commission proposals are not binding and so one must not rely upon them until the Council has in fact legislated upon them.

(iv) DELEGATED LEGISLATION: The Commission may also exercise such legislative powers as are conferred upon it by the Council of Ministers. Whilst the Council is the main legislative body of the EEC, it may delegate legislative powers to the Commission for the implementation of certain EEC policies. This often happens in relation to complex areas like common customs tariffs, competition rules and the Common Agricultural Policy where the Council will often lay down the basic framework in its Regulations and delegate legislative power to the Commission to fill out the necessary details. Therefore, although the bulk of secondary Community legislation comprises Regulations, Directives and Decisions made by the Council of Ministers, it is not unusual to find some made by the Commission. Such

legislative measures of the Commission have the same binding force as those of the Council and all are to be found in the "L" section of the Official Journal of the European Communities. (The Official Journal is explained in more detail in the next chapter).

In light of this examination of the Commission's functions one can appreciate the great influence the Commission has upon both the legislative workload of the Council of Ministers and the case-load of the Court of Justice. One can also understand why the Commission has been nicknamed the "power-house" or executive of the EEC. Its relations, and those of the Council of Ministers, with the European Parliament need now to be considered.

3 THE EUROPEAN PARLIAMENT (OR EUROPEAN ASSEMBLY)

Articles 137 and 144 of the EEC Treaty as amended by the Merger Treaty and the Treaties of Accession govern the European Assembly, or rather the "European Parliament" as it has styled itself since 1962. These titles may be used interchangeably, but it is now common parlance to refer to this body as the European Parliament. The Parliament is considered by many commentators to be the weakest of the Community institutions, and has frequently been labelled as a "mere talking-shop". A close look at its composition and, in particular, at its functions will show however that this is not an altogether accurate assessment of this institution.

(a) COMPOSITION

Until mid-1979 when the first direct elections to the Parliament were held, it was composed of 198 delegates, designated by the respective parliaments of the member states. The drafters of the EEC Treaty had not envisaged that the Parliament should remain such an undemocratic body and so Article 138 of the Treaty provides that it should draw up proposals for elections by "direct universal suffrage in accordance with a uniform procedure in all member states". The Council of Ministers was then required to lay down the appropriate provisions for these elections. After many years of procrastination by the Council of Ministers, it finally agreed on 20 September 1976 to an Act concerning the Election of the Representatives of the Assembly by Direct Universal Suffrage. This Act left it up to each member state to decide on its own national electoral provisions for the first election to the European Parliament but the Act required that in future elections to the Parliament, to be held every five years, there should be a uniform system of electing members. In the 1979 elections eight of the then nine member states used some form of proportional representation while the United Kingdom used two forms of voting. In Great Britain the "first-past-the-post" system was used as is usual in its national elections, while the single-transferable vote system was used in Northern Ireland. Those elections resulted in a much enlarged Parliament of 410 members meeting for the first time at Strasbourg on 17 July 1979. After Greece acceded to the European Communities on 1 January 1981, 24 Greek MEPs joined the European Parliament. Since the Council of Ministers could not agree on a uniform electoral system for the second direct elections to the European Parliament in June 1984, Great Britain again operated the first-past-the-post system while in Northern Ireland and in all the other member states some form of proportional representation was used. As a result of those elections 434 MEPs were returned to the European Parliament, but this number will again be increased in 1986 when Spain and Portugal join the European Communities. There will be 60 seats in the Parliament for Spain and 24 for Portugal, bringing the overall total membership to 518.

MEPs may serve for five years and are eligible to stand for re-election as many of them did in the second direct elections in 1984. Members of the European Parliament may at the same time be members of their own national parliaments, and thus hold what is called a dual-mandate. However, a person would be disqualified as an MEP if he or she became a member of a national government. The number of MEPs varies from one member state to another as follows: the "Big Four" member states—France, Italy, West Germany and the United Kingdom—each have 81; Netherlands has 25; Belgium and Greece have 24 each; Denmark has 16; the Republic of Ireland has 15; and finally Luxembourg has 6.[8] This division of seats between member states was not made solely on the basis of the population of each country but rather it was the result of a compromise between the need for the population of each country to be the main determining factor and the desire to give each state, even the smallest, Luxembourg, meaningful representation within the European Parliament. Within the United Kingdom its 81 seats are divided again so that Northern Ireland has 3, Wales 4, Scotland 8 and England 66. The three Northern Ireland MEPs are Mr John Hume (SDLP), Rev Ian Paisley (DUP) and Mr John Taylor (OU); all three hold a dual-mandate as they are also members of the Westminster Parliament. As such they are entitled to one salary plus ⅓ of the other salary as well as an MEP's secretarial, attendance and travel allowances.

Since its enlargement in 1979 the European Parliament has held most of its plenary sessions, now about ten per year for roughly a week each time, in purpose-built accommodation in Strasbourg. This move away from its alternative venue in Luxembourg greatly annoyed its service staff, most of whom live in Luxembourg and have therefore had to commute to Strasbourg for each plenary session. However, the European Court of Justice has held

[8] Art 138 (1) EEC Treaty.

in *Grand Duchy of Luxembourg* v *European Parliament (No. 1)*[9] that the Parliament is at liberty to decide upon its own place of work in the absence of any decision by the Council of Ministers fixing a permanent venue. Since three of the Council members, namely France, Belgium and Luxembourg, would each like to have the European Parliament based in their respective countries, they seem reluctant to forsake their individual claims to this particular institution and therefore the Council seems unlikely to agree in the near future on a permanent place of work for the Parliament. In the meantime the Court of Justice considers that the European Parliament is entitled to hold its plenary sessions in Strasbourg, its committee meetings in Brussels and to retain its secretariat in Luxembourg.

At the European Parliament's plenary sessions in Strasbourg, the MEPs do not sit in national blocs but instead most of them belong to one of the Parliament's eight multi-national, political groups within which they can meet and discuss issues with like-minded representatives from other EEC countries. After the second direct elections to the European Parliament in June 1984, the main political groups, in decreasing order of size, are as follows: the Socialists, (including John Hume (SDLP)); the European People's Party; the European Democrats, (including John Taylor (OU)); the Communists and Allies; the Liberals; the European Democratic Alliance (formerly the European Progressive Democrats); the Rainbow Group (formerly the Group for the Technical Co-Ordination and Defence of Independent Groups and Members); and an entirely new political grouping called the Group of the European Right. As members of a group, MEPs gain more speaking time in debates and greater access to secretarial assistance than if they remain independent. However, some MEPs, like Rev. Ian Paisley (DUP), do prefer to sit as independents and so are known as "non-attached" members. Further details of the composition of the European Parliament are set out in the tables on pp. 30-1.[10] The agenda and business of the European Parliament are organised by a Bureau comprising the President and twelve Vice-Presidents of the Parliament, who are elected by the MEPs by secret ballot to serve for two and a half years. The Presidency of the European Parliament is currently held by Monsieur Pflimlin, a French MEP.

Although the European Parliament only meets in full session for about sixty-five days per year, the organisation of the Parliament into various specialised standing committees, meeting regularly in Brussels and each dealing with a particular aspect of the EEC's activities, ensures that there is continuity in the work of the Parliament. The standing committees' main tasks are to discuss proposals for EEC legislation and to prepare reports for debate by the full Parliament, which will then give its opinion on them. For

[9] [1983] ECR 283; [1983] 2 CMLR 726. *See also Grand Duchy of Luxembourg* v *European Parliament (No 2)*. [1984] ECR 1945.

[10] Supplied by Mr Ken Collins, MEP.

example, at the instigation of the European Parliament's Socialist Group, the Political Affairs Committee of the European Parliament undertook an inquiry into the situation in Northern Ireland in order to explain its problems to the European Parliament and to see how the EEC could further assist the Province. The ensuing report, prepared by the Danish MEP on the Committee, Niels Haagerup, was discussed and adopted by the European Parliament in March 1984 by 124 votes to 3. Nevertheless, it should be stressed that since the European Parliament has no power to make binding legislation for the EEC, the Haagerup Report and the Parliament's subsequent Resolution adopting it are not legally enforceable documents.

(b) FUNCTIONS

The main functions of the directly-elected European Parliament are the same as those of the former nominated Parliament although it would seem that since being directly elected, the Parliament has, as explained below, flexed its muscles with much greater effect than before. Its basic powers are conferred by Article 137 of the EEC Treaty, which states that the Parliament shall exercise "the advisory and supervisory powers conferred on it by the Treaty". It is indeed very important to note that the European Parliament is only an advisory and supervisory body; unlike national parliaments, such as the Westminster Parliament, it is not a legislative body and so its Resolutions, Reports and Opinions are not legally binding.

The advisory and supervisory powers of the European Parliament may be exercised by it in four different ways:

(i) CONSULTATION ON LEGISLATION: In relation to EEC legislation, the Parliament should be consulted by the Council of Ministers, the main legislative body of the European Communities, on all important matters and must be consulted whenever the EEC Treaty so requires. In the recent case of *Roquette Freres* v *Council* (or *The Isoglucose Case)*[11] the Court of Justice emphasised that this consultation process is not a mere formality that can be ignored by the Council without serious consequences. The Court held that a Council Regulation concerning isoglucose was void because of the failure of the Council to obtain the Opinion of the Parliament about it as required by Article 43 of the EEC Treaty. It is suggested that this judgment enhances the powers of the European Parliament in that the Parliament may delay its Opinion on legislative proposals as a trade-off for other concessions from the Council of Ministers. It is also worth noting that the Parliament has initiated legislation by making suggestions to the Commission. For example, after its debate on the Haagerup Report on Northern Ireland, the European Parliament called upon the EEC Commission, *inter alia,* to assume greater responsibility for economic and social development in Northern Ireland. In response the Commission is expected to present legislative proposals to the Council of Ministers to increase economic aid to Northern Ireland.

[11] [1980] ECR 3333. For further details see p 37 *post*.

(ii) BUDGETARY POWERS: Perhaps the European Parliament's most important power is in relation to the European Community's budget, which involved around £17,000m in 1984. The Community's financial resources comprise a small percentage of Value Added Tax (approximately 1.4%) contributed by each member state plus customs duties and agricultural levies charged on goods imported from non-EEC countries or levied on some agricultural produce exported from the EEC. Articles 203 to 205 of the EEC Treaty as amended by the Budgetary Treaties of 1970 and 1975 give the European Parliament substantial powers over this budget. Briefly, Community expenditure is divided between compulsory (or obligatory) expenditure and non-compulsory (or non-obligatory) expenditure. The former denotes expenditure *necessarily arising* under the EEC Treaty or implementing legislation, most of which goes on financing the Common Agricultural Policy, representing about 65% of the total. The latter, the non-compulsory expenditure, relates mainly to expenditure on the Regional and Social Policies of the EEC.

The financial year of the EEC runs from 1 January to 31 December. Each of the Community institutions must draw up before 1 July an estimate of its expenditure for the next financial year. The Commission must then consolidate these estimates into a preliminary draft budget and present this to the Council of Ministers by 1 September. The Council, acting by a qualified majority, must confirm the draft budget and then send it to the European Parliament by 5 October. The Parliament may amend the non-compulsory expenditure part of the draft budget but may only propose "modifications" to the compulsory expenditure part of it. If the Parliament approves the draft budget or within 45 days *has not amended it nor proposed any modification thereto,* the budget is deemed to have been finally adopted. If, however, the Parliament does amend it or propose "modifications", then the draft budget must be sent back to the Council. If within a further 15 days, the Council has not changed the amendments adopted by the Parliament and has accepted the "modifications" proposed by the latter, then again the budget is deemed to be adopted. If, on the other hand, the Council makes any changes to the amendments or "modifications", the draft budget must again be returned to the Parliament. At this stage the Parliament may only alter the Council's changes, if any, to the Parliament's amendments to the non-compulsory expenditure and it has 15 days within which to do so; thus the Parliament has the final say over amendments to the non-compulsory expenditure while the Council has the last say about amendments to the compulsory expenditure. If, however, there are important reasons, the Parliament may reject the entire draft budget and ask for a new draft to be submitted to it. This drastic action was taken by the European Parliament in December 1979 because MEPs objected so strongly to the inordinately high level of expenditure on the CAP compared to that on regional and social policies. Again in December 1984 the draft budget was rejected because the

Parliament knew then that the EEC's present financial resources would not be sufficient to cover the total 1985 expenditure proposed in the budget; the resources would only cover ten out of twelve months and the Parliament insisted that it only had power to approve a budget for the full financial year. Until final approval, the Community survives from month to month on one twelfth of the preceding financial year's budget allocation. These incidents demonstrate that the European Parliament is willing to use its power of veto over the entire Community budget to force concessions on expenditure by the Council of Ministers. The European Parliament has also used its budgetary powers to withhold rebates due to the United Kingdom in order to persuade the British Government to change its objections to a supplementary budget for 1984.

(iii) MOTIONS OF CENSURE: As well as having considerable control over the Community budget, the Parliament has another important power in that it may pass a motion of censure on the activities of the entire Commission. (It should be noted that this power cannot be used by the Parliament to dismiss an individual Commissioner.) Under Article 144 of the EEC Treaty the Commission must resign *en bloc* if the motion of censure is carried by a two-thirds majority of the votes cast, representing a majority of the members of the European Parliament. Pursuant to this Article various motions of censure have been tabled but so far they have either been withdrawn before a vote by the Parliament or have been defeated in the vote. Motions of censure have been tabled castigating a wide variety of activities by the Commission such as sales of cheap butter to Eastern Europe.

(iv) SUPERVISION: The European Parliament also has power to question members of the Council of Ministers and the Commission either orally or in writing. In this way European Community policies may be more openly discussed in debate on the floor of the Parliament and further information extracted from the Commission about EEC activities. In addition the Commission is also required to submit to the Parliament an Annual General Report on the activities of the European Communities. The presentation of this Report is followed by a debate during which MEPs may air their views on the various areas of Community activity. The Annual General Report of the Commission is available on request from European Commission Information Offices and is also supplied to libraries which are depositaries or documentation centres for European Community materials. The debates of the Parliament, the written questions posed by MEPs and the corresponding answers to such questions are published in the Official Journal of the European Communities, in its "C" section. The OJ, as it's commonly known, is published virtually daily and provides a ready and useful source of information about the current state of business being conducted by the European Parliament as well as by the other Community institutions.

Finally we turn to consider the work of the European Court of Justice to see in particular what contribution it makes in respect of the development of EEC law.

4 THE EUROPEAN COURT OF JUSTICE

The composition and functions of the European Court of Justice (often referred to as the ECJ or simply the Court of Justice) are governed by Articles 164 to 188 of the EEC Treaty as amended by the Accession Treaties.

(a) COMPOSITION

The ECJ presently consists of eleven judges, assisted by five advocates-general. There is one judge from each of the ten member states and in addition, because an uneven number is required an eleventh judge was appointed as from 1 April 1981. This extra judgeship will be rotated through the "Big Four" member states every few years. Of the five advocates-general, there is one from each of the "Big Four" member states and the fifth one, also newly created on 1 April 1981, will be rotated amongst the smaller member states. Lord MacKenzie-Stuart, a former judge of the Scottish Court of Session and judge from the United Kingdom since its accession is now President of the Court. The present advocate-general from the United Kingdom is Sir Gordon Slynn, formerly chairman of the Employment Appeal Tribunal. He replaced Jean-Pierre Warner, who has returned to the Bench in England. The Court will have one Spanish and one Portuguese judge when these countries join the Communities, bringing the total to thirteen. There will also be six advocates-general instead of five.

According to Article 167 of the EEC Treaty both the judges and the advocates-general must be chosen by the "common accord" of the governments of all the member states. Article 167 of the Treaty requires that they be chosen from persons:

> whose independence is beyond doubt and who possess the qualifications required for appointment to the highest judicial offices in their respective countries or who are jurisconsults of recognised competence.

This formulation covers the practice of judicial appointments in common law countries like the United Kingdom and also the civil law practice in, for example, France where leading legal academics may be appointed as members of the judiciary. As the same qualifications are required of judges and advocates-general, a person who has held office as a judge may subsequently become an advocate-general and *vice versa*. For example, Judge Capotorti later served as an advocate-general. Judges and advocates-general are appointed for a term of six years and are eligible for reappointment. During an appointment a judge or advocate-general may voluntarily submit his resignation, as did Judge O'Dalaigh in 1975 to enable him to become President of Ireland. Apart from voluntary retirement, a judge or advocate-general can only be dismissed from his post by the unanimous agreement of the other judges and advocates-general if he no longer fulfils the requisite conditions or obligations of office. This procedure helps to maintain the independence of the ECJ from undue influence from the other institutions or from the member states. The independence of the Court of Justice has gained it enormous respect. A quorum of seven judges is necessary when the Court sits in plenary session. However, the Court may sit in chambers unless the case is of particular importance. A chamber, or division, of the Court comprises of three or five judges and an advocate-general. The Court may now subdivide into five chambers, which enables it to cope with a greater number of cases; two chambers of five judges or three chambers of three judges.

The role of the advocate-general requires some explanation as there is no direct analogy in the domestic systems of the member states. As already mentioned, advocates-general have equal status with the judges and the advocate-general assigned to a particular case does in fact sit together with the judges on the bench on the left-hand side. The role of an advocate-general is primarily to assist the judges. As each new case comes before the Court it is allocated to a particular advocate-general who studies it in depth. Having researched a case, it is his duty under Article 166:

> acting with complete impartiality and independence, to make, in open court, reasoned submissions on [the] cases brought before the Court of Justice, in order to assist the Court . . .

Although the "reasoned submission" of the advocate-general is not binding on the Court it will be considered carefully by the judges when they adjourn alone to reach their decision. The "reasoned submission" is printed together with the facts of the case and the judgment of the Court in the European Court Reports, which are the Court's official reports. The "reasoned submission", although not binding, can prove very useful as it is much more informative and certainly easier to read than the actual judgment. The latter is written in the terse style of continental judgments, without any dissenting judgment being recorded; the Court's judgment is a collective one, reached in secret by the judges and signed by all those judges who took part in the deliberations. Often one's understanding of a judgment of the Court of Justice can be greatly enhanced by first reading through the reasoned submission of the advocate-general, but one must always remember that it is only the actual judgment of the Court itself that is binding.[12]

There are two other important points to remember about the judgments of the ECJ. The first point is that there is no appeal from its judgments; they are final and binding on the parties. This emphasises the need for the Court, assisted by an advocate-general, to get the law right first time. The only scope for revision of a judgment is provided for in Article 41 of the Protocol

12 See Dashwood, "The Advocate-General in the Court of Justice of the European Communities" (1982) 2 *Legal Studies* 202.

on the Statute of the ECJ. An application for revision of a judgment may be made to the Court only on discovery of a fact which is of such a nature as to be a "decisive factor" and which, when the judgment was given, was unknown to the Court and to the party claiming the revision. There is a time-limit of ten years for making applications for reviews of this kind. In fact they rarely occur.

The second important point is that the Court of Justice is not bound by precedent. Nevertheless, it does tend to follow its earlier judgments but it is not unknown for it to change its attitude towards a particular subject. For example, as regards the protection of fundamental human rights by Community law, the ECJ at first declared that it had no jurisdiction to consider such matters as the EEC Treaty only concerned economic matters but later, when the development of economic policies by the EEC allegedly encroached upon fundamental rights the Court did claim jurisdiction to consider such cases.[13]

The Court sits in the Palais de Justice, Kirchberg in Luxembourg. Its judgments are, as already mentioned, published in the European Court Reports (ECR) in all the Community's official languages.[14] In addition, the Information Office of the Court of Justice publishes weekly Information Sheets entitled "Proceedings of the Court of Justice of the European Communities", summarising the cases that have been decided by the Court during that particular week. The Information Office also publishes annual synopses of the work of the Court, under the heading "Synopsis of the Work of the Court of Justice of the European Communities" in 1983, 1984 etc. The Information Office may be contacted at PO Box 1406, L-2920, Luxembourg.

(b) FUNCTIONS

The task of the Court as stated in Article 164 of the EEC Treaty is to ensure that "in the interpretation and application of this Treaty the law is obeyed". Given this task the ECJ has certainly played a very influential part in developing EEC law since all its major characteristics such as its supremacy over all conflicting legislation, the direct effectiveness of some of its provisions and its protection of fundamental rights have been introduced and developed by the Court; these characteristics are not written into the Treaty itself but are inventions of the Court designed to further the scope and effectiveness of Community law. The Court has been able to do this mainly by using the Article 177 preliminary ruling procedure, whereby a national court or tribunal refers points of Community law to the ECJ for interpretation and the ECJ then sends its ruling back to the referral body for

[13] See *Stork* v *High Authority* [1959] ECR 17 and compare *Stauder* v *City of Ulm* [1969] ECR 419.

[14] English, French, German, Italian, Dutch, Danish and Greek but not Irish. Spanish and Portuguese will become official languages in 1986.

application to the facts of the case. This Article 177 procedure is an indirect action where the case begins and ends with the national court and reference to the ECJ is only an intermediary step. As this Article has been used so much to develop EEC law it will be examined more fully in Chapter 7, *post*.

As well as this indirect action, certain Articles of the Treaty give the ECJ jurisdiction in direct actions where a Community institution, a member state or, in certain instances, individuals or companies may bring a case directly before the ECJ. It is important to note that the Court has no inherent jurisdiction and there are only a few Articles of the EEC Treaty that give the Court jurisdiction to hear a case. These Articles will be examined in Chapter 8. A case must, therefore, come within the precise terms of one or other of these Articles, otherwise the Court will declare the case inadmissible. In fact much of the Court's proceedings are taken up by arguments about admissibility. Legal advisers should therefore take particular care to ensure that any proceedings brought before the Court of Justice satisfy the admissibility criteria of the relevant Treaty Article(s).

Under the EEC Treaty, the ECJ may act in several capacities in order to see that Community law is obeyed. Firstly, it may act as an administrative court dealing with the legality of Community measures. If, for example, the Council of Ministers or the Commission makes a Regulation or Directive without following the proper procedures, a member state or an individual who believes it to be invalid, may then bring an action before the ECJ under specific Articles of the EEC Treaty challenging the validity of that Regulation or Directive. Articles 173, 175 and 184 give the Court jurisdiction in such cases. Other internal administrative matters, which take up a great deal of the Court's time, are staff cases concerning complaints by employees of the Community institutions about their terms and conditions of employment. Such cases form the bulk of the workload of the Court and arise under Article 179 of the EEC Treaty. Another aspect of the Court's jurisdiction in administrative matters is its power to dismiss an individual Commissioner under Article 13 of the Merger Treaty if he no longer fulfils the conditions required for the performance of his duties or if he has been guilty of serious misconduct. This power has not yet been exercised, but it is nevertheless available to the Court should it be necessary.

Secondly, the ECJ may be regarded as an international court since the European Communities' treaties are instruments of international law being agreements between states. As disputes between states and breaches of those treaties are matters for international courts, the EEC Treaty gives the ECJ jurisdiction to rule in cases where member states fail to fulfil their EEC Treaty obligations. For example, in the so-called "Lamb War" between France and the United Kingdom, where France operated a ban on imports of British sheepmeat, the ECJ ruled that such action was contrary to EEC law. Articles 169 and 170 of the Treaty give the Court jurisdiction in such cases, where proceedings are brought before the Court of Justice by the Commission or by a member state.

Thirdly, the ECJ is a court of civil jurisdiction whenever it deals with the liability of the European Community. If, for instance, a Council Regulation has been declared invalid, then under Article 215 of the EEC Treaty the ECJ may order that compensation be awarded to the plaintiff for loss caused by the Regulation. Clearly then the jurisdiction conferred on the ECJ by the EEC Treaty is wide ranging, but note that it is also specialised because the powers of the Court are confined to European Community law alone. Thus the ECJ does not have power to declare a national law void if it conflicts with Community law. Instead the ECJ would rule that European Community law should prevail over any conflicting rule of national law because Community law is supreme. It is then up to the national authorities and domestic courts to implement that ruling. Many of these points, including supremacy, will be examined more fully in Chapter 5.

5 OTHER ADVISORY BODIES

EUROPEAN COUNCIL

Besides the four main institutions of the EEC, there are two other bodies which are influential in the formation of EEC legislation and which therefore merit some consideration in order to provide as complete a picture as possible of how EEC law is made. The first of these bodies is called the "European Council",[15] which comprises the Heads of Government or State of each of the member states together with their respective Foreign Ministers. They began meeting informally at "summit meetings" in the early 1970s during the oil crisis and the formation of the European Council in 1974 was really the institutionalisation of these informal meetings. The European Council (which should not be confused with the Council of Ministers described at p 12 *ante*) meets three times per year to discuss not only Community matters but also other international affairs such as tensions in the Middle East and relations with the Soviet Union. Over recent years it has become the trend for the European Council to resolve crises that have previously deadlocked the Council of Ministers' meetings and to initiate Community action in particular areas. The practice has been that if legislation is required to implement the initiatives of the European Council, then it is done through the normal channels with a Commission proposal being adopted by the Council of Ministers.

[15] See Lauwaars, "The European Council" (1977) 14 *CML Rev* 25.

ECONOMIC AND SOCIAL COMMITTEE

The second body that deserves some mention is the Economic and Social Committee (the ESC) which performs important advisory functions. It was set up under Article 193 of the EEC Treaty and has more than 150 members made up of representatives of trades unions, employers' organisations, farmers, consumer groups, professional people and the general public. The members of the Committee are appointed by the Council of Ministers from lists of candidates suggested by the member states. An appointment is for four years and is renewable. The ESC *must* be consulted by the Council or by the Commission where the EEC Treaty so provides. Moreover, the Committee *may* be consulted by these institutions in all cases in which they consider it appropriate. The Committee gives its opinions on proposed EEC legislation but such opinions are advisory only; the Committee has no decision-making or legislative powers of its own. Its opinions may be found in the Official Journal, "C" section.

TABLE 1

MEMBERSHIP OF THE EUROPEAN PARLIAMENT'S POLITICAL GROUPS

AFTER JUNE 1979 ELECTIONS (WITHOUT GREECE)

	Total	B	DK	F	G	IRL	I	L	NL	UK
Socialists	113	7	4	22	35	4	13	1	9	18
European People's Party	107	10	—	8	42	4	30	3	10	—
European Democrats	64	—	3	—	—	—	—	—	—	61
Communists	44	—	1	19	—	—	24	—	—	—
Liberals	40	4	3	17	4	1	5	2	4	—
European Progressive Democrats	22	—	1	15	—	5	—	—	—	1
Group for the Technical Co-ordination and Defence of Independent Groups and Members	11	1	4	—	—	1	5	—	—	—
Non-attached	9	2	—	—	—	—	4	—	2	1
Total	410	24	16	81	81	15	81	6	25	81

BEFORE JUNE 1984 ELECTIONS

	Total	B	DK	D	GR	F	IRL	I	L	NL	UK
Socialists	125	7	4	35	10	23	4	14	1	9	18
EPP (Christian Democrats)	117	10	1	42	8	9	4	30	3	10	—
European Democrats (Conservatives) . .	63	—	2	—	—	—	—	—	—	—	61
Communists and Allies	48	—	1	—	4	19	—	24	—	—	—
Liberals and Democrats	38	4	3	4	—	15	1	5	2	4	—
European Progressive Democrats . . .	22	—	1	—	—	15	5	—	—	—	1
Group for Technical Co-ordination . . .	11	2	4	—	—	—	1	4	—	—	—
Independents	10	1	—	—	2	—	—	4	—	2	1
Total	434	24	16	81	24	81	15	81	6	25	81

AFTER JUNE 1984 ELECTIONS

	Total	B	DK	D	GR	F	IRL	I	L	NL	UK
Socialists	131	8	4	33	10	20	—	12	2	9	33
EPP (Christian Democrats)	110	6	1	41	9	9	6	27	3	8	—
European Democrats (Conservatives) . .	50	—	4	—	—	—	—	—	—	—	46
Communists and Allies	41	—	1	—	4	10	—	26	—	—	—
Liberals and Democrats	31	5	2	—	—	12	1	5	1	5	—
European Democratic Alliance	29	—	—	—	—	20	8	—	—	—	1
Rainbow	20	4	4	7	—	—	—	3	—	2	—
European Right	16	—	—	—	1	10	—	5	—	—	—
Non-attached	6	1	—	—	—	—	—	3	—	1	1
Total	434	24	16	81	24	81	15	81	6	25	81

CHAPTER 4

THE SOURCES OF COMMUNITY LAW AND HOW TO FIND THEM

1 TREATIES

The original treaties establishing the three European Communities form the primary source of Community law. Those treaties together with subsequent amending treaties, provide the very foundations of the Communities.[1] The complete list of treaties is as follows:

(a) Treaty of Paris, 1951 establishing the European Coal and Steel Community (ECSC);

(b) Treaty of Rome, 1957 establishing the European Atomic Energy Community (EURATOM);

(c) Treaty of Rome, 1957 establishing the European Economic Community (EEC) (to avoid confusion with the EURATOM Treaty, this particular Treaty of Rome is referred to as the EEC Treaty throughout the text of this Guide);

(d) Convention on Certain Institutions Common to the European Communities, 1957 establishing a single Court of Justice and a single Assembly for all three Communities;

(e) Merger Treaty, 1965 establishing a single Council and a single Commission for all three Communities;

(f) First Budgetary Treaty, 1970 amending certain budgetary provisions of the original treaties establishing the Communities and of the Merger treaty;

(g) First Treaty of Accession, 1972 concerning the accession of the United Kingdom, Republic of Ireland and Denmark to the three European Communities;

(h) Second Budgetary Treaty, 1975 again amending certain financial provisions of the treaties establishing the Communities and of the Merger Treaty;

(i) Second Treaty of Accession, 1979 concerning the accession of Greece to the European Communities;

[1] In addition to these treaties there are several important Decisions of the Council of Ministers which have altered the constitutional structure of the European Communities. These include: Council Decision of 21 April 1970 on "own resources" (JO 1970 L 94); Council Decision of 20 September 1976 on direct elections to the European Parliament by direct universal suffrage, (OJ 1976 L 278/1).

(j) Treaty Amending The Treaties Establishing The European Communities, 1985, making those minor amendments necessary for Greenland's withdrawal from the Communities (having been granted home rule in May 1979 by Denmark, Greenlanders then decided in a referendum in 1982 to withdraw from the European Communities);

(k) Third Treaty of Accession, 1985 concerning the accession of Spain and Portugal as of 1 January 1986.

As this Guide focuses upon the EEC it is item (c), the Treaty of Rome of 1957 establishing that particular Community, as subsequently amended or supplemented by items (d) to (k), which will henceforth be considered. The EEC Treaty may be regarded as a *traité cadre,* or a skeleton treaty, requiring secondary legislation to put the flesh on the bare, general principles laid down by the Articles of the Treaty; there are some 248 Articles in the Treaty, many of which are concerned with establishing the Community's institutions. So the Treaty itself only provides the basic policies of the Community.

Where to find the Treaties

The main treaties governing the European Communities are available in English from HMSO[2] or alternatively they can be found in *European Community Treaties* (4th ed, 1980) published by Sweet and Maxwell. There is also the useful Clarendon Press publication *Basic Community Laws* (1st ed, 1980), edited by Rudden & Wyatt, which contains not only the text of the principal treaties but also extracts from some of the most important EEC Regulations and Directives relating to, for example, the competition rules, and the social security provisions of the EEC.

2 *MEASURES TAKEN BY THE COMMUNITY INSTITUTIONS*

Measures taken by the Council of Ministers and by the Commission under the EEC Treaty form the most important secondary source of Community law. In this regard Article 189 of the EEC Treaty is of vital importance. It states that in order to carry out their tasks the Council and Commission shall, in accordance with the provisions of the Treaty, "make Regulations, issue Directives, take Decisions, make Recommendations or deliver Opinions".[3] Article 189 then describes the main characteristics of each of these five measures and it will be helpful at this stage to consider each of them in turn.

[2] The London HMSO provides a full list of EEC publications.

[3] Capital letters are used throughout this book for EEC Regulations, Directives, Decisions etc in order to distinguish them from national regulations etc.

(a) REGULATIONS

> A Regulation shall have general application. It shall be binding in its entirety and directly applicable[4] in all Member States.

Regulations are the most important source of secondary Community law. As Regulations are binding in their entirety, a member state cannot pick and choose the provisions it wishes to obey, ignoring the rest. Doing so may well result in the country being taken before the Court of Justice by the Commission as happened in 1979 when the United Kingdom only partially implemented the EEC tachograph Regulations because of trade union opposition.[5] Thus Regulations are normative in character and bind an indeterminable number of people throughout the Community as they have general application. They have direct application in all the member states without any act of incorporation by those states. Therefore one will not find Regulations being duplicated in the statute book at Westminster; rather the full texts of EEC Regulations are only found in the Official Journal of the European Communities, "L" section (considered further below). It is not only superfluous but quite improper for a member state to repeat verbatim a Regulation in a statute thereby hiding its special character as Community law and confusing its status with that of ordinary national legislation within the domestic legal system.[6] A member state may, nevertheless, be permitted by an EEC Regulation itself to introduce certain measures to implement the administrative details of the Regulation.

(b) DIRECTIVES

> A Directive shall be binding, as to the result to be achieved, upon each Member State to which it is addressed, but shall leave to the national authorities the choice of form and methods.

Directives differ from Regulations in that Directives do not have general application; instead a Directive is binding only on the particular member state(s) to which it is addressed and even then only binding as to the result to be achieved, leaving the method of implementation to the discretion of the member state(s) concerned. Directives are most frequently used in those areas where the objective is the gradual approximation or harmonisation of the national laws of the member states, for example in achieving equal access for men and women to vocational training and equal treatment for them in social security matters. A Directive invariably stipulates a time-limit, frequently eighteen months or two years, for implementation by member states. If a member state has not complied with the Directive within the requisite period, the Commission may well bring proceedings before the European Court of Justice under Article 169 of the EEC Treaty for a declaration that that country has failed to fulfil its obligations under

[4] The term "directly applicable" is considered in Ch 5 *post*.

[5] *Commission* v *UK (Re Tachographs)* [1979] ECR 419; [1979] 2 CMLR 45.

[6] *Eg Variola* v *Amministrazione Italiana delle Finanze* [1973] ECR 981.

Community law. Such action has been taken recently against the United Kingdom for failing to comply with the Equal Pay Directive.[7] Moreover, if provisions of a Directive are directly effective an individual may rely upon them before a national court even if the member state has not implemented the Directive within the time-limit. This concept of "directly effective" provisions of Community law is considered in the next chapter. Directives are also published in the "L" section of the Official Journal of the European Communities.

(c) DECISIONS

> A Decision shall be binding in its entirety upon those to whom it is addressed.

Decisions are administrative measures and thus a Decision differs from a Regulation in that the former does not have general application nor is it directly applicable. Decisions also differ from Directives since the former can be addressed to private individuals as well as to member states whereas Directives are only addressed to member states. Moreover Decisions, unlike Directives, are binding in their entirety and not just as to the result to be achieved. One will often find Decisions addressed by the Commission to companies which it has found to be in breach of the EEC's competition rules. Decisions, like Regulations and Directives, are published in the Official Journal, "L" section.
section.

(d) and (e) RECOMMENDATIONS AND OPINIONS

> Recommendations and Opinions shall have no binding force.

Council or Commission Recommendations and Opinions are of persuasive or informative value only. As they are not binding, they are published in the "C" section (for communications) in the Official Journal. Other acts of the Community institutions, which are not listed in Article 189, like Notices, Communications and Information for example, give general information but do not constitute binding legislation and so they too appear in the "C" section of the Official Journal.

Therefore, of the five measures listed in Article 189, only three are legally binding—Regulations, Directives and Decisions—and these can all be found in the "L" section of the Official Journal. There are a number of important points which must be made about these three forms of secondary Community legislation. First, although the distinctions between the three types of measures seem quite clear as set out above, one should be wary of the label attached to a particular measure. For example, a measure may be designated a "Council Regulation" or "Commission Regulation" but may in reality be a Decision as it binds a specific number of persons, instead of having general application as a true Regulation should have. The European

[7] *Commission* v *UK (Re Equal Pay)* [1982] ECR 2601; [1982] 3 CMLR 284.

Court of Justice will look at the substance of the measure, and not just at the label given to it.[8] The true nature of the measure is of vital importance especially when it comes to cases of judicial review of Community action by the Court of Justice as ordinary individuals only have limited *locus standi* to challenge Decisions and may only indirectly challenge a Regulation in very special circumstances. Thus it may be crucial for an individual to show that a so-called "Regulation" is in substance a bundle of individual Decisions in order to challenge its validity. Further consideration is given to the topic of judicial review of Community measures in Chapter 8 *post.*

Secondly, unlike the legislature of the United Kingdom, the Council and Commission of the European Communities are required by Article 190 of the EEC Treaty to state in the preamble to their Regulations, Directives and Decisions the reasons on which they are based and to refer to any proposals or opinions which were required to be obtained pursuant to the EEC Treaty. For an illustration, consider the text of the Council Directive of 19 December 1978 on the progressive implementation of the principle of equal treatment for men and women in matters of social security[9] as set out below:

> The Council of The European Communities.
>
> Having regard to the Treaty establishing the European Economic Community, and in particular Article 235[10] thereof,
>
> Having regard to the proposal from the Commission,
>
> Having regard to the opinion of the Economic and Social Committee,
>
> Whereas Article 1 (2) of Council Directive 76/207 EEC of 9 February 1976 on the implementation of the principle of equal treatment for men and women as regards access to employment, vocational training and promotion, and working conditions provides that, with a view to ensuring the progressive implementation of the principle of equal treatment in matters of social security,the Council, acting on a proposal from the Commission, will adopt provisions defining its substance, its scope and the arrangements for its application;
>
> Whereas the Treaty does not confer the specific powers required for this purpose;
>
> Whereas the principle of equal treatment in matters of social security should be implemented in the first place in the statutory schemes which provide protection against the risks of sickness, invalidity . . .
>
> Whereas . . .
>
> Has adopted this Directive:
>
> Article 1 The purpose of this Directive is the progressive implementation, in the field of social security and other elements of social protection provided for in Art. 3 of the principle of equal treatment for men and women in matters of social security . . .

[8] See *International Fruit Co* v *Commission* [1971] ECR 411.

[9] Council Directive 79/7 EEC (OJ 1979 L 6/24).

[10] Art 235 EEC Treaty gives the Council of Ministers a very general grant of power to take appropriate measures if "action by the Community should prove necessary to attain, in the course of the operation of the common market, one of the objectives of the Community and this Treaty has not provided the necessary powers".

Clearly then, by reading the preamble to a measure, one can learn a considerable amount about its development. For instance, from the above one can see that the Directive was made by the Council, acting under Article 235 of the Treaty, upon a proposal of the Commission and that the Economic and Social Committee had been consulted.

The reasons for the measure are also stated. Failure to comply with Article 190 of the EEC Treaty constitutes an infringement of an essential procedural requirement and is therefore a ground for annulment of the measure of the Council or Commission under Article 173 of the EEC Treaty. Likewise failure by the Council or Commission to consult other bodies where so required by the EEC Treaty would also constitute a breach of an essential procedural requirement. *Roquette Frères* v *Council (The Isoglucose Case)*[11] illustrates this point well. According to Article 43 (2) of the EEC Treaty, the Council is required to obtain an Opinion from the European Parliament prior to making Regulations concerning agricultural products. In March 1979 the Council proposed a Regulation concerning quotas and production levies for isoglucose which were to come into force on 1 July 1979. The Council did refer the proposed Regulation to the European Parliament for its Opinion but no such Opinion had been received by the Council before the end of the parliamentary session, which just happened to be the last one before the first direct elections to the European Parliament. However, the Bureau of the Parliament had earlier decided that an extraordinary session of the Parliament could be called by the Council if necessary. Instead of following this emergency procedure, the Council, without obtaining the necessary Opinion, simply went ahead and made the Regulation on isoglucose. Roquette Frères, a French company manufacturing isoglucose, asked the European Court of Justice to declare the Regulation void on the ground that the Council had adopted the Regulation without having received the Opinion of the Parliament as required by Article 43 (2) of the EEC Treaty. In its judgment the Court made some very important points about the consultation processes involved in making secondary Community legislation. The Court stated that:

> The consultation provided for in the third subparagraph of Article 43 (2), as in other similar provisions of the Treaty, is the means which allows the Parliament to play an actual part in the legislative process of the Community. Such power represents an essential factor in the institutional balance intended in the Treaty. Although limited, it reflects at Community level the fundamental democratic principle that the people should take part in the exercise of power through the intermediary of a representative assembly. Due consultation of the Parliament in the cases provided by the Treaty therefore constitutes an essential formality disregard of which means that the measure concerned is void.[12]

It followed that in the absence of the Opinion of the European Parliament as required by the Treaty, the isoglucose Regulation was declared void.

[11] [1980] ECR 3333.

[12] *Ibid,* at p 3360.

In conclusion, it can be seen that when confronted with secondary Community legislation in the form of an EEC Regulation, Directive or Decision of either the Council or Commission, one can discover from its preamble the reasons why it was made, the Article of the Treaty on which it was based and of course, one should check to see that the proper procedural requirements have been followed like consultation with the European Parliament and/or the Economic and Social Committee as this can be a ground for challenging its validity before the ECJ.

HOW SECONDARY EEC LAW IS MADE

As explained in the previous chapter, the Council of Ministers is the main legislative body of the EEC with the Commission having a certain amount of legislative power delegated to it by the Council. Whether a measure has been made by the Council or Commission will be indicated in the exact title of the measure as printed in the Official Journal. Regulations, Directives and Decisions of the Commission have the same binding force as those of the Council and should not be regarded as somehow inferior just because the Commission's legislative powers are more limited than those of the Council.

Having made those preliminary points, one may well ask how are these EEC Regulations, Directives etc made? The bulk of Community law is of a secondary nature, designed to fill out the details of the policies laid down in general terms by the EEC Treaty. Much of this secondary legislation is enacted by the Council of Ministers acting upon proposals from the Commission. A long consultation process invariably precedes the drawing up of the Commission's proposal. During this period it will consult various interested groups and experts in the particular area. The Economic and Social Committee, an advisory body, is frequently consulted. Where the EEC Treaty so requires, the European Parliament's Opinion on the proposal must be obtained[13] and in other cases where important matters are being legislated upon it has become common practice to consult the Parliament. One or more of the European Parliament's Specialised Committees concerned by the proposal will discuss it, appointing a rapporteur to give a report on it which will subsequently be discussed by the whole Parliament. After all the necessary consultation, the Commission's proposal is sent to COREPER, the Committee of Permanent Representatives whose job it is to prepare the work of the Council of Ministers and the agenda for the meetings of the Council. When COREPER has managed to reach agreement on a proposal it is listed as an "A Point" on the agenda for the next Council meeting whereas if no agreement on it yet exists, the proposal is held over as a "B Point". In this way COREPER greatly assists the Council of Ministers in its work but COREPER cannot

[13] There are seventeen occasions when the Parliament's Opinion must be obtained. Arts 7, 14, 43, 54, 63, 75, 87, 100, 126, 127, 201, 203, 203a, 228, 235, 236 and 238 EEC Treaty.

fully eliminate disagreements even over proposals at "A point". Due to the increased reliance on the Luxembourg Accords, requiring the unanimous vote of the Council members on a proposal which a member state feels will affect a very important national interest, the legislative process within the EEC has been greatly slowed down. When the Accords were first introduced in 1966 unanimity was easier to achieve because there were only six members of the Council of Ministers but as a result of the two enlargements of the EEC there are now ten members and obviously unanimity will be even more difficult to achieve when two more voices are added to the Council with the accession of Spain and Portugal. Calls for the abandonment of the Luxembourg Accords have been growing louder and it is expected that in the near future the Council will revert to the voting procedures stipulated in the EEC Treaty itself, that is to voting by simple majority unless the Treaty itself requires unanimity or a qualified vote.

According to Article 149 (2) of the Treaty, if the Council wants to amend a Commission proposal, then it must be unanimous. In view of the Council's difficulty in reaching unanimity as explained above, a proposal has a better chance of being enacted unchanged than amended by the Council. Since before presenting a proposal to the Council, the Commission has usually consulted widely and taken account of the views of various bodies, it is not necessarily unfortunate that the Council cannot easily amend the considered proposal of the Commission. As the Commissioner most concerned with the particular proposal is able to attend (but without having a vote) the relevant Council meeting to support the proposal, the Commission is in a strong position in relation to Community legislation.

Entry into Force

Draft proposals for Community legislation are published in the "C" section of the Official Journal of the European Communities. When the proposed measures are eventually passed by the Council, or by the Commission on those occasions when the latter has legislative powers conferred on it by the Council, the measures are published in the "L" section of the Journal. Article 191 of the EEC Treaty requires Regulations to be published in the OJ and provides that Regulations enter into force on the date specified therein or if no such date is specified, then on the twentieth day after their publication. As for Directives and Decisions, Article 191 requires that they be notified to the addressee(s) and they take effect upon notification. Although not required by Article 191, they too are invariably published in the Official Journal with commencement dates. Particular attention should always be paid to the date of entry into force of a Community Regulation, Directive or Decision not only because there are strict time-limits (often as short as 2 months) within which to challenge the validity of such measures[14] but also because it may be necessary to know exactly when one can rely upon a particular Community measure as being directly effective. (The concept of direct effectiveness of Community law and judicial review of Community legislation will be considered later in Chapters 5 and 8 respectively).

Where to find Secondary Legislation

The measures taken by the Community institutions are published in the Community's official languages[15] in the "Official Journal of the European Communities" which appears virtually daily. As from 1 January 1968 the Journal was divided into two separate sections, one marked "L" for Legislation and the other marked "C" for Communications. Since then the legally binding measures—Regulations, Directives and Decisions of the Council and Commission—are located in the "L" section of the Journal, while the non-binding acts of the institutions such as Commission proposals for legislation, the proceedings of the European Parliament and information about cases before the ECJ are contained in the "C" section. In addition a new "S" section, or supplement section, of the Official Journal was introduced in 1976 and in it one finds invitations for tenders to EEC contracts.

It was not until 1 January 1973 when the United Kingdom, Denmark and the Republic of Ireland joined the European Communities, that the Journal was first published in English and referred to as the "Official Journal of the European Communities", or the "OJ" for short, rather than the "Journal Officiel" (JO). References to publications in the Journal after 1 January 1973 are made by stating the year, then "L" or "C" section followed by the number of the issue and finally the page. (*Eg* Council Directive 79/7 EEC, OJ 1979 L 6/24 refers to an EEC Directive made by the Council of Ministers that can be located in the "L" section of the OJ, issue number 6 of 1979 at page 24.) As for the measures of the institutions in force before the United Kingdom's accession on 1 January 1973, most of these were published in English in the "Special Editions of the Official Journal". Hence there are now authentic English translations of all the most important Community measures.

One last point about the citation of these measures of the Council and Commission should be noted and that is their individual peculiar style of numbering which is as follows:

Regulations—The number of the Regulation precedes the year of publication *eg* Regulation 1234/82 refers to the Regulation numbered 1234 issued in 1982.

[14] *Eg* Arts 173, 175 EEC Treaty.

[15] Danish, Dutch, English, French, German, Greek and Italian. Spanish and Portuguese will be added in 1986.

Directives —The year of publication precedes the number of the Directive *eg* Directive 82/567 refers to Directive number 567 issued in 1982.

Decisions —Same as for Directives.

3 DECISIONS OF THE EUROPEAN COURT OF JUSTICE (ECJ)

There is absolutely no doubt that through its jurisprudence the European Court of Justice has played a very significant part in the development of European Community law and its decisions must be regarded as a vital source of Community law. In fact the most important principles of Community law have been established by the ECJ rather than stipulated in the EEC Treaty or laid down in some form of secondary Community legislation. The principle of the supremacy of Community law was established by the Court in *Costa* v *ENEL*[16] in 1964 and has been reiterated many times since then. Similarly, the principle of the direct effectiveness of provisions of Community law was first explained by the Court in 1963 in *Van Gend en Loos.*[17] Moreover it was the ECJ which first asserted in 1969 in *Stauder* v *City of Ulm*[18] that the protection of fundamental human rights forms part of the general principles of Community law of which the Court ensures respect. These three decisions alone well illustrate the importance of decisions of this Court as a source of European Community law. Although the ECJ knows no rule of binding precedent, it does in the main follow principles established by it in earlier cases. It is worth remembering that the "reasoned submission", delivered by the advocate-general to the Court of Justice in every case, is not binding upon the Court. Therefore, while such reasoned submissions are extremely informative and may legitimately be referred to in argument, it must be borne in mind that the submissions are not authoritative *per se.*[19]

Where to find Decisions of the European Court of Justice

The European Court Reports (ECR) which are published in English as well as in the other official languages are the only authentic source of citation of the judgments of the Court of Justice. The early volumes of the ECR from 1954 to 1973, published before the United Kingdom's accession, have been translated into English. Alternatively, the main judgments of the Court

[16] [1964] ECR 585; [1964] 425.

[17] [1963] ECR 1; [1963] CMLR 105.

[18] [1969] ECR 419; [1970] CMLR 112.

[19] See Dashwood, "The Advocate-General in the Court of Justice of the EEC" (1982) 2 *Legal Studies* 202.

together with those of the United Kingdom's own domestic courts involving points of EEC law are published in the Common Market Law Reports (CMLR), published by the European Law Centre in London. Individual copies of a "reasoned submission" and/or judgment may be obtained directly from the Court's Information Office in Luxembourg on payment of a small fee.

A 1984 publication, the *Gazetteer of European Law* by Neville Hunnings also provides useful indices of cases concerning European Community law. For example if one only has a case name, like the *"UHT Milk Case"*, one can easily trace it through the indexes in the *Gazetteer* to find its ECR and/or CMLR references.

4 GENERAL PRINCIPLES OF LAW

"General principles of law" are forming an increasingly important, albeit still rather vague, source of European Community law. Again it is through the innovation of the European Court of Justice that certain "general principles" have been culled from the national laws of the member states[20] and used by the Court both as an aid to the interpretation of Community law and as a standard by which to measure the legality of acts of the Community institutions. Such general principles include the principle of proportionality[21] (certainly more familiar to the legal system of the Federal Republic of Germany than to that of the UK), the principle of legal certainty,[22] respect for fundamental human rights (mentioned above in the 1969 *Stauder* case) and certain rules of natural justice (more familiar to the UK system) such as *audi alteram partem*[23] and *nulla poena sine lege.*[24] Where does one find these general principles? In this area there is no ready source as they appear at random in cases decided by the Court of Justice.

Other Publications and Sources of Information

The Community institutions produce a great range of publications besides the aforementioned. Of particular note are the monthly Bulletins of the European Communities, the Annual General Reports of the activities of the European Communities and the reports of the various committees of the European Parliament. An Annual Synopsis of the work of the European Court of Justice also provides useful notes on some of its judgments for a particular year as well as giving more general information about the Court.

20 See Usher, "The Influence of National Concepts in decisions of the European Court", (1975-76) *EL Rev* 359.

21 *Eg Internationale Handelsgesellschaft* v *EVST* [1970] ECR 1125; [1972] CMLR 255.

22 *Eg Brasserie de Haecht* v *Wilkin (No. 2)* [1973] CMLR 287.

23 *Eg Transocean Marine Paint* v *Commission* [1974] ECR 1063; [1974] 2 CMLR 459.

24 Raised in *Hoffmann-La Roche* v *Commission* [1979] ECR 461; [1979] 3 CMLR 211.

Many of these publications are obtainable free of charge from the Office for Official Publications of the European Communities, L-2985, Luxembourg. In addition, the Information Offices of the European Commission of the European Communities, four of which have been established in the United Kingdom, are very helpful when it comes to tracing and supplying particular publications.[25] The Information Office of the European Commission in Northern Ireland is located in Windsor House, Bedford Street, Belfast. If an Information Office does not have a copy of the requested publication in stock, it can normally obtain a copy from the Official Publications Office or the Statistical Office in Luxembourg. Apart from local Information Offices, there are over forty European Documentation Centres (EDCs) throughout the United Kingdom, including ones at the University of Ulster, Coleraine and also at The Queen's University in Belfast. There are also several depository libraries for Community materials in the United Kingdom, mainly in London. Both the EDCs and the depository libraries receive most of the European Community's publications and these publications should be available to the general public during normal opening hours. They are therefore the most easily accessible source of information about the European Communities. In The Queen's University Library, Deck 3 is devoted to European Community materials and there is available a useful guide to explain the contents of the various publications and assist readers in finding them.[26]

Finally, with the recent developments in computerised information retrieval systems EUROLEX and LEXIS can retrieve EEC legislation and decisions of the European Court of Justice very rapidly indeed.

[25] European Commission Information Offices in the UK are at: Windsor House, 9/15 Bedford Street, Belfast BT2 7EG; 7 Alva Street, Edinburgh EH2 4PH; 8 Storey's Gate, London SW1 3AT; 4 Cathedral Road, Cardiff CF1 9SG. There are additional European Parliament Information Offices in the UK.

[26] Kirkpatrick, *Guide to the EEC and its Publications.*

CHAPTER 5

NATURE OF COMMUNITY LAW

Several characteristics of European Community law make it quite unique when compared to Public International law and to the national laws of the EEC's member states. As the Court of Justice explained in an oft-cited passage in *Van Gend en Loos:*

> . . . the Community constitutes a new legal order in international law, for whose benefit the States have limited their sovereign rights, albeit within limited fields, and the subjects of which comprise not only member-States but also their nationals.[1]

Unlike traditional International law under which, for the most part, states are its subjects and individuals merely its objects, Community law imposes duties and creates rights not only for the member states of the EEC but also for the citizens of those states. The other peculiar characteristics of Community law that require more detailed consideration are considered below.

1 AUTONOMY

The European Community's legal system is an autonomous legal system, different from those of the members states which comprise the EEC. The Court of Justice emphasised this point in the leading case of *Costa* v *ENEL* holding that:

> As opposed to other international treaties, the Treaty instituting the EEC has created its own order which was integrated with the national order of the Member States the moment the Treaty came into force; as such, it is binding upon them. In fact, by creating a Community of unlimited duration, having its own institutions, its own personality, and its own capacity in law, apart from having international standing and more particularly, real powers resulting from a limitation of competence or a transfer of powers from the States to the Community, the member-States, albeit within limited spheres, have restricted their sovereign rights and created a body of law applicable both to their nationals and to themselves.[2]

This statement certainly made it clear to member states that membership of the EEC involved not only a limitation of their sovereign rights as mentioned in *Van Gend en Loos* above, but also a transfer of real power to the Community in those areas covered by the EEC Treaty. Since the Community legal system is an autonomous and yet an integral part of the legal systems of the member states, there will inevitably be times when conflicts arise between these legal systems. In cases of conflict the crucial question is which legal system is to prevail, which is to be given supremacy over the other?

[1] *Van Gend en Loos* v *Nederlandse Belastingadministratie* [1963] CMLR 105, 129.

[2] *Costa* v *ENEL* [1964] CMLR 425, 455.

2 *SUPREMACY*

Whenever there is a conflict between Community law and the domestic legislation of a member state, whether it be ordinary legislation, or legislation of a higher constitutional status, Community law must always prevail. This particular characteristic of Community law was emphasised by the Court of Justice in the leading case of *Amministrazione delle Finanze dello Stato* v *Simmenthal (No. 2)* where an Italian company importing beef from France challenged the legality of Italian legislation of 1970, imposing a fee for the veterinary and public health inspection of this imported beef, on the ground that it was incompatible with earlier provisions of EEC law. In considering the relationship between EEC law on the one hand and national laws of the member states on the other, the Court of Justice was quite emphatic that in accordance with the principle of the precedence of Community law, it would not only:

> . . . render automatically inapplicable any conflicting provision of current national law but . . . also preclude the valid adoption of new national legislative measures to the extent to which they would be incompatible with Community provisions. Indeed any recognition that national legislative measures which encroach upon the field within which the Community exercises its legislative power or which are otherwise incompatible with the provisions of Community law had any legal effect would amount to a corresponding denial of the effectiveness of obligations undertaken unconditionally and irrevocably by member states pursuant to the [EEC] Treaty and would thus imperil the very foundations of the community.[3]

It is the supremacy of Community law in every case of conflict with national legislation of the member states that is of fundamental importance to the whole Community legal system. The justification for this claim of supremacy is well explained by the ECJ in the following passages taken from its early judgment in *Costa* v *ENEL*. Here an Italian lawyer was trying to challenge the legality of an Italian law of 1962 that nationalised the production and sale of electricity on the ground that it conflicted with provisions of the EEC Treaty of 1957. On an Article 177 reference to the Court of Justice, the Court in introducing the concept of the supremacy of Community law, explained that:

> The reception, within the laws of each member-state, of provisions having a Community source, and more particularly of the terms and of the spirit of the Treaty, has as a corollary the impossibility, for the member-state, to give preference to a unilateral and subsequent measure against a legal order accepted by them on a basis of reciprocity. In truth the executive strength of Community laws cannot vary from one State to the other in favour of the later internal laws without endangering the realisation of the aims envisaged by the Treaty in Article 5 (2) . . . The transfer, by member-states, from their national order in favour of the Community order of the rights and obligations arising from the Treaty,

[3] [1978] 3 CMLR 263, 283.

> carries with it a clear limitation of their sovereign rights upon which a subsequent unilateral law, incompatible with the aims of the Community, cannot prevail.[4]

By emphasising the supremacy of Community law, the Court of Justice ensures its uniformity throughout all member states thus enabling the aims of the EEC to be fulfilled because a Common Market wherein goods, people and so on can move freely would never be achieved if the member states were free to give priority to their own legislation whenever they thought fit. As Article 5 of the EEC Treaty requires member states to take "all appropriate measures, whether general or particular, to ensure fulfilment of the obligations arising out of this Treaty or resulting from action taken by the institutions of the Community" and "abstain from any measure which could jeopardise the attainment of the objectives of this Treaty," it would seem to follow that the national courts of those states are obliged to abide by the ECJ's exhortation that they give precedence to Community law if it conflicts with domestic legislation in a case before them. This of course presents a dilemma for courts in the United Kingdom as they have to try to reconcile in some way the principle of supremacy of Community law with the principle of UK parliamentary sovereignty. To see how the United Kingdom courts have faced up to this problem so far, the next chapter will deal with the relationship between Community law and the domestic law of the United Kingdom.

3 DIRECT APPLICABILITY AND DIRECT EFFECT

As well as being supreme, provisions of Community law are frequently described as being "directly effective" and/or "directly applicable". Both terms are particularly important from the point of view of an ordinary individual or firm trying to rely upon EEC law before the local courts and therefore they require fuller examination. The concepts of "direct applicability" and "direct effect" of Community law have been developed by the ECJ in recent years and have generated a considerable amount of confusion as well as literature on the subject.[5] Much of the confusion actually stems from the fact that the ECJ tends to use the two terms interchangeably, as illustrated in *Van Gend en Loos,* considered below.

Basically "direct applicability" refers to the mode of reception, or incorporation, of Community law into the domestic legal systems of the

[4] [1964] CMLR 425, 456.

[5] See *eg* Winter, "Direct Applicability and Direct Effect: Two Distinct and Different Concepts of Community Law" (1972) 9 *CML Rev* 425; Steiner, "Direct Applicability in EEC Law—A Chameleon Concept" (1982) 98 *LQR* 229; and see in particular the excellent examination of the topic by a judge of the European Court of Justice, Judge Pescatore, "The Doctrine of Direct Effect: An Infant Disease of Community Law" (1983) 8 *EL Rev* 155.

member states. As the term itself suggests, it means that certain provisions of Community law apply directly within the national legal systems of the member states without further action by their legislatures. In other words, no further act of incorporation is required by a member state to make "directly applicable" provisions of Community law part and parcel of its national legal order. Regulations are the only provisions of Community law which are expressly said by Article 189 of the EEC Treaty to be "directly applicable" (see p 34 *ante*). Therefore it is totally unnecessary for the Westminster Parliament to duplicate EEC Regulations on the statute book. In fact it is quite wrong for it to do so as such reproduction would obscure the special characteristics, in particular the supremacy, of EEC Regulations.[6]

Member states, may, however, be required by an EEC Regulation to pass implementing legislation to comply with its terms as in the case of the EEC tachograph Regulation, Article 21 of which obliged member states to adopt such laws or administrative provisions as were necessary, *inter alia,* to check compliance with its terms and impose penalties in cases of non-compliance.[7]

The ECJ has, however, over the years held that in addition to Regulations certain Articles of the EEC Treaty and certain provisions of EEC Directives and Decisions may also be "directly applicable". For example, in *Van Gend en Loos* Dutch importers challenged the re-classification of, and thereby the increased rate of import duty levied on, certain chemicals imported by them from West Germany. on the ground that the increased duty was prohibited by Article 12 of the EEC Treaty. The case was referred to the ECJ asking if Article 12 of the Treaty had direct application within the Dutch national legal system. In answering this question the ECJ ruled that Article 12 not only had direct application within the member states but, moreover, it should be interpreted as producing "direct effects" and thus creating individual rights which domestic courts should protect.[8]

Thus it was in the *Van Gend en Loos* ruling of February 1963 that the ECJ introduced the concept of "direct effect" of certain provisions of Community law. This concept is an invention of the European Court of Justice since the term "direct effect" was not used at all in the EEC Treaty itself. If a provision of Community law is held by the ECJ to be "directly effective", it means that it creates immediate rights that individuals may enforce before the local domestic courts. The rationale for the development of this concept is that the effectiveness (or as appears in the Court's judgments, *l'effet utile)* of Community law is brought home to ordinary individuals when they can rely upon it in their local courts in order to overcome inconsistent domestic law. Therefore it is of crucial importance

[6] *Eg Variola* v *Amministrazione Italiana delle Finanze* [1973] ECR 981.

[7] Council Regulation 1463/70 EEC (OJ 1970 L 164/1) implemented in N Ireland by the Passenger and Goods Vehicles (Recording Equipment) Regulations (NI) 1979.See ch 14 *post* for further comment.

[8] *Op cit, supra* n l, at p 130.

for individuals to know which provisions of Community law are "directly effective" because they increase the number of remedies and defences available to ordinary individuals before their own local courts and, coupled with the principle of supremacy of Community law, such provisions do, of course, provide an effective means of overriding conflicting domestic legislation. In *Van Gend en Loos,* for instance, the Dutch importers were immediately able to invoke the aid of Article 12 of the EEC Treaty directly to overcome the Dutch legislation, which had reclassified particular imported chemicals so that they fell within a higher tariff level. Similarly in *R* v *Bouchereau*[9] when a French citizen working in England was threatened with deportation for illegal possession of controlled drugs, he was able to rely upon certain directly effective provisions of Community law to challenge his recommended deportation from the United Kingdom with the result that he was merely fined instead.

Having emphasised the importance of knowing which provisions of Community law are "directly effective", it may initially be somewhat disconcerting to learn that their exact number is uncertain. This uncertainty results from the fact that, having invented the concept, the ECJ decides on a purely *ad hoc* basis whether a particular provision of Community law has direct effect. What is certain though is that the ECJ has held not only Articles of the EEC Treaty to be "directly effective",[10] but also particular provisions of Regulations,[11] of Directives[12] and of Decisions[13] to have this peculiar characteristic. In deciding which provisions of Community law are "directly effective", the Court of Justice applies certain tests. To be "directly effective" a provision must be "complete and legally perfect", that is to say a provision must be:

(i) sufficiently clear and precise for judicial application;

and (ii) unconditional. Therefore, if there is a time-limit for implementation, as is invariably the case with Directives, that time-limit must have passed[14];

and (iii) require no further act of implementation by the member states or by the Community institutions.

If there is not already a ruling by the ECJ on whether or not a particular provision of Community law is "directly effective", then by applying these

[9] [1977] ECR 1999; [1977] 2 CMLR 800.

[10] *Eg* Arts 7, 12, 13, 16, 31, 32, 33, 34, 48, 85 (1) and (2), 86, EEC Treaty. See Collins, *European Community Law in the United Kingdom* (3rd ed, 1984) pp 89-92 for a full list.

[11] *Bertholet* [1966] CMLR 191.

[12] See *eg Van Duyn* v *Home Office* [1974] ECR 1337; [1975] 1 CMLR 1; *Pubblico Ministero* v *Ratti* [1979] ECR 1629; [1980] 1 CMLR 96.

[13] See *eg Grad* v *Finanzamt Traunstein* [1970] 2 ECR 825; [1971] CMLR 1.

[14] *Op cit, supra* n 12.

tests to that provision and finding them to be satisfied, one can predict with a certain degree of reliability that, given an opportunity, the ECJ will probably rule such provision to have "direct effect". To resolve the issue conclusively, however, an Article 177 reference should be made by the national court to the ECJ, asking it to rule on the point as the ECJ is the only court having competence to rule on the interpretation of Community law. Thus, for instance, in *Johnston* v *Chief Constable of the Royal Ulster Constabulary*[15] a Northern Ireland Industrial Tribunal recently made an Article 177 reference to the European Court of Justice to ascertain whether a provision of Directive 76/207[16] on equal treatment for men and women as regards access to employment was directly effective, thus giving a woman the right to have her contract as a full-time RUC police reservist renewed as had happened in the case of the male police reservists.

When the distinction between "direct applicability" (which goes to incorporation of Community law into the national legal systems of the EEC's member states) and "direct effect" (which goes to remedies before the national courts) is explained as above, one may ask why there is such confusion and controversy about these two concepts.[17] The common explanation is that much of it is caused by the ECJ itself using the terms interchangeably as if there is no distinction. For example, in the same sentence the ECJ may say, as it did in *Van Gend en Loos*, that:

> Article 12 of the EEC Treaty has direct application within the territory of a member-state and enures the benefit of citizens whose individual rights the internal courts should protect.[18] (sic)

This apparent carelessness of expression by the Court of Justice may be explained by looking again at the three tests used by the Court to determine whether a provision of Community law is "directly effective". The third test is that the provision must require no further act of implementation by the member states or Community institutions. Now recall the meaning of "directly applicable"—it too means that a provision of Community law requires no act of incorporation by the member state to make the provision part of its domestic law. Thus if a provision of Community law complies with all three tests and is held by the ECJ to be "directly effective", it must follow that the provision is also "directly applicable". The converse, however, is not true; for example, although a Regulation is "directly applicable", as expressly stated by Article 189 of the EEC Treaty, it does not follow that every provision of that Regulation must be "directly effective" because some of its provisions may require implementation (like Article 21 of the tachograph Regulation) or may be of a general, descriptive nature and therefore could not be "complete and legally perfect" as is required of

15 Unreported NI judgment of 17 May 1982, preliminary ruling expected 1986.

16 (OJ 1976 L 39/40). Set out in Rudden and Wyatt, *Basic Community Laws* (1980) pp 281-284.

17 See Hartley, *The Foundations of European Community Law* (1981) ch 7 for details.

18 *Op cit. supra* n 1, at p 132.

"directly effective" provisions. In conclusion, it can be said that while all provisions of an EEC Regulation have direct application and the national courts should take judicial notice of them in their entirety, not every provision of a Regulation will necessarily produce "direct effects" giving immediate rights to individuals which they may rely upon before those courts. In practice, this does not cause problems because all EEC Regulations are directly applicable in member states. They are therefore part and parcel of the domestic legal system of the United Kingdom and since Regulations like all Community law are supreme, they will prevail over inconsistent United Kingdom implementing measures or other conflicting United Kingdom legislation.

4 GENERAL APPLICATION IN ALL MEMBER STATES

Another important feature of Community law is that it is common to all the member states of the EEC. In order to bring about a Common Market and achieve common policies in areas like agriculture and more recently fisheries, it is obviously essential that Community law should have uniform and general application in all member states. The supremacy of Community law over all conflicting types of national legislation is intended to ensure its uniformity and common application throughout the European Community. Since a characteristic of EEC Regulations is their general application, they are the most appropriate means of bringing about common policies for the whole of the EEC and so one should expect to find Regulations establishing common market organisations for agricultural products, implementing the competition rules and the so-called "fundamental freedoms of the EEC" like the free movement of people and of goods within the EEC.

CONCLUSION

Of all the characteristics of Community law, the one to be emphasised is that of its supremacy over all conflicting national laws. Therefore, once EEC law is mentioned, the word "supremacy" should immediately spring to mind. The importance of this point is well-illustrated by reference to *Pigs Marketing Board (Northern Ireland)* v *Redmond.*[19] In this case Redmond was prosecuted for moving bacon pigs within Northern Ireland without the proper transportation documents issued by the Pigs Marketing Board (NI) pursuant to the Movement of Pigs Regulations (Northern Ireland) 1972. When this case came before the Resident Magistrate in Armagh, he decided to refer it to the European Court of Justice for a preliminary ruling, making it in fact the first such reference from a Northern Ireland court. The Court

[19] [1978] ECR 2347; [1979] 1 CMLR 177.

of Justice ruled that the Movement of Pigs (Northern Ireland) Regulations were incompatible with the EEC's provisions on the free movement of goods and in particular a 1975 Regulation governing the common organisation of the market in pigmeat. Consequently, when this ruling was returned to the Resident Magistrate to apply to the facts of the case, the proceedings against Redmond were dismissed as being ill-founded.[20]

Another useful illustration of the advantages derived from invoking EEC law is *Macarthy's Ltd* v *Wendy Smith*,[21] an English case where a female store manager, who was paid £10 less than her male predecessor for doing broadly similar work, was able to rely upon Article 119 of the EEC Treaty in order to obtain the same pay as the man. She had been employed four months after the man had left the job and, therefore, a majority in the Court of Appeal felt that she was not entitled to the same pay as the man under the Equal Pay Act 1970, as she had not worked contemporaneously with her male predecessor. She relied upon Article 119 of the Treaty which had already been held by the ECJ to be directly effective.[22] It states the bare principle that "men and women should receive equal pay for equal work" without any qualification as to the time of the employment. On an Article 177 reference to the Court of Justice, the Court ruled that as long as the essential nature of the work done by the woman was the same as that done by the man, then she was entitled to the same pay as him since Article 119 was not confined to situations in which men and women are contemporaneously doing equal work for the same employer. Thus, by virtue of reliance upon Article 119 of the EEC Treaty, Mrs Smith was eventually awarded the same pay as her predecessor, a result that would not have occurred had she only been able to rely on the Equal Pay Act 1970.[23]

These two cases clearly indicate the benefits that may be derived from pleading points of Community law and the need, therefore, for legal practitioners to have a working knowledge of substantive provisions of EEC law in order to advise clients properly.

20 [1979] 3 CMLR 118.

21 [1979] 3 All ER 325 and [1981] 1 All ER 111 (CA); [1980] 2 CMLR 205 (ECJ).

22 See *Defrenne* v *SABENA* [1978] ECR 1365; [1978] 3 CMLR 312.

23 See Szyszczak, "Pay Inequalities and Equal Value Claims" (1984) 48 *MLR* 139. See also *Garland* v *British Rail Engineering Ltd* [1982] ECR 359; [1982] 1 CMLR 696.

CHAPTER 6

RELATIONSHIP BETWEEN COMMUNITY LAW AND UK DOMESTIC LEGISLATION

In the previous chapter the main characteristics of Community law were discussed. Aware that the Community legal system is autonomous, and that Community law must be given precedence over every kind of domestic legislation in the member states, courts and legal practitioners in the United Kingdom may well ask what they should do if confronted with a conflict between some domestic legislation and an Article of the EEC Treaty or an EEC Regulation or Directive? Must they now ignore the basic constitutional principle of the sovereignty of the United Kingdom Parliament in order to give precedence to some Community legislation "concocted" in Brussels? Moreover, clients may seek advice from legal practitioners about the existence of additional rights and remedies available to them by virtue of directly effective and directly applicable provisions of Community law. In this chapter these questions will be resolved by considering the relationship between Community law and domestic legislation of the United Kingdom.[1]

In the United Kingdom it is a prerogative of the Crown to enter into international treaties. In practice this prerogative is exercised by government ministers, acting on behalf of the Crown. Once entered into, a treaty is binding on the United Kingdom Government at an international level but a treaty will not form part of the United Kingdom's domestic law unless and until an Act of Parliament is passed giving effect to it. In this way the fundamental constitutional principle of the sovereignty of the United Kingdom Parliament is maintained. This was well explained by Lord Denning MR in *McWhirter* v *Attorney-General,* a case decided after the signing of the EEC Treaty but before an Act had been passed to incorporate it into United Kingdom domestic law:

> Even though the Treaty of Rome has been signed, it has no effect, so far as these courts are concerned, until it is made an Act of Parliament. Once it is implemented by an Act of Parliament, these courts must go by the Act of Parliament. Until that day comes, we take no notice of it.[2]

The European Communities Act 1972 (ECA 1972) was the Act passed by the United Kingdom Parliament to give effect to the provisions of the European Community treaties. In other words, the ECA 1972 is, to use Lord Denning's phraseology, the Act of Parliament by which the United Kingdom courts must go. As its long title states, the European Communities Act is an Act:

[1] For a detailed account see Collins, *European Community Law in the United Kingdom* (3rd ed, 1984) Chs 1 and 2.

[2] [1972] CMLR 882, 886.

to make provision in connection with the enlargement of the European Communities to include the United Kingdom, together with (for certain purposes) the Channel Islands, the Isle of Man and Gibraltar.

The Act has two parts and four Schedules. Part I entitled "General Provisions" deals with, *inter alia,* the general implementation of Community Treaties, and decisions on and proof of the Treaties, and other Community measures. Part II contains amendments to existing United Kingdom legislation and makes provision for such matters as customs duties, sugar, the common agricultural policy, companies, cinematograph films, restrictive trade practices and "Community offences" whereby a person who makes a false statement before the ECJ may be punished by a UK court. For present purposes it is Part I of the ECA 1972 and in particular sections 1, 2 and 3 which are relevant. These sections may be examined under the following headings.

1 DIRECT APPLICATION OF COMMUNITY LAW

Section 1 (2) defines "Community Treaties" very widely to include both pre-accession and post-accession treaties. They include the original Treaties establishing the three European Communities and according to section 1 (2) (d):

> . . . any other treaty entered into by any of the Communities, with or without any of the Member States, or entered into, as a treaty ancillary to any of the treaties, by the United Kingdom.

If, by Order in Council, Her Majesty declares a treaty to be a "Community Treaty", then, according to section 1 (3), the Order shall be conclusive on that point; but a treaty entered into after the United Kingdom's accession on 22 January 1972 shall not be so regarded unless a draft of the Order in Council has been approved by resolution of both Houses of Parliament. For example, late in 1984 when the EEC had virtually run out of financial resources, member states agreed to give additional money to the Community. In the United Kingdom this was done by making the European Communities (Definition of Treaties) (Undertaking on Supplementary Finance for the Community) Order 1984 which was to be regarded as a "Community Treaty" and therefore any Community obligations arising therefrom could be charged on the United Kingdom's Consolidated Fund. When a British taxpayer sought to challenge this by way of judicial review on the ground that a full Act of Parliament, rather than delegated legislation, should have been used, the Court of Appeal dismissed the case holding that the 1984 Order would not be *ultra vires* section 1 (3) of the ECA 1972.[3]

[3] *R* v *HM Treasury, ex parte Smedley* [1985] 1 All ER 589.

As to the effect of these Community Treaties within the United Kingdom, section 2 (1) states:

> All such rights, powers, liabilities, obligations and restrictions from time to time created or arising by or under the Treaties, and all such remedies and procedures from time to time provided for by or under the Treaties, *as in accordance with the Treaties are without further enactment to be given legal effect or used in* the United Kingdom shall be recognised and available in law and be enforced, allowed and followed accordingly; and the expression "enforceable Community right" and similar expressions shall be read as referring to one to which this subsection applies. [Emphasis supplied]

This provision requires further comment to highlight its significance. First, section 2 (1) is extremely widely drafted to include "rights, powers, liabilities, obligations and restrictions" plus "remedies and procedures" which already exist or may arise in the future ("from time to time created or . . . provided for"). Secondly, it includes all rights, remedies and so forth arising under both the Community Treaties and secondary Community legislation which are regarded by Community law as directly applicable ("as in accordance with the Treaties are without further enactment . . ."). They are immediately available in the United Kingdom without further ado.

Thus section 2 (1) of the ECA 1972 makes directly applicable Community law part and parcel of the law of the United Kingdom which cannot be ignored by United Kingdom courts, lawyers and law enforcement agencies; they must always be aware that through section 2 (1) of the ECA 1972 springs a constant source of Community rights, obligations and remedies, which may have considerable influence upon the wide range of activities now affected by Community law.

2 IMPLEMENTATION OF COMMUNITY OBLIGATIONS

As some provisions of Community law, especially Directives, require implementation by the member states, it is section 2 (2) of the ECA 1972 that provides for such implementation of Community obligations in the United Kingdom. It provides that implementation of any Community obligation may be by subordinate legislation in the form of Orders in Council or regulations made by any designated Minister or department. In this context "designated Minister or department" means such Minister of the Crown or government department as may from time to time be designated by Order in Council for a particular matter or purpose. For example, it is the Department of Agriculture that is designated to deal with the implementation of EEC agricultural obligations. However, it is important to note that the powers conferred by section 2 (2) of the ECA 1972 are limited by Schedule 2 of the Act and consequently do not include the power—

(a) to impose or increase taxation
(b) to enact retrospective legislation
(c) to sub-delegate legislative power other than rules of procedure for any court or tribunal
(d) to create any new criminal offence punishable with imprisonment for more than two years or punishable on summary conviction with imprisonment for more than three months or with a fine of more than £2,000 (if not calculated on a daily basis) or with a fine of more than £100 a day.[4]

If implementation of a Community obligation makes it necessary to do any of these four things a full Act of Parliament is required, rather than subordinate legislation.

3 SUPREMACY OF COMMUNITY LAW

Having by section 2 (1) incorporated within the United Kingdom directly effective Community law and by section 2 (2) implemented other provisions of Community law, section 2 (4) of the ECA 1972 attempts to deal with potential conflicts between these Community law provisions and United Kingdom domestic legislation. The supremacy of Community law, its most fundamental characteristic, which had been developed by the European Court of Justice long before the United Kingdom's accession to the EEC, had to be accommodated when the Westminster Parliament passed the ECA in 1972. Regrettably, the accommodation provided by section 2 (4) is still uncertain, not least because the section is so badly drafted. It reads as follows:

> The provision that may be made under subsection (2) above includes, subject to Schedule 2 to this Act, any such provision (of any such extent) as might be made by Act of Parliament, *and any enactment passed or to be passed,* other than one contained in this Part of this Act, *shall be construed and have effect subject to the foregoing provisions of this section* . . . [Emphasis supplied]

If this section was intended to help United Kingdom courts in cases of a conflict between Community law and domestic United Kingdom legislation, then it is arguable that its complex wording makes it more of a hindrance than a help. Differing interpretations of section 2 (4) have been postulated by various writers but its full implications have not yet been worked out by the United Kingdom courts. It may be that by providing that "any enactment passed or to be passed . . . shall be construed and have effect subject to the foregoing provisions" of section 2, which include the

[4] The levels of fines originally provided in the ECA 1972 were increased by arts 4 (6) (a) and 8 of the Fines and Penalties (NI) Order 1984, SI 1984/703 (NI 3) and by s 32 (3) of the Criminal Law Act 1977 respectively. Art 17 of the 1984 Order contains power to "inflation proof" the level of fines and under this the £1,000 fine was doubled by SR 1984/253 as from 1 Sept. 1984.

recognition and application of directly effective provisions of Community law under section 2 (1), that Parliament intended that all United Kingdom domestic legislation, both past and future, should be subordinated to Community law in every case of conflict. If this interpretation is correct and the ECA 1972 is protected by section 2 (4) from even express repeal by a subsequent Act of Parliament it necessarily involves the death of the principle of parliamentary sovereignty. If such a radical change in United Kingdom Constitutional law was really intended by Parliament in enacting the ECA 1972 one could not be criticised for expecting it to have been carried out more clearly, and certainly more openly, instead of having it tucked away in the middle of a subsection as complex as section 2 (4).

However. the interpretation of section 2 (4), which seems to have the most widespread support,[5] is that it not only gives Community law precedence over existing United Kingdom law, but it also protects Community law against implied repeal by a subsequent United Kingdom statute. In other words in accordance with section 2 (4) of the ECA 1972 Community law should be given precedence over conflicting United Kingdom legislation unless Parliament *expressly* provides in a later statute that it should prevail over Community law. This interpretation has been supported by, *inter alia,* Lord Denning MR, albeit *obiter,* in a 1979 case on equal pay, *Macarthy's Ltd* v *Wendy Smith* where he observed:

> If the time should come when our Parliament deliberately passes an Act—with the intention of repudiating the [EEC] Treaty or any provision in it—or intentionally of acting inconsistently with it—and says so in express terms—then I should have thought that it would be the duty of our courts to follow the statute of our Parliament. I do not however envisage any such situation . . . Unless there is such an intentional and express repudiation of the Treaty, it is our duty to give priority to the Treaty.[6]

Such an interpretation is, however, quite contrary to the European Court of Justice's exhortation that in every case of conflict between national laws of member states and Community law, it is Community law which should prevail. In the leading case of *Amministrazione delle Finanze dello Stato* v *Simmenthal* (No 2), where there was a conflict between provisions of the EEC Treaty on the abolition of customs duties on goods between member states, and a subsequent Italian law imposing a veterinary charge on the import of meat from France the Court of Justice stressed that:

> A national court which is called upon, within the limits of its jurisdiction, to apply provisions of Community law is under a *duty* to give full effect to those provisions, *if necessary refusing of its own motion to apply any conflicting provisions of national legislation, even if adopted subsequently, and it is not necessary for the Court to request or await a prior setting aside of such provision by legislative or other Constitutional means.*[7] [Emphasis added]

[5] See de Smith, *Constitutional and Administrative Law* (5th ed, 1985) p 90 *et seq;* Ellis, "Supremacy of Parliament and European Law" (1980) 96 *LQR*. 511.

[6] [1979] 3 CMLR 44, 47.

[7] [1978] ECR 629, 644.

The Court of Justice could hardly have made clearer its instructions to national courts. It remains to be seen whether United Kingdom courts will follow these instructions or uphold the fundamental principle of Parliamentary sovereignty when it comes to a head-on conflict between Community law and a subsequent Act of Parliament, which expressly contradicts the former. In reality it seems that unless the United Kingdom Government had decided to withdraw from the European Communities, it is unlikely that Parliament would deliberately pass conflicting legislation with the intention of repudiating the EEC Treaty.

4 DECISIONS ON, AND PROOF OF, COMMUNITY LAW

It is suggested that United Kingdom courts, confronted with a conflict between Community law and domestic law, should bear in mind the ECJ's clear exhortation in *Simmenthal,* particularly in light of the instructions given to them by Parliament in section 3 (1) of the ECA 1972. Section 3 (1) of the 1972 Act provides:

> For the purposes of all legal proceedings any question as to the meaning or effect of any of the Treaties, or as to the validity, meaning or effect of any Community instrument, shall be treated as a question of law (and, if not referred to the European Court, be for determination as such *in accordance with the principles laid down by and any relevant decision of the European Court).* [Emphasis supplied]

Therefore, where a point of Community law is in issue before a United Kingdom court it should either be referred to the Court of Justice under Article 177 of the EEC Treaty for a preliminary ruling (as explained in the next chapter) or, if not so referred, be decided upon "in accordance with the principles laid down by and any relevant decision of the Court of Justice". As such principles undoubtedly include that of the supremacy of Community law, reiterated so often by the Court of Justice, section 3 (1) adds strength to the interpretation that by section 2 (4) of the ECA 1972 Parliament did intend that its legislation, past and future, should be made subordinate to Community law.

Moreover, by section 3 (2) of the ECA 1972 United Kingdom courts are required to take judicial notice of the Community Treaties, of the Official Journal of the Communities (see p 40 *ante*) and of any decision of, or expression of opinion by, the European Court of Justice on any questions as to the meaning or effect of provisions of Community law. The Official Journal is admissible as evidence of any instrument or other act thereby communicated of any of the three European Communities or of any of the Community institutions.

5 CHARGE ON THE CONSOLIDATED FUND

Section 2 (3) of the ECA 1972 provides for a charge on, and payment out of, the United Kingdom Consolidated Fund or, if so determined by HM Treasury, the National Loans Fund, of the amounts required to meet this country's financial obligations to the Community.[8] Northern Ireland's contribution to such payments is allowed for by section 13 of the Northern Ireland Constitution Act 1973, but the details of this are beyond the scope of this Guide.

RELEVANT STATUTORY PROVISIONS

For reference purposes the full text of the relevant sections of the European Communities Act 1972 are set out below.

EUROPEAN COMMUNITIES ACT 1972 as amended by the European Communities (Greek Accession) Act 1979

1. SHORT TITLE AND INTERPRETATION

1. (1) This Act may be cited as the European Communities Act 1972.

(2) In this Act and, except in so far as the context otherwise requires, in any other Act (including any Act of the Parliament of Northern Ireland):

'the Communities' means the European Economic Community, the European Coal and Steel Community and the European Atomic Energy Community;

'the Treaties' or 'the Community Treaties' means, subject to subsection 3 below, the pre-accession treaties, that is to say, those described in Part I of Schedule 1 to this Act, taken with:

(a) the treaty relating to the accession of the United Kingdom to the European Economic Community and to the European Atomic Energy Community, signed at Brussels on the 22 January 1972; and

(b) the decision, of the same date, of the Council of the European Communities relating to the accession of the United Kingdom to the European Coal and Steel Community; and

(c) the treaty relating to the accession of the Hellenic Republic to the European Economic Community and to the European Atomic Energy Community, signed at Athens on 28 May 1979; and

(d) the decision, of 24 May 1979, of the Council relating to the accession of the Hellenic Republic to the European Coal and Steel Community;

and any other treaty entered into by any of the Communities, with or without any of the Member States, or entered into, as a treaty ancillary to any of the Treaties, by the United Kingdom;

and any expression defined in Schedule 1 to this Act has the meaning there given to it.

(3) If Her Majesty by Order in Council declares that a treaty specified in the Order is to be regarded as one of the Community Treaties as herein defined, the Order shall be conclusive that it is to be so regarded; but a treaty entered into by the United Kingdom after the 22 January 1972, other than a pre-accession treaty to which the United Kingdom accedes on terms settled on or before that date, shall not be so regarded unless it is so specified, nor be so specified unless a draft of the Order in Council has been approved by resolution of each House of Parliament.

(4) For purposes of subsections (2) and (3) above, 'treaty' includes any international agreement, and any protocol or annex to a treaty or international agreement.

[8] *Op cit, supra* n 3.

2. GENERAL IMPLEMENTATION OF TREATIES

2. (1) All such rights, powers, liabilities, obligations and restrictions from time to time created or arising by or under the Treaties, and all such remedies and procedures from time to time provided for by or under the Treaties, as in accordance with the Treaties are without further enactment to be given legal effect or used in the United Kingdom shall be recognised and available in law, and be enforced, allowed and followed accordingly; and the expression 'enforceable Community right' and similar expressions shall be read as referring to one to which this subsection applies.

(2) Subject to Schedule 2 of this Act, at any time after its passing Her Majesty may by Order in Council, and any designated Minister or department may by regulations, make provision:

(a) for the purpose of implementing any Community obligation of the United Kingdom, or enabling any such obligation to be implemented, or of enabling any rights enjoyed or to be enjoyed by the United Kingdom under or by virtue of the Treaties to be exercised; or

(b) for the purpose of dealing with matters arising out of or related to any such obligation or rights or the coming into force, or the operation from time to time, of subsection (1) above;

and in the exercise of any statutory power or duty, including any power to give directions or to legislate by means of orders, rules, regulations or other subordinate instrument, the person entrusted with the power or duty may have regard to the objects of the Communities and to any such obligation or rights as aforesaid.

In this subsection 'designated Minister or department' means such Minister of the Crown or government department as may from time to time be designated by Order in Council in relation to any matter or for any purpose, but subject to such restrictions or conditions (if any) as may be specified by the Order in Council.

(3) There shall be charged on and issued out of the Consolidated Fund or, if so determined by the Treasury, the National Loans Fund the amounts required to meet any Community obligation to make payments to any of the Communities or Member States, or any Community obligation in respect of contributions to the capital or reserves of the European Investment Bank or in respect of loans to the Bank, or to redeem any notes or obligations issued or created in respect of any such Community obligation; and, except as otherwise provided by or under any enactment:

(a) any other expenses incurred under or by virtue of the Treaties or this Act by any Minister of the Crown or government department may be paid out of moneys provided by Parliament; and

(b) any sums received under or by virtue of the Treaties or this Act by any Minister of the Crown or government department, save for such sums as may be required for disbursements permitted by any other enactment, shall be paid into the Consolidated Fund or, if so determined by the Treasury, the National Loans Fund.

(4) The provision that may be made under subsection (2) above includes, subject to Schedule 2 to this Act, any such provision (of any such extent) as might be made by Act of Parliament, and any enactment passed or to be passed, other than one contained in this Part of this Act, shall be construed and have effect subject to the foregoing provisions of this section; but, except as may be provided by any Act passed after this Act, Schedule 2 shall have effect in connection with the powers conferred by this and the following sections of this Act to make Orders in Council and regulations.

(Sections 2(5) and (6) omitted.)

3. DECISIONS ON, AND PROOF OF, TREATIES AND COMMUNITY INSTRUMENTS ETC.

3. (1) For the purposes of all legal proceedings any question as to the meaning or effect of any of the Treaties, or as to the validity, meaning or effect of any Community instrument, shall be treated as a question of law (and, if not referred to the European Court, be for determination as such in accordance with the principles laid down by and any relevant decision of the European Court).

(2) Judicial notice shall be taken of the Treaties, of the *Official Journal of the Communities* and of any decision of, or expression of opinion by, the European Court on any such question as aforesaid; and the *Official Journal* shall be admissible as evidence of any instrument or other act thereby communicated of any of the Communities or of any Community institution.

(Final provisions omitted.)

CHAPTER 7

REFERENCES FOR PRELIMINARY RULINGS FROM THE EUROPEAN COURT OF JUSTICE

Since the European Communities Act 1972 charges courts in the United Kingdom with the duty of recognising, allowing and enforcing European Community law, it is inevitable that in doing so they will encounter difficulties involving the interpretation and validity of provisions of EEC law. For instance, a court or tribunal may be faced with problems concerning the compatibility of United Kingdom legislation with Community law as was the Armagh Magistrates' Court in *Pigs Marketing Board (NI)* v *Redmond*[1], or the direct effectiveness of provisions of a Council Directive as occurred recently before a N Ireland Industrial Tribunal in *Johnston* v *The Chief Constable of the Royal Ulster Constabulary*[2], or concerning the validity of a Commission Decision on the ground, *inter alia,* that it infringes the fundamental human rights enshrined in the general principles of Community law as in *R* v *Kent Kirk*[3] a case that arose before Newcastle-Upon-Tyne Crown Court. Judging by these few examples, one can appreciate that questions concerning Community law may arise in a variety of ways before United Kingdom courts and tribunals.

However national courts and tribunals of the member states may not themselves rule upon the validity or the interpretation of Community law; it is the European Court of Justice, and it alone, which has competence to interpret and to determine the validity of Community law. This point was justified by the Court of Justice in the leading case of *Internationale Handelsgesellschaft* v *EVST* where a German exporter wanted to challenge the validity of certain EEC Regulations on the ground that they conflicted with fundamental rights guaranteed by the German Constitution. The Court of Justice refused to allow the German courts to test EEC law in this way. The Court explained that:

> . . . Recourse to legal rules or concepts of national law to judge the validity of instruments promulgated by Community institutions would have the effect of harming the unity and efficacy of Community law. The validity of such instruments can only be judged in the light of Community law. In fact, the law born from the [EEC] Treaty, the issue of an autonomous source, could not, by its very nature, have the Courts opposing to it rules of national law of any nature whatever without losing its Community character and without the legal basis of the Community itself being put in question.[4]

[1] [1978] 2 CMLR 697; ECJ ruling [1978] ECR 2347; [1979] 1 CMLR 177.

[2] Unreported NI decision of 17 May 1982. Eventually referred to ECJ on 8 August 1984.

[3] [1984] 3 CMLR 522.

[4] [1972] CMLR 255, 283.

The converse is also true in that it is for the national courts of the member states to interpret and rule on the validity of their own domestic legislation while the Court of Justice is not competent to declare national legislation void.

Thus while the national courts of the member states are bound to apply Community law, it is the Court of Justice in Luxembourg which is bound to interpret and rule upon the validity of that law. In this context it is Article 177 of the EEC Treaty which provides the essential means of co-operation between the Court of Justice and the national courts.

Article 177 provides:

> The Court of Justice shall have jurisdiction to give preliminary rulings concerning:
>
> (a) the interpretation of this Treaty;
>
> (b) the validity and interpretation of acts of the institutions of the Community;
>
> (c) the interpretation of the statutes of bodies established by an act of the Council, where those statutes so provide.
>
> Where such a question is raised before any court or tribunal of a Member State, that court or tribunal may, if it considers that a decision on the question is necessary to enable it to give judgment, request the Court of Justice to give a ruling thereon.
>
> Where any such question is raised in a case pending before a court or tribunal of a Member State, against whose decisions there is no judicial remedy under national law, that court or tribunal shall bring the matter before the Court of Justice.

This Article 177 reference procedure enables a national court or tribunal, when confronted with questions about the meaning or validity of a provision of Community law, to stay its own proceedings and refer these questions to the Court of Justice in Luxembourg for an authoritative ruling, which is then handed back down to the referral court to apply to the facts of the case. Therefore, although the Article 177 procedure is commonly called the "preliminary" reference procedure, this is something of a misnomer as the reference to the Court of Justice is in fact an intermediate step in the proceedings, which begin and end in the national court.

Some general comments may be made about the Article 177 procedure before examining it in more detail. Firstly, the whole aim or purpose of the Article 177 procedure is to ensure the uniform interpretation and proper application of Community law in all the EEC countries. Clearly it would be wholly incompatible with the fundamental characteristic of Community law, namely its general and uniform application throughout the EEC (see *ante* Chapter 5), if the national courts simply took it upon themselves to interpret or rule on the validity of Community law. As the Court of Justice has explained:

> Article 177 is essential for the preservation of the Community character of the law established by the [EEC] Treaty and has the object of ensuring that in all circumstances this law is the same in all States of the Community.
>
> Whilst it thus aims to avoid divergences in the interpretation of Community law which the national courts have to apply, it likewise tends to ensure this application by making available to the national judge a means of eliminating difficulties which may be occasioned by the requirements of giving Community law its full effect within the framework of the judicial systems of the member States.[5]

Secondly, the Article 177 preliminary reference procedure has been immensely influential in the development of Community law by the Court of Justice. It has been the vehicle used by the Court to develop all the main features of Community law; the principles of the supremacy of Community law,[6] the direct effect of certain of its provisions[7] and the protection of fundamental rights within its general principles[8] have all been established by the Court of Justice on Article 177 references from national courts. Indeed preliminary rulings make up a considerable amount of the workload of the Court of Justice. From recent statistics about the Court's work, which are set out on page 89 one can see that out of a total of 1,839 judgments delivered before the end of 1985, well over half of them (1,146) were preliminary rulings. Some 116 of the 229 judgments given during 1985 alone were preliminary rulings, while in 1982 the figure was 94 out of 185 judgments.[9]

With these two general comments in mind, one may now consider the particular prerequisites for a preliminary reference.[10] Consideration of these will involve a detailed examination of Article 177 under the following headings:

(1) Questions which may be referred
(2) Courts and tribunals that may make references
(3) When to make a reference
(4) Duty or discretion to make a reference
(5) Procedure for making references
(6) Effect of preliminary rulings

[5] *Rheinmühlen-Düsseldorf* v *EVST* (No 1) [1974] 1 CMLR 523,577.

[6] See *Costa* v *ENEL* [1964] ECR 585.

[7] See *Van Gend en Loos* [1963] ECR 1.

[8] See *Stauder* v *City of Ulm* [1969] ECR 419; [1970] CMLR 112.

[9] Statistics taken from *Synopsis of the work of the Court of Justice of the European Communities in 1983,* published by the Office for Official Publications of the European Communities.

[10] For a detailed analysis see Collins, *European Community law in the United Kingdom* (3rd ed, 1984) Ch 3; Hartley, *The Foundations of European Community Law* (1981) pp 247-282; Brown and Jacobs, *The Court of Justice of the European Communities* (2nd ed, 1983) Ch 9.

1 QUESTIONS WHICH MAY BE REFERRED

The first paragraph of Article 177 of the EEC Treaty confers jurisdiction on the Court of Justice to give preliminary rulings concerning:

(a) the interpretation of the Treaty
(b) the interpretation and validity of acts of the Community institutions
(c) the interpretation of the statutes of bodies established by an act of the Council of Ministers where such statutes so provide.

As subparagraph (c) is so restrictive, covering only statutes of bodies set up by acts of the Council which expressly permit references to the Court of Justice, it is in fact of little practical importance and may therefore be disregarded. Subparagraphs (a) and (b) of Article 177 (1) are in practice the important ones. Under these subparagraphs courts in the United Kingdom may, and in some cases must, refer questions of interpretation and validity of Community law to the Court of Justice. Under Article 177 (1) (a) they *may* ask the Court of Justice to interpret an Article of the EEC Treaty itself, its annexes and amendments made to it by other treaties like the Accession Treaties. For example, in *Pigs Marketing Board (NI)* v *Redmond,* the Resident Magistrate asked if certain Articles of the Treaty were "directly applicable so as to confer upon individuals rights enforceable by them in the courts of the United Kingdom".[11] Note that Article 177 (1) (a) does not envisage national courts challenging the validity of provisions of the EEC Treaty; they may only ask for interpretations of provisions of the Treaty since its validity is taken for granted.

On the other hand, subparagraph (b) of Article 177 (1) does enable United Kingdom courts to ask the Court of Justice to interpret and also to rule on the validity of "acts" of Community institutions. This is widely interpreted to include all binding measures of the Council and Commission like Regulations, Directives and Decisions, as well as other binding *sui generis* acts such as Council Resolutions[12] and association agreements concluded by the Council with non-EEC countries.[13] It must be stressed that the ability of national courts to challenge the validity of such a wide variety of "acts" of the Community institutions by using the Article 177 procedure is extremely important, particularly for individual litigants. This is because the other methods prescribed by the EEC Treaty for individuals to challenge directly the legality of EEC Regulations, Directives and so on are limited by strict rules of *locus standi* and by short limitation periods, usually only two

[11] [1978] 2 CMLR 697, 709. "Directly applicable" in this quotation is understood by the writer to be more properly "directly effective". See Ch 5 *ante* for detailed discussion.

[12] See *Re ERTA* [1971] ECR 263 where the ECJ held that a Council Resolution on the European Road Transport Agreement (ERTA) was a *sui generis* act for the purposes of Art 173 EEC Treaty. Arguably it also follows that it is an "act" for the purposes of Art 177.

[13] See *Haegeman* v *The Belgian State* [1974] ECR 449, 459 where the ECJ stated that an Association Agreement between Greece and the EEC was an "act" of the Community institutions within the meaning of Art 177 (1) (b).

months[14] (See Chapter 8 *post*). There are no such limitations in the case of preliminary rulings. Thus for the private litigant Article 177 provides a useful means of challenging the legality of measures taken by the Community institutions. It is, however, an indirect method of challenge for private parties because the reference must be made by the domestic court or tribunal; an individual cannot himself make an Article 177 reference directly to the Court of Justice. To summarise thus far, it is questions concerning *the interpretation of the EEC Treaty* as well as *the interpretation and validity of acts of Community institutions* that may be referred to the Court of Justice under Article 177. Obviously the interpretation or validity of domestic law of the United Kingdom cannot be the subject of a preliminary ruling and so if a United Kingdom court or tribunal asks the Court of Justice to rule on such aspects of United Kingdom legislation or administrative practices, the Court of Justice will not do so. Rather, it will extract those parts of the questions that concern Community law and rule upon them, thus enabling the United Kingdom court or tribunal itself to decide upon the compatibility of the national law or administrative practices with Community law.

2 COURTS AND TRIBUNALS THAT MAY MAKE REFERENCES

According to Article 177 of the EEC Treaty questions about the interpretation or validity of Community law may only be referred to the Court of Justice from "a court or tribunal of a Member State". It goes almost without saying that courts and tribunals of non-EEC countries may not make references to the Court of Justice. It is also clear from the wording of Article 177 that references may be made by the United Kingdom's civil and criminal courts. What though is the position as regards references from administrative tribunals, arbitrators, ombudsmen and professional bodies such as the Law Society of Northern Ireland? The question of what constitutes a "court or tribunal of a Member State" for the purposes of Article 177 is determined by the Court of Justice by reference to Community law rather than by focusing on the national labels or designations given to these bodies. The ECJ has given the phrase a wide interpretation for Article 177 purposes. The factors that the Court of Justice has taken into account when classifying a body as a "court or tribunal of a Member State", include the degree of *public* recognition given to the body, whether it decides points of law and whether its decisions are legally binding rather than merely advisory.[15] It appears therefore from the case-law of the Court of Justice that *private* arbitration tribunals and professional bodies like the Law Society of Northern Ireland[16] would not constitute a "court or tribunal" within the meaning of Article 177. Within the United Kingdom references have in

[14] In particular, Arts 173 and 175 of the EEC Treaty.

[15] See *Vaassen-Göbbels case* [1966] ECR 261; CMLR 508.

[16] See *Broekmeulen case* [1981] ECR 2311; [1982] 1 CMLR 91 and also *Re Borker* [1980] ECR 1975; [1980] 3 CMLR 638. *Cf Nordsee* v *Nordstern AG* [1982] ECR 1095.

fact been made and accepted by the Court of Justice from a wide spectrum of bodies, ranging from the House of Lords right down to the National Insurance Commissioner.[17] It should be noted that where a body has a right to make a reference by virtue of the wide interpretation of Article 177 (2), that right cannot be abrogated by national law. Since Community law is supreme, the ECJ's interpretation of a "court or tribunal of a Member State" will prevail over any national interpretation of the phrase.

3 WHEN TO MAKE A REFERENCE

Not every question of Community law that is raised before United Kingdom courts and tribunals should be referred to the Court of Justice for a preliminary ruling. As Article 177 paragraph 2 explains, a reference need only be made where a national court or tribunal considers that a decision on a question of Community law is *necessary* to enable it to give judgment in the case. When then should a reference be made? There can be no definitive answer to this question as it is for the particular national court or tribunal itself, and not the parties, to make that assessment. In their work on preliminary references Jacobs and Durand warn that:

> Greater caution may be necessary in the United Kingdom courts before deciding that a reference is unnecessary, because the technique of interpreting Community law is somewhat different from that to which the United Kingdom courts are accustomed. For example, in order to interpret a particular provision of the Treaty, the European Court will first examine the general propositions containing the aims of the Treaty, and the system of the Treaty with its divisions into parts and chapters . . . Next the Court will look at the structure of the article in question, in its context. Lastly and with far less emphasis than in a United Kingdom court the words of the provision in question are examined. The interpretation of regulations and other acts of Community institutions follows a similar pattern.[18]

Therefore the word "necessary" should not be construed too narrowly by United Kingdom courts and tribunals.

While it is up to the national court to determine when it is "necessary" to have the Court of Justice rule on a particular point of Community law, the Court has recently stressed in two related, and rather extraordinary cases, that it will only have jurisdiction to give a ruling in the case of "a genuine dispute". Therefore, the Court of Justice will not give a ruling under Article 177 in a hypothetical case, nor apparently where the parties involved in the case before the national court have in some way arranged a dispute in order for a reference to be made. As these two cases are noteworthy from the point of view of the Court's interpretation of Article 177, they merit closer analysis.

[17] The first reference from the House of Lords was in *R* v *Henn and Darby* [1979] 2 CMLR 495. For a reference from the Nat. Insurance Commissioner see *Brack* v *Insurance Officer* [1976] ECR 1429; [1976] 2 CMLR 592.

[18] *References to the European Court: Practice and Procedure*, (1975) p 161.

Both cases, *Foglia* v *Novello (No. 1)*[19] and *(No. 2)*[20], arose out of the same set of facts. Novello, an Italian, contracted with an Italian wine merchant, Foglia, for the delivery of fortified wines from Italy to France. A clause in their contract relieved Novello of any charges imposed by French or Italian authorities that were contrary to Community law. A similar clause was inserted in the contract between Foglia and the carrier. Nevertheless the carrier paid the French tax on the imported wines to the French authorities without protest. Foglia repaid the tax to the carrier and then claimed reimbursement from Novello, who then relied upon the clause in their contract. Before an Italian magistrates' court, Foglia sought to rely upon Article 95 of the EEC Treaty which prohibits member states from imposing on the products of other member states any internal taxation of any kind in excess of that imposed on similar domestic products. The magistrate decided to make an Article 177 reference to the Court of Justice, requesting an interpretation of Article 177 itself and of Article 95 of the Treaty. In *Foglia* v *Novello (No. 1)* the Court of Justice declared itself to have no jurisdiction to give a ruling on the questions asked by the Italian court. The Court of Justice felt that the dispute had been fabricated by the parties for neither the carrier nor Foglia had tried to rely upon the clauses in the contracts when asked to pay the levies nor had the parties contested the legality of the levy before the French courts. Instead the two Italians were seeking to rely on Community law before an *Italian* court, in particular upon the direct effectiveness of Article 95 of the Treaty, in order that the Court of Justice should declare *French* tax legislation inapplicable. The Court baulked at this prospect and refused to give a ruling, saying:

> The duty of the Court of Justice under Article 177 of the EEC Treaty is to supply all courts in the Community with the information on the interpretation of Community law which is necessary to enable them to settle *genuine disputes* which are brought before them.[21]

As the parties were in agreement that the French tax was contrary to Article 95 of the EEC Treaty, there was no "genuine dispute" and therefore the Court considered that no ruling was necessary.

When the decision was sent back to the Italian magistrate, he made a second reference to the Court of Justice, including more information this time, to try to show the genuineness of the dispute between the parties. Nevertheless in *Foglia* v *Novello (No. 2)* the Court of Justice again declined to give a ruling under Article 177 since the magistrate had not revealed any new facts which would justify the Court taking a different view of its jurisdiction. The Court emphasised:

[19] [1980] ECR 745; [1981] 1 CMLR 45.

[20] [1981] ECR 3045; [1982] 1 CMLR 585.

[21] [1981] 1 CMLR 45, 58. Emphasis added.

> . . . that Article 177 gives the Court of Justice the task, not of formulating advisory opinions on general or hypothetical questions, but of contributing to the administration of justice in Member States. Consequently it would not have jurisdiction to answer questions of interpretation submitted to it as part of a procedural arrangement by the parties with a view to procuring the Court to comment on certain problems of Community law which do not satisfy an objective need inherent in the decision of a dispute.[22]

Both cases have attracted adverse criticism[23], because they are regarded as an unwelcome change in the Court of Justice's previous liberal policy towards accepting references from national courts. It should, however, be added that the facts in *Foglia* v *Novello* were quite extraordinary in that there were two Italian citizens, who were not in a real dispute about Community law, but were seeking to rely upon it before one of their own national courts in order to challenge the legislation of another member state, France. The Court of Justice clearly felt that it would have to be particularly vigilant in such "extraordinary circumstances" to ensure that the Article 177 procedure was not misused by individuals. To assist the Court of Justice in this respect, national courts or tribunals should take cognisance of the introduction by the Court in the course of its judgment in *Foglia* v *Novello (No. 2)* of a requirement that:

> . . . it is essential for national courts to explain the *reasons,* unless the reasons are beyond any doubt clear from the file, why they consider that a reply to their questions is *necessary* for a decision in the case.[24]

Consequently it is submitted that one should not draw the far-reaching conclusion from *Foglia* v *Novello* that the Court of Justice has suddenly decided to restrict references from national courts as subsequent cases have demonstrated its continuing readiness to accept references.[25]

4 DUTY OR DISCRETION TO MAKE A REFERENCE

The lower courts and tribunals in the United Kingdom, as in all the member states, *may* under Article 177 (2) make a reference to the Court of Justice if a decision on a question of interpretation or validity of Community law is necessary for them to reach a judgment in the case before them; thus lower courts have a discretion to refer.[26] In 1974 in *Bulmer* v *Bollinger*[27] in

[22] [1982] 1 CMLR 585, 609.

[23] See *eg* Barav, "Preliminary Censorship? The Judgment of the European Court in Foglia v Novello", (1980) 5 *EL Rev* 443. See also Bebr, "The Existence of a Genuine Dispute: An Indispensable Precondition of the Jurisdiction of the Court under Article 177 EEC Treaty?" (1980) 17 *CML Rev* 523 and Bebr. "The Possible Implications of Foglia v Novello (2)" (1982) 19 *CML Rev* 525.

[24] [1982] 1 CMLR 585, 608. Emphasis added.

[25] See *Chemial Faemaceutici* v *DAF* [1981] ECR 1; [1981] 3 CMLR 350.

[26] See *Rheinmühlen-Düsseldorf* v *EVST* (No 1) [1974] ECR 33; [1974] 1 CMLR 523 and (No 2) [1974] ECR 139; 1974 1 CMLR 578.

[27] [1974] 2 All ER 1226; [1974] Ch 401.

the Court of Appeal Lord Denning MR laid down certain guidelines for the exercise of this discretion by the lower courts in the United Kingdom. He urged them to take into account such factors as:

— the time it would take to obtain a ruling from the Court of Justice;
— the importance of not overloading the Court;
— the need to formulate the questions clearly;
— the difficulty and importance of the point;
— the expense of obtaining a ruling; and
— the wishes of the parties in the dispute.

It must, however, be pointed out that these guidelines are not binding upon the lower courts. Although one suspects that having being provided by the Master of the Rolls, the guidelines must at that time have deterred the lower courts from making references to the Court of Justice, the evidence of the annual increase in the number of references by the lower courts in the United Kingdom since then indicates that any deterrent effect of the guidelines has certainly waned. This can be seen from the Table on page 73 showing the number, and break-down by type of court, of Article 177 references from the United Kingdom since accession to the Communities on 1 January 1973.

As for the higher courts, paragraph 3 of Article 177 imposes a *duty* to refer on courts or tribunals of a member state "against whose decisions there is no judicial remedy under national law". Two theories exist as to the meaning of this phrase. According to one, "the abstract theory", the phrase only covers the highest court in each member state and so, for instance, only the House of Lords in the United Kingdom would be obliged to refer. According to the other theory, "the concrete theory", the phrase extends to whichever court or tribunal happens to be the final one in any particular case and so, for example, the Court of Appeal would come within Article 177 (3) in a case where leave to appeal to the House of Lords had been refused.

There seems to be no agreement between the judges in the United Kingdom courts as to which of these theories is correct. In *Bulmer* v *Bollinger,* Lord Denning MR preferred the abstract theory, and declared, albeit *obiter,* that the Court of Appeal is never obliged to make an Article 177 reference. However, in a more recent Court of Appeal case in 1980, *Hagen* v *Fratelli D and G Moretti S N C,* Buckley L J stated *obiter* that:

> . . . when a case reaches the ultimate court of appeal in any domestic jurisdiction—and that, in the case of this country, is either this court if leave to appeal to the House of Lords is not obtainable, or the House of Lords [a reference should be made].[28]

[28] [1980] 3 CMLR 253, 255.

This view, in support of "the concrete theory", certainly seems preferable to "the abstract theory" and has considerable support from academics and from the Court of Justice itself. Jacobs and Durand contend that:

> The determining factor should be whether the court's decision on the question of Community law in that case is subject to appeal; for only if it is, can an erroneous interpretation of Community law be corrected, either by the appeal court or on a reference from the appeal court.[29]

It is submitted that this offers the best guidance for a court or tribunal in the United Kingdom, which wishes to know if it is obliged to make an Article 177 reference.

Even courts of last instance are under a duty to make references only when a decision on the interpretation or validity of Community law is *necessary* to enable them to give judgment. This point was settled recently by the Court of Justice in *CILFIT* v *Italian Ministry of Health*[30] which is now regarded as the main authority on the duty of courts or tribunals of last instance to make references. The case involved questions of interpretation of Community legislation to ascertain whether or not wool was an "animal product". The question arose before the Italian Supreme Court of Cassation where it was argued that since it was a court of last resort within the meaning of Article 177 (3), it had a duty to refer any questions of Community law raised before it, whether or not they were necessary to enable it to give judgment in the case. The Court of Cassation then submitted questions to the Court of Justice for a ruling on the meaning of Article 177 (3) of the Treaty. The Court of Justice explained that:

> . . . the courts or tribunals referred to in paragraph (3) have the same discretion as any other national court or tribunal to ascertain whether a decision on a question of Community law is *necessary* to enable them to give judgment. Accordingly, those courts or tribunals are not obliged to refer to the Court of Justice a question concerning the interpretation of Community law raised before them *if that question is not relevant,* that is to say, if the answer to that question, regardless of what it may be, can in no way affect the outcome of the case.[31]

If, however, courts or tribunals of last instance consider that a decision on a point of Community law is necessary to enable them to decide the case, then as a general rule Article 177 (3) imposes an obligation on them to refer the case to the Court of Justice. To this general rule the Court listed, in the *CILFIT* case, certain exceptions where courts and tribunals covered by Article 177 (3) have a discretion rather than a duty to make a reference. The first exception is when the question of Community law raised before the national court or tribunal has already been interpreted by the Court of Justice. In such cases, courts and tribunals of last instance are not under a duty to make references, but instead have a discretion to do so. As the Court explained:

[29] *Op cit, supra* n 18 at p 163.

[30] [1983] 1 CMLR 472; [1982] ECR 3415.

[31] [1983] 1 CMLR 472, 490. Emphasis added.

> . . . it must not be forgotten that in all such circumstances national courts and tribunals, including those referred to in paragraph (3) of Article 177, remain entirely at liberty to bring a matter before the Court of Justice if they consider it appropriate to do so.[32]

This is an important point to remember since the Court of Justice is not bound by precedent and may, therefore, change or elaborate upon its view on a point of Community law that it has dealt with earlier.

The other exception to the general rule that references must be made by courts or tribunals of last resort is where, as the Court pointed out in *CILFIT:*

> . . . the correct application of Community law may be so obvious as to leave no scope for any reasonable doubt as to the manner in which the question raised is to be resolved. Before it comes to the conclusion that such is the case, the national court or tribunal must be convinced that the matter is equally obvious to the courts of the other member-States and to the Court of Justice. Only if those conditions are satisfied, may the national court or tribunal refrain from submitting the question to the Court of Justice and take upon itself the responsibility for resolving it.[33]

Since Community law uses terminology that is quite peculiar to it and is drafted in several official languages, national courts and tribunals should be very careful indeed in deciding that a point of Community law is so clear *(acte clair)* that a reference need not be made to the Court of Justice under Article 177.

5 PROCEDURE FOR MAKING REFERENCES[34]

In the United Kingdom rules have been made governing the procedure for certain courts making references to the Court of Justice under Article 177 of the EEC Treaty. It should be added of course that even in the absence of special rules, any court or tribunal in the United Kingdom, is empowered by Article 177 itself to make a reference to the Court in Luxembourg.

In N Ireland the procedure to be followed by the Court of Appeal and the High Court when making references to the Court of Justice is laid down by Order 114 of the Rules of the Supreme Court (Northern Ireland) 1980, which is set out in Appendix I of this book. In addition Order 23 of the County Court Rules (Northern Ireland) 1981[35], laying down the procedure for County Courts making references, is set out in Appendix II.

Once a reference is made, it may take between nine and twelve months for the ECJ to give a ruling in the case and return it to the referral court to apply to the facts of the case.

[32] *Ibid.*

[33] *Ibid,* at p 491.

[34] *Op cit, supra* n 10, Collins at p 155 *et seq*. See also Usher, *European Court Practice,* (1983) p 154 *et seq*.

[35] County Court Rules (NI), SR 1981 No 225.

COSTS: Under Article 72 of the ECJ's Rules of Procedure proceedings before the Court of Justice are not normally subject to court fees. Moreover the Court will not make an order as to costs on an Article 177 reference. It leaves the question of such costs to be determined by the referral court since the reference is regarded as an integral part of the national proceedings. This means that in the United Kingdom courts costs will, as normal, be at the discretion of the court.

LEGAL AID: Again since an Article 177 reference is regarded as part of the national proceedings it follows that in the United Kingdom legal aid may be available to cover preliminary references.[36] In certain special circumstances, under Article 104 of the Rules of Procedure of the Court of Justice, the Court may grant as legal aid, assistance to meet the costs of representation.[37] For example, if legal aid is not available in the national proceedings, the Court may grant it.[38]

6 EFFECT OF PRELIMINARY RULINGS

After the Court of Justice gives its ruling, a certified copy of it is sent back to the referral court, which will then recommence its proceedings from where they were adjourned. Strangely enough however Article 177 of the EEC Treaty is silent about the effect of a preliminary ruling by the Court of Justice. This silence gives rise to questions like—Does a ruling on the validity or interpretation of EEC law bind only the referral court or all the courts and tribunals throughout the member states? From the standpoint of the Court of Justice itself, the answer to such questions seem to depend upon whether it is a preliminary ruling on the interpretation of Community law or a ruling on the validity of an act of the Community institutions. If the Court of Justice gives a ruling on the interpretation of a provision of Community law, then that ruling should be followed by the referral court and also by all other national courts and tribunals if they have to apply that particular provision to a case before them. However, they are not precluded from making yet another reference under Article 177 for an interpretation of the same provision if the previous ruling is not sufficiently clear or in case the Court of Justice has changed its view on the particular matter in the light of intervening events.

On the other hand, if the Court holds in a preliminary ruling that an act of a Community institution, for instance a Council Regulation, is invalid, the effect of that ruling is that it is binding only on the particular referral court;

[36] See *R* v *Bouchereau* [1977] ECR 1999.

[37] Article 104 ECJ Rules of Procedure provides:

"As regards the representation and attendance of the parties to the main action in the preliminary ruling procedure the Court shall take account of the rules of procedure applicable before the national court or tribunal which made the reference.

In special circumstances the Court may grant, as legal aid, assistance for the purpose of facilitating the representation and attendance of a party".

[38] See *Lee* v *Minister of Agriculture* [1980] ECR 1495; [1980] 2 CMLR 682.

the ruling does not invalidate that measure *erga omnes* unlike the effect of a successful action for annulment of a Community measure under Article 173 of the EEC Treaty, which does render the measure void *erga omnes*. Nevertheless, if an act of an institution is declared invalid under Article 177, the Court has recently declared that:

> . . . it is sufficient reason for any other national court to regard that act as void for the purposes of a judgment which it has to give. That assertion does not however mean that national courts are deprived of the power given to them by Article 177 of the Treaty and it rests with those courts to decide whether there is a need to raise, once again, a question which has already been settled by the Court where the Court has previously declared an act of a Community institution to be void. There may be such a need in particular if questions arise as to the grounds, the scope and possibly the consequences of the invalidity established earlier.[39]

As far as United Kingdom courts are concerned section 3 (1) of the European Communities Act 1972 provides assistance as to the effect of previous preliminary rulings by the Court of Justice. It states that:

> For the purposes of all legal proceedings any question as to the *meaning* or *effect* of any of the Treaties, or as to the *validity*, meaning or effect of any Community instrument, shall be treated as a question of law *(and, if not referred to the European Court,* be for determination as such in accordance with the principles laid down by and any relevant decision of the European Court). [Emphasis added.]

This section suggests that if a United Kingdom court or tribunal decides not to refer to the Court of Justice questions of Community law under Article 177, then it is bound by other relevant rulings of the Court both on interpretation and validity of Community law.

39 *SpA International Chemical Corporation* v *Amministrazione delle Finanze dello Stato* [1981] ECR 1191, 1223.

TABLE 2

REFERENCES BY UNITED KINGDOM COURTS AND TRIBUNALS TO EUROPEAN COURT OF JUSTICE

	YEAR OF ORDER TO MAKE REFERENCE											
UK COURT	1973	1974	1975	1976	1977	1978	1979	1980	1981	1982	1983	1984
House of Lords							1		1		1	
Court of Appeal					1		1	3				2
High Court		1	1		3	1	2	1	2		3	2
High Court of Justiciary										1		
Crown Court											1	
County Court										1		
Magistrates' Court					1		1		1			
Employment Appeal Tribunal								1	1			
Industrial Tribunal											1	1
National Insurance Commissioner				1	2		2	1				
Social Security Commissioners										2		
Special Commissioners for Inland Revenue					1						1	1
VAT Tribunal										1		

CHAPTER 8

PROCEEDINGS AGAINST COMMUNITY INSTITUTIONS

There may well be occasions when an individual feels so aggrieved by the action of a particular Community institution that he may wish to challenge the legality of that action. If, for example, the Council of Ministers makes a Regulation imposing quotas on vegetable growers but fails to follow the proper procedure in making that Regulation, or the Commission misuses its powers to make a Decision imposing a super-levy on Northern Ireland's dairy farmers, or the European Parliament orders stationery from a Northern Ireland printer but refuses to pay for it, the persons aggrieved by such actions would obviously want to know what proceedings, if any, they could bring against the particular Community institution involved.

There are in fact only a few specific articles of the EEC Treaty that allow ordinary individuals and companies, as well as member states and certain Community institutions, to bring proceedings in cases such as those outlined above, *directly* before the European Court of Justice in Luxembourg. The importance of these articles lies in the fact that they allow individuals to bring direct actions before the Court of Justice. Thus, they differ from Article 177 of the Treaty which provides for an indirect form of action in which the individual brings his case before a domestic court or tribunal which may, or if it is one of last instance *must,* refer the case to the Court of Justice (See Chapter 7 *ante* for details). Some words of caution must though be given from the outset; the few articles of the Treaty that confer jurisdiction upon the Court of Justice in direct actions are complicated by time-limits, *locus standi* requirements, and specific grounds for challenge. If a plaintiff brings proceedings before the Court under one or other of these articles but fails to come within the precise terms of the particular article, then the case will simply be dismissed by the Court as inadmissible without going on to look at its substance. A great amount of the Court's time is in fact taken up with arguments about the admissibility of proceedings and if one looks at the Table on p 89 *post,* one can see just what a large proportion of cases are dismissed as inadmissible. To avoid wasting the Court's time and that of a client, legal practitioners ought to have an awareness of the main features of each of the relevant articles.

The articles of the EEC Treaty giving the Court of Justice jurisdiction to review the acts and omissions of the Community institutions may be divided into two main groups—one group concerns the *legality* of the action or inaction of the Community institutions while the other concerns their *liability*.

A. LEGALITY OF COMMUNITY ACTION

In this first group there are four articles of the EEC Treaty, giving the Court of Justice power to review the legality of Community action.

They are as follows:

(1) Article 172—appeal against fines
(2) Article 173—action for annulment
(3) Article 175—action for failure to act (or the action for inactivity)
(4) Article 184—the plea of illegality (or the defence of inapplicability)

Each of these articles will be considered in turn in order to highlight their primary features.[1]

1 APPEAL AGAINST FINES

Article 172 of the Treaty enables the Council of Ministers in its Regulations to give the Court of Justice plenary, or full, jurisdiction in respect of penalties provided for in those Regulations. Perhaps the most important of such Regulations so far made is Council Regulation 17/62,[2] relating to the EEC's competition rules. Article 17 of this Regulation expressly states that:

> The Court of Justice shall have unlimited jurisdiction within the meaning of Art. 172 of the [EEC] Treaty to review decisions whereby the Commission has fixed a fine or periodic penalty payment; it may cancel, reduce or increase the fine or periodic penalty payment imposed.

If, therefore, the Commission investigates the activities of a Northern Ireland firm, decides that it has infringed the EEC's competition rules and imposes a fine, that firm may bring proceedings before the Court of Justice seeking the annulment of that Commission Decision under Article 173 of the Treaty (discussed below) and also requesting the Court to review the fine pursuant to Article 17 of Regulation 17/62 and Article 172 of the Treaty. (For further details of the EEC competition rules, fines etc see Chapters 15 and 16 *post*).

2 ACTION FOR ANNULMENT

Article 173 of the EEC Treaty is a very important provision indeed as it allows the Court of Justice to annul certain acts of the Community institutions. In accordance with Article 173, paragraph 1 the Court can ". . . review the legality of *acts* of the Council and the Commission, *other than* recommendations and opinions".

[1] For a detailed analysis of each Article, see Hartley, *The Foundations of European Community Law* (1981) Part IV; Brown & Jacobs, *The Court of Justice of the European Communities* (2nd ed, 1983) Chs 6 & 7; Usher, *European Court Practice* (1983); Collins, *European Community Law in the United Kingdom* (3rd ed, 1984) Ch 4.

[2] (OJ Sp Ed 1959-62, p 87).

Clearly, the Court can review all Regulations, Directives and Decisions of the Council of Ministers and the Commission. It should be noted that acts of the European Parliament cannot be reviewed under Article 173 (1),[3] nor can acts of the Court of Justice itself. However, it appears from the case-law of the Court that it will also review the legality of other binding acts of the Council and Commission under Article 173, regardless of the label attached to the particular act. The case of *Commission* v *Council (Re ERTA)*[4] serves as authority for this point. Here the Commission challenged the legality of Council negotiations and conclusions concerning the European Road Transport Agreement on the ground that the Council lacked competence to act in this area. The Court of Justice held the case to be admissible under Article 173 as it opened to review by the Court all measures adopted by the institutions that were intended to have legal force and in this particular case the Council's act was regarded as binding by the member states. The Court, however, went on to dismiss the case on its merits.

Consequently, the Court of Justice may review the legality of all *binding* acts of the Council and Commission under Article 173. Actions may be brought by a member state, the Council of Ministers or by the Commission or, in certain circumstances, by private parties under Article 173. Thus, for instance, the United Kingdom could seek the annulment of a Commission Decision addressed to France, or the Commission could bring an Article 173 action to challenge the legality of the Council's action as in *Re ERTA* discussed above. Member states, the Council and the Commission are, therefore, presumed to have *locus standi* to bring proceedings under Article 173 before the Court of Justice. This is not, however, the case for private parties. Ordinary individuals and companies have limited *locus standi* in that they may only bring an action under Article 173 to challenge specific kinds of acts of the Council and Commission; an individual or company may only challenge certain Decisions of the Council and Commission. According to Article 173, paragraph 3, a private party may only challenge the legality of: (i) a Decision addressed to him personally; or (ii) a Decision which, although disguised as a Regulation, is of direct and individual concern to him;[5] or (iii) a Decision, which although addressed to another person, is of direct and individual concern to him. Individuals and companies *cannot* challenge the legality of true EEC Regulations nor can they challenge the legality of Directives under Article 173 of the Treaty; they may only use Article 173 to challenge certain Decisions of the Council or Commission.

[3] See *Grand Duchy of Luxembourg* v *European Parliament, (No 1)* [1983] ECR 283; [1983] 2 CMLR 726.

[4] [1971] ECR 263; [1971] CMLR 335.

[5] See for example *International Fruit Co* v *Commission* [1971] ECR 411. See also Harding, "The Review of EEC Regulations and Decisions" (1982) 19 *CML Rev* 311.

As for the first type of Decision, one addressed to the applicant himself, it may be recalled that under Article 189 of the EEC Treaty, a Decision is binding in its entirety upon the addressee and so it is understandable that he should be regarded as having sufficient interest to challenge its legality under Article 173. If a Northern Ireland company, for instance, has a Commission Decision addressed to it, saying that the firm has infringed the EEC's competition rules, it may seek the annulment of that Decision under Article 173 of the Treaty.

It is much harder however for an individual or company to challenge the second and third types of Decisions because it is so difficult for a private party to satisfy the cumulative tests of "direct and individual concern". The Court of Justice has given this phrase a very restrictive interpretation. If, for example, a Decision is addressed to the United Kingdom Government, then in order for an individual to show that it concerns him "directly", he must show that there is no intervening act required of the Government before that Decision affects him. Moreover, to show that that Decision "individually" concerns him, he must prove that *at the time the Decision was made,* he was within a clearly defined group of persons affected by it.[6] As a result of this narrow interpretation few individual applicants have successfully surmounted what has been described as the "almost insurmountable barrier of direct and individual concern".[7] In a few successful cases, the fact that the Decision involved had retroactive effect has been decisive in establishing individual concern, the harder of the two tests.[8] Consequently many of the applications brought by individuals or companies under Article 173 to challenge a Decision addressed to another person, particularly one addressed to a member state, are dismissed as inadmissible since it is so hard for applicants to show that such a Decision directly and individually concerns them. Where a decision is addressed to another company or individual, rather than to a member state, the court has tended to give the test of "direct and individual concern" a more liberal interpretation.[9]

[6] See *eg Plaumann* v *Commission* [1963] ECR 95; [1964] CMLR 29, especially the reasoned submission of Advocate-General Roemer.

[7] Barav. "Direct and Individual Concern: An Almost Insurmountable Barrier to the Admissibility of Individual Appeal to the EEC Court" (1974) 11 *CML Rev* 191.

[8] See *Toepfer & Getreide Import* v *Commission* [1965] 1 ECR 405; [1966] CMLR 111 and *Bock* v *Commission* [1971] ECR 897; [1972] CMLR 160.

[9] *Cf Metro* v *Commission* [1977] ECR 1875; [1978] 2 CMLR 1, where the ECJ gave a more liberal interpretation to the phrase "direct and individual concern" in a case involving EEC competition rules, and a company challenging a Decision addressed to another company, rather than to a member state.

Apart from the important difference between the types of acts of the Council and Commission that may be challenged by private parties and those that may be challenged by member states, the Council or the Commission, the other requirements of Article 173 of the Treaty about time-limits and grounds for annulment are the same for all applicants.

Article 173 (3) stipulates a time-limit of two months; proceedings must be instituted before the Court of Justice within two months of publication of the measure in the Official Journal of the European Communities or of its notification to the applicant, or in the absence thereof, of the day on which it came to the knowledge of the applicant. The need for legal certainty makes such a short time-limit justifiable. Timing is certainly an important feature to remember about this action for annulment under Article 173.

The grounds for annulment of an act of the Council or Commission are set out in Article 173, paragraph 1.[10] They are:

(a) lack of competence;
(b) infringement of an essential procedural requirement;
(c) infringement of the EEC Treaty or of any rule of law relating to its application; or
(d) misuse of powers.

It seems from the case-law of the Court of Justice that grounds (a) and (d) are very difficult to prove; the Court may imply competence to the Council or Commission to take certain action if ground (a) is invoked, while for an applicant to succeed on ground (d) it must be shown that the Council or Commission intended to use its powers for a purpose other than those for which they were conferred upon it. Consequently grounds (b) and (c) are much more commonly invoked by applicants. Ground (b) (procedural infringement) is often argued. It is up to the Court of Justice to decide if the infringement was of an *essential* requirement. In *Roquette Frères* v *Council,*[11] for instance, the company contended that a Council Regulation, laying down quotas for isoglucose producers, should be annulled as the Council had failed to follow the proper procedure for making the Regulation; it had not obtained the prior Opinion of the European Parliament as required by Article 43 of the EEC Treaty. The Court of Justice agreed that obtaining the Opinion of the Parliament was an essential procedural requirement and consequently the Council's Regulation was annulled.

Ground (c) (infringement of the EEC Treaty or of any rule of law relating to its application), has been given a liberal interpretation by the Court of Justice. The phrase "any rule of law relating to [the application of the Treaty]" has been interpreted to include such general principles of law as the

[10] *Op cit supra,* n 1, Hartley, Ch 15 for details; Collins, 199 *et seq.*

[11] [1980] ECR 3333.

protection of fundamental human rights. Thus, in 1974 in *Nold* v *Commission*[12] the Court for the first time accepted that an infringement of fundamental rights by an act of the Council or Commission would be a ground for its annulment.

Assuming that an applicant's case is admissible under Article 173 and that he succeeds on the merits of his case, what are the consequences of a successful action for annulment? According to Article 174 of the EEC Treaty, if an action for annulment is well founded the Court of Justice shall declare the act concerned to be void. If, however,an EEC Regulation is annulled, Article 174 (2) allows the Court if it considers it necessary, to state which effects of that Regulation shall be considered as definitive. This is an important power for the Court because the annulment of an entire Regulation would have very far-reaching consequences. The case of the *Commission* v *Council (Re Civil Service Salaries)*[13] illustrates the point. Here a Council Regulation laying down salaries for Community civil servants was annulled because it conflicted with an earlier policy decision. In order that salaries could continue to be paid to staff until a valid Regulation was made, the Court of Justice ordered that the old Regulation should continue in force until the Council made the new one.

Article 174 (2) only gives this power in respect of Regulations but in cases where a company has successfully challenged part of a Commission Decision finding it in breach of the EEC's competition rules, the Court of Justice is accustomed to annulling certain parts of the Decision and reducing any fine accordingly.[14]

The Community institution, whose act has been declared void by the Court of Justice, is required by Article 176 of the EEC Treaty to take the "necessary measures" to comply with the judgment of the Court. This often means introducing a new measure. It should be noted that this requirement does not affect any further obligation that might result from an action for damages brought by the aggrieved person against the Community under Article 215 (2) of the Treaty, further details of which are discussed below.

As can be seen from the statistics in Table 3 on p 89, individual applicants have not had a high rate of success in actions for annulment under Article 173 of the EEC Treaty.[15] By comparison Article 175 of the Treaty (action against Community institutions for their inactivity) holds out an even smaller chance of success for individual plaintiffs. That said, the threat of instituting an Article 175 action against a Community institution may provoke it into action to avoid such litigation.

12 [1974] ECR 491; [1974] 2 CMLR 338. See also Ch 18 *post* for further details.

13 [1973] ECR 575; [1973] CMLR 639.

14 *Eg Consten and Grundig* v *Commission* [1966] ECR 299; [1966] CMLR 418.

15 See Rasmussen, "Why is Article 173 Interpreted Against Private Plaintiffs?" (1980) *EL Rev* 112.

3 ACTION FOR INACTIVITY

While Article 173 of the Treaty allows the Court of Justice to review positive acts of the Community institutions, it is equally important for the Court to be able to review those situations where the institutions have failed to act, since an omission on their part may produce consequences just as serious as those of a wrongful act of commission. It is Article 175 of the EEC Treaty, commonly known as the "action for inactivity", which allows the Court of Justice to review failures by the Community institutions to take action.[16] Article 175 (1) provides that:

> Should the Council or the Commission, in infringement of this Treaty, fail to act, the Member States and the other institutions of the Community may bring an action before the Court of Justice to have that infringement established.

Again it should be noted that it is only a failure to act on the part of the Council of Ministers or the Commission that may be challenged under Article 175 and then only when such failure constitutes an infringement of the EEC Treaty. In other words, it seems that an action for inactivity may only be brought against the Council or Commission where they have been under a duty to take action under the Treaty so that their failure to do so amounts to a breach of that duty.

Proceedings may be brought by a member state, the Council of Ministers, the Commission or by the European Parliament as it is one of "the other institutions of the Community". The European Parliament did threaten to bring Article 175 proceedings against the Council of Ministers in the early 1970s when the Council failed to adopt proposals for direct elections to the Parliament and is currently pursuing an action against the Council for its failure to adopt a Common Transport Policy.[17] Ordinary individuals and companies may also bring proceedings under Article 175 but only in very limited circumstances. Article 175, paragraph 3 allows a private party to bring an action if the Council or Commission, in infringement of the Treaty, has failed "to address to *that* person any act other than a recommendation or an opinion". Since EEC Regulations and Directives are never addressed to private parties, Article 175 (3) only permits a private party to bring proceedings when the Council or Commission has failed to address a Decision to him *personally* where the Treaty so requires it.

Therefore, as far as individual plaintiffs are concerned, Article 175 limits the *locus standi* of individuals even more than the action for annulment under Article 173. At least under Article 173 an individual could challenge Decisions addressed to other persons provided that he could show that the Decision in question directly and individually concerned him. By contrast, Article 175 may only be used by an individual where the Council or

[16] *Op cit supra,* n 1, Hartley, Ch 13.

[17] *European Parliament* v *Council (Re Common Transport Policy)* (ECJ) *The Times,* 27 May 1985.

Commission has failed in its duty to address a Decision directly to him. A good illustration of this point is provided by *Lord Bethell* v *Commission.*[18] Lord Bethell, an English Member of the European Parliament and Chairman of an association called the "Freedom of the Skies Campaign", complained to the EEC Commission about the high fares charged by aviation companies on flights within Europe. He asked the Commission to investigate the agreements between aviation companies and to take a Decision as regards their possible breach of the EEC's competition rules. When the Commission refused to take such action, Lord Bethell brought proceedings before the Court of Justice under Article 175 of the Treaty, alleging the Commission's failure to act. The Court of Justice dismissed his application as inadmissible because what Lord Bethell was seeking from the Commission was not a Decision addressed to himself, but rather one in respect of third parties, the aviation companies. Even though he was an airline user and Chairman of an airline users organisation, he was still not in the position of a potential addressee of a Decision which the Commission had a duty to address to him; therefore he failed to satisfy the strict *locus standi* requirements of Article 175 (3).

As well as satisfying the *locus standi* requirements, any applicant, whether a private party, a member state or a Community institution, must come within the time-limits specified in Article 175 (2). The action will be admissible only if the institution in default has first been called upon to act by the applicant. If, within a further two months of being so called upon, the institution has not "defined its position", the action must be brought within a further period of two months. Therefore, it is important to note that if the defaulting institution has been called upon to act and has defined its position within two months, that terminates the action for inactivity under Article 175. What is meant by "defining its position" was considered by the Court of Justice in *Alfons Lutticke* v *Commission*[19] where the applicants were German companies which imported dried milk products into the Federal Republic of Germany. They had complained to the Commission that the turnover tax imposed by their government on imports of powdered milk was contrary to the EEC Treaty and they requested that the Commission take proceedings against the Federal Republic under Article 169 of the Treaty. Within two months the Commission replied by letter to the companies, refusing to take such action. The companies then brought proceedings before the Court of Justice under Article 175. The Court dismissed their case as inadmissible since the Commission had "defined a position" within the requisite two month period by a letter simply informing the companies why it would not take action against the German Government. Thus it would seem that as long as the institution gives the plaintiff a clear statement of its

[18] [1982] ECR 2277; [1982] 3 CMLR 300.

[19] [1966] ECR 19; [1966] CMLR 378. See also n 17 *supra*.

stance on the complaint, that amounts to a definition of its position. Another point that arose in the *Lütticke* case that is also worth noting is that the institution may "define its position" in such a form that it does not amount to a proper Decision and cannot, therefore, form the basis of annulment proceedings under Article 173 of the Treaty.[20] This results in a gap in the remedies available to private parties under the EEC Treaty.

Obviously it is very difficult indeed for individuals to succeed in an Article 175 action as the statistics in Table 3 confirm (see p 89 *post*). However, in the event of a successful action under Article 175, the Court will declare that the Council or Commission has failed to act where the Treaty so required. In accordance with Article 176, the defaulting institution must then take the necessary measures to comply with the judgment of the Court.

4 THE PLEA OF ILLEGALITY (OR THE DEFENCE OF INAPPLICALITY)

Of all the actions that may be brought before the Court of Justice, that of Article 184 is probably the strangest for legal practitioners in the United Kingdom.[21] Article 184 states:

> Notwithstanding the expiry of the period laid down in the third paragraph of Article 173, any party may, in proceedings in which a regulation of the Council or Commission is in issue, plead the grounds specified in the first paragraph of Art 173, in order to invoke before the Court of Justice the *inapplicability* of that regulation. [Emphasis supplied.]

Article 184 was, therefore, designed to overcome the two major limitations of an action for annulment under Article 173 of the Treaty namely, that private parties may not use Article 173 to challenge the legality of true Regulations and that no one may challenge the legality of a Regulation after two months from the date of its publication in the Official Journal. By relying upon Article 184, a party may, despite his status or the passage of time, seek a declaration from the Court of Justice that a Regulation should be declared inapplicable to him on any of the four grounds listed in Article 173 (1) which are misuse of powers, lack of competence, infringement of an essential procedural requirement, or infringement of the EEC Treaty or any rule of law relating to its application. The brevity of Article 184 has left the Court of Justice to develop its scope and the Court has given it some curious features. First, Article 184 can only be raised as an ancillary action in the course of legal proceedings based upon another article of the Treaty. It is, therefore, important to remember that Article 184 is not a separate form of action but must instead be coupled with another action, normally an action for annulment under Article 173.

[20] There have been recent cases where the Commission has defined its position in a different form. See *eg Gema* v *Commission* [1979] ECR 3173; [1980] 2 CMLR 177.

[21] *Op cit supra*, n 1, Hartley, Ch 14; Collins, 221-5.

Hence Article 184's title of "the defence of illegality" is most appropriate as it forms a shield, not a sword, against the application of a Regulation. Since it is only an ancillary action, Article 184 is dependent upon the success of the other supporting action; if the supporting action fails, so too does Article 184. Secondly, Article 184 can only be raised in proceedings before the Court of Justice where a Regulation (or other general act) is in issue.[22]

Thus, for example, if a Regulation has been made some months ago by the Council misusing its powers, a private party might bring an action under Article 173 of the Treaty seeking the annulment of any Decision based upon that Regulation on the ground that the illegality of the parent Regulation has also tainted that Decision. The applicant would still have to satisfy the *locus standi* requirements and time-limits of Article 173 to challenge that Decision but in the same proceedings, the applicant might also invoke Article 184 before the Court of Justice, seeking a declaration that the parent Regulation be declared *inapplicable* to him. Article 184 is, therefore, an indirect way to challenge the applicability of an EEC Regulation. The outcome of a successful case would mean not only the annulment of the Decision but also a declaration that the Regulation should not be applied to the party before the Court. Under Article 184 the Regulation would not be declared void *erga omnes*. In practical terms, though, if a Regulation has been declared inapplicable the institution responsible would have to replace it; otherwise there would be a flood of cases from other parties affected by it. The restrictions on the operation of Article 184 mean that it is of very limited usefulness for ordinary individuals.

Having considered those articles of the EEC Treaty that give the ECJ jurisdiction to review the legality of Community action, one may now consider those articles concerned with the liability of the Community.

B. LIABILITY OF THE COMMUNITY

In Northern Ireland and perhaps elsewhere in the United Kingdom, it is widely, but mistakenly, believed that the EEC is immune from liability. In fact the EEC claims no special immunities or privileges and so it may be liable in contract and in tort. The relevant provision of the EEC Treaty on this topic is Article 215, which distinguishes between the "contractual", and "non-contractual" liability of the Community. The use of this terminology, common in continental Europe, is strange to United Kingdom lawyers and those of the Republic of Ireland. The term "non-contractual" is wide enough to embrace the Community's liability in tort and quasi-contract. Legal practitioners need an understanding of Article 215 as they may have to advise a client, who has for example supplied goods or services under a

[22] See *Wohrmann & Lütticke* v *Commission* [1962] ECR 501; *Simmenthal* v *Commission* [1979] ECR 777.

contract with a Community institution but cannot recover payment for them, or has paid certain agricultural levies but believes they were wrongfully collected from him and seeks their repayment.

1 CONTRACTUAL LIABILITY OF THE EEC

Article 215, paragraph 1 of the EEC Treaty governs the contractual liability of the Community.[23] It states:

> The contractual liability of the Community shall be governed by the law applicable to the contract in question.

"The law applicable to the contract" will be whatever national law governs that contract as its proper law chosen in accordance with the Private International law rules. A litigant, complaining of a breach of contract by a Community institution, may bring proceedings before a national court, rather than the Court of Justice as Article 215 (1) does not give it exclusive jurisdiction in every case of contractual liability of the Community.

Thus if, as suggested at the beginning of this chapter, a Belfast printer supplied stationery to the European Parliament, which then refused to pay for it, the printer could bring proceedings in a Belfast court to decide liability under Northern Irish law of contract.

To this basic rule there are some exceptions. First, if the contract contains a clause conferring exclusive jurisdiction upon the Court of Justice in cases of disputes arising from that contract, then obviously a litigant may only bring proceedings before the Court of Justice in Luxembourg. This may produce the curious result that the Court of Justice, although having jurisdiction, must, nevertheless, apply the national law of contract agreed by the parties in a choice of law clause in the contract.[24] As Plender points out:

> . . . there are in existence a very few contracts which reserve jurisdiction to the European Court but specify as the governing law systems foreign to the Communities, and presumably foreign to the knowledge of the . . . judges. In the event of a dispute over such a contract the Court would probably rely on expert evidence of the chosen law.[25]

The second exception to the general proposition that the national courts of the member states have jurisdiction to hear disputes involving the contractual liability of the Community is in respect of contracts of employment of the staff of the Community institutions. Article 179 of the EEC Treaty gives the Court of Justice exclusive jurisdiction in any disputes between the Community and its servants within the limits and under the conditions laid down in the Staff Regulations and the Conditions of Employment. Staff disputes may, therefore, only be decided by the Court of

[23] *Op cit, supra,* n 1, Hartley, Part V—"*Community Liability*"*;* Collins, 221-5.

[24] See *eg Pellegrini* v *Commission* [1976] ECR 1807; [1977] 2 CMLR 77.

[25] Plender, *A Practical Introduction to European Community Law* (1980) p 30.

Justice. Staff cases do in fact take up a considerable amount of the Court's time; about a third of the cases brought before it in its first 25 years were staff cases. They are now dealt with by one of the chambers of the Court. Recommendations have however been made that a special Staff Tribunal be set up to relieve the Court of Justice of such cases.

The contractual liability of the EEC is, therefore, relatively straightforward. By contrast, the principles governing the non-contractual liability of the Community are much more complicated.

2 NON-CONTRACTUAL LIABILITY OF THE EEC

Article 215 paragraph 2 of the EEC Treaty provides:

> In the case of non-contractual liability, the Community shall, in accordance with the general principles common to the laws of the Member States, make good any damage caused by its institutions or by its servants in the performance of their duties.

From the wording of Article 215 (2) one can understand why this form of action is commonly referred to as "an action for damages", rather than one to establish the "non-contractual liability" of the Community. Unlike cases of contractual liability the Court of Justice in Luxembourg is given exclusive jurisdiction by Article 178 of the Treaty in all disputes relating to the non-contractual liability of the Community provided for in Article 215 (2). In dealing with claims for damages under Article 215 (2), the Court of Justice has developed, and continues to develop, complex rules about when compensation should be paid by the Community.

Nevertheless the action for damages has become much more popular since 1971, when the Court of Justice first accepted it as an autonomous and independent form of action. Prior to that, the Court had treated it as a supplementary form of action that had to be coupled with another action such as an Article 173 action for annulment. This had the unfortunate consequence that if the supplementary action failed, then so too did the action for damages. In April 1971 in *Lütticke* v *Commission*[26] the Court of Justice acknowledged, however, that the action for damages had its own particular function of compensating an individual who had suffered damage because of the wrongful action of a Community institution, whereas the purpose of Article 173 was the annulment of an act of a Community institution *erga omnes*.

The increasing popularity of actions for damages, demonstrated by Table 3 on p 89 *post,* may be explained on various grounds. Firstly, Article 215 (2) does not lay down strict rules about *locus standi.* Secondly the period of limitation for actions for damages, according to Article 43 of the Protocol on the Statute of the European Court of Justice, is;

[26] [1971] ECR 325.

> . . . five years from the occurrence of the event giving rise thereto. The period of limitation shall be interrupted if proceedings are instituted before the Court or if prior to such proceedings an application is made by the aggrieved party to the relevant institution of the Community.[27]

In order to succeed in a claim for damages, the basic rule is that the plaintiff must show that he has suffered damage caused by a wrongful act or omission of a Community institution or of its servants acting in the performance of their duties. To this general proposition the Court of Justice has developed many limitations as regards the circumstances that render the Community liable and the kinds of damages that are recoverable from the Community. It is especially difficult to prove the causal connection between an allegedly wrongful act of a Community institution and the damage suffered by the plaintiff, particularly since so much Community legislation is implemented by the national authorities of the member states. For example, in *Haegeman* v *Commission*[28] a Belgian wine importer alleged that certain countervailing duties, imposed by Commission Regulations on wine imported from Greece, were wrongfully collected as they were contrary to the Association Agreement then in force between Greece and the EEC. The company brought an action before the Court of Justice under Article 215 (2) of the Treaty seeking, *inter alia,* the repayment of those duties by the Commission. The Court dismissed this claim explaining that the plaintiff should have brought proceedings before a national court for the recovery of the levies since it had been the national authorities, and not the EEC Commission, that had collected those levies. If the national court wanted to determine the legality of the Commission's Regulations, then it could do so by making a reference to the Court of Justice under Article 177 of the EEC Treaty.

Therefore, to save a client time and expense, one must be very careful indeed about choosing the correct forum in which to bring his claim for damages—it may be a local court or the Court of Justice in Luxembourg.[29] It has been suggested that choosing the right court depends very much on the nature of the claim. If it is really a claim for compensation for damage (an unliquidated sum), caused by a wrongful act or omission of a Community institution, then the Court of Justice alone has jurisdiction under Articles 215 (2) and 178 to determine the case.[30] If, however, the claim is for the recovery of a specific sum, like countervailing or export duties collected by the national authorities in implementation of EEC legislation, then proceedings should be brought before a national court which can use the

[27] The Protocol on the Statute of the Court of Justice of the European Communities is reproduced in Rudden & Wyatt, *Basic Community laws* (1980) p 102. See also *Kampffmeyer* v *Commission* [1976] ECR 245, and *Adams* v *Commission, The Times,* 8 November 1985.

[28] [1972] ECR 1005; [1973] CMLR 365.

[29] See Harding, "The Choice of Court problem in Cases of Non-Contractual Liability under EEC Law" (1979) 16 *CML Rev* 389.

[30] *Eg Merkur* v *Commission* [1973] ECR 1055.

preliminary reference procedure of Article 177 to establish the legality of the EEC legislation in issue.

As a result of the limitations developed by the Court of Justice about the operation of Article 215 (2) it is not surprising that few plaintiffs have actually succeeded in obtaining damages from the Community. An example of a successful action for damages under Article 215 (2) may be found in what is familiarly known as the *Quellmehl* case.[31] Here the applicant company sought compensation from the Community for the loss it had suffered on account of the abolition by the Council of Ministers of production refunds for quellmehl, which is derived from maize or wheat and is used mainly in bread-making. The Court of Justice had already ruled that the Council was wrong to withdraw production refunds for quellmehl while maintaining them for starches which could also be used in the bakery industry; the Council had failed to observe the principle of equality, as required by Article 40 (3) of the EEC Treaty, between producers of quellmehl and starch. Consequently, the Court ordered damages to be paid to the applicant together with 6 per cent interest from the date of its judgment. It is interesting to note that the Court took, as the basis for the assessment of the damage suffered, the amount of production refunds the applicant would have received had they not been abolished. On this basis the Court accepted that if the applicant had passed on his losses in higher prices, then his damage would be diminished accordingly. As the Court explained:

> . . . it must be admitted that if the loss from the abolition of the refunds has actually been passed on, or could have been passed on, in the prices the damage may not be measured by reference to the refunds not paid. In that case the price increase would take the place of the refunds, thus compensating the producer.[32]

From the statistical data produced before the Court, it was shown that the applicant had not passed on, nor could have passed on, in its selling prices the losses resulting from the abolition of the production refunds. The Court's method of assessing damages, payable under Article 215 (2) has been severely criticised by academics.[33] The *Quellmehl* case illustrates well the difficulties an applicant may encounter in trying to obtain compensation for damage caused by the Community. Nevertheless, it should be noted that even if an applicant is not eventually awarded damages by the Court of Justice, bringing an Article 215 (2) action is yet another method whereby a private party is able to have secondary Community legislation in the form of Council or Commission Regulations, Directives and Decisions reviewed by the Court.

[31] *Ireks-Arkady GmbH* v *Council and Commission* [1979] ECR 2955. See also *Moulins et Huileries de Pont-à-Mousson* v *ONIC (Gritz Case)* [1977] ECR 1795; [1979] 2 CMLR 445 and *Adams* v *Commission, The Times,* 8 November 1985.

[32] *Ireks-Arkady GmbH* v *Council and Commission (Quellmehl case)* [1979] ECR 2955, 2974.

[33] *Eg* Rudden and Bishop, "Gritz and Quellmehl: Pass it On" (1981) 6 *EL Rev* 243.

Finally, in cases of concurrent liability, where both the member state authorities and the Community institutions have acted wrongfully and thus caused damage to a plaintiff, he should first seek redress before his local courts and then only if he is not compensated, or is insufficiently compensated, should he bring an action for damages under Article 215 (2) before the Court of Justice. The leading authority on this point is *Kampffmeyer* v *Commission*[34] where the Commission and the West German authorities were both liable for the damage caused to German grain importers. Together they had miscalculated the rate of levy to be applied to grain imports, and fixed the rate at zero. When the plaintiffs sought import permits from the German authorities they refused their applications and this refusal was later endorsed by the Commission. Only when the Commission had calculated a new rate, did the German authorities issue import permits. Consequently the plaintiffs had suffered by having to pay higher levies and to cancel some contracts. In proceedings brought under Article 215 (2), the Court of Justice agreed that both the Commission and the German authorities had acted wrongfully. Nevertheless, the Court directed the plaintiffs to return to the German courts to claim damages there first and only if they were insufficiently compensated there, should they return to the Court of Justice. The Court's rationale for this was that it would avoid:

> . . . the applicants' being insufficiently or excessively compensated for the same damage by the different assessment of two different courts applying different rules of law.[35]

This decision has also received much criticism as it forces litigants to go on what has become known as "the long march" through the domestic courts and then possibly to the Court of Justice as well. In such cases the litigant should of course be careful to observe the five year limitation period for instituting an action for damages under Article 215 (2) before the Court of Justice. One of the difficulties with cases of concurrent liability lies in the fact that the EEC Treaty does not itself contain any provision allowing for the apportionment of liability between the Community institutions and national authorities. The Court of Justice has therefore attempted to resolve the problem by placing the primary responsibility on the national authorities to compensate the plaintiff, leaving the Community with a secondary rôle to play. Despite the criticism of the Court's attitude, the *Kampffmeyer* approach still represents the current position in cases of concurrent liability.[36]

[34] [1967] ECR 245.

[35] *Ibid,* p 266.

[36] *Op cit, supra,* n 29. See also Hartley, "Concurrent Liability in EEC Law: A Critical Review of the Cases" (1977) 2 *EL Rev* 249.

TABLE 3

CASES BROUGHT SINCE 1958—31 DECEMBER 1985 BEFORE THE ECJ[1] *UNDER THE EEC TREATY*

(ANALYSED BY TYPE)

TYPE OF CASE	PROCEEDINGS BROUGHT UNDER													
			ARTICLE 173					ARTICLE 177						
	Arts. 169[2] and 93	Art. 170	By Govern-ments	By Com-munity Institu-tions	By Indi-viduals	Total	Art. 175	Validity	Inter-pretation	Total	Art. 181[3]	Art. 215	Proto-cols, Conven-tions Art. 220	GRAND TOTAL
Cases Brought . . .	412	2	81	8	361	450	30	202	1,180	1,382	9	206	55	2,559
Cases Not Resulting in a Judgment	114	1	9	3	42	54	5	5	69	74	3	29	3	286
Cases Decided . . .	165	1	39	5	253	297	24	175	971	1,146	3	152	48	1,839
In Favour of Applicant .	149	1	13	2	70	85	3	—	—	—	3	12	—	256
Dismissed on Substance .	15	—	25	3	125	153	3	—	—	—	—	124	—	295
Dismissed as Inadmissible	1	—	1	—	58	59	18	—	—	—	—	16	—	94
Cases Pending	133	—	33	—	66	99	1	22	140	162	3	25	4	434

[1] Excluding staff cases. These statistics were kindly supplied by the Information Office of the ECJ.

[2] Cases brought by Commission against Member States for failing to fulfil their general Community obligations or under Art. 93 for granting state aids which are considered incompatible with the Common Market.

[3] Arbitration clauses in contracts giving the ECJ jurisdiction in case of disputes.

CHAPTER 9

FREE MOVEMENT OF GOODS WITHIN THE EEC

There were many different economic barriers between France, Italy, West Germany and the three Benelux countries before they formed the EEC in 1957. These barriers ranged from customs duties and quotas on imports and exports of each others goods and immigration controls on the movement of their respective citizens through to monetary controls on the flow of capital between the countries. Such barriers clearly hindered the attainment of a Common Market in Western Europe. The drafters of the EEC Treaty, consequently, included in it specific provisions concerning those freedoms that were regarded as fundamental for the establishment of the Common Market. These so-called "fundamental freedoms of the EEC" are, therefore, aimed at removing the economic barriers that divide and separate member states into national markets. One can identify six such freedoms provided for in the EEC Treaty, namely:

- freedom of movement of goods between member states
- freedom of movement of capital
- freedom of movement of payments
- freedom of movement for workers
- freedom of movement for self-employed persons providing their services
- freedom of establishment for self-employed persons and companies.

As each of these freedoms covers a variety of activities, it is not considered appropriate to use the standard common law headings like Trade, Immigration, Companies etc. Hence the usual Community law terminology will be used throughout the next few chapters of this Guide as each of these fundamental freedoms of the EEC is examined.

PROBLEMS INVOLVING THE FREE MOVEMENT OF GOODS

The fact that Northern Ireland shares a land frontier with the Republic of Ireland, a member state of the EEC, means that in any cross-border trading activity the Community law provisions on the free movement of goods will be applicable. These provisions will therefore be relevant in a whole variety of situations, not only where there is trade with the Republic but also where there is trade between Northern Ireland and any other member country of the European Community. The following illustrations, taken from decided cases, give an indication of the range of activities covered by the EEC's rules on the free movement of goods:

— the Northern Ireland Pigs Marketing Board's requirements about transportation documents for the movement of bacon pigs within the Province;[1]
— the smuggling into Northern Ireland from the Irish Republic of citizen band radios having a prohibited frequency;[2]
— the payment by an importer of compulsory veterinary and public health inspection fees on a consignment of beef brought from one member state into another;[3]
— the complete ban on the importation into the United Kingdom of pornographic films and literature from other member states;[4]
— the destruction of and trade in British sixpences, florins and half-crowns within the EEC;[5]
— state protection of historic and artistic treasures by the requirement of a fee when exported to other member states;[6]
— the import licences and processing requirements for ultra heat treated (UHT) milk coming from other member states into the United Kingdom.[7]

This random selection of cases should alert the reader to the diverse ways in which Community law may affect import and export transactions to and from the Province. In order to explain how European Community law may be involved in such transactions, one needs to consider the main EEC provisions on the free movement of goods.

THE MAIN PROVISIONS ON THE FREE MOVEMENT OF GOODS

Article 9-37 of the EEC Treaty contain the main provisions governing the free movement of goods. These articles provide for the establishment of a Community Customs Union which, according to Article 9 of the Treaty, forms the very basis or foundation of the EEC. This Community Customs Union (CCU) covers all trade in goods and involves the prohibition of customs duties and quantitative restrictions and of all charges and other measures having equivalent effect on imports and exports moving between member states. The CCU also requires the adoption of a "common customs tariff" by the member states on goods imported from non-EEC countries.

The "goods" referred to in Article 9 include products originating in the

[1] *Pigs Marketing Board (NI)* v *Redmond* [1978] ECR 2347; [1979] 1 CMLR 177.

[2] *McAfee* v *Smyth and Quigley* [1981] 1 CMLR 410.

[3] *Amministrazione delle Finanze dello Stato* v *Simmenthal SpA (No 2)* [1978] ECR 629; [1978] 3 CMLR 263.

[4] *R* v *Henn and Darby* [1979] ECR 3795; [1980] 1 CMLR 246.

[5] *R* v *Thompson, Johnson and Woodiwiss* [1979] 1 CMLR 47; [1978] ECR 2247.

[6] *Commission* v *Italy (Art Treasures Cases)* [1968] ECR 423 and [1972] ECR 527.

[7] *Commission* v *UK (Re UHT Milk)*[1983] 2 CMLR 1.

member states as well as products coming from countries outside the European Community, which are "in free circulation in the Member States". The latter goods are defined by Article 10 as being goods which have complied with the import formalities of a member state, and on which any customs duties or equivalent charges have been levied if they have not benefited from any reimbursement of such duties or charges.[8] The term "goods" has been widely interpreted by the Court of Justice to include all items having a monetary value and capable of being the object of a commercial transaction.[9] Coins themselves are not, however, regarded by the Court as "goods" if they are still legal tender but instead are treated as "means of payment" and as such are covered by other provisions of the EEC Treaty.[10] Chapter 10 *post* looks in more detail at the movement of payments and capital within the European Community.

The Community Customs Union envisaged by Article 9 of the Treaty can thus be distinguished from an ordinary free trade area like that operated by the European Free Trade Association (EFTA[11]) as the former comprises not only a free trade area for industrial and agricultural products within the Community itself but also a Common Customs Tariff[12] towards all countries outside the Community. By comparison, EFTA is a free trade area for industrial goods produced by its own member countries, leaving them free to fix their own rates of tariffs for goods coming from countries outside the Association.

Articles 12-29 of the EEC Treaty explain how the Community Customs Union was to be established. Basically, member states are obliged by Article 12 to refrain from introducing as between themselves any new customs duties or any charges having equivalent effect on imports or exports. They were also prohibited from increasing any existing customs duties. In one of its earliest and most important judgments, *Van Gend en Loos,* the Court of Justice ruled that Article 12 was directly effective, creating immediate rights which individuals could rely upon before their national courts or tribunals. Van Gend en Loos was a Dutch company engaged in importing chemicals into the Netherlands. In 1960 it imported a quantity of ureaformaldehyde from the Federal Republic of Germany and was charged a higher customs duty in accordance with a recent Dutch law of 1959, which had reclassified this particular product. The company objected to paying the higher duty and sought, before a local tribunal, to rely upon Article 12 of the Treaty which

[8] For details see Parry and Dinnage, *EEC Law* (2nd ed, 1981) pp 167 *et seq;* Wyatt and Dashwood, *The Substantive Law of the EEC* (1980) pp 78-80. See also Oliver, *Free Movement of Goods in the EEC* (1982).

[9] *Commission* v *Italy (Art Treasures) Re Export Tax on* (No 1) [1968] ECR 423; [1969] CMLR 1.

[10] *Op cit, supra,* n 5.

[11] See Ch 1 *ante.*

[12] Also sometimes referred to as the Common External Tariff, or CET.

prohibited both the introduction of new customs duties on goods traded between member states and any increase in existing ones. On an Article 177 reference to the Court of Justice, the Court emphasised that:

> . . . Article 9, which bases the Community upon a customs union, includes as an essential provision the prohibition of these customs duties and charges . . . It is applied and explained by Article 12 . . . [which] must be interpreted as producing direct effects and creating individual rights which national courts must protect.[13]

Furthermore, the Court emphasised that since Community law was supreme, it would prevail over any conflicting national law. As a result of this ruling, an individual in a member state may rely upon Article 12 of the EEC Treaty before a local court in order to challenge national legislation, which has imposed any *new* customs duty or charge having an equivalent effect on goods traded between the EEC's member states.

Rather than impose straightforward customs duties, a member state might impose inspection fees, or administration charges on imports from other member states, but such charges are not permissible. Thus in the *Variola* case where the Italian authorities imposed unloading charges on certain imports and used the income for the provision and maintenance of port installations, the Court of Justice was quite categorical in its condemnation of such charges. It declared that:

> The prohibition of all customs duties and charges having equivalent effect covers *any charge levied at the time or by reason of importation* and which, specifically affecting the imported product and not the home-produced product, has the same restrictive effect on the free movement of goods as a customs duty.
>
> The levying of such a charge, however small, together with the administrative formalities which it occasions, constitute an obstruction of the free movement of goods.[14]

Clearly the amount of the import charge and the purpose for charging it are irrelevant; even a small import fee that goes towards some worthy cause like port improvement or medical research cannot be justified by a member state.

That part of Article 12 which prohibited any increases in *existing* customs duties on intra-Community trade has in fact been overtaken by Articles 13-17 of the Treaty which laid down a timetable for the gradual abolition of such customs duties. For "the Original Six" member states existing customs duties were abolished by 1 July 1968 and for the three new member states, including the United Kingdom, which joined the EEC in 1973 they were eliminated by 1 July 1977. During these years the Common Customs Tariff (CCT) was also being established whereby member states charged the same level of tariffs on all goods from non-EEC countries.[15] The CCT was finally

[13] [1963] ECR 1, 13.

[14] *Variola* v *Amministrazione Italiana delle Finanze* [1973] ECR 981, 989. Emphasis supplied.

[15] Council Regulation 950/68 EEC (OJ Sp ed, 1968(1), 275) sets out the level of tariffs and goods covered by the CCT. This Regulation is regularly amended by the Commission. For details see Parry and Dinnage, *EEC Law* (1981) pp 172 *et seq;* Plender, *A Practical Introduction to European Community Law,* (1980) ch 4.

established for these nine member states by 1 July 1977 and so for them the Community Customs Union has been in existence since that date. As for Greece which joined the EEC in 1981, the progressive dismantling of internal tariff barriers and adjustment to the CCT are scheduled to be completed by 1 January 1986. Similarly, Spain and Portugal will have transitional periods in which to adapt to the Community Customs Union and the CCT.

Besides customs duties, the founders of the EEC realised that member states could hinder trade between themselves just as effectively by imposing so-called "quantitative restrictions", meaning bans or quotas by the weight, value or number of goods. Consequently, Articles 30-34 of the EEC Treaty provide for the abolition of quantitative restrictions and measures having equivalent effect on goods traded between member states. The prohibition of "quantitative restrictions", imposed by Articles 30 to 34 of the Treaty, has been interpreted by the European Court of Justice as covering "measures which amount to a total or partial restraint of, according to the circumstances, imports, exports or goods in transit".[16] Thus, for example, in *R* v *Henn and Darby*[17] the Court of Justice ruled that the complete ban imposed by the United Kingdom on the importation of pornographic articles from all countries, including member states of the European Community, amounted to a "quantitative restriction", although doubts had earlier been expressed on this point in the English Court of Appeal.[18] In this case the appellants had been involved in importing into the United Kingdom pornographic materials from the Netherlands and were convicted under section 42 of the Customs Consolidation Act 1876 which imposes a complete ban on the importation into the United Kingdom of indecent and obscene articles. They appealed on the ground that this ban constituted a quantitative restriction on goods coming from another EEC member state and was therefore contrary to Article 30 of the EEC Treaty. Their appeal went eventually to the House of Lords which felt it necessary to refer the case to the Court of Justice for a preliminary ruling under Article 177 of the Treaty. (This was in fact the first case in which the House of Lords made a reference to the European Court of Justice and illustrates that on points of Community law it is superior to the House of Lords). The Court of Justice ruled that even though the United Kingdom's ban on these materials did constitute a "quantitative restriction" within the meaning of Article 30 of the Treaty, it could nevertheless be justified on grounds of public morality under Article 36 of the Treaty (See below for details).

16 *Eg Geddo* v *Ente Nazionale Risi* [1973] ECR 865, 879; [1974] 1 CMLR 13, 42.

17 [1979] ECR 3795; [1980] 1 CMLR 246.

18 Arguments had been raised before the Court of Appeal that since "quantitative restriction". related to quantity, a complete ban could not amount to a "quantitative restriction". See CA decision in *R* v *Henn and Darby* [1978] 3 All ER 1190.

While the meaning of "quantitative restrictions" is therefore quite clear, the concept of "measures having an equivalent effect to quantitative restrictions" is much more complicated and has given rise to a great many cases being brought before the Court of Justice for an interpretation of the phrase. The oft-quoted interpretation is that given by the Court in *Procureur du Roi* v *Dassonville* where it stated:

> All trading rules enacted by Member States which are capable of hindering, directly or indirectly, actually or potentially, intra-Community trade are to be considered as measures having an effect equivalent to quantitative restrictions.[19]

By applying this very broad definition one can now understand how it is that the variety of national measures, mentioned at the beginning of this chapter, may be prohibited by EEC law. This is why, for instance, the United Kingdom's recent policy of controlling the spread of fowl-pest by introducing a slaughter policy in Great Britain and then prohibiting the import of poultry or poultry products from any country which vaccinated against the disease rather than slaughtered, was held by the Court of Justice to constitute a measure having an effect equivalent to a quantitative restriction.[20]

Similarly, licensing systems for imports of goods like UHT milk and poultry entering the United Kingdom from other member states have been condemned by the Court of Justice. For example, in a decision of 31 January 1984, *Commission* v *Great Britain and Northern Ireland (Re: Import Licences for Poultry)*[21] the Court of Justice declared that by operating a system ot specific import licences for poultry entering Great Britain, the United Kingdom was acting in breach of its Community's obligations. The requirement of a licence, even as a formality, was held to be contrary to Article 30 of the Treaty. One should therefore always be extremely wary of such disguised restrictions on trade between member states, as they are less obvious than the straightforward quota or customs duty on the export or import of certain goods.

That said, one should also bear in mind the fact that Article 36 of the EEC Treaty allows member states to make certain derogations from the otherwise strict prohibition of quantitative restrictions and equivalent measures imposed by Articles 30 to 34. Article 36 states that:

> The provisions of Arts 30 to 34 shall not preclude prohibitions or restrictions on imports, exports or goods in transit justified on grounds of public morality, public policy or public security; the protection of health and life of humans, animals or plants; the protection of national treasures possessing artistic, historic or archaeological value; or the protection of industrial and commercial property. Such prohibitions or restrictions shall not, however, constitute a means ot arbitrary discrimination or a disguised restriction on trade between Member States.

19 [1974] ECR 837, 852; [1974] 2 CMLR 436, 453-4.

20 *Commission* v *UK (Re Imports of Poultry)* [1982] 3 CMLR 497; [1982] ECR 2793.

21 [1984] 1 ECR 283.

Several points should be noted about this important derogation clause.[22] The first point to note about Article 36 is that because it allows exceptions to the fundamental principle of freedom of movement of goods within the EEC, it will always be interpreted strictly by the Court of Justice. Secondly, the introductory words of Article 36 show that it can only be used by member states to justify certain quantitative restrictions imposed by them; it can never be relied upon by individuals or companies, who may enter agreements to restrict trade between member states, nor can a member state use Article 36 to justify customs duties on goods from other member states. Authority for this point is *Commission* v *Italy (First Art Treasures Case)*[23] where Italy tried unsuccessfully to rely upon Article 36 to justify an export charge on certain historic works. The Court of Justice immediately rejected this argument, stressing that Article 36 does not relate to customs duties or charges having an equivalent effect and therefore cannot be used to justify them.

Thirdly, the Court of Justice has recognised that, since the member states have different values, concepts such as "public policy" and "public morality" will vary from one country to another. Thus they are permitted a margin of appreciation, subject of course to the overall review of the Court. A good illustration of this is *R* v *Henn and Darby* where the United Kingdom was able to rely upon Article 36 to justify its ban on the import of pornographic materials from other member states, despite the fact that within the United Kingdom itself there were differences between the laws in force to control obscene literature. The Court of Justice accepted that the United Kingdom's ban could be justified on the ground of public morality. Since there was no lawful trade within the United Kingdom in such goods, such a prohibition could not amount to a means of arbitrary discrimination or a disguised restriction on trade.

The case of *McAfee* v *Smyth and Quigley*[24], decided in 1980 by the Belfast Recorder's Court, serves as a useful illustration of the impact of the Community law provisions on the free movement of goods, and in particular of Article 36, in the Northern Ireland context. The RUC had intercepted a lorry-load of citizen band radios in County Tyrone after they had been smuggled across the border from the Republic of Ireland. The lorry driver and a passenger were charged, *inter alia,* with being knowingly concerned in the fraudulent evasion of the prohibition on the importation of such radios imposed by section 7 of the Wireless Telegraphy Act 1967 and the Radiotelephonic Transmitters (Control of Manufacture and Importation) Order 1968. The defendants contended that those provisions constituted a

[22] For details see *op cit, supra,* n 8, Wyatt and Dashwood, pp 106-108; Parry and Dinnage, pp 181-183. Art 100 of the Treaty may be used by the Council to harmonise national measures concerning animal health etc.

[23] *Op cit, supra,* n 9.

[24] *Op cit, supra,* n 2.

quantitative restriction on imports or a measure having equivalent effect, within the meaning of Article 30 of the EEC Treaty and were thus contrary to Community law. Counsel for the Crown accepted that the legislation did constitute a ban contrary to Article 30 but sought to justify the prohibition by reference to Article 36 of the Treaty "on grounds of public morality, public policy, public security and the protection of health and life of humans". Evidence was produced to show that citizen band radios with the particular frequency of those concerned had been used by terrorists in Northern Ireland over recent years to detonate bombs and that such radios were also capable of interfering with radio equipment used by hospital and other emergency services. On this evidence the judge found the prohibition on the import of such radios justified on grounds of public policy and public security. Whilst admitting the possibility that the prohibition might also be justified on the ground of public morality, the judge did not consider that there was enough evidence to show that the incidence of soliciting by prostitutes or their procurers was to any great extent increased by the existence of citizen band radios. The judge concluded that the prohibition was not an arbitrary discrimination or disguised restriction on trade between member states; it was not imposed for the purpose of fostering any United Kingdom industry, but was genuinely imposed for public policy and public security reasons. Accordingly the appeals were dismissed.

The importance of this case lies not only in the fact that it clearly demonstrates the relevance of Community law in Northern Ireland but also in the fact that the judge decided that it was not necessary to refer the case to the Court of Justice for a preliminary ruling. By considering the judgment of the Court of Justice in *R* v *Henn and Darby,* the judge in this case felt himself able to apply Articles 30 and 36 of the EEC Treaty to the facts.

Finally as far as Northern Ireland is concerned, it is also worth noting that in *Commission* v *Great Britain and Northern Ireland (Re: Import Licences for Poultry)* decided on 30 January 1984, the Court of Justice took account of the different conditions pertaining in Northern Ireland compared to Great Britain as regards the importance of the poultry industry in the Province and the fact that a slaughter policy to control fowl-pest had been in existence here for several years before the United Kingdom joined the EEC. The Court held that while the requirement of an import licence, even as a mere formality, was a quantitative restriction contrary to Article 30 of the Treaty, it did not necessarily follow that a licensing system could not be justified under Article 36. It was necessary to see if the system was disproportionate to the objective pursued, namely the protection of the health of animals like poultry in this case. The Court stated that:

> . . . whether or not national measures on animal health may include an import licensing system without infringing Article 36 of the Treaty depends upon the relationship in an individual case between, on the one hand, the inconvenience caused by the administrative and financial burdens imposed under such a system and . . . on the other hand the dangers and risks for animal health resulting from the imports in question.[25]

It seems, therefore, that certain import licensing systems operated in Northern Ireland may be compatible with Article 36 provided their purpose is to protect one of the interests listed therein and the licences are not too expensive or inconvenient to obtain.

As well as the exceptions permitted by Article 36 of the EEC Treaty, the free movement of goods within the European Community is frequently curtailed by non-tariff barriers. These are technical and commercial barriers to free trade and include such things as different national health and safety standards for all sorts of products, different types of ingredients permitted for manufacturing particular domestic products and so on. For example, if under consumer legislation it was only lawful within the United Kingdom to manufacture and sell ice-cream made from vegetable fats then that would exclude ice-cream made in any other EEC member state from animal fats being marketed within the United Kingdom. Obviously such non-tariff barriers could block free trade just as effectively as a quota or customs duty on the goods. To try to overcome such technical barriers there are over 200 Directives harmonising technical standards for various products so that they are acceptable to all the member states. Thus we have, for example, a Directive setting the maximum acceptable level of noise emitted from lawnmowers and EEC standards for vegetable and flower seeds etc. All of these measures are intended to facilitate the free movement of goods between the member states. Obtaining agreement amongst the members of the Council of Ministers for such Directives has proved a very slow process indeed.

Against this background, the Court of Justice's decision in 1979 in *Cassis de Dijon*[26] represents a very significant step towards liberalising trade within the EEC. In this case the Court ruled that obstacles to the free movement of goods between member states resulting from national rules about the *marketing* of goods have to be accepted in so far, but only in so far, as they can be regarded as *necessary* to satisfy certain "mandatory requirements" like the protection of health, the fairness of commercial transactions, and the protection of consumers. Where such rules cannot be regarded as necessary to satisfy any of these requirements, they amount to measures having an equivalent effect to quantitative restrictions within the meaning of

[25] [1984] 1 ECR 283, 301.

[26] The full title of this case is *Rewe-Zentral AG* v *Bundesmonopolverwaltung für Branntwein* [1979] ECR 649; [1979] 3 CMLR 494.

Article 30 of the EEC Treaty and as such are prohibited. In this particular case, the plaintiff was a German company wishing to import a French fruit liqueur called "Cassis de Dijon" from France where it was lawfully produced and freely marketed. The German authorities, however, refused to allow its sale in West Germany because under German law fruit liqueurs could only be marketed in the country if they had a minimum alcoholic content of 25 per cent and this Cassis de Dijon liqueur only had between 15 and 20 per cent alcoholic content. The Court of Justice ruled that since the German legislation governing the alcoholic content of such liqueurs was not necessary in order to satisfy any mandatory requirements, it fell within the prohibition of Article 30 of the EEC Treaty. (In this case, Article 36 of the Treaty was not even argued to save this type of *marketing* restriction. It would seem, therefore, that Article 36 can only be raised to defend restrictions on the *import or export* of goods from or to other member states).

This ruling of the Court, delivered on 20 February 1979, was followed on 3 October 1980 by a Commission Communication[27] to the member states. In this the Commission stated its interpretation of the Court's ruling in the *Cassis de Dijon* case and in light of this, the Commission declared its revised policy towards technical barriers to trade between the member states of the Community. The Commission's view is that:

> Whereas Member States may, with respect to domestic products and in the absence of relevant Community provisions, regulate the terms on which such products are marketed, the case is different for products imported from other Member States. Any product imported from another Member State must in principle be admitted to the territory of the importing state if it has been *lawfully produced,* that is, conforms to rules and processes of manufacture that are customarily and traditionally accepted in the exporting country, and is marketed in the territory of the latter . . . Only under very strict conditions does the Court accept exceptions to this principle; barriers to trade resulting from differences between commercial and technical rules are only admissible:
>
> — if the rules are necessary, that is appropriate and not excessive, in order to satisfy mandatory requirements (public health, protection of consumers or the environment, the fairness of commercial transactions, etc).[28]

Although a Communication is not one of the legally binding measures mentioned in Article 189 of the EEC Treaty, Communications provide useful guidance. This particular one should not be ignored by member states for it serves as a polite warning to them of the kinds of trade barriers that, if employed by them, may well lead to a case being brought against them by the Commission under Article 169 of the EEC Treaty. Alternatively, the national measures may be challenged by an individual before a local court since Articles 30-34 are directly effective giving rise to immediate rights that ought to be enforced by domestic courts. From now on the Commission's

[27] (OJ 1980 C 256/2); [1981] 1 CMLR 177.

[28] *Ibid,* [1981] 1CMLR 177, 178.

work on harmonisation of standards will be mainly directed at those national provisions about public health, consumer protection, and so on that are permissible under the Court's criteria set out in *Cassis de Dijon*.

INTERNAL TAXATION

Finally, it should be added that the United Kingdom, like the other member states, is still entitled to impose its own domestic taxes, like value added tax, on imports from other EEC countries. Nevertheless, Article 95 of the EEC Treaty lays down strict conditions about the imposition of such taxes. Article 95 provides:

> No Member State shall impose, directly or indirectly, on the products of other Member States any internal taxation of any kind *in excess* of that imposed directly or indirectly on similar domestic products. Furthermore, no Member State shall impose on the products of other Member States any internal taxation of such a nature as to afford indirect protection to other products. [Emphasis supplied.]

Thus, for example, the United Kingdom authorities may continue to impose value added tax on cars imported into Northern Ireland from the Republic of Ireland provided that the tax is not imposed in a discriminatory manner on the imported cars as compared to home-produced ones.[29]

[29] For details see *op cit, supra,* n 8, Wyatt and Dashwood, pp 87 *et seq*. See also Plender, *A Practical Introduction to European Community Law* (1980) pp 49 *et seq*.

CHAPTER 10

FREE MOVEMENT OF CAPITAL AND PAYMENTS WITHIN THE EEC

Not so long ago the Irish punt was aceptable in Northern Ireland and one did not have to worry about differences in exchange rates between the pound sterling and the punt when crossing the border into the Republic of Ireland. Then in 1979, because of something called the EMS (the European Monetary System) parity between the two currencies ended. Why did this happen? What exactly is the EMS? These are some of the questions raised by members of the Northern Ireland public, who regard this move as building barriers between the member states rather than removing them as was expected as a result of membership of the Common Market. Other queries may arise about the legality of restrictions on the amount of currency one can take out of the country when going on holiday or doing business in another EEC country; although the United Kingdom Government lifted all exchange control regulations as of midnight of 24 October 1979, other member states like France and Italy still have strict exchange controls. For United Kingdom courts there is also the question of whether or not they may order judgment in the currency of another member state, instead of in sterling, whenever the successful plaintiff is a national of another EEC country. Questions like these make it necessary to consider the EEC Treaty provisions relating to the movement of capital and payments within the European Community.

THE MAIN PROVISIONS ON THE FREE MOVEMENT OF CAPITAL

Articles 67 to 73 of the EEC Treaty govern the free movement of capital between the member states. Basically these articles provide two separate, but complementary, ways in which to free capital movements within the Community; one places the onus upon the member states, while the other places it upon the Council of Ministers. Article 67 (1) states that:

> During the transitional period and *to the extent necessary* to ensure the proper functioning of the common market, Member States shall progressively abolish between themselves all restrictions on the movement of capital belonging to persons resident in Member States and any discrimination based on the nationality or on the place of residence of the parties or on the place where such capital is invested.

This provision is complemented by Article 69 of the Treaty, which requires the Council of Ministers to issue the necessary Directives for the progressive implementation of Article 67. To date only two Directives have been issued by the Council to give effect to Article 67. The first of these Directives was adopted on 11 May 1960[1] and the second, adding to and amending the first, on 18 December 1962[2]. These two Directives categorise capital movements into four groups, referred to as Lists A, B, C, and D. As regards the capital movements in Lists A and B, the member states must grant general or individual authorisations for these transactions as they are unconditionally liberalised. The capital movements in List C are only liberalised whenever a member state judges that such movement would not interfere with its economic or monetary policy. Lastly the capital movements in List D, including the import and export of banknotes, are not yet liberalised. Therefore, while an individual member state may decide unilaterally to remove all of its currency restrictions, these Directives still permit member states to impose certain restrictions. Consequently, although the United Kingdom removed all its exchange control regulations in October 1979, other countries like France and Italy may legitimately retain some.

The imprecision of these Council Directives and the discretionary wording of Article 67 (1) itself, which only requires member states to remove restrictions "on capital *to the extent necessary* to ensure the proper functioning of the Common Market", have led the Court of Justice to conclude that Article 67 of the Treaty is not directly effective. An individual cannot, therefore, rely upon Article 67 of the EEC Treaty as giving him an immediate right to move sums of money freely between member states. This point was established in the *Casati*[3] case where an Italian national, living in West Germany, was charged with attempting to export from Italy, without the authorisation prescribed by Italian exchange control legislation, large sums of Italian and German banknotes. He claimed that he had gone to Italy to buy equipment from a certain factory for his business in West Germany and had taken the money with him for that purpose. On finding that the factory was closed, he then had to take the money home with him to West Germany. Under Italian exchange control legislation, Casati was liable to a fine and, or imprisonment. He sought to rely, *inter alia,* upon Article 67 of the EEC Treaty, arguing that as of the end of the transitional period the restrictions on the movement of capital should be deemed to be abolished regardless of whether the necessary Directives had been issued under Article 69. The Court of Justice rejected that argument, declaring that:

> . . . Article 67(1) must be interpreted as meaning that restrictions on the exportation of bank notes may not be regarded as abolished as from the expiry of the transitional period, irrespective of the provisions of Article 69.[4]

[1] (OJ Special Ed. 1959-62, p49). Directive 921/60.

[2] (OJ Special Ed. 1963-64, p 5). Directive 62/63.

[3] *Casati, Criminal proceedings Against* [1981] ECR 2595; [1982] 1 CMLR 365. See the article by Louis, "Free Movement of Capital in the Community: The Casati Judgement" (1982) 19 *CML Rev* 443.

[4] *Casati,* [1981] ECR 2595, 2615.

A propos the impact of EEC law upon the criminal process of the member states, (considered in relation to the United Kingdom's criminal process in Chapter 14 *post*) it is significant that in the *Casati* case the Court of Justice ruled that the power of member states to impose penalties could only be limited in respect of those transactions that had been liberalised by Community law; in this particular case, since there was no liberalisation as regards banknotes, then Community law could not apply to limit the full rigour of the penalties that Italian criminal law might impose on Casati.

Further Council Directives will, therefore, be necessary to liberalise capital movements between the member states. The fact that capital movements are so closely related to the economic and monetary policies of the member states means that the Council of Ministers will probably be slow in agreeing upon further liberalising Directives as there is always the fear that if capital could move completely freely between the member states, the economy of one or other of them would be undermined.

Outside the EEC Treaty provisions, the member states have nevertheless been working towards closer co-ordination of their monetary policies. It was realised that with the removal of customs duties on goods traded between them, their economies would become increasingly inter-dependent and that currency fluctuations in any member state could have serious implications for the others. Therefore, after much debate, the member states eventually brought into operation the European Monetary System, or the EMS, as the first step towards "a zone of monetary stability in Europe". The EMS is an exchange rate system.[5] The currency of each member state that participates in the system is given a central rate against the ECU, that is the European Currency Unit. The exchange rates of the various currencies are then pegged round that central rate so that X amount of a French franc equals so much of a West German Deutschmark, equals so much of an Irish punt and so on. The currencies are allowed to fluctuate up or down by 2.25 per cent approximately from that central rate, except for the Italian lira which is permitted to fluctuate by 6 per cent. If the currency of a member state goes down against another, then the central banks of the states concerned are supposed to intervene to buy up the weaker currency and sell the stronger one. Thus the EMS represents a flexible, yet stable, exchange rate system.

The United Kingdom, however, refused to join the EMS in 1979, believing then that it would drag the pound sterling down in value. The Republic of Ireland, on the other hand, did decide to join, having been offered loans and grants to compensate for economic difficulties resulting from joining the system. Breaking the link between the Irish punt and the pound sterling soon afterwards was necessary because the pound sterling rose in value while the Irish punt had to remain within 2.25 per cent of its

[5] For details about the EMS, see Rey, "The European Monetary System" (1980) 17 *CML Rev* 7.

central exchange rate against the ECU. It seems a strange irony that the European Monetary System, designed to bring a European Monetary Union closer, has in fact created an economic barrier between Northern Ireland and the Republic of Ireland. Business transactions are now more complicated; Irish punts are no longer acceptable as legal tender in Northern Ireland and before going into the Republic people from Northern Ireland now exchange their pounds for punts. Although the United Kingdom is keeping "under review" its attitude towards joining the EMS, the country still does not participate fully in the system.

THE MAIN PROVISIONS ON THE FREE MOVEMENT OF PAYMENTS

In order to facilitate the free movement of goods, services, capital and people within the European Economic Community, the drafters of the EEC Treaty regarded it as important to include a provision to ensure that payments for goods, services and so on could be made in the currency of the most appropriate member state. The main Treaty provision governing the liberalisation of payments is Article 106. In accordance with Article 106(1), each member state:

> . . . undertakes to authorise, in the currency of the Member State in which the creditor or the beneficiary resides, any payments connected with the movement of goods, services or capital, and any transfers of capital and earnings, *to the extent* that the *movement of goods services, capital and persons* between Member States has been *liberalised* pursuant to this Treaty. [Emphasis supplied.]

The term "payments" is not defined in the Treaty, but has been interpreted by the Court of Justice. In *R* v *Thompson, Johnson and Woodiwiss*[6], a case referred under Article 177 of the Treaty by the English Court of Appeal (Criminal Division) to the Court of Justice, the latter had its first opportunity to rule on what constitutes "payments" within the meaning of Article 106. In this case the defendants had been convicted of the illegal importation of kruggerrands into the United Kingdom and the illegal export from the United Kingdom of silver coins, including florins, sixpences and half-crowns. They appealed against their convictions on the ground that the United Kingdom legislation imposing restrictions on the import and export of these coins constituted a quantitative restriction on the free movement of goods, contrary to Article 30 of the EEC Treaty. The Court of Justice ruled that coins that were not legal tender, like the half-crowns, constituted "goods" and although the United Kingdom's ban on their export amounted to a restriction contrary to Article 30, it could nevertheless be justified on public policy grounds under Article 36 of the Treaty. The remaining coins, which were legal tender, constituted "means of payment" within Article 106 rather than "goods". Therefore, the prohibition of quantitative restrictions on "goods" imposed by Article 30 of the Treaty simply did not apply to such coins. Coins that are legal tender in any of the member states are "means of payment", not goods.

[6] [1978] ECR 2247; [1979] 1 CMLR 47.

Within the United Kingdom, Article 106 has been considered by the courts. In 1975 Lord Denning MR applied Article 106 of the EEC Treaty in *Schorsch Meier* v *Hennin*[7] when the plaintiffs, dealers in car parts in West Germany, requested judgment in Deutschmarks. The defendant, who lived in England, had ordered spare parts from the plaintiffs and then refused to pay the bill. By the time the case came before the Court of Appeal, the pound sterling had been devalued so the plaintiffs sought payment in Deutschmarks. They relied upon Article 106 of the Treaty as they were creditors resident in another member state and they had supplied goods to the defendant in the United Kingdom. Lord Denning MR treated Article 106 as if it was directly effective, giving rise to immediate rights that could be enforced before the domestic courts, even though the Court of Justice had not yet ruled on this point. He decided that, by virtue of Article 106, the United Kingdom's courts were no longer bound by the old rule that judgments had to be given in sterling at the prevailing exchange rate when the debt became due.

This judgment was subsequently criticised by the House of Lords in *Miliangos* v *George Frank Textiles Ltd*[8], particularly by Lord Wilberforce, who felt that other United Kingdom courts should not regard Article 106 as directly effective unless and until the Court of Justice said so since it alone has jurisdiction to rule on the meaning and effect of Community Law.

Given an opportunity to do just this in the *Casati* case, the Court of Justice did not rule that Article 106 was sufficiently clear and precise and unconditional to be directly effective.

[7] [1975] 1 All ER 152; [1975] QB 416.

[8] [1975] 2 CMLR 585; [1976] AC 443; [1975] 3 All ER 801.

CHAPTER 11

FREEDOM OF MOVEMENT FOR WORKERS WITHIN THE EEC

The EEC Treaty contains specific provisions designed to facilitate the movement of people between member states for one of the main aims of the EEC is to achieve a common market within which people can move freely. It is worth remembering that at the time when the EEC Treaty was being drafted in the mid 1950s there were industrial areas in Northern Europe, such as that of the Ruhr in West Germany, which desperately needed to attract a larger workforce while at the same time there were areas, like Southern Italy, where unemployment was rife and where people were eager to move elsewhere in search of work. It was recognised that people would not be encouraged to move from their own country to another member state if there were numerous formalities at national borders and so Community law tries to minimise such formalities. In addition, it also strives to eliminate discrimination in obtaining employment, housing, education, social security and so on on grounds of nationality, which migrant workers might otherwise suffer on settling in another member state. It was with these objectives in mind that the EEC rules on the free movement of persons were developed.

In the EEC Treaty the provisions on the free movement of persons are in fact subdivided into two chapters, one dealing with the free movement of workers, that is employed persons, and the other dealing with the freedom, or right, of establishment of self-employed persons and of companies, enabling them to move from their own country and set up in business in another EEC country. Consequently, a similar division will be used in this Guide with this particular chapter devoted to the free movement of workers, leaving consideration of the right of establishment to the next chapter.

The European Community law rules concerning the free movement of workers are particularly relevant for Northern Ireland, not just because of the daily movement of workers between the North and South of Ireland but also because the high rate of unemployment in the Province means that many people actively contemplate going to another EEC country to find work. The provisions on the free movement of workers may be applicable in all sorts of ways, which are not immediately obvious as the following examples, taken from decided cases, will illustrate.

PROBLEMS INVOLVING FREEDOM OF MOVEMENT OF WORKERS

The EEC's provisions on the free movement of workers have been involved in the following instances:

- the refusal of entry into the United Kingdom of a Dutch woman who wanted to take up employment with the Church of Scientology, a cult formerly considered by the Home Office as socially harmful;[1]
- the threatened deportation from the United Kingdom of a French citizen with previous criminal convictions for illegal possession of controlled drugs;[2]
- the provision of vocational training in the United Kingdom for a citizen of the Irish Republic without the three years residence requirement and for fees at the "home" rate rather than overseas rate;[3]
- the availability to migrant Community workers of social security benefits in another member state, after having left their own home state;[4]
- the refusal by court order to allow a Northern Ireland girl to enter England or Wales for three years following a conviction in England for theft;[5]
- equal rights to trade union membership and the same social and tax advantages for migrant workers from other EEC countries as for nationals of the member state to which they have come to work;[6]
- equal rights in housing allocation for migrant workers from other EEC countries;[7]
- and right of a migrant worker from another EEC country and his family to remain permanently in the host member state after he has retired or been incapacitated at work through an accident or occupational disease.[8]

[1] *Van Duyn* v *Home Office* [1974] ECR 1337; [1975] 1 CMLR 1.

[2] *R* v *Bouchereau* [1977] ECR 1999; [1977] 2 CMLR 800.

[3] *MacMahon* v *Department of Education and Science* [1982] 3 CMLR 91; [1982] 3 WLR 1129. See also *R* v *Inner London Education Authority, ex parte Hinde and ex parte Duverley* and *R* v *Knowsley Metropolitan Borough Council, ex parte Phillips,* QBD, reported *The Times* 19 Nov 1984.

[4] See *eg Hoekstra (née Unger)* v *Bestuur* [1964] ECR 177. See also Ch 13 *post* on Social Security for Persons Moving within the EEC.

[5] *R* v *Saunders* [1979] ECR 1129; [1979] 2 CMLR 216.

[6] See Arts 8 and 7(2) Council Regulation 1612/68 (OJ Special ed, 1968 (II) 475).

[7] *Ibid,* Art 9.

[8] Commission Regulation 1251/70, (OJ Special ed, 1970 (II) 402).

From these illustrations one can appreciate more readily the variety of ways in which a working knowledge of the EEC rules on the free movement of workers is essential in order properly to advise people leaving Northern Ireland to work in another EEC country as well as workers coming to the Province from other member states.

THE MAIN PROVISIONS ON THE FREE MOVEMENT OF WORKERS

The basic reference point is Article 48 of the EEC Treaty, which is the main provision on the free movement of workers within the European Community. The first paragraph of Article 48 states the bold objective that freedom of movement of workers should be secured within the Community by the end of the transitional period. That period has passed for nine of the ten member states; Greece still has until 1988 to adapt to these provisions. When Spain and Portugal join the EEC in 1986, they too will have transitional periods. Article 48(2) explains that this freedom entails the abolition of any discrimination based on nationality between workers of member states as regards employment, remuneration and other conditions of work and employment. Subject to important limitations, justified on grounds of public policy, public security and public health (which will be considered at the end of this chapter) Article 48(3) goes on to explain in more detail that freedom of movement for workers includes the following rights:

The right—

(a) to accept offers of employment actually made;

(b) to move freely within the territory of Member States for this purpose;

(c) to stay in a Member State for the purpose of employment in accordance with the provisions governing the employment of nationals of that State laid down by law, regulation or administrative action;

(d) to remain in the territory of a Member State after having been employed in that State, subject to conditions which shall be embodied in implementing regulations to be drawn up by the Commission.

The provisions of Article 48 paragraphs 1 and 2 were declared by the Court of Justice in *Van Duyn* v *Home Office*[9] (see below) to be directly effective, thus creating immediate rights for individuals, which they may rely upon before the domestic courts of the member states. Before examining Article 48 further, some important preliminary comments must be made.

The first point to note is that the EEC Treaty provisions on the free movement of workers cannot be applied to situations which are *wholly* internal to one member state; in other words, Article 48 is designed to benefit workers who are moving between member states but does nothing for persons moving within the territory of their own country. Authority for

[9] *Op cit, supra,* n 1.

this point is the case of *R* v *Saunders*.[10] Briefly the facts were as follows: Miss Saunders, a British national and a native of Northern Ireland, had been convicted of theft in December 1977 by Bristol Crown Court. For that offence she was liable to imprisonment but she expressed to the court a wish to go back to live in Northern Ireland and a willingness to be bound over on condition that she should do so. The court ordered her to be bound over in her own recognisance of £50 to come up for judgment on or after 16 January 1978 unless she proceeded to Northern Ireland before that date and did not enter England or Wales for a period of three years. She did not, however, comply with the terms of this order and was arrested in Wales in June 1978 and was brought again before the Crown Court. During the court proceedings the question was raised whether as a "worker" within the meaning of European Community law, the court order of 1977 might have infringed her rights under Article 48 of the Treaty. The Crown Court decided to stay its proceedings and refer this question to the Court of Justice for a preliminary ruling under Article 177 of the EEC Treaty. The Court of Justice ruled that:

> The provisions of the [EEC] Treaty on the freedom of movement for workers cannot . . . be applied to situations which are *wholly internal to a member-state,* in other words where there is no factor connecting them to any of the situations envisaged by Community law. The application by an authority or court of a member-State to a worker who is a national of that same State of measures which deprive or restrict the freedom of movement of that worker within the territory of that State as a penal measure provided for by national law by reason of acts committed within the territory of that State is a *wholly domestic situation which falls outside the scope of the rules contained in the [EEC] Treaty on freedom of movement for workers.*[11]

If there had been some factor connecting Saunders with another member state, then it seems the Court would have regarded Article 48 of the Treaty as relevant.

Another important point to bear in mind is that the provisions governing the free movement of workers only benefit workers, who are *nationals* of the EEC's member states; as yet these provisions do nothing to benefit workers from non-EEC countries like the Algerian and other "Gastarbeiters" in West Germany. Although Article 48 itself does not make this explicit, its implementing measures are written in terms of workers who are nationals of a member state.[12] Hence the use of the phrase "migrant Community worker" throughout this chapter serves to emphasise that the EEC provisions benefit those workers who are nationals of one of the EEC's member states and are migrating within the EEC. However, to encourage workers to move from their own country for employment in another

[10] *Op cit, supra,* n 5. See also casenote by Watson, (1979) 3 *EL Rev* 195.

[11] [1979] 2 CMLR 216, 227 (Emphasis supplied). This principle has again been reiterated by the Court of Justice in *Moser* v *Land-Baden Württemberg* [1984] 3 CMLR 720.

[12] See *eg* Art 1, Council Regulation 1612/68 EEC (OJ Sp ed, 1968 (11), 475); Art 1, Council Directive 68/360 EEC (OJ Special ed, 1968 II, p 485).

member state the EEC provisions do extend to members of the worker's family, *irrespective* of their nationality since the family's rights flow from the worker's status and so it is his or her nationality that is crucial. The worker's family is defined as: (a) his spouse and their descendants who are under the age of 21 years or are dependants as well as (b) dependent relatives, in an ascending line, of the worker and his spouse. They have the right to install themselves with a worker who is a national of one member state *and* who is employed in the territory of another member state. If a spouse, who is a non-EEC national, becomes divorced from his/her partner, he/she does not have a separate, independent right of residence in the host country.[13]

Although the Community legislation is written in terms of a male worker, the provisions apply equally if the worker is a woman.

Since Article 48 of the EEC Treaty only lays down the basic principles about the free movement of workers one must also refer to its associated implementing Regulations and Directives for further details of the rights given to migrant Community workers and their families under Community law.[14] It is worth repeating that if there is a conflict between these EEC provisions and the domestic law of the United Kingdom, it is the EEC law that should prevail since it has supremacy over all conflicting national legislation. EEC law has been incorporated into the United Kingdom's legal system by the European Communities Act 1972. (See ch 6 *ante.*)

ENTRY AND RESIDENCE IN ANOTHER MEMBER STATE

If one is confronted with a problem concerning restrictions on a worker's movement and residence within a member state, then one should look at Council Directive 68/360.[15] This Directive complements subparagraphs (a), (b) and (c) of Article 48(3) of the EEC Treaty as it elaborates upon the rights of a migrant Community worker and his family to leave their own member state, to enter another and to reside there for the purpose of employment. An essential feature of Directive 68/360 is that it abolished the requirement of work permits for migrant Community workers and their families; these persons may no longer be required by member state authorities to obtain work permits. Consequently at the end of the United Kingdom's transitional period, the former Safeguarding of Employment Act (NI) 1947, requiring non-residents of Northern Ireland to obtain work permits, could not have been enforced against EEC nationals. This Act was repealed by the Employment Miscellaneous Provisions (NI) Order 1981. Instead, as *proof*

[13] See Art 10(1), Regulation 1612/68 EEC (OJ Special ed, 1968 (11), 475). See *Diatta* v *Land-Berlin* (ECJ) *The Times* 12 March 1985.

[14] For a detailed commentary see Evans, *Immigration Law* (1st ed, 1983), Ch 4. Relevant extracts of these Regulations and Directives are set out in Rudden and Wyatt (eds) *Basic Community Laws.*

[15] (OJ Special ed, 1968 (II), 485). For a detailed commentary on Directive 68/360 EEC see Wyatt and Dashwood, *The Substantive Law of the EEC* (1980) 127-135.

of their right of residence in another member state a document called a "Residence Permit for a National of a Member State of the EEC" should be issued by the relevant national authorities.[16] In the United Kingdom it is the Home Office which issues such residence permits. If a migrant Community worker's job in the host member state is going to last for more than twelve months he is entitled to receive this residence permit on production of his valid passport or identity card, together with his future employer's confirmation of a job. His family should receive residence permits, valid for the same length of time as his, by producing the document with which they entered the country and another issued by their state of origin or from whence they came proving their relationship and, where appropriate, one testifying their dependence upon the worker. The residence permit must be valid throughout the territory of the member state which issued it and must be valid for at least five years from the date of issue and be automatically renewable. Member states are therefore prohibited from imposing formalities such as frequent periodical renewals of these residence permits. Authority on this point is *R* v *Pieck*[17] where United Kingdom immigration officials had stamped a Dutch worker's passport with the words "Given leave to enter the UK for six months". Pieck, who was employed as a printer in Wales, had forgotten to renew this permission for entry and was threatened with deportation. He held no residence permit. However, when the case was referred by Pontypridd Magistrates' Court for a preliminary ruling by the Court of Justice under Article 177 of the Treaty, it held that such formalities were obstacles to the basic freedom of movement of workers and as such were prohibited. The Court emphasised that the right of a worker to reside in the host country arises directly from the EEC Treaty and its implementing Directives; the right of residence does not flow from, and is not therefore dependent upon, the issue of a residence permit. The case was subsequently dismissed by the Magistrates.

A residence permit may be withdrawn on grounds of prolonged absence.[18] Thus, for example, if an Italian came to Northern Ireland to work but hated the weather and went back to Italy for sunshine and stayed there for more than 6 consecutive months, his permit could be withdrawn. Voluntary unemployment[19], and in certain circumstances involuntary unemployment,

[16] See Art 4, Council Directive 68/360 EEC.

[17] [1980] ECR 2171; [1980] 3 CMLR 220.

[18] See Art 6(2), Council Directive 68/360 EEC. Breaks in residence less than six months and absence on military service shall not affect the validity of the permit.

[19] See *eg R* v *Secchi* [1975] 1 CMLR 383—a decision of Marylebone Magistrates' Court. A person who becomes voluntarily unemployed may no longer be considered a "worker" within the meaning Art 48 of the EEC Treaty.

may also mean that a permit is withdrawn.[20] Moreover, Article 10 of Directive 68/360 repeats verbatim the limitations laid down in Article 48(3) of the EEC Treaty. Therefore a person may be refused entry to a country or have his/her residence permit withdrawn and be deported on grounds of public policy, public security or public health (see below).

The residence permits so far discussed are those issued to workers and their families where the worker has confirmation of a job in the host member state which is expected to last more than twelve months. Although Article 48 of the EEC Treaty is silent about the rights of workers seeking work in another member state, it should be noted that at the Council of Ministers' negotiations about Directive 68/360, it was informally agreed that the member states would allow each others nationals, who had not yet obtained a job, to enter and remain in the host country for up to three months to look for work. Such persons are not entitled to a residence permit and if after three months they have still not found employment, they may be required to leave. The United Kingdom is in fact more generous than this informal agreement requires since it allows such persons up to six months to look for work. The right to enter another EEC country and remain there to search for work has been recognised by the Court of Justice in *Procureur du Roi* v *Royer*[21]. The Court was of the opinion that it would not be in keeping with the spirit and purpose of Article 48 of the EEC Treaty to interpret it strictly so that rights only accrued to those actually having employment in another member state. In addition, the EEC Regulations on social security (examined in Chapter 13 *post*), make provision for unemployment benefits to be paid to nationals of another member state for up to three months while they are looking for work in another member state.

Apart from the workers who have confirmation of a job lasting more than twelve months and those who are seeking employment, there are so-called "frontier workers" and "seasonal workers" to whom rather different rules about residence permits apply. A "frontier worker" is one who lives in one member state, but who travels daily or at least once a week across the border to his work in another member state. These frontier workers may be issued with "special permits" at the option of the host member state. Similarly workers, who go to another member state to work for more than three but less than twelve months or who are only seasonal workers, for example going only to help with the harvest, should be issued with "temporary residence permits" the validity of which is limited to the expected period

[20] Under Art 7(2) of Directive 68/360 upon the first renewal of a residence permit the next period of residence may be restricted to a period of not less than twelve months, if the worker has been involuntarily unemployed for more than twelve consecutive months. After this second, shorter period of residence expires, it appears the worker has no automatic right to renewal of his permit. But see Commission Regulation 1251/70 EEC (OJ Sp ed, 1970 (11), 402) on the rights of migrant workers to remain in the host member state after retirement or incapacity to continue working.

[21] [1976] ECR 497; [1976] 2 CMLR 619.

of employment.[22] For historical reasons Irish nationals living and working in the United Kingdom are not required to obtain residence permits.

The benefit of having a residence permit lies in the fact that its bearer can offer immediate proof of his/her right to reside in the host state and entitlement to the equality of treatment bestowed on migrant Community workers by Article 48 of the Treaty and its implementing measures as outlined below. As emphasised in *R* v *Pieck* the permit is merely proof or evidence of these rights, rather than the source of them.[23]

EQUALITY OF TREATMENT FOR MIGRANT COMMUNITY WORKERS

If one has to deal with a problem concerning the eligibility of a migrant Community worker for a job in Northern Ireland or one about discrimination on the ground of nationality as regards the terms and conditions of employment between workers from other member states and those in the United Kingdom, then one must refer to Council Regulation 1612/68.[24] As EEC Regulations are incorporated into the domestic law of the United Kingdom by section 2(1) of the European Communities Act 1972, Regulation 1612/68 is part and parcel of its law, to be given effect and enforced by United Kingdom courts. This Regulation complements Article 48(2) of the EEC Treaty in that it lays down the detailed provisions for the abolition of discrimination based on nationality between workers in respect of terms and conditions of employment. The Regulation is divided into three sections: eligibility for employment; employment and equality of treatment; and the workers' families. The salient points about each of these sections follows in the order adopted by the Regulation.

Under the first section of Regulation 1612/68 the general rule is that migrant Community workers are entitled to take up available employment in another member state with the same priority as nationals of that country. Article 3(1) states quite clearly that provisions laid down by law or administrative action or practices of a member state shall not apply:

> . . . where they limit application for and offers of employment, or the right of foreign nationals to take up and pursue employment or subject these to conditions not applicable in respect of their own nationals; or
>
> — where, though applicable irrespective of nationality, their exclusive or principal aim or effect is to keep nationals of other Member States away from the employment offered.

22 Art s6 (3) and 8, Council Directive 68/360 EEC.

23 [1980] ECR 2171; [1980] 3 CMLR 220 and *Procureur du Roi* v *Royer* [1976] ECR 497; [1976] 2 CMLR 619.

24 (OJ Sp ed, 1968 (11), 475). Relevant extracts are contained in Rudden and Wyatt (eds), *Basic Community Laws.*

An exception is made where linguistic knowledge is required by reason of the nature of the post to be filled. Beyond that, however, United Kingdom restrictions by number or percentage of foreign nationals taking up jobs here do not apply to nationals of other EEC countries although jobs in the "public service" form an exception to this general rule (see below).

The next section of the Regulation provides the details for the abolition of discrimination based on nationality in respect of conditions of employment.[25] In particular Article 7(1) thereof means that as regards any conditions of employment like remuneration or dismissal, the migrant Community worker who takes up a job in the United Kingdom must not be treated differently from British workers because of his nationality. This provision is probably of more practical value for migrant Community workers coming to work in Northern Ireland rather than in Great Britain since the latter's Race Relations legislation does not apply in the Province. Therefore Article 7(1) is an important source of protection against discrimination on grounds of nationality in Northern Ireland.

Moreover, under Article 7(2) of Regulation 1612/68 a migrant Community worker is entitled to "the same social and tax advantages as national workers". This provision may prove to be very important indeed for migrant Community workers coming to the United Kingdom, seeking supplementary and other social security benefits.[26] (This point is examined more thoroughly in Chapter 13 on Social Security for Persons Moving within the EEC.)

According to Article 7(3) of this Regulation migrant Community workers are also entitled to "access to training in vocational schools and retraining centres" in the host member state under the same conditions as nationals of that state. The significance of this provision has been recently highlighted in *MacMahon* v *Department of Education and Science,*[27] a decision of the English High Court, Chancery Division. MacMahon, an Irish citizen, went to England in 1978 to work in a car factory. Soon afterwards he decided to train as a teacher at St. Mary's College, Strawberry Hill, in England and applied to the relevant education authority for a further education award to do so. The local authority refused his application as he had not been ordinarily resident in the United Kingdom for the preceding three years. In addition he was considered to be "an overseas student" and was going to be charged a higher rate of fees than home students. He challenged this decision relying, *inter alia,* on Article 7(3) of Council Regulation 1612/68 which guarantees that migrant workers, who are nationals of other member states, shall have access to training in vocational schools under the same conditions as nationals of the host country. Dillon J considered him to be a

[25] For a detailed examination of Regulation 1612/68 see Wyatt and Dashwood, *The Substantive law of the EEC* (1980) 135-143.

[26] *Ibid,* pp 164 *et seq.*

[27] [1982] 3 CMLR 91; [1982] 3 WLR 1129.

"worker" before he decided to study as a teacher, and therefore, MacMahon could rely upon Article 7(3) of the EEC Regulation. It was held that St. Mary's College was a "vocational school" and that the residence requirement constituted covert discrimination against nationals of other EEC countries. Therefore MacMahon should be charged the same fees as home students, despite the fact that he did not meet the three years' residence requirement. This decision has subsequently been applied by the High Court, Chancery Division, in *R* v *Inner London Educational Authority, ex parte Hinde and Duverley* and *R* v *Knowsley Metropolitan Borough Council, ex parte Phillips*[28] where it was held that both education authorities, in denying two of the applicants access to postgraduate certificate of education courses at vocational schools in England under the same conditions as British nationals, had acted in breach of Article 7(3) of Regulation 1612/68. However, the third applicant, Hinde, had his application dismissed. He was an Irish citizen, who had been accepted to read for an LLB degree at Queen Mary College, London, but was refused an education award by ILEA on the grounds that he did not satisfy the three year residence requirement and that the LLB course was not a vocational course, nor Queen Mary College a vocational school. Taylor J agreed that the LLB course was not vocational training. The test, he said, was whether the training was intended to prepare or qualify a person for a particular vocation or job. Since the faculty of law of a university did not concentrate its teaching specifically on training barristers and solicitors, the LLB course was the academic stage while that which followed at law school was the vocational stage. Accordingly Hinde could not avail himself of the rights guaranteed by Article 7(3) of Regulation 1612/68 as Queen Mary College was not a vocational school. Clearly the implications of Article 7(3) of Regulation 1612/68 must be borne in mind by all vocational training bodies in the United Kingdom.

Subsequent provisions of Part II of Regulation 1612/68 deal with equality of treatment for migrant workers as regards membership of trade unions and housing. Housing authorities in member states, for instance the Northern Ireland Housing Executive, should take account of Article 9 of Regulation 1612/68 which states that migrant Community workers who are employed in another member state, like a French worker employed in Belfast, . . . "shall enjoy all the rights and benefits accorded to national workers in matters of housing, including ownership of the housing he needs. Such workers may, with the same right as nationals, put his name down on the housing lists in the region in which he is employed . . .".[29]

The migrant worker's family—the spouse and descendants, who are under twenty-one or dependent on him—also have the right to take up any

[28] *The Times,* 19 Nov 1984.

[29] Art 9 (1)–(2), Regulation 1612/68.

activity as an employed person in that same country, *even if they are not nationals of any member state.*[30] Children of a migrant worker, are entitled to be admitted to the host country's ". . . general educational, apprenticeship and vocational training courses under the same conditions as the nationals of that State".[31] In this context the recent case of *Morson and Jhanjan* v *The Netherlands*[32] is significant. Here the Court of Justice ruled that if a worker stays in his own country, in this case, the Netherlands, and has never exercised his rights under EEC law to move to another member state for work, he is not covered by the Community law provisions on the free movement of workers. Consequently his spouse and relatives derive no rights under Community law either. In this case Mrs Morson and Mrs Jhanjan, nationals of the former Dutch colony of Surinam, sought to rely upon Article 10 of Regulation 1612/68 to enter and reside in the Netherlands where their children, Dutch nationals, worked and lived. They failed in their efforts as their children had never exercised their rights as workers to freedom of movement within the European Community.

It should by now be clear that the rights conferred directly on migrant Community workers and their families by Regulation 1612/68 are indeed extensive. As the preamble to the Regulation explains, these rights had to be wide-ranging to ensure that many of the obstacles to the free movement of workers from one country to another within the EEC were eliminated. Employers, education authorities, housing organisations and lawyers in Northern Ireland should recognise the implications of this Regulation in their dealings with nationals from other EEC countries who come to the Province to work.

RESIDENCE AFTER RETIREMENT OR INCAPACITY TO WORK

If one is asked to advise a worker from another EEC country about his rights to remain here after his employment ends through illness or an accident at work, then Commission Regulation 1251/70[33] provides important guidance in such matters. This particular Regulation supplements Article 48(3) sub-paragraph (d) of the EEC Treaty and deals with the rights of the migrant worker and his family to remain in the host member state *after* having been employed in that state. The Regulation grants the right to remain permanently in the host country to two categories of workers—firstly, the retired and secondly the incapacitated.[34] Thus, for example, a French citizen, who has worked in Northern Ireland, acquires a right to

[30] Art 11, Regulation 1612/68 EEC. But this provision does not give them an independent right of residence in the host state. See *Diatta* v *Land-Berlin, supra* n 13.

[31] Art 12, Regulation 1612/68 EEC.

[32] [1983] 2 CMLR 221; [1982] ECR 3723.

[33] (OJ Special ed, 1970 (II), 402).

[34] For a detailed analysis see Wyatt and Dashwood, *The Substantive Law of the EEC* (1980) 143 *et seq.*

remain in the United Kingdom permanently when he reaches the age for entitlement to an old-age pension provided (a) he has been employed here for at least the last twelve months and (b) he has resided here continuously for more than three years.[35]

Similarly if a French citizen, employed in Northern Ireland, ceases work because of permanent incapacity he is entitled to remain in the country if he has resided continuously here for more than two years. If, however, the permanent incapacity was caused, either as a result of an accident at work or an occupational disease entitling him to a pension for which an institution of the host state (the United Kingdom in this instance) is entirely or partially responsible, he is entitled to remain here permanently irrespective of the length of his residence here.[36] Members of the worker's family are also covered by Regulation 1251/70 for it would clearly discourage a worker from taking up employment in another state if he knew that when he retired or became unfit to work, he himself could remain in that country but his family could not. Therefore Article 3(1) gives the members of a worker's family the right to remain permanently in the host country if the worker has acquired that right in accordance with the above mentioned conditions and they may stay even after his death. If the worker dies during his working life but before acquiring the right to remain permanently in the host country, his family may still remain provided certain liberal requirements are satisfied, such as the worker having continuously resided in the host country for at least two years or his death having resulted from an accident at work or occupational disease.[37]

Finally, it should be noted that the voluntarily unemployed migrant Community worker and his family are outside the scope of Commission Regulation 1251/70 and therefore do not acquire a right to reside permanently in the host state. As explained above, if a worker from another EEC country becomes voluntarily unemployed in the host member state, he may be required by the national authorities to leave the country.

LIMITATIONS ON THE FREE MOVEMENT OF WORKERS PROVISIONS

As well as providing important rights for workers moving within the EEC, Article 48 of the EEC Treaty also permits member states to limit such rights in certain circumstances. First of all, Article 48(4) of the EEC Treaty provides a far-reaching restriction for it states that the provisions of Article 48 of the Treaty do not apply "to employment in the public service". The Treaty therefore, recognises that member states may regard certain public posts as of such a sensitive nature that they may legitimately wish to exclude foreigners from them. The Treaty does not, however, define what is meant

[35] Art 2(1)(a), Regulation 1251/70 EEC.

[36] Art 2(1)(b), Regulation 1251/70 EEC.

[37] See Art 3(2), Regulation 1251/70 EEC.

by "public service" and so it has been left to the Court of Justice to determine which jobs fall within this public service exception. In line with its view that any exceptions to the fundamental freedoms of the EEC should be strictly construed, recent decisions of the Court of Justice indicate that it will only countenance a narrow interpretation being given to "public service" posts.[38] In *Sotgiu* v *Deutsche Bundespost,*[39] a case involving the payment of an allowance to an Italian national by his employer, the West German Post Office, the Court of Justice ruled that Article 48(4) of the EEC Treaty could only be used to restrict the *admission* of foreign nationals to certain activities in the public service; it could not be used to justify discrimination against them as regards their remuneration or other conditions of employment once appointed.

As well as this important exception to the Community rules on the freedom of movement of workers within the European Community it should also be noted that, according to Article 48(3) of the EEC Treaty, limitations on such movement may be justified by member states on the grounds of public policy, public security or public health. If, for example, the United Kingdom immigration authorities refused entry to a worker from another member state because he was a drug addict or if a national court recommended the deportation of a migrant Community worker because he had been convicted of serious criminal offences, how should one advise the worker in these circumstances? Is drug addiction a legitimate ground for refusal of entry into the United Kingdom? Does a worker have a right of appeal under EEC law against a deportation order?

The answers to such questions lie first and foremost in the appropriate legislation and secondly in the relevant case-law of the Court of Justice. While Article 48(3) of the EEC Treaty provides the basic proposition that limitations may be justified by member states on grounds of public policy, public security and public health, the details of this Treaty provision are worked out in secondary Community legislation. One must, therefore, refer to Council Directive 64/221,[40] a very important Directive indeed, which co-ordinates the measures that member states may take on these grounds concerning the entry into their territory, the issue or renewal of residence permits or expulsion of migrant Community workers and their families. This Directive prevents member states from using the grounds listed in Article 48(3) of the Treaty for purely economic reasons. Instead, Article 3 (1) of Directive 64/221 requires that measures taken on grounds of public policy or public security by member states to restrict entry into their territory, to refuse the issue or renewal of residence permits, or to expel from their

[38] See *eg Commission* v *The Belgian State (Re:Public Employees) (No 1)* [1980] ECR 3881; [1981] 2 CMLR 413 and *(No 2)* [1982] ECR 1845; [1982] 3 CMLR 539.

[39] [1974] ECR 153.

[40] (OJ Sp ed, 1963-64, 117). Relevant extracts are set out in Rudden and Wyatt (eds) *Basic Community Laws.*

territory migrant Community workers and members of their families, must be based "exclusively on the personal conduct of the individual concerned".

In the leading case of *Van Duyn* v*Home Office*[41] the Court of Justice ruled that Article 3 (1) of Directive 64/221 was directly effective, giving rise to immediate rights which individuals can rely upon before national courts. Van Duyn was a Dutch national and a practising member of the Church of Scientology. She came to the United Kingdom to take up employment as a secretary at the Church's headquarters in East Grinstead, Sussex, but United Kingdom immigration officials refused her permission to enter the country. Before the High Court she sought to rely upon Article 48 of the EEC Treaty, claiming that since she was both a worker and a national of an EEC country, she was entitled to move freely between member states for the purpose of taking up an offer of a job. On an Article 177 reference to the Court of Justice, the first made by a United Kingdom court, the Court said that while as a general rule a person's past conduct could not alone justify refusal of entry, present association with an organisation could be considered as part of a person's "personal conduct". The Court emphasized that any exceptions to one of the basic fundamental freedoms of the EEC, namely the free movement of workers, had to be construed strictly. Nevertheless member states were allowed a margin of discretion since the concept of "public policy" varied from one country to another and from time to time. The exercise of their discretion would, however, be reviewed by the Court of Justice to ensure that member states did not go too far. The Court accepted that since the United Kingdom had for several years considered that Scientology was a socially harmful cult and had had an established policy of discouraging the growth of the Church of Scientology by refusing entry to foreign members of the Church, this policy came within the margin of discretion. This was so even though the United Kingdom's own nationals were not restricted from membership of or employment with the Church. It may be noted that on 16 July 1980 Mr Whitelaw, then Home Secretary, said in a House of Commons written reply that the twelve year old ban on the entry of foreign Scientologists into the United Kingdom was to be lifted. He added, however, that individuals associated with Scientology whose presence was considered not to be conducive to the public good would continue to be liable to be refused entry.

Another important provision of Directive 64/221 is Article 3(2), which stipulates that previous criminal convictions shall not in themselves constitute grounds for the taking of measures on grounds of public policy or public security. In *R* v *Bouchereau*[42] the Court of Justice considered this phrase and stressed that:

[41] [1974] ECR 1337; [1975] 1 CMLR 1.

[42] [1977] ECR 1999; [1977] 2 CMLR 800.

> The existence of a previous criminal conviction can . . . only be taken into account in so far as the circumstances which gave rise to that conviction are *evidence* of personal conduct constituting a *present* threat to the requirements of public policy.
>
> Although, in general, a finding that such a threat exists implies the existence in the individual concerned of a propensity to act in the same way in the future, it is possible that past conduct alone may constitute such a threat to the requirements of public policy.
>
> It is for the authorities and, where appropriate, for the national courts, to consider that question in each individual case. . . .
>
> . . . Recourse by a national authority to the concept of public policy presupposes, in any event, the existence, in addition to the perturbation of the social order which any infringement of the law involves, of a genuine and sufficiently serious threat to the requirements of public policy affecting one of the fundamental interests of society.[43]

In this particular case a French national, who had been working in England, was convicted by Marylebone Magistrates' Court for unlawful possession of a small quantity of controlled drugs and given a twelve month conditional discharge and ordered to pay £5 costs. Within six months he was again found guilty, this time by Marlborough Street Magistrates' Court, of a similar offence. The Magistrates' Court recommended his deportation from the United Kingdom but Bouchereau maintained that such deportation of an EEC worker would be contrary to the EEC provisions on the free movement of workers. The Magistrates then decided to refer the case to the Court of Justice for a preliminary ruling under Article 177 of the EEC Treaty. Following the Court of Justice's narrow interpretation of the "public policy" exception, outlined above, the Magistrates' Court fined him £35 instead of deporting him as they did not regard him as a sufficiently serious threat to the requirements of public order. This case again illustrates how EEC law may mitigate the criminal sanctions that would otherwise be imposed by United Kingdom courts. (See chapter 14 *post.*)

A person's right of appeal against refusal of entry or deportation from a member state or refusal of a residence permit is laid down in Article 9 of Directive 64/221. The Court of Justice has recently stressed that a lapse of time between a recommendation to deport and its confirmation might deprive a person of a proper appeal as guaranteed by this provision. This point arose in *R* v *Secretary of State for Home Affairs ex parte Santillo,*[44] where an Italian national, who had been working in the United Kingdom since 1967, was convicted in 1974 by the Central Criminal Court of serious offences, including buggery, rape and indecent assault, and was sentenced to eight years imprisonment. When giving judgment, the court recommended his deportation under the Immigration Act 1971. Some four years later the Home Secretary confirmed the deportation order against him, expelling him from the United Kingdom when his sentence was

[43] [1977] ECR 1999, 2012 *et seq.* Emphasis added.

[44] [1980] ECR 1585; [1980] 2 CMLR 308.

completed. Santillo appealed against this order on the ground that it contravened EEC law especially his right of appeal guaranteed by Article 9 of Directive 64/221; he applied to the High Court for judicial review to quash the order. The court referred questions about the interpretation of Article 9 of the Directive to the Court of Justice for a preliminary ruling under Article 177 of the Treaty. The Court of Justice warned that a lapse of time of several years between a recommendation to deport and the confirmation of such a recommendation might be contrary to Article 9 of Directive 64/221. It stated that:

> . . . a lapse of time amounting to several years between the recommendation for deportation and the decision by the administration is *liable* to deprive the recommendation of its functions as an opinion within the meaning of Article 9. It is indeed essential that the social danger resulting from a foreigner's presence should be assessed at the very time when the decision ordering expulsion is made against him as the factors to be taken into account, particularly those concerning his conduct, are likely to change in the course of time.[45]

In this particular case the High Court did not feel that the lapse of time had affected his right of appeal under Article 9 and his deportation was confirmed.[46] The Court of Appeal subsequently confirmed this decision.[47]

Certain diseases or disabilities may constitute public health grounds justifying refusal of entry into a member state or refusal to issue a first residence permit. These are listed in the Annex of Directive 64/221. In addition, drug addiction is listed therein as an illness which might threaten public policy or public security.

As regards the limitation on the entry and residence of migrant Community workers and their families Directive 64/221 has very far-reaching implications. It is, therefore, worthy of detailed study by United Kingdom courts, the police and legal practitioners alike for in any case involving restrictions on the movement of EEC citizens, they can no longer simply look to United Kingdom legislation; they should have regard to the relevant EEC legislation and case-law of the Court of Justice in this area, which will have primacy in any cases of conflict with the United Kingdom's own domestic legislation.[48]

45 [1980] ECR 1585, 1601.

46 See Paisley, "European Community Law Flows Across the Channel into UK Immigration Law" (1982) 33 *NILQ* 85.

47 [1981] 1 CMLR 569.

48 See Wyatt and Dashwood, *The Substantive Law of the EEC* (1980) 146-54; Wooldridge, "Free Movement of EEC Nationals: The Limitation based on Public Policy and Public Security" (1977) *E L Rev* 190; Evans, "Court Recommendations to Deport etc" (1981) *E L Rev* 139; O'Keeffe, "Practical Difficulties in the Application of Article 48 EEC Treaty" (1982) 19 *CML Rev* 35.

CHAPTER 12

FREE MOVEMENT OF SELF-EMPLOYED PERSONS WITHIN THE EEC

The EEC Treaty not only seeks to encourage the free movement of workers within the European Community, but also tries to ensure that self-employed persons, such as lawyers, vets, plumbers, etc may pursue their particular occupations with as few obstacles as possible in a member state other than their own. A self-employed person may want to go to another member state either to provide his services for a short time only or to set himself up in business there on a more permanent basis. The drafters of the EEC Treaty realised that member states would accept more readily the free movement of non-professional workers than they would the free movement of self-employed persons since each country had, and still has, different training periods, examination systems and professional rules of conduct for its doctors, lawyers, vets and the like. The mutual recognition by the member states of their varying qualifications and training requirements for those skilled occupations could only be brought about gradually. Consequently the Treaty contains separate provisions governing the free movement of self-employed persons, which are slightly different in various respects from those concerning workers. As employment opportunities for professionally qualified people in the United Kingdom become scarcer, and since many have to do business in other European countries, it has become more attractive for accountants, lawyers and others to undertake temporary, or even long-term, employment in other EEC countries. For such reasons the relevant EEC legislation assumes increasing importance.

PROBLEMS INVOLVING FREEDOM OF MOVEMENT OF SELF-EMPLOYED PERSONS

The EEC provisions relating to self-employed persons moving from one member state to another on either a temporary or permanent basis may be relevant in a variety of ways. The following examples, gleaned from cases already decided by the European Court of Justice, serve to illustrate this:

- a British self-employed accountant, disqualified from cash sickness benefit under United Kingdom social security legislation for a period of illness while on holiday in France, was nevertheless entitled to such benefits by the operation of EEC Regulations[1];

[1] See *Brack* v *Insurance officer*[1976] ECR 1429; [1976] 2 CMLR 592.

— a Dutch national, educated in Belgium and having acquired a diploma in law there, was able to overcome the disqualification from admission to the Belgian Bar on grounds of his Dutch nationality by relying upon provisions of the EEC Treaty[2];

— a French national, initially refused permission to practise as a vet in his own country and prosecuted for doing so because the authorities refused to recognise his Italian veterinary qualifications, was held to be entitled to practise by virtue of an EEC Directive[3];

— under Community law a Dutch lawyer should not have been disqualified from representing his client before a Dutch tribunal merely because the lawyer changed his residence to live in a neighbouring member state[4];

— two French ladies, accused of operating as prostitutes in Belgium, were entitled to rely upon Community law to avoid deportation from Belgium.[5]

From these examples one can understand how national rules relating to social security entitlement, residence, nationality, professional qualifications and public policy may create obstacles to the free movement of self-employed persons within the European Community. One now needs to know where to find the relevant EEC legislation in order to be able to advise someone confronted by such obstacles.

THE MAIN PROVISIONS CONCERNING FREE MOVEMENT OF SELF-EMPLOYED PERSONS

The EEC Treaty in fact contains two sets of Articles concerning self-employed persons; one set concerns the right, or freedom, of establishment and the other concerns the freedom to provide services. The right of establishment is the right of a natural or legal person, (an ordinary individual or a company) to move to, and settle permanently in, a member state to carry on business there. It includes the right to take up and pursue activities as self-employed persons and to set up and manage undertakings *under the same conditions as nationals of the member state* where such establishment is effected.[6] For present purposes, only the right of establishment of natural

[2] See *Reyners* v *The Belgian State* [1974] ECR 631; [1974] 2 CMLR 305.

[3] See *Ministère Public* v *Auer* [1979] ECR 437; [1979] 2 CMLR 373 and *Auer* v *Ministère Public* [1985] 1 CMLR 123.

[4] *Van Binsbergen* v *Bedrijfsvereniging voor de Metaalnijverheid* [1974] ECR 1299; [1975] 1 CMLR 298.

[5] *Adoui and Cornuaille* v *Belgian State* [1982] ECR 1665; [1982] 3 CMLR 631.

[6] Para 2 of Art 52 of the EEC Treaty.

self-employed persons will be examined. The position as regards companies will be considered at the end of the chapter. The right of establishment is to be distinguished from the freedom to provide services. The former implies that the self-employed person settles permanently in another member state, whereas the latter applies to a self-employed person established in one member state, who provides services on a temporary basis in another. For example, in the case of a barrister qualified in Northern Ireland who goes to Dublin to represent a client in a particular case there, the EEC provisions on freedom to provide services would apply. If instead the barrister decided that he wanted to settle in the Republic of Ireland and practise there permanently, then the right of establishment provisions, in so far as they apply to lawyers, would be apposite.

The distinction between the two is not always easy to draw because the regular provision of services borders closely on establishment.[7] The Court of Justice has on several occasions ruled that it is up to the national court hearing a particular case to decide, on the basis of the facts before it, which of the EEC Treaty provisions on the free movement of workers or the provision of services or the right of establishment should apply.[8] In so far as a particular activity is not governed by the provisions relating to the free movement of workers and the right of establishment, then those provisions on the freedom to provide services apply since they are expressed in Article 59 of the EEC Treaty to be of a residual nature. It should, however, be remembered that while there are technical differences between the freedom to provide services and the right of establishment, they have of course the same ultimate goal, namely achieving the fullest possible freedom of movement for self-employed persons within the European Community.

THE RIGHT OF ESTABLISHMENT OF SELF-EMPLOYED PERSONS[9]

Articles 52 to 57 of the EEC Treaty are the main provisions on the right of self-employed persons to establish themselves in an EEC country other than their own. As explained above, Article 52 includes the right of persons who are *nationals* of EEC countries to take up and pursue activities as self-employed persons in a member state other than their own on the same conditions as nationals of that other state. Article 52 of the EEC Treaty provided for the progressive abolition of any restrictions on the right of establishment during the transitional period. Moreover, the Council of Ministers was required by Article 54(1) of the Treaty to draw up a General Programme for the abolition of existing restrictions on the right of

[7] See Wyatt & Dashwood, *The Substantive Law of the EEC* (1980) 182-3.

[8] *Eg* see *The State (Italy)* v *Watson and Belmann* [1976] ECR 1185; [1976] 2 CMLR 552.

[9] *Op cit, supra,* n 7, Wyatt & Dashwood, pp 183-195 give a detailed account. See also Plender, *A Practical Introduction to European Community Law* (1980) Ch 6.

establishment within the Community. The Council did produce such a Programme at the end of 1961[10], setting out the general conditions under which the right of establishment was to be attained. Since a "General Programme" is not one of the legally binding forms of secondary Community legislation listed in Article 189 of the EEC Treaty, the Programme only provided guidelines to be implemented by further Council Directives. These Directives were for the abolition of restrictions any member state had imposed on self-employed nationals of other member states coming to its territory to pursue a particular activity. In addition the Council was required by Article 57(1) of the Treaty to issue Directives on "the mutual recognition of diplomas, certificates and other evidence of formal qualifications" in order to make it easier for persons to take up and pursue activities as self-employed persons in other member states.

As the Council was trying to cover scores of different activities, ranging from plumbing, wholesale trading and so on right through to veterinary surgery and other professions, production of both sets of Directives was a very slow process. As if to speed up this legislative process, and indeed to circumvent the need for so many Council Directives, the Court of Justice made an important intervention in the 1974 case of *Reyners* v *The Belgian State.*[11] Here Reyners, a Dutch national, born and educated in Belgium and having obtained the Belgian diploma in law giving him the right to practise at the Belgian Bar, was nevertheless excluded from that profession on the ground of his nationality since Belgian law only permitted Belgian nationals to practise. On an Article 177 reference to the Court of Justice, the Court emphasised that the abolition of discrimination between citizens of EEC countries on grounds of nationality was one of the fundamental legal principles of Community law. Consequently the Court declared that Article 52 of the EEC Treaty was directly effective as of the end of the transitional period, and therefore the Council's Directives had become ". . . superfluous with regard to implementing the rule on nationality since this is henceforth sanctioned by the Treaty itself with direct effect."[12] The transitional periods have passed for all of the present member states except Greece. There will be a few transitional periods for professions in Spain and Portugal to allow them to adjust to the right of establishment of self-employed persons.

This ruling has significant implications for it means that if an EEC citizen is disqualified from following a particular profession or business in another member state on the ground of nationality, then that person may rely directly upon Article 52 of the Treaty before the local courts in order to overcome such discrimination.[13] While obstacles based on nationality can be

[10] (OJ Special ed, 1961 (II), 7). Extracts set out in Rudden & Wyatt, *Basic Community Laws* (1980), pp 231 *et seq.*

[11] [1974] ECR 631; [1974] 2 CMLR 305.

[12] [1974] ECR 631, 652.

[13] *Op cit, supra,* n 9 Wyatt & Dashwood, pp 186-188; Plender, 74-80. See also *Paris Bar* v *Klopp* [1985] 1 CMLR 99.

overcome by relying directly on Article 52 of the Treaty, there are other ways of excluding foreigners from pursuing certain professions or activities. For example, refusing to recognise their qualifications or training periods as equivalent to those of nationals of the host country or requiring registration with professional bodies may be more subtle forms of discrimination against nationals of other EEC countries than blatant ones based on foreign nationality. However such forms of discrimination are just as detrimental to the achievement of freedom of establishment for self-employed persons within the EEC. The Court of Justice, foreseeing just such difficulties, concluded in the *Reyners* case that the Council of Ministers still had to issue Directives to introduce into the law of member states provisions "to make easier the effective exercise" of the right of establishment. Since then the Council has been endeavouring to produce Directives on the mutual recognition of qualifications, diplomas and training periods for various professions.

As an illustration of the benefits self-employed persons may derive from Council Directives on the mutual recognition of qualifications and training periods one may consider the 1979 case of *Knoors* v *Secretary of State for Economic Affairs*.[14] Here a Dutch national, who had resided and worked in Belgium as a plumber for seven years, applied to the relevant Dutch authorities for authorisation to carry on business as a plumber in his own country, the Netherlands. His application was, however, refused on the ground that he did not possess the qualifications for the plumbing trade required by Dutch law. Knoors then sought to rely upon Council Directive 64/427 EEC, which was intended to facilitate the right of establishment of tradesmen like plumbers by requiring the member states to accept, as sufficient evidence of the knowledge and ability to plumb, the fact that the person in question had carried on that trade in another member state for a certain period. The Dutch Secretary of State for Economic Affairs kept refusing Knoors' applications because he maintained the Directive was only intended to benefit nationals of other EEC countries, but not a state's own nationals as in the instant case. On an Article 177 reference, the Court of Justice ruled that Directive 64/427 applied not only to nationals of other member states but also to a national of the host state, who had been a plumber in another EEC country and wanted to return to his home country to pursue that trade there. The Court declared that:

> Although it is true that the provisions of the Treaty relating to establishment and the provision of services cannot be applied to situations which are *purely internal* to a member-State, the position nevertheless remains that the reference in Article 52 [of the EEC Treaty] to 'nationals of a member-State' who wish to establish themselves 'in the territory of another member-State', cannot be interpreted in such a way as to exclude from the benefit of Community law a given member-State's own nationals when the latter, owing to the fact that they have lawfully resided on the territory of another member-State and have there

14 [1979] ECR 399; [1979] 2 CMLR 357.

> acquired a trade qualification which is recognised by the provisions of Community law are, with regard to their State of origin, in a situation which may be assimilated to that of any other persons enjoying the rights and liberties guaranteed by the Treaty.[15]

It should, therefore, be noted that the EEC's provisions on the right of establishment and those on the provision of services will not apply if the situation is *wholly internal* to one member state; these provisions are to ensure the free movement of self-employed persons *moving within the European Community*. In this respect the principles applicable to self-employed persons are the same as those applicable to workers (See p 108 *ante.*) One should also note that the Treaty provisions are aimed at abolishing restrictions imposed on EEC nationals by private bodies as well as by government authorities. For example, United Kingdom sporting associations may not be allowed to exclude nationals from other EEC countries from playing in their teams unless they are national sports teams or amateur competitions.[16]

Therefore if, for instance, one is asked to advise a doctor, nurse, or veterinary surgeon who has trained and qualified in the United Kingdom about the possible difficulties of practising in another EEC country like the Republic of Ireland, one should check the Official Journal, "L" section, for any relevant Directives on the mutual recognition by member states of qualifications, training periods etc and on the right of establishment.[17] There has not yet been a Directive upon the mutual recognition of lawyers' qualifications nor one on the right of establishment of lawyers, although the CCBE (the French acronym for Consultative Committee of European Bar and Law Societies) is working on draft proposals.[18] For the time being a qualified Northern Ireland lawyer may only provide his services on a temporary basis in another member state under the Lawyers' Services Directive (Council Directive 77/249) which will be considered below. In the meantime, the Court of Justice has stressed in *Paris Bar* v *Klopp*[19] that the absence of Directives to co-ordinate national provisions governing access to, and practice in, the legal profession does not mean that a Bar Council or similar professional body of a member state can exclude a lawyer from practising in that country just because he retains chambers in another member state. Here the Paris Bar Council had tried, unsuccessfully, to

[15] [1979] 2 CMLR 357, 367. But see also *Ministère Public* v *Auer* [1979] 2 CMLR 373.

[16] See *Walrave and Koch* v *Union Cycliste Internationale* [1974] ECR 1405 and *Donà* v *Mantero* [1976] ECR 1333.

[17] See *eg* Council Directive 77/452 EEC (OJ 1977 L 176/1) on the Mutual Recognition of Diplomas . . . of Nurses; Council Directive 78/1026 EEC (OJ 1978 L 362/1) on the Mutual Recognition of Diplomas . . . in Veterinary Surgery.

[18] The CCBE has also initiated the drafting of a common code of professional conduct as a step towards attaining the right of establishment for lawyers within the EEC. *(Eurolaw Community Intelligence* No 13/83).

[19] [1985] 1 CMLR 99.

exclude a German barrister from practising as an advocat in Paris by reason of the fact that he had retained his chambers in Düsseldorf, which was contrary to the Paris Bar Council's own internal rules.

FREEDOM OF SELF-EMPLOYED PERSONS TO PROVIDE SERVICES

Articles 59 to 66 of the EEC Treaty are the main provisions on the freedom of self-employed persons to provide their services within the European Community. It is the right of an EEC national, who is established in a member state, to provide his services temporarily in another member state under the same conditions as those imposed by that state on its own nationals. It bears repeating that the basic distinction between the right of establishment and the freedom to provide services is that the former allows an EEC citizen to take up a business or profession as a self-employed person in another member state on a permanent basis, whereas the latter means that the person remains established in one member state, while temporarily pursuing his business or providing professional services in another. The EEC rules about the provision of services cover three different sets of circumstances:[20]

(a) where the person providing the service lives in State A and travels to State B to perform the service there—for example, a Northern Ireland solicitor travels from Belfast, where he is established, to Dublin to advise a client; or

(b) where the recipient of the service travels from State B to State A where the person provides the particular service—for example, the client travels from Dublin to Belfast for advice from the solicitor; or

(c) where the person giving the service supplies it from State A, where he is based, across the border to State B without actually going there—for example, the Belfast solicitor sends advice to his client in Dublin.

The "services" covered by the Treaty are defined in Article 60 as those "normally provided for remuneration". In particular Article 60 goes on to explain that "services" covered by the Treaty include activities of an industrial or commercial character, of craftsmen and of the professions; this is not, however, an exhaustive list. Restrictions, like those based upon nationality or residence requirements, on the freedom to provide such services within the EEC were to be abolished progressively during the transitional period. As in the case of the right of establishment, the EEC Treaty once again required the Council of Ministers to draw up a General Programme for the member states, giving them guidance on the abolition of these restrictions. This Programme was completed by the end of 1961. It set out the general conditions under which, and the stages by which, each type

[20] See Wyatt & Dashwood, *The Substantive Law of the EEC* (1980) 199-200.

of service was to be liberalised.[21] In order to implement this General Programme, the Council was obliged to issue Directives. When the Council proved to be too slow in adopting these Directives, the Court of Justice hastened progress in this area in 1974 just as it had done in *Reyners* v *Belgian State* six months earlier in relation to the right of establishment. In *Van Binsbergen*[22] a legal representative, Kortmann, who was a Dutch national established in the Netherlands, had been employed by Van Binsbergen to bring an appeal on his behalf before a Dutch social security court. Under Dutch law only persons established in the Netherlands could act as legal representatives or advisers before such courts. Consequently when Kortmann transferred his habitual residence to Belgium during the hearing of Van Binsbergen's appeal, the court informed Kortmann that he was no longer entitled to appear as a legal representative in the case. Kortmann sought to rely upon Article 59, which required the abolition of such restrictions on the freedom to provide services. On an Article 177 reference, the Court of Justice declared that Articles 59 and 60 were directly effective as of the end of the transitional period. The provisions of Article 59, the Court said:

> . . . abolish all discrimination against the person providing the service by reason of his nationality or the fact that he is established in a Member State other than that in which the service is to be provided. Therefore, as regards at least the specific requirement of *nationality or of residence,* Articles 59 and 60 impose a well-defined obligation, the fulfilment of which by the Member States cannot be delayed or jeopardised by the absence of [the implementing Council Directives].[23]

This ruling means that nationals of other EEC countries who are, by reason of their nationality or residence, prevented from providing services in the host member state, may rely directly upon Articles 59 and 60 before the local courts to overcome such discrimination.

One must, however, be careful when relying upon the *Van Binsbergen* decision because the Court did not give a *carte blanche* to every self-employed business or professional person, allowing him to provide his services in any member state irrespective of all requirements imposed by the authorities or professional bodies in those countries. In its ruling the Court of Justice did add the important caveat that member states were still entitled to impose some restrictions on nationals from other member states pursuing certain professional activities. As the Court explained in *Van Binsbergen:*

[21] Some provisions of this General Programme are reproduced by Rudden and Wyatt, *Basic Community Laws,* pp 234 *et seq.*

[22] *Op cit, supra,* n 4. [1974] ECR 1299; [1975] 1 CMLR 298.

[23] [1974] ECR 1299, 1311-1312. Emphasis supplied.

> . . . taking into account the particular nature of the services to be provided, specific requirements imposed on the person providing the service cannot be considered incompatible with the [EEC] Treaty where they have as their purpose the application of professional rules justified by the general good—in particular rules relating to organisation, qualifications, professional ethics, supervision and liability—which are binding upon any person established in the State in which the service is provided, where the person providing the service would escape from the ambit of these rules by being established in another Member State.[24]

The Court was in fact drawing a distinction between on the one hand ordinary business activities such as those of laundry-cleaners, café owners and the like, who are not bound by professional rules of conduct and on the other hand professions like legal and medical ones, which are bound by such rules. As for the latter, a member state might impose certain restrictions on nationals of other EEC countries providing such services in order to ensure that they observe the professional rules of conduct which would be applicable to them if they were permanently settled there but which they could evade because they are actually established in another country. The Court suggested that restrictions falling short of residence requirements would suffice.

The ruling in the *Van Binsbergen* case only overcomes obstacles based on nationality or residence and here again Council Directives are still necessary to facilitate the effective exercise of the freedom to provide services. Directives on the mutual recognition of professional qualifications, training and the like are just as necessary for facilitating the provision of services as they are for the right of establishment.[25] Therefore if one is asked to advise a doctor, veterinary surgeon, plumber or lawyer about the obstacles that exist against the provision of their particular services in another EEC country, one should again check the Official Journal "L" section, for any relevant Directives and then look for United Kingdom implementing legislation made under section 2(2) of the European Communities Act 1972. Even if no United Kingdom implementing measures have been taken, it should be remembered that provisions of any Directives may be directly effective if the time-limit for their implementation has passed and if directly effective, they give rise to immediate rights enforceable before the local courts.[26]

At present, if a lawyer from another EEC country wants to provide his services in Northern Ireland, the person in question should be advised to consult Council Directive 77/249 on the Lawyers' Freedom to Provide

[24] *Ibid,* p 1309.

[25] Art 66 of the EEC Treaty states: "The provisions of Arts 55 to 58 [on the Right of Establishment] shall apply to the matters covered by [the Chapter on Services]." Therefore Article 57 of the Treaty on the mutual recognition of qualifications etc applies equally to the provision of services as it does to establishment.

[26] See the useful article by Leenen in (1980) 17 *CML Rev* 259.

Services[27] and also the United Kingdom's implementing measure, the European Communities (Services of Lawyers) Order 1978.[28] This applies to the whole of the United Kingdom and came into operation at the beginning of March 1979. Council Directive 77/249 only deals with measures to facilitate the effective pursuit of the activities of lawyers by way of the provision of services. Member states were given two years to implement it. It does not contain provisions on the mutual recognition of qualifications, nor on the right of establishment for lawyers, both of which will require more detailed legislation. Made in 1977, the Directive takes account of the *Van Binsbergen* decision and the Court's concern therein for respect for professional rules of conduct. The lawyer from another EEC country coming to the United Kingdom to provide his services must retain the professional title he uses in the member state in which he is established.[29] By virtue of Article 4(1) of the 1977 Directive a visiting lawyer may not be disqualified from representing a client in a court in the host country by reason only of his nationality or the fact that he has not registered with the professional body in that country. However, he must respect the professional rules of conduct of the host country and may be disciplined by the professional ruling body for breach of them. In implementation of a proviso in the Directive, the United Kingdom has restricted visiting EEC lawyers from undertaking conveyancing and probate work for remuneration.[30] They may, however, represent clients in other legal proceedings provided that throughout they are instructed and act in conjunction with a lawyer fully entitled to practise before the particular British court or tribunal.[31] Barristers and solicitors from the Republic of Ireland are further limited in the services they may provide in the United Kingdom.[32] One may already deduce that in practical terms, the application of the Lawyers' Services Directive is indeed limited. Consequently, much depends on the long-awaited Council Directive on the right of establishment of lawyers if the present limitations on the mobility of members of this particular profession within the European Community are to be overcome.

PROVISIONS COMMON TO BOTH THE RIGHT OF ESTABLISHMENT AND THE FREEDOM TO PROVIDE SERVICES

It should be obvious from the foregoing discussion that the EEC rules on the provision of services and the right of establishment of the self-employed

[27] (OJ 1977 L 78/17). The Directive's main provisions are reproduced in Rudden and Wyatt, *Basic Community Laws* (1980) pp 246-249. It is annotated by Bronkhorst in (1977) 2 *EL Rev* 224.

[28] SI 1978 No 1910.

[29] See Art 3 of Directive 77/249 and Art 11 of EC (Services of Lawyers) Order 1978.

[30] *Ibid,* Art 1 of the Directive and Art 9 of the Order.

[31] See Art 5 of the Directive 77/249 and Art 5 of the EC (Services of Lawyers) Order 1978.

[32] See Art 6 of the EC (Services of Lawyers) Order 1978. See generally Walters, "Uncertain Steps Towards a European Legal Profession" (1978) 3 *EL Rev* 265.

within the European Community have much in common. This is hardly surprising since they share the same aim; that of securing the fullest possible freedom of movement for self-employed persons within the EEC. With this point in mind, one can readily understand why several EEC Treaty provisions and associated implementing secondary legislation apply both to those providing services and those seeking to establish themselves in a member state other than their own.

1 ENTRY AND RESIDENCE OF SELF-EMPLOYED PERSONS

If one is asked to advise a self-employed person from the United Kingdom about rights of entry and/or residence in another EEC country or advise a person coming to Northern Ireland to work, then one should consider Council Directive 73/148 EEC.[33] This Directive concerns the abolition of restrictions on the movement and residence within the EEC of nationals of member states with regard to the right of establishment or the provision of services. It brings the law governing the entry and residence of self-employed persons into line with that applying to workers and its provisions are similar to those of Directive 68/360, considered in Chapter 11 *ante* on the Freedom of Movement of Workers within the European Community.

Subject to exceptions based on public policy, public security and public health, (to be discussed below) Article 1 of Directive 73/148 requires the member states to abolish restrictions on the movement and residence of *(a) nationals* of a member state who are established or who wish to establish themselves in another member state in order to pursue activities as self-employed persons, or who wish to provide services in that state and *(b)* nationals of member states wishing to go to another member state as *recipients* of services. According to paragraphs (c) and (d) of Article 1 the members of the family, who are entitled to accompany them, include their spouse and their children under twenty-one years of age and dependent ascendants and descendants of themselves or their spouses, *irrespective* of nationality. As in the case of workers, it is the nationality of the self-employed person or the recipient of the particular service that is all important since the family's rights flow from his status, and so the nationality of members of the family is irrelevant.

Persons covered by Article 1 of Directive 73/148 are entitled to enter another EEC country merely on production of a valid passport or identity card. When it comes to residence, there is a difference between those providing services and those wishing to establish themselves. For the latter Article 4(1) states that:

[33] (OJ 1973 L 172/14). Its main provisions are reproduced by Rudden and Wyatt in *Basic Community Laws* (1980) pp 237-240.

> Each member state shall grant the right of permanent residence to nationals of other member states who establish themselves within its territory in order to pursue activities as self-employed persons, *when the restrictions on these activities have been abolished pursuant to the [EEC] Treaty*. (Emphasis supplied)

This wording suggests that in the absence of Directives made under Article 57 of the Treaty on mutual recognition of qualifications etc for lawyers and the like, such persons do not have a right of permanent residence. If however, such restrictions have been removed, they are to be issued with a "Residence Permit for a National of a Member State of the European Communities" as *proof* of their right of residence. This residence permit shall be valid for five years and shall be automatically renewable. As for self-employed persons who are only providing their services temporarily in another member state and also for recipients of such services, they have a right of residence co-terminous with the period of their service. Where that period exceeds three months, the person should be issued with "a right of abode" permit as proof of the right of residence.[34] The Home Office is responsible for issuing such documents in the United Kingdom.

Self-employed persons are not to be deported or excluded from the host country simply for failing to inform the authorities of that country of their presence or failure to comply with the state's administrative formalities for the control of aliens. Authority on this point is *Procureur du Roi* v *Royer*[35] where a tradesman of French nationality was ordered to leave Belgium on the grounds, *inter alia,* that he had not completed the administrative formalities of entry on the population register and had no permit to establish himself in Belgium. On an Article 177 reference, the Court of Justice ruled that:

> . . . the right of nationals of a member-State to enter the territory of another member-State and reside there for the purposes intended by the Treaty—in particular *to look for* or pursue an occupation or activities as employed or self-employed persons, or to rejoin their spouse or family—is a right conferred *directly* by the Treaty, or, as the case may be, by the provisions adopted for its implementation. It must therefore be concluded that this right is acquired *independently* of the issue of a residence permit by the competent authority of a member-State. The grant of this permit is therefore to be regarded not as a measure giving rise to rights but as a measure by a member-State serving to prove the individual position of a national of another member-State with regard to the provisions of Community law.[36]

The Court concluded that the mere failure by an EEC national to comply with entry and residence requirements was not of such a nature in itself to constitute conduct threatening public policy and thus justifying deportation

[34] See Art 4 of Council Directive 73/148. See also commentary by Wyatt & Dashwood, *The Substantive Law of the EEC* (1980) 184-185.

[35] [1976] ECR 497; [1976] 2 CMLR 619. See also *The (Italian) State* v *Watson and Belmann* [1976] ECR 1185; [1976] 2 CMLR 552.

[36] [1976] 2 CMLR 619, 639. Emphasis added.

or temporary imprisonment. This case is yet another reminder of how the criminal law of member states may be influenced by the application of Community law.

2 RIGHT TO REMAIN AFTER EMPLOYMENT CEASES

If one has to deal with a problem about the right of a self-employed person, who is a national of an EEC country, and his family to remain permanently in another member state after his retirement or after being incapacitated, one should turn to Council Directive 75/34.[37] Their rights are virtually the same as those of a worker and his family as specified in Commission Regulation 1251/70 EEC considered at p 116 *ante*. Similarly, where a self-employed person becomes entitled to an old-age pension in the host country, or reaches 65 in a host state without old-age pensions for self-employed persons, or becomes incapacitated at work through accident or occupational illness, he may remain permanently in the host member state provided certain liberal conditions about length of residence and work therein are satisfied.

3 SOCIAL SECURITY PROVISIONS FOR SELF-EMPLOYED PERSONS

To encourage self-employed people to move from their home country to another one within the European Community it is important to maintain their pension rights etc once they leave their own country. Strangely however, the EEC Treaty omitted to make provision for self-employed persons' social security entitlement; Article 51 of the Treaty only applies to migrant Community workers. In fact it was not until quite recently that Council Regulation 1390/81,[38] which came into operation in July 1982, extended the EEC provisions on social security to include self-employed persons and their families moving within the European Community. This represents a very significant development towards the greater mobility of self-employed people within the Community as the Regulation preserves their social security entitlement when they move from one EEC country to another. The EEC social security Regulations are examined in more detail in Chapter 13.

[37] (OJ 1975 L 14/10). See Rudden & Wyatt, *Basic Community Laws,* pp 243-246.

[38] (OJ 1981 L 143/1).

4 *LIMITATIONS ON THE RIGHT OF ESTABLISHMENT AND PROVISION OF SERVICES*

Just as Article 48(3) of the EEC Treaty allows member states to impose restrictions on the free movement of workers on the grounds of public policy, public security and public health, restrictions may also be imposed on self-employed persons moving within the European Community. Article 56(1) of the EEC Treaty provides that the EEC legislation, guaranteeing self-employed persons the right of establishment:

> . . . shall not prejudice the applicability of provisions laid down by law, regulation or administrative action providing for special treatment for foreign nationals on grounds of public policy, public security or public health.

By virtue of Article 66 of the Treaty these limitations also limit the freedom of self-employed persons to provide services. The most important implementing Directive in this area is again Council Directive 64/221 which co-ordinates the measures that member states may impose on any of these three grounds on migrant Community workers and their families and also on self-employed EEC nationals and their families. With a single Directive to co-ordinate such measures one may conclude that the public policy, public security and public health provisos in Article 56(1) (and thereby Article 66) will be interpreted by the Court of Justice in the same strict manner as those in Article 48(3) of the Treaty.[39] Such a conclusion is borne out by the recent ruling of the Court of Justice in *Adoui and Cornuaille* v *The Belgian State*[40] where the Court was questioned about the interpretation of the "public policy" proviso in Articles 48 and 56 of the EEC Treaty. The questions arose in proceedings brought by two French women against the Belgian State when the authorities there recommended that they be excluded from Belgium on the ground that the women's conduct was considered to be contrary to public policy. They worked as waitresses in a bar which was suspect from the point of view of morals and in which waitresses displayed themselves in the windows. Although prostitution itself was not unlawful in Belgium, certain incidental activities, such as soliciting, incitement to debauchery, exploitation of prostitution and living on immoral earnings were prohibited. The Court of Justice ruled that:

> Although Community law does not impose upon the member-States a uniform scale of values as regards the assessment of conduct which may be considered as contrary to public policy, it should nevertheless be stated that conduct may not be considered as being of a sufficiently serious nature to justify restrictions on the admission to or residence within the territory of a member-State of a national of another member-State in a case where the former member-State does not adopt, with respect to the same conduct on the part of its own nationals, repressive measures or other genuine and effective measures intended to combat such conduct.[41]

[39] Directive 64/221 (OJ Special ed (1963-64) 117. See Ch 11 *ante*.

[40] *Op cit, supra,* n 5. [1982] ECR 1665; [1982] 3 CMLR 631.

[41] [1982] 3 CMLR 631, 662.

In the light of this decision in 1982 it would seem that the Court has narrowed the margin of appreciation allowed to member states since *Van Duyn* in 1974 (see p 119 *ante*).

It seems clear, that a member state may not, by virtue of the "public policy" proviso in Articles 48, 56 and 66 of the EEC Treaty expel, or refuse entry to, a national of another EEC country, whether an employed or self-employed person, because of conduct which, if attributable to that country's own nationals, does not incur harsh penalties. For further details of the Court's narrow interpretation of the public policy, public security and public health provisos one should refer again to Chapter 11 *ante* on the Freedom of Movement of Workers.

In addition to these restrictions on the free movement of self-employed persons, there is yet another very important exception. Article 55 of the EEC Treaty states that the provisions on the right of establishment do not apply so far as any given member state is concerned *"to activities* which in that State *are connected, even occasionally, with the exercise of official authority."* Again Article 66 of the Treaty extends this same exception to those providing services within the European Community. In other words, the *activities* of certain professions may be so closely connected to official state authority that the member state would only permit its own nationals to enter such professions. In the *Reyners* case the Court of Justice expressed the view that under Article 55:

> . . . the exclusion of [non-]nationals is limited to *those activities* which, taken on their own, constitute a *direct and specific connection with the exercise of official authority.*
>
> An extension of the exception . . . to a whole profession would be possible only in cases where such activities were linked with the profession in such a way that freedom of establishment would result in imposing on the Member State concerned the obligation to allow the exercise, even occasionally, by non-nationals of functions appertaining to official authority. The extension is . . . not possible when within the framework of an independent profession, the activities connected with the exercise of official authority are separable from the professional activity in question taken as a whole.[42]

In this particular case it had been argued that the profession of "advocat" in Belgium came within the Article 55 exception of "official authority" and could therefore be properly restricted to Belgian nationals. The Court rejected this argument, declaring that the activities of an "advocat", such as representation and defence of parties in court, did not constitute such "a direct and specific connection to official authority" to justify the exclusion of the whole profession.

By analogy, in the United Kingdom the whole legal profession could not be excluded from the EEC's provisions on the right of establishment and reserved for British nationals just because certain activities of some of its

[42] [1974] ECR 631, 654. Emphasis supplied.

lawyers may be connected with the exercise of official authority as is the case when they perform judicial functions in industrial tribunals. These particular activities could it seems be severed from the legal profession as a whole and be restricted to United Kingdom nationals alone.[43] The Court of Justice is obviously consistent when construing any of the permitted limitations to those freedoms regarded as "fundamental" to the attainment of the Common Market; whether they be in relation to the free movement of goods, workers or self-employed people they must be construed narrowly in order to ensure, as far as possible, real freedom of movement within the European Community.

COMPANIES

The right of establishment and the freedom to provide services in different member states of the European Community extend to companies and firms as well as to natural self-employed persons. As explained earlier, Article 52 of the EEC Treaty declares that the right of establishment:

> . . . shall include the right to take up and pursue activities as self-employed persons and to set up and manage undertakings, in particular companies or firms within the meaning of . . . Art 58, under the conditions laid down for its own nationals by the law of the country where such establishment is effected.

The businesses that can benefit from the Treaty provisions are defined in Article 58 thereof as those:

> Companies or firms formed in accordance with the law of a Member State *and* having their registered office, central administration or principal place of business within the Community . . . . 'Companies or firms' means companies or firms constituted under civil or commercial law, including cooperative societies, and other legal persons governed by public or private law, save for those which are non-profit making.

Judging by this definition, one can see that the list of intended beneficiaries of these EEC provisions is very wide indeed with the exception of non-profit making bodies such as charities and religious and political organisations.

As Article 66 of the EEC Treaty extends the provisions on the right of establishment in Articles 52 to 58 of the Treaty to the matters covered by the chapter on the freedom to provide services, it is intended that companies and firms should be able either to establish themselves permanently in a member state that is not their own or at least be able to provide their services on a temporary basis in another member state. Nevertheless, the differences between the company law provisions of the various EEC member states create substantial obstacles for companies established in one member state, wanting to set up branches or subsidiaries in another member state. The harmonisation of European company laws is therefore of paramount

[43] Wyatt & Dashwood, *The Substantive Law of the EEC* (1980) 190-192; Plender, *A Practical Introduction to European Community Laws* 79-80.

importance in order to make these fundamental freedoms practical realities for companies within the European Community. In this respect the 1968 Convention on the Mutual Recognition of Companies and Legal Persons tried to overcome the obstacles caused by the different national rules on the recognition of foreign companies. For instance some EEC countries, like the United Kingdom, observe the "law of incorporation" rule in that a company will be recognised if it is formed in accordance with the law of the country of incorporation. Other countries prefer the "law of the real seat" whereby a company would be recognised if it was formed in compliance with the law of the place of its central management.[44]

As well as this Convention, a whole series of Council Directives has been adopted in order to comply with Article 54(3) (g) of the EEC Treaty, which requires the Council of Ministers to co-ordinate:

> . . . to the necessary extent the safeguards which, for the protection of the interests of members and others, are required by Member States of companies or firms within the meaning of . . . Art 58 with a view to making such safeguards equivalent throughout the Community.

Of the Council Directives issued so far—and one should anticipate more in respect of companies—the First Directive[45] deals with public disclosure of such matters as the company's memorandum and articles of association, and the validity of acts carried out by persons acting *ultra vires* the company. In the United Kingdom this latter provision is reflected in section 9 (1) of the European Communities Act 1972.

The Second Directive [46] concerns the formation of public companies, and the allotment and maintenance of their share capital. This Directive was implemented in Great Britain by the Companies Act 1980 and in Northern Ireland by the Companies (NI) Order 1981, some of the provisions of which cover private companies also. The Third Directive[47] is concerned with the merger of public companies while the Fourth Directive[48] on company law has serious implications for accountants as it deals with the format and disclosure of company accounts. It has been implemented in Great Britain by the 1981 Companies Act and in Northern Ireland by the Companies (NI) Order 1982. The Sixth Directive on company law deals with the process of scission whereby an existing company divides into smaller entities.[49]

[44] See Wyatt & Dashwood, pp 195-199. See also European File, "Company Law in the European Community" 4/85.

[45] Directive 68/151 (JO 1968 L 65/8).

[46] Directive 77/91 (OJ 1977 L 26/1).

[47] Directive 78/855 (OJ 1978 L 295/36).

[48] Directive 78/660 (OJ 1978 L 222/11).

[49] Directive 82/891 (OJ 1982 L 378/47).

The Seventh Directive concerns group financial statements.[50] It harmonises accounting practices for groups of companies and is complementary to the Fourth Directive on the annual accounts of companies.

The recent Eighth Directive of 1984 defines the qualifications required by Community law of persons who audit accounts.[51] Consequently the Fourth, Seventh and Eighth Directives have far-reaching implications for the local accountancy profession.

The Fifth Directive, dealing with company structures, is still under negotiation.[52]

[50] Directive 83/349 (OJ 1983 L 193/1). See Cooke, "The Seventh Directive—An Accountant's Perspective" (1984) 9 *EL Rev* 143.

[51] Directive 84/253 (OJ 1984 L 126/20).

[52] See Welch, "The Fifth Directive—A False Dawn?" (1983) 8 *EL Rev* 83.

CHAPTER 13

SOCIAL SECURITY FOR PERSONS MOVING WITHIN THE EUROPEAN COMMUNITY

The founding fathers of the EEC realised that a worker would be greatly discouraged from leaving his own member state and moving to another to take up employment there if it meant that his social security entitlement in his home country terminated as soon as he ceased to reside there and if simultaneously he was disqualified, on such grounds as foreign nationality or insufficient contributions, from receipt of social security benefits in another member state. Similarly a worker's family would not be keen to accompany him to another member state if they too were to lose their entitlement to benefits because of their foreign residence or nationality. Consequently Article 51 was included in the EEC Treaty, requiring the Council of Ministers "to adopt such measures in the field of social security as are necessary to provide freedom of movement for workers". It is worth noting that the drafters of the Treaty did not widen the scope of Article 51 to cover the social security entitlement of self-employed persons. This omission has been subsequently remedied, initially by the jurisprudence of the Court of Justice and more recently by secondary Community legislation in the form of Council Regulations. The following examination of Article 51 and its implementing Regulations should, therefore, be seen as complementary to the provisions on the free movement of persons within the European Community, discussed in the previous two chapters. With the increase in unemployment throughout the United Kingdom and Ireland, both North and South, it is clearly important to be aware of the social security implications of a person's migration between member states of the EEC.[1]

PROBLEMS INVOLVING THE EEC PROVISIONS ON SOCIAL SECURITY

The EEC rules on social security entitlement may be relevant in a variety of situations as the following examples illustrate:

— an Irish national, while seeking work in Northern Ireland, finds that he/she is disqualified from United Kingdom supplementary benefit because of the five-year residence requirement applicable only in Northern Ireland;

[1] See generally Watson, *Social Security Law of the European Communities* (1980). This book is helpful as regards the position of migrant workers but requires updating to cover self-employed persons.

— in deciding whether an Irish national, who had been living in England and entitled to sickness benefit there, was disqualified from that benefit while imprisoned in the Republic of Ireland;[2]
— in authorising the continued payment of unemployment benefit for up to three months while a person looks for a job in another EEC country;[3]
— in providing for free or reduced cost medical care for British nationals while on holiday or on short business trips in another EEC country.[4]

THE MAIN EEC PROVISIONS ON SOCIAL SECURITY

As mentioned above, Article 51 is the basic provision in the EEC Treaty dealing with social security. It requires the Council of Ministers to adopt the measures *necessary* to support the free movement of workers by making arrangements to secure for migrant workers and their dependants:

(a) aggregation (that is totalisation), for the purpose of qualifying for and calculating the amount of benefit, of all periods taken into account by the social security legislation of the member states; and
(b) payment of benefits to those persons whilst resident in any EEC country.

This Article was in fact implemented very quickly by the Council of Ministers in 1958 by the making of Regulations 3 and 4. As these were amongst the earliest EEC Regulations made by the Council, they reflect to some degree the realisation that EEC social security provisions were an essential incentive if workers were to be encouraged to migrate from the less prosperous areas of the Community to those areas where labour was then scarce. However, the frequency with which the Court of Justice was subsequently called upon to give preliminary rulings upon the interpretation of these Regulations showed that their drafting had created many difficulties. Consequently, these two 1958 Regulations were replaced by Council Regulation 1408/71[5], setting out the substantive rules for the provision of social security benefits for migrant Community workers and their families, and by Council Regulation 574/72[6], detailing the

[2] *Kenny* v *Insurance officer* [1978] ECR 1489; [1978] 3 CMLR 651. See also the subsequent decision of the High Court in *R* v *National Insurance Commissioner, ex parte Warry, The Times,* 26 July 1980.

[3] See Council Regulation 1408/71 EEC, Arts 67-69.

[4] DHSS Leaflet SA 30/1982 is obtainable free from local Social Security offices and gives details of what is available. The essential form to take when going to another EEC country is Form E 111.

[5] (OJ Special ed, 1971 (11) p 416).

[6] (OJ Special ed, 1972 (I) p 160).

administrative procedures necessary to give effect to these rules. Both Regulations have been in effect since October 1972.

At present Article 51 of the EEC Treaty together with Regulations 1408/71 and 574/72 are the main provisions of European Community law regarding social security benefits for migrant workers, who are nationals of an EEC country, and their families moving within the EEC.[7] In 1981 these Regulations were amended by extending their provisions to cover self-employed persons and their families moving within the European Community. As EEC Regulations they are directly applicable and binding in their entirety in all the member states. In accordance with section 2(1) of the European Communities Act 1972, these EEC Regulations are part and parcel of the domestic law of the United Kingdom, forming a significant element of our social security system and have to be applied by the Department of Health and Social Services and other relevant authorities. From the outset it is important to appreciate that these EEC social security provisions do not attempt to impose a uniform social security system for the whole of the European Community. Rather, they aim to co-ordinate the national social security systems of the individual member states in order to preserve for the migrant EEC citizen rights to benefits, which he has earned or paid for before migrating, and to allow him to carry them over into the member state of immigration.[8] The Regulations are thus designed to ensure that the person maintains a continuous record of social security entitlement when he moves between member states of the EEC.

One can distinguish certain general principles that provide guidance as to the operation of the EEC provisions in this area. These general principles are briefly as follows:

(i) a person is not to be disqualified from entitlement to benefits on the grounds of his nationality, or change of residence when he moves to another EEC country;

(ii) a person may in fact become entitled to benefits in one member state by aggregating relevant insurance contributions or periods of employment made or completed in other member states; and

(iii) a person should not be placed in a more advantageous position by moving within the EEC than if he had stayed at home. There are provisions in the EEC Regulations dealing with the possibility of overlapping benefits.[9]

[7] For detailed analysis see Watson, *Social Security Law of the European Communities*(1980); Wyatt & Dashwood, *The Substantive Law of the EEC*(1980), Ch 14 and Ogus and Barendt, *The Law of Social Security*, (2nd ed, 1982), Ch 16.

[8] Watson, *Social Security Law of the European Communities*, Chs 3 and 4 provide a very useful analysis of the position as regards social security benefits for migrant workers.

[9] See Wyatt & Dashwood, *The Substantive Law of the EEC* (1980), 179-181.

Subject to the EEC rules about non-discrimination and aggregation for entitlement to benefits, member states may still lay down their own conditions for entitlement. For example, the Court of Justice ruled in *Kenny* v *Insurance Officer*[10] that the United Kingdom authorities were entitled, though not obliged, to take into account factors such as lawful detention or imprisonment in another EEC country, Ireland, which, if they had occurred within the United Kingdom, would have meant disqualification from cash sickness benefit. In this case an Irish citizen working in England claimed sickness benefit, upon his return there, for a period of sickness which had occurred whilst in Ireland. He sought, unsuccessfully, to rely upon the EEC Regulations to overcome the disqualification from cash sickness benefit imposed by the Social Security Act 1975 in respect of periods of illness suffered whilst in "lawful detention or imprisonment".

The generality of these guidelines must not disguise the fact that the EEC social security Regulations are complicated, not least by the fact that the generality of their wording leaves many questions unanswered. Consequently the application of these complex social security Regulations by national courts and tribunals has resulted in numerous Article 177 references being made by them to the Court of Justice for guidance on the interpretation of the provisions.[11] One such reference in 1976 by the United Kingdom National Insurance Commissioner in *Brack* v *Insurance Officer*[12] will serve as a useful illustration of the implications of the EEC social security Regulations within our domestic system. Brack, a British citizen and resident in the United Kingdom, had been insured under the British insurance scheme since 1948, paying contributions as a salaried employee for the first nine years only and thereafter as a self-employed accountant. In September 1974, on medical advice, he went on a holiday to France. He fell seriously ill there and had to receive immediate medical treatment. In October 1974 he returned to England and claimed cash sickness benefit for the period spent in France. He would have been entitled to full benefit if his contributions as a self-employed person and as an employed person were counted together.

However, payment was refused by the Insurance Officer because section 49(1) of the then National Insurance Act 1965 (replaced by section 85(5), Social Security Act 1975) provided that a person was disqualified from benefit for any period of absence from Great Britain. Moreover, the Insurance Officer was of the opinion that Brack could not avail himself of EEC Regulation 1408/71 to overcome this disqualification as the Regulation then only concerned "workers", rather than self-employed persons and Brack had been self-employed for the past seventeen years of his life. Article

[10] *Op cit, supra,* n 2.

[11] For a very useful summary of the ECJ's decisions and of Regulation 1408/71, see the *Compendium of Community provisions on Social Security* (1981) published by E. Commission.

[12] [1976] ECR 1429; [1976] 2 CMLR 592.

2 of Regulation 1408/71 provided that it applied to "... workers who are or have been subject to the legislation of one or more Member States and who are nationals of one of the Member States ... and also to the members of their families and their survivors". On appeal to the National Insurance Commissioner, an Article 177 reference was made to the Court of Justice for a preliminary ruling on the definition of "worker" within the meaning of Regulation 1408/71. The Court ruled that Regulation 1408/71 applied to persons:

> ... who are not 'employed persons' within the meaning of the law of employment but who must be treated as such for the purposes of applying Regulation 1408/71, taking account on the one hand of the objectives and of the spirit of this Regulation and of Articles 48 to 51 of the [EEC] Treaty which form its basis and, on the other hand, of *the special features of the administration or financing of the scheme to which such persons are affiliated* and of the changes which have taken place in the nature of such affiliation.[13]

In other words, the Court was stressing that the term "worker" has a special Community meaning, which is not confined to the national concept of a "worker" as defined by employment law, nor is it limited to the notion that the movement between member states must be for the purposes of employment. Brack was, after all, on holiday in France, on "a frolic of his own" to use the terminology of labour lawyers. Instead of relying upon these strict national rules about the identification of a "worker", the Court of Justice preferred to give the term a much wider interpretation in order to fulfil the aims and spirit of Articles 48 to 51 of EEC Treaty, namely, to make the movement of people within the Community as free as possible. In *Brack* the Court chose, as it had done in earlier cases[14], to identify a claimant as a "worker" by considering whether the national social security system was "administered or financed" in such a way that the person was covered by it. Applying this criterion in the *Brack* case, the Court concluded that since, under the British social security scheme, the whole working population, whether self-employed or employed, had to pay contributions to the same overall scheme, then all such employed persons could be identified as "workers" within the meaning of EEC Regulation 1408/71. Thus Brack could rely upon Regulation 1408/71, and in particular upon Article 22(1) thereof, which entitles a worker, who satisfies the conditions of the legislation of the competent state (in this case the United Kingdom) for entitlement to sickness benefits, and whose condition necessitates immediate benefits during a stay in the territory of another member state, to receive benefits. Consequently Brack's absence from the United Kingdom could not be used to disqualify him from cash sickness benefit. Moreover he was entitled to benefit at the full-rate as his contributions as a self-employed person could be counted together with those made as an employed person.

[13] [1976] ECR 1429, 1442; [1976] 2 CMLR 592, 617. Emphasis and words in brackets supplied.

[14] This is in line with previous ECJ rulings in *Hessische Knappschaft* v *Maison Singer* [1966] CMLR 82 and *Hoekstra* (nee *Unger)* v *Bestuur* [1964] ECR 177.

This particular case in 1976 highlighted the precarious position of self-employed persons moving from one EEC country to another. Although Regulation 1408/71 was designed to cover migrant "workers" and their families moving within the Community, the Court of Justice only construed the term "workers" to include self-employed persons *provided* they were insured under the same general social security scheme as applied to employees. As Watson explains in *Social Security Law of the European Communities:*

> In the case of a Member State, like the United Kingdom, which has a social security system which covers the entire population, Regulation 1408/71 has a potentially far greater scope than in countries like France and Belgium where the employed and self-employed are insured under different insurance schemes.[15]

To remedy this particularly unfair situation, the Council of Ministers subsequently made Regulation 1390/81[16], extending Regulation 1408/71 specifically to include self-employed persons, who are nationals of an EEC country, and their families moving within the European Community. In addition, Council Regulation 574/72, containing the detailed administrative procedures for co-ordinating these benefits, was amended by Council Regulation 3795/81[17] to cover migrant self-employed persons and their families as well as migrant workers. Again it must be remembered that Regulations 1390/81 and 3795/81 are directly applicable in the United Kingdom as in all member states. Since July 1982, when Regulation 1390/81 came into force, the persons covered by the EEC social security provisions include employed persons and self-employed persons, who are nationals of a member state, and members of their families irrespective of their nationality, moving within the Community.

PROBLEMS CONCERNING EEC SOCIAL SECURITY LEGISLATION

If one has to advise a foreign claimant about his/her entitlement under EEC legislation to social security benefits in Northern Ireland, then one should first check that the claimant comes within the scope of the persons covered by the Regulations as outlined above. The claimant should be a national of an EEC country and either an employed or self-employed person or else a member of the family of such a person.[18] If the claimant is a person covered by the EEC Regulations, for example an Irish national, one should next check that the benefits he seeks to claim fall within the scope of EEC Regulations. It is important to note that Regulation 1408/71 remains unchanged by Regulation 1390/81 in respect of the benefits it covers. By

[15] Watson, *Social Security Law of the European Communities* (1980), 71.

[16] (OJ 1981 L 143/1).

[17] (OJ 1981 L 378/1).

[18] "Member of the family" is defined by Art 1(f) of Regulation 1408/71 as amended by Council Regulation 1390/81, Art 2(c).

Article 4(1), Regulation 1408/71 applies to all national legislation of the member states concerning the following branches of *social security:*

— sickness and maternity benefits;
— invalidity benefits, including those for the maintenance or improvement of earning capacity;
— old-age benefits;
— survivors' benefits;
— benefits in respect of accidents at work and occupational diseases;
— death grants;
— unemployment benefits;
— family benefits.

As one commentator has remarked, Regulation 1408/71 covers a life blighted with misfortune from the cradle to the grave. Regulation 1408/71 applies to all general and special social security schemes, whether contributory or non-contributory.[19] For specific guidance on how this EEC Regulation affects the availability of each of these benefits to nationals of other EEC countries coming to Northern Ireland and also people from Northern Ireland going to another EEC country, it is advisable to contact the Overseas Branch of the DHSS in Belfast.[20]

For present purposes, it is sufficient to make some general comments about the operation of Regulation 1408/71 in relation to the benefits covered by it. First, Regulation 1408/71 only co-ordinates the national legislation of the member states in relation to the eight particular types of "social security" benefits listed in Article 4(1) thereof; this list is an exhaustive one.[21] "Social and medical assistance" are specifically excluded by Article 4(4) from the scope of Regulation 1408/71. Herein lies considerable controversy for the Regulation itself contains no definition of what amounts to "social security" as opposed to "social assistance". Traditionally, "social security" benefits were ones paid for by insurance contributions and awarded as of right, whereas "social assistance" was a discretionary payment made gratuitously by the state to its most needy citizens. Today, however, this distinction has become blurred. In the United Kingdom for example, supplementary benefit, although not earned through insurance contributions, is awarded as of right to any person whose needs exceed his/her resources and whose capital does not exceed £3,000.[22] On this basis are

[19] See Art 4(2), Council Regulations 1408/71.

[20] Department of Health & Social Services, Overseas Branch, Castle Grounds, Stormont, Belfast, BT4 3SN. See also Wyatt & Dashwood, *The Substantive Law of the EEC* (1980), 162-181 and two separate articles by Knorpel in (1981) 18 *CML Rev* 133-154 and (1982) 19 *CML Rev* 105-152.

[21] *Hoeckx* v *Openbarr Centrum voor Maatschappelijk,* (ECJ) *The Times,* 11 April 1985.

[22] Supplementary Benefit (Resources) Regulations (Northern Ireland) 1984.

supplementary benefits to be classified as "social assistance" and therefore outside the scope of Regulation 1408/71 or are they "social security" and within its scope? The answer could be very important, especially within Northern Ireland because a person claiming supplementary benefit here is not entitled to it if he has not been resident within the United Kingdom for a period of five years immediately preceding the date on which he claims benefit. Therefore if an Irish citizen came to Northern Ireland tomorrow, he would be disqualified from receiving supplementary benefit here on the grounds of an insufficiently long period of residence whereas, if he went to England instead and claimed there, he would be entitled to the benefit as there is no equivalent residence requirement for receipt of supplementary benefit in Great Britain. Since the aim of the EEC social security provisions is to overcome such residence requirements for persons moving within the Community, it would clearly be advantageous to that Irish citizen if United Kingdom supplementary benefits were classified as "social security" and thus covered by Regulation 1408/71. On several occasions the Court of Justice has been asked to rule on whether a particular welfare benefit falls within the "social security" category or the "social assistance" one.[23] So far the Court has not offered a clear-cut definition of these two categories of benefit. Instead the Court regards as "social security" benefits those which "confer a legally defined status on beneficiaries not involving any individual and discretionary assessment of needs or personal circumstances".[24] Moreover, if the benefit income is claimed in addition to other social security benefits, then to classify the former, the Court looks at, for example, the extent to which it is reduced by the receipt of the other benefits.

Although the official British Government view is that United Kingdom supplementary benefits and family income supplement constitute "social assistance" and are therefore beyond the scope of Regulation 1408/71[25], this is not conclusive of the issue as the Court of Justice may, if required to give a ruling on the point in an Article 177 reference, declare otherwise. Just as the Court of Justice gives the term "worker" a special Community meaning, likewise the Court may give a special Community meaning to "social security" benefits.

Even if supplementary benefit is classified as "social assistance" and outside the EEC social security Regulations, a migrant worker coming to Northern Ireland may possibly be able to rely upon Article 7(2) of Council Regulation 1612/68 on the freedom of movement of workers within the

[23] See *eg Callemeyn* v *Belgian State* [1974] ECR 553; *Frilli* v *The Belgian State* [1972] ECR 457; *Biason* [1975] 1 CMLR 59.

[24] *Paola Piscitello* v *Istituto Nazionalle della Previdenza,* [1984] 1 CMLR 108.

[25] Art 5 of Regulation 1408/71 requires member states to specify the social security legislation covered by the Regulation. See Council Information (OJ 1973 C 43/1) for the legislation specified by the United Kingdom Government.

Community, considered in Chapter 11 *ante.* By virtue of Article 7(2) of Regulation 1612/68 a migrant worker is entitled to "the *same social* and tax *advantages as national workers*". In 1976 in the *Inzirillo* case the Court of Justice ruled that:

> ... the matters covered by Article 7(2) must be defined in such a way as to include every social and tax advantage whether or not linked to a contract of employment.[26]

In this particular case the son of a migrant worker could therefore receive an allowance for a handicapped person, which was awarded as of right to nationals of the host country.

However, the recent decision by the Court of Justice in the *Hoeckx*[27] case, decided in April 1985, throws some light on the problem of classification of benefits. Here a Dutch national was refused a minimum subsistence allowance by the Belgian authorities because she failed to satisfy a five-year residence requirement imposed on foreign claimants. The Court ruled that the list of social security benefits in Article 4 of Regulation 1408/71 was exhaustive and did not include a benefit like this particular Belgian one. However, the Court went on to rule that an allowance, which guaranteed a minimum means of subsistence, constituted a "social advantage" within the meaning of Article 7(2) of Regulation 1612/68 and could not be denied to a migrant worker from another EEC country because of insufficient residence.

On this basis it is arguable that social assistance benefits, like supplementary benefit, should be available to migrant Community workers in Northern Ireland under Article 7(2) of Regulation 1612/68.

Another important feature to note about the operation of the EEC social security Regulation 1408/71 is that many benefits within its scope are calculated on the basis of aggregation of periods of insurance or employment in various EEC countries. If faced with a particular problem about a certain benefit, one should check the Regulation for the specific provisions relating to each type of benefit and also consider any relevant cases decided by the Court of Justice.[28] For present purposes, unemployment benefits may be used to illustrate this principle of aggregation.[29] Articles 67 to 71 of Regulation 1408/71, as amended by Regulation 1390/81 to include self-employed people, govern the rights of migrant EEC nationals to claim unemployment benefit on the basis of aggregated insurance or employment periods in different member states. A member state, like the United Kingdom, whose legislation makes the right to unemployment benefit subject to *the completion of insurance periods,* is required by Article 67(1):

[26] *Inzirillo* v *Caisse d'Allocations Familiales de l'Arrondissement de Lyon* [1976] ECR 2057, 2068.

[27] *Hoeckx* v *Openbaar Centrum voor Maatschappelijk,* (ECJ) *The Times,* 11 April 1985. See Watson, *Social Security Law of the European Communities,* 100 *et seq;* Wyatt and Dashwood, *The Substantive Law of the EEC,* 162 *et seq.*

[28] Consult the subject-index of Hunnings, *Gazetteer of European Law,* Vols 1 and 2, (1983).

[29] See Watson, *Social Security Law of the European Communities,* Ch 14.

> . . . [to] take into account, to the extent necessary, periods of insurance or employment completed under the legislation of any other Member State, as though they were periods completed as an employed person under the legislation which it administers, *provided,* however, that the periods of employment would have been counted as insurance periods had they been completed under that legislation.

If, on the other hand, a member state's legislation makes the right to unemployment benefit subject to the *completion of periods of employment,* then under Article 67(2) it must, to the extent necessary, take account of periods of insurance or employment completed as an employed person under the legislation of any other member state as if they were periods of employment completed under the law that it administers. As Watson explains:

> Apart from complying with these rules relating to the type of periods of employment and insurance periods which may be aggregated the claimant must actually be subject to the law of the country in which he makes his claim for unemployment benefit at the time when he makes his claim in accordance with [Article 67(3) of Regulation 1408/71]. Thus in the case of a man who claims unemployment benefit in the United Kingdom, he must prior to his claim have paid or been credited with insurance contributions under United Kingdom law.[30]

Where, on the other hand, a person is wholly unemployed *and* is entitled to unemployment benefit under the law of one member state, for instance the United Kingdom, and goes to another EEC country to seek work there, Article 69 of Regulation 1408/71 ensures that he retains his entitlement to unemployment benefit for a maximum of three months provided that:

(1) before his departure, he registers with the employment services (the DHSS in the United Kingdom) as a person seeking work and is available for work for at least four weeks before leaving this country; and

(2) that within seven days of leaving (in this case the United Kingdom) for another EEC country, he registers as a person seeking work in that country.[31] These particular provisions support the view that a national of any EEC country is entitled under Community law to go to look for work in another member state for up to three months and that the advantages of the EEC provisions on the free movement of people are not confined to those who actually have offers of employment in another member state as a strict interpretation of Article 48(3) of the Treaty might suggest. It is important to note that if a person returns to the United Kingdom before the end of the three months, his entitlement to unemployment benefit continues in this country. As a general rule he will lose all such entitlement if he fails to return to the United Kingdom before the expiry of that time. In exceptional circumstances, however, this time limit may be extended.[32]

[30] *Ibid,* p 231.

[31] Art 69(1), Council Regulation 1408/71 as amended by Council Regulation 1390/81.

[32] *Ibid,* Art 69(2).

The Regulations contain additional rules about the calculation and payment of benefits. Persons leaving the United Kingdom to seek jobs in other Common Market countries are advised to collect form E303 explaining these EEC Regulations. It should be remembered that these EEC social security Regulations are indeed complex and have given rise to much case-law before the Court of Justice. The Northern Ireland Department of Health and Social Services has produced reference leaflets on "Social Security for Migrant Persons within the EEC" and these provide useful guidance.[33]

[33] See also Wyatt and Dashwood, *The Substantive Law of the EEC* (1980), 170 *et seq.*

CHAPTER 14

THE INFLUENCE OF EUROPEAN COMMUNITY LAW UPON THE UNITED KINGDOM'S CRIMINAL PROCESS

The impact of European Community law upon the United Kingdom's domestic criminal process is often overlooked, presumably because Community law is expected to operate exclusively in the economic sphere, leaving criminal matters untouched. Community law does, however, move in subtle ways encroaching gradually here and there upon the United Kingdom's criminal process. The fact that these encroachments are not of the sensational kind—European Community law does not, and will not, affect major criminal offences such as murder or manslaughter—further explains why its impact in the field of criminal law passes virtually without comment.[1] Nevertheless, this unsensational, but creeping, influence of Community law upon the criminal law merits examination here.

Community law has already been involved in several criminal proceedings before United Kingdom courts and the following illustrations are but a random selection of these:

- prosecutions brought against vehicle users, who have failed to install a tachograph in the vehicle as required by EEC Regulations and, since January 1980, by the implementing Northern Ireland regulations;[2]
- the recommended deportation from the United Kingdom of a French national for the illegal possession of controlled drugs was mitigated to a small fine after reliance upon EEC provisions governing the free movement of migrant Community workers;[3]
- the complete dismissal of the prosecution of a man charged with illegally transporting bacon pigs within Northern Ireland without the proper documentation as required by Northern Ireland legislation;[4]

[1] See the excellent article on this topic by Hartley, "The Impact of European Community Law on the Criminal Process" (1981) *Crim L Rev* 75. With Professor Hartley's permission, the writer has adopted the threefold division employed by him in this article.

[2] The Passenger and Goods Vehicles (Recording Equipment) Regulations (NI) 1979, implementing Council Regulations 1463/70 EEC (OJ 1970 L 164/1).

[3] *R* v *Bouchereau* [1977] ECR 1999; [1977] 2 CMLR 800.

[4] *Pigs Marketing Board (NI)* v *Redmond* [1978] ECR 2347; [1979] 1 CMLR 177.

— the dismissal of an appeal against the conviction of two men for smuggling citizen band radios into Northern Ireland from the Republic of Ireland, even though a ban on the import of such goods from another member state was *prima facie* contrary to the EEC rules on the free movement of goods.[5]

These cases indicate that Community law does affect the United Kingdom criminal process and may do so in one of three ways. Community law may (i) provide a complete defence to a criminal charge; or (ii) mitigate the sentence that would otherwise be imposed; or (iii) create a completely new criminal offence. It is appropriate to examine each of these more closely.

1 EEC LAW AS A COMPLETE DEFENCE TO A CRIMINAL CHARGE

The supremacy of European Community law over any conflicting domestic legislation of the United Kingdom, or of any other member state, is crucial to a proper understanding of the influence of Community law in this area. Of similar importance is the fact that certain provisions of Community law have direct effect. This means that they give rise to immediate rights which individuals may rely upon in proceedings before national courts and tribunals of the member states. Consequently, if United Kingdom legislation criminalises certain action but European Community law endorses the same action and is directly effective, the latter legislation will prevail, giving the defendant an instant defence. These points are well-illustrated by the local case of *Pigs Marketing Board (Northern Ireland)* v *Redmond*[6] which arose in 1977. The defendant was charged with transporting bacon pigs within Northern Ireland without the proper transportation documents issued by the Pigs Marketing Board pursuant to the Movement of Pigs Regulations (Northern Ireland) 1972. For this offence the defendant was liable to a £200 fine and/or three months imprisonment and/or forfeiture of the pigs involved. On an Article 177 reference from the Resident Magistrate in Armagh, the European Court of Justice ruled that the Movement of Pigs Regulations were incompatible with Articles 30 and 34 of the EEC Treaty, prohibiting quantitative restrictions on the movement of goods between member states, and Council Regulation 2759/75, establishing the common organisation of the market in pigmeat. The Court stated that these provisions of Community law were directly applicable and directly conferred on individuals immediate rights which the courts of the member states were obliged to protect. Consequently, in applying this ruling to the facts of the case, the Resident Magistrate dismissed the summons against the defendant as being ill-founded. European Community law had thus provided Redmond with a complete defence to a criminal offence created by Northern Ireland legislation.

[5] *McAfee* v *Smyth and Quigley* [1981] 1 CMLR 410.

[6] *Op cit, supra*, n 4.

Similarly in the recent case, *R* v *Kent Kirk*[7], the captain of a Danish fishing vessel, who was convicted by North Shields Magistrates' Court and fined £30,000 for illegally fishing within twelve miles of the United Kingdom's coast line, was successful in challenging the legality of the relevant British legislation on the ground that it was incompatible with Community law as it was, *inter alia,* discriminatory.

In the light of such cases as these one can readily appreciate why these so-called "Euro-defences" have become increasingly popular before United Kingdom courts. One should, therefore, consider whether there is an EEC dimension, particularly when dealing with offences connected with agriculture, fishing, or the movement of goods and people between the United Kingdom and other Common Market countries. Of course pleading points of EEC law is not always successful since Community law permits certain limitations in respect of the free movement of goods, people and so on and may tolerate criminal sanctions imposed by the member states in these areas. For example, Article 36 of the EEC Treaty does allow member states to impose complete bans or other quantitative restrictions on imports and exports from other member states on grounds, *inter alia,* of the protection of the life and health of humans and animals or public morality, public policy or public security. Thus, for instance, the defendants in *McAfee* v *Smyth and Quigley*[8] were unsuccessful in their appeal in October 1980 to the Belfast Recorder's Court against their convictions and fines for smuggling some citizen band radios of a certain prohibited frequency into Northern Ireland from the Republic of Ireland, thereby evading the ban on the import of such radios into the United Kingdom, imposed by the Wireless Telegraphy Act 1967.[9] The judge held that even though the United Kingdom legislation, prohibiting the import of such citizen band radios, did amount to a quantitative restriction on imports within the meaning of Article 30 of the EEC Treaty, it was nevertheless justified under Article 36 of the Treaty on the grounds of public policy and public security. There was sufficient evidence to show that citizen band radios of this particular frequency had been used by terrorists to detonate bombs in Northern Ireland during the last ten years and interfered with communications of the security and hospital services.

The onus is upon the Crown to justify, within the terms of Article 36 of the Treaty, any restrictions by the United Kingdom on the import and export of goods from other member states.[10] Thus, for example, criminal legislation controlling the importation into the United Kingdom of pornographic

[7] [1984] 3 CMLR 522.

[8] *Op cit, supra,* n 5. See also *Criminal Proceedings against Casati* [1981] ECR 2595; [1982] 1 CMLR 365.

[9] S 7 of the Wireless Telegraphy Act 1967 and the Radio-telephonic Transmittors (Control of Manufacture and Importation) Order 1968.

[10] See the speech by Lord Diplock in *R* v *Goldstein* (H L) [1983] 1 All E R 434; [1983] 1 WLR 151; [1983] 1 CMLR 244.

materials[11], certain citizen band radios and kruggerrands as well as the exportation of silver coins[12] has been justified by the Crown as coming within the exceptions permitted by Article 36 of the EEC Treaty. Similarly, Article 48(3) of the EEC Treaty allows the United Kingdom and other member states to limit the movement and residence of migrant Community workers and their families on grounds of public policy, public security and public health. Likewise Articles 56 and 66 of the Treaty permit member states to impose restrictions on self-employed persons and their families on the same grounds. The scope of those important limitations has been considered in Chapters 11 and 12 *ante*. Their impact on the criminal process will be examined below.

2 EEC LAW AS A MITIGATING FACTOR IN SENTENCING

There have been other cases before United Kingdom courts where Community law, though not providing a complete defence to a criminal charge, has been invoked in order to mitigate the sentence that would otherwise have been imposed. In *R* v *Bouchereau*[13], for instance, the defendant, a French national, who had worked in England for some months, relied upon the EEC rules governing the free movement of workers in Article 48 of the Treaty and Council Directive 64/221 in order to avoid deportation from the United Kingdom. In January 1976 he had pleaded guilty before a magistrates' court to a charge of unlawful possession of certain controlled drugs contrary to section 5(2) of the Misuse of Drugs Act 1971 and had been given a twelve-month conditional discharge. Six months later he was again found guilty of the unlawful possession of a small quantity of controlled drugs and this time the magistrates' court was minded to make a recommendation for his deportation from the United Kingdom. Bouchereau maintained that such a recommendation would be contrary to Community law as his previous criminal conviction did not manifest a present or future intention to act in a manner contrary to public policy or public security and thus justify deportation. Article 3(2) of Council Directive 64/221 states that previous criminal convictions shall not, *per se,* constitute grounds for excluding a person on grounds of public policy or public security. On an Article 177 reference to the Court of Justice, the Court ruled that previous criminal convictions could only be taken into account if they indicated a propensity to act in the same way in the future. For national authorities to justify recourse to the concept of "public policy" to limit the free movement of workers within the EEC, the Court explained that the person's presence in the country had to constitute ". . . a genuine and sufficiently serious threat to the requirements of public policy affecting

[11] *R* v *Henn and Darby*[1979] ECR 3795; [1980] 1 CMLR 246.

[12] *R* v *Thompson, Johnson & Woodiwiss* [1978] ECR 2247; [1979] 1 CMLR 47.

[13] *Op cit, supra,* n 3.

one of the fundamental interests of society".[14] The Court regards the free movement of persons within the European Community as a fundamental freedom of the EEC and therefore any restrictions on grounds such as public policy must be strictly interpreted. When the Court's ruling was handed back to the magistrates' court, it considered that the possession of a small amount of drugs by Bouchereau did not make him a sufficiently serious threat to the requirements of public policy in the United Kingdom. Consequently they fined him £35 instead of recommending his deportation.

The fact that the Court of Justice construes "public policy" so narrowly is a point that the United Kingdom's criminal courts must bear in mind when recommending deportation of EEC nationals and their families. The courts should also ensure that they comply with the appeal procedure laid down by Article 9 of Council Directive 64/221 and should, unless security reasons prevent it, give reasons for recommending deportation.[15] A lapse of time between the recommendation to deport and its confirmation by the Home Secretary may not comply with this procedure.[16] Moreover, the penalties that may be imposed upon citizens of other member states for failure to comply with entry and residence formalities must be modified to comply with Community law. This point was emphasised by the Court of Justice recently in *R* v *Pieck*.[17] In this case Pieck, a Dutch national, had been working in Wales for some time but had neglected to obtain a "Residence Permit for an EEC National" to which he was entitled as of right under Community law. When he first entered the United Kingdom the British immigration authorities had also stamped his passport with the words "given leave to enter the UK for six months", but he had failed to renew this permission to reside in the United Kingdom. On an Article 177 reference from Pontypridd Crown Court, the Court of Justice ruled that the failure by a migrant Community worker, in this case by a Dutch national, to comply with United Kingdom immigration formalities could not be punished by deportation. Pieck's right of residence in the United Kingdom arose directly from the EEC Treaty and implementing Community legislation; it was not dependent upon a document—a Residence Permit—which simply indicated proof of his right of residence. In addition the Court ruled that:

> As regards other penalties such as fines and imprisonment, whilst the national authorities are entitled to impose penalties in respect of failure to comply with the terms of provisions relating to residence permits which are comparable to those attaching to minor offences by nationals, *they are not justified in imposing a penalty so disproportionate to the gravity of the infringement* that it becomes an

[14] [1977] ECR 1999, 2013-2014.

[15] See *Dannenberg* v *Secretary of State for Home Affairs* [1984] 2 CMLR 456.

[16] See *R* v *Secretary of State for Home Affairs, ex parte Santillo* [1980] ECR 1585. See the note by Paisley on *R* v *Bouchereau* and *R* v *Secretary of State for Home Affairs, ex parte Santillo* in (1982) 33 *NILQ* 85-91.

[17] [1980] ECR 2171; [1980] 3 CMLR 220.

> obstacle to the free movement of persons. This would be especially so if that penalty included imprisonment.[18]

Accordingly, the charges against Pieck were subsequently withdrawn by the Crown Court. This principle of proportionality, that penalties should not be more onerous or severe than strictly necessary, is one of the general principles of law adopted by the Court of Justice as a source of Community law and features regularly throughout the jurisprudence of the Court.[19]

The fact that the Court of Justice does defend so strenuously the fundamental principle of freedom of movement of workers within the EEC is a point that United Kingdom criminal courts and immigration officials should note very carefully when considering deportation of EEC nationals. With this in mind, one could in fact speculate about the compatibility of exclusion orders made under the Prevention of Terrorism (Temporary Provisions) Act 1984 and the EEC rules on the free movement of persons. What would be the outcome if, for example, an Irish citizen entered Northern Ireland to look for work and finding none, he went across to Liverpool to take up an offer of employment there but was met with an exclusion order made under the 1984 Act excluding him from entering Great Britain? He might seek to rely upon the supremacy of Community law, in particular upon the EEC provisions on the free movement of workers to try to overcome the obstacles to his freedom of movement within the United Kingdom as created by the Prevention of Terrorism Act 1984. The United Kingdom authorities would presumably rely upon the limitations on the free movement of workers provided by Article 48(3) of the EEC Treaty, especially the ground of public security, to justify the exclusion order preventing him moving freely within the United Kingdom. As he is an Irish national, the situation is not wholly internal to one member state and can thus be distinguished from the situation in *R* v *Saunders*[20] where all the factors of the case involved only one member state, the United Kingdom alone. There a British citizen and native of Northern Ireland was bound over by Bristol Crown Court to return to Northern Ireland and not re-enter Great Britain for 3 years. She had been convicted of theft of a savings bank account book. However, she later came up for judgment before the Crown Court as she had been detained in Great Britain within months of being confined to Northern Ireland. She contended that as a national of an EEC country and a worker, she was entitled to rely upon the EEC Treaty provisions guaranteeing freedom of movement for workers within the European

18 [1980] 3 CMLR 220, 242. Emphasis supplied. See also *Procureur du Roi* v *Royer* [1976] ECR 497; [1976] 2 CMLR 619 and *Adoui and Cornuaille* v *Belgian State* [1982] ECR 1665; [1982] 3 CMLR 631.

19 *Eg* in relation to fundamental human rights, *Internationale Handelsgesellschaft* v *EVST* [1970] ECR 1125; [1972] CMLR 255, and in respect of agriculture, *Bela-Mühle Josef Bergmann* v *Grows-Farm* [1977] ECR 1211; [1979] 2 CMLR 83.

20 [1979] ECR 1129; [1979] 2 CMLR 216. For details see Chapter 11 on The Freedom of Movement of Workers. Reaffirmed in *Moser* v *Land-Baden Wurttenberg* [1984] 3 CMLR 720.

Community. On an Article 177 reference, the Court of Justice ruled that since this was a *wholly* internal situation—a British national, committing a theft in Great Britain and being confined to Northern Ireland—without any factors connecting Saunders to any other member state, it fell outside the scope of the EEC rules on the free movement of workers. These EEC provisions were designed to assist workers moving between member states within the Community.

In the light of the very strict interpretation given by the Court of Justice to the "public policy" exception in Article 48(3) of the EEC Treaty, one could expect a rigorous review by the Court of the "public security" reasons offered by the United Kingdom officials in the hypothetical case considered above. As against that, one must also add that it is uncertain how much disclosure of the reasons for deportation would be required by the Court of Justice in cases involving national security since the meaning of "public security" in this context has not yet been interpreted by the Court of Justice. Obviously the full potential of how far EEC law may mitigate United Kingdom criminal sanctions that would otherwise be imposed has not yet been fully worked out. This is, therefore, an area ripe for further development.

3 EEC LAW AS A SOURCE OF NEW CRIMINAL OFFENCES

There have been occasions when Community law has obliged member states to introduce criminal sanctions in order to implement their Community obligations. Perhaps the best known example is Council Regulation 1463/70 EEC,[21] which required tachographs to be fitted in certain commercial vehicles in an effort to improve transport safety standards throughout the European Community. Article 21(1) of Regulation 1463/70 required member states to adopt:

> . . . such law, regulations or administrative provisions as may be necessary for the implementation of this Regulation. Such measures shall cover, inter alia, the reorganisation of, procedure for, and means of carrying out, checks on compliance and the *penalties* to be imposed in case of breach.

Although the United Kingdom Government, as the result of strong trade union opposition, delayed introducing the necessary measures to make the fitting of tachographs in lorries compulsory, it eventually complied with the Regulation after being brought before the Court of Justice under Article 169 of the Treaty. The United Kingdom was censured by the Court for failing to fulfil its Community obligations, as laid down in the EEC tachograph Regulation.[22] Subsequently, in Northern Ireland the Passenger and Goods Vehicles (Recording Equipment) Regulations (Northern Ireland) 1979 were introduced. These impose a penalty of £200 for failure to install a tachograph in vehicles over 3 tonnes in weight although there are specific

[21] (OJ Special ed, 1970, p 482).

[22] *Commission* v *United Kingdom (Re: Tachographs)* [1979] ECR 419; [1979] 2 CMLR 45.

exemptions. It bears repetition here that the general provisions of the EEC Regulations governing tachographs are directly applicable and by virtue of section 2(1) of the European Communities Act 1972 are part and parcel of the United Kingdom's domestic law. If there is any discrepancy between the governing EEC Regulations and the implementing Northern Ireland legislation, the former must prevail as EEC law has supremacy over all forms of conflicting domestic law. Therefore, it may well be that a defendant could successfully rely upon the EEC tachograph Regulation to avoid conviction under the Northern Ireland measures, especially as there are some exemptions permitted by the EEC Regulation over and above those contained in the implementing local regulations. In such cases the police and any legal advisers would be well advised to consult the governing EEC Regulation in the Official Journal of the European Communities.

Where, however, EEC Regulations in other areas, in particular agriculture, are silent about sanctions for non-compliance, member states may introduce criminal sanctions if appropriate. The Suckler Cow Premium Regulations 1981,[23] for instance, stipulate that a person is liable for a fine not exceeding £400 on summary conviction if he knowingly or recklessly makes a false statement to obtain a premium payable under the Council Regulations, which introduced the scheme of payment of premiums for suckler cows.[24]

Finally, in this particular context it is worth noting that under section 2(2) of the European Communities Act 1972, if a minister or government department is required to introduce legislation in order to implement Community obligations, they may do so by means of regulations or Orders in Council *unless* the matter falls within the Schedule 2 exceptions. Originally, under Schedule 2 paragraph 1(d) of the 1972 Act, where implementation of an EEC obligation would result in the creation of "any new criminal offence punishable with imprisonment for more than two years or punishable on summary conviction with imprisonment for more than three months or with a fine of more than £400 (if not calculated on a daily basis) or with a fine of more than £5 a day", a full Act of Parliament was required. This is why, for example, delegated legislation in the form of regulations could be used to comply with the obligation laid down by Article 21(1) of the EEC tachograph Regulation as the fines for non-compliance here were set at £200, below the £400 limit in Schedule 2, paragraph 1(d) of the 1972 Act. This sub-paragraph has recently been amended, increasing the level of fines to £2,000 or a fine of £100 a day respectively.[25]

[23] Art 6, SI 1981/1700. See also *Amsterdam Bulb BV* case [1977] ECR 137.

[24] See Council Regulation 1357/80 (OJ 1980 L 140/1) for premiums in the United Kingdom and Council Regulation 1056/81 EEC (OJ 1981 L 142/6) which provided an additional premium for maintaining suckler cows in Northern Ireland.

[25] Arts 4(6)(a), 8 and 17, Fines and Penalties (NI) Order 1984, SI 1984/703 (NI 3) and s32(3) Criminal Law Act 1977 respectively.

CHAPTER 15

THE EEC COMPETITION RULES: PROHIBITION OF RESTRICTIVE TRADE PRACTICES

The main aim of the EEC Treaty is to bring about a Common Market in which the formerly distinct national markets of the member states are replaced by one large free-trade area in which goods, persons, services and capital may move freely, subject only to the minimum of restrictions.[1] Having required member states to abolish customs duties and quantitative restrictions on goods traded between them, the Treaty must also ensure that individual traders and companies do not hinder this free trade by employing restrictive trade agreements and practices. Thus it is the free movement of goods provisions in the early part of the EEC Treaty which most need to be reinforced by its later rules on competition. The EEC competition rules are additional to the United Kingdom's own domestic legislation on monopolies and other restrictive practices.[2] The latter controls anti-competitive practices restricting trade within the United Kingdom, while the former are concerned only with practices which affect trade between member states of the European Community. However, an important point to bear in mind from the beginning is that the Court of Justice has given the phrase "affect trade between member states" a very wide interpretation indeed, as will be explained later. Thus it is possible for the EEC competition rules to apply even if all the parties to the particular arrangement are based in, and conduct their business within, only one member state[3] or, alternatively, if all or some of the parties are based outside the EEC but carry on business within the European Community.[4] Therefore, it may well be that a trading arrangement between a firm in Northern Ireland and another in the Republic of Ireland, or even one purely between firms established in the Province, may contravene the EEC competition rules. It would be unwise for traders here to regard Northern Ireland as so small and so far from the hub of the EEC Commission's Directorate-General IV on Competition in

[1] For examples of such restrictions see the public policy, public security and public health exceptions in Articles 36, 48(3), 56 and 66 of the EEC Treaty considered in the chapters on the Free Movement of Goods, Workers and Self-Employed Persons.

[2] See the Restrictive Trade Practices Acts 1976 and 1977 and the Competition Act 1980. See the very useful recent text by Merkin and Williams, *Competition Law: Antitrust policy in the United Kingdom and the EEC (1984)*.

[3] See *Vereeniging van Cementhandelaren* v *Commission* [1972] ECR 977; [1973] CMLR 7.

[4] See *Béguelin Import Co* v *Import-Export S A* [1971] ECR 949; [1972] CMLR 81.

Brussels that they can safely ignore the Community's rules on free competition. Since the EEC Commission may impose on parties who intentionally, or even negligently, breach these competition rules, fines of up to 10 per cent of their turnover in the previous year, the financial consequences of turning a blind eye to the rules may be very severe indeed. Consequently some basic knowledge of how and when the EEC competition rules apply is certainly of the utmost importance for business people and for legal advisers acting for firms of any size in Northern Ireland.

PROBLEMS INVOLVING THE EEC COMPETITION RULES

The EEC competition rules may apply to a wide variety of business arrangements and the situations discussed below offer but a few illustrations of arrangements where traders and their legal advisers should be particularly careful. The following transactions may infringe the EEC competition rules:

— several simultaneous price increases of the same rate for certain products by different companies operating in various EEC countries;[5]

— the refusal by a leading manufacturer of particular raw materials,[6] or of spare parts for equipment,[7] to supply one of its customers;

— the use of a network of exclusive distribution agreements throughout various EEC countries giving territorial protection to each individual distributor;[8]

— a discriminatory pricing policy for the same foods sold in different EEC countries;[9]

— the take-over by a major manufacturing company of a smaller one manufacturing the same products, thus eliminating a competitor;[10]

— the charging of excessive prices for goods or services by a major company;[11]

— the granting of loyalty rebates by a major manufacturer of vitamins to its customers on the basis of the amount of their requirements obtained from it.[12]

These examples, taken from cases decided by the Court of Justice, will be considered in more detail in this and the following chapter.

[5] See *eg ICI* v *Commission* [1972] ECR 619; [1972] CMLR 557.

[6] See *eg Istituto and Commercial Solvents* v *Commission* [1974] ECR 223; [1974] 1 CMLR 309.

[7] See *Camera Care Ltd* v *Commission* [1980] ECR 119; [1980] 1 CMLR 334.

[8] See *eg Consten and Grundig* v *Commission* [1966] ECR 299; [1966] CMLR 418.

[9] See *eg United Brands* v *Commission* [1978] ECR 207; [1978] 1 CMLR 429.

[10] See *eg Europemballage Corporation and Continental Can Co* v *Commission* [1973] ECR 215; [973] CMLR 199.

[11] See *eg General Motors Continental* v *Commission* [1975] ECR 1367; [1976] 1 CMLR 95 and also *United Brands, op cit, supra,* n 9.

[12] See *Hoffmann-La Roche* v *Commission* [1979] ECR 461; [1979] 3 CMLR 211.

THE MAIN EEC COMPETITION RULES[13]

The starting point must be Article 3 paragraph (f) of the EEC Treaty which lists amongst the activities of the Community "the institution of a system ensuring that competition in the common market is not distorted". It is important to note that the Court of Justice often refers to Article 3(f) to enlarge the scope of application of the main competition rules in the Treaty. The detailed provisions implementing this very general provision are found in Articles 85 to 94 of the EEC Treaty under the heading of "Rules on Competition". These Articles are subdivided into three sections—"Rules applying to Undertakings" (Articles 85 to 90), "Dumping" (Article 91) and "Aids Granted by States" (Articles 92 to 94). Since this Guide is primarily concerned with the activities of individual companies and traders concentration will be focused on the "Rules applying to Undertakings" rather than the specialised topics of "Dumping" and "State Aids". For details of these, reference should be made to other materials.[14]

Of the "Rules Applying to Undertakings", Articles 85 and 86 are the main provisions designed to control anti-competitive practices by undertakings, and for easy reference the full text of each Article is set out in Appendices III and IV. Article 85 governs restrictive trade practices operated by undertakings, while Article 86 governs any abuse by an undertaking of its dominant position. Before examining each of these Articles in separate chapters, one very important point must be stressed. Article 85, paragraphs (1) and (2) and Article 86 of the EEC Treaty are directly applicable provisions of Community law, having direct effects. By virtue of section 2(1) of the European Communities Act 1972, they are therefore part and parcel of the United Kingdom's domestic law, giving rise to immediate rights, which individuals may enforce before the national courts and tribunals. Thus, for example, a United Kingdom firm, seeking to challenge the validity of a particular business agreement, might rely upon Article 85 of the EEC Treaty before a local court, claiming that the agreement is void because it distorts competition within the EEC and affects trade between member states. Alternatively, a firm might rely upon Article 86 to claim damages or an injunction by asserting that the other party has abused its dominant position in the EEC or a substantial part thereof.[15] In all United Kingdom legal proceedings a claim based upon these articles must be treated as a

[13] For general reference see Bellamy and Child, *Common Market Law of Competition,* (2nd ed, 1978) which needs up-dating but is still a useful basic text. More up-to-date are Merkin and Williams, *Competition Law: Antitrust Policy in the United Kingdom and the EEC* (1984); Swann, *Competition and Industrial Policy in the European Community* (1983).

[14] See Wyatt and Dashwood, *The Substantive Law of the EEC* on State Aids at pp 322 *et seq* and on Public Undertakings at pp 363 *et seq;* Merkin and Williams, *Competition Law: Antitrust Policy in the United Kingdom and the EEC,* pp 373 *et seq* on State Aids.

[15] See *Garden Cottage Foods Ltd* v *Milk Marketing Board* (HL) [1983] 3 CMLR 43; [1983] 2 All ER 770.

question of law and, if the point is not referred to the Court of Justice for a preliminary ruling, it must be dealt with in accordance with the principles laid down by, and any relevant decision of, the Court of Justice.[16] In other words, United Kingdom courts must consider the arguments based on Articles 85 or 86 of the EEC Treaty alongside those based purely on United Kingdom contractual principles. The main features of Article 85 of the EEC Treaty will now be considered, leaving examination of Article 86 to the following chapter.

RESTRICTIVE TRADE PRACTICES[17]

Paragraph (1) of Article 85 of the EEC Treaty prohibits as being incompatible with the Common Market:

> . . . all agreements between undertakings, decisions by associations of undertakings and concerted practices which may affect trade between Member States and which have as their object or effect the prevention, restriction or distortion of competition within the common market.

It then lists five particular types of arrangement which are likely to fall within this prohibition. They are agreements, decisions or concerted practices which:

(a) directly or indirectly fix purchase or selling prices or any other trading conditions;
(b) limit or control production, markets, technical development or investment;
(c) share markets or sources of supply;
(d) apply dissimilar conditions to equivalent transactions with other trading parties, thereby placing them at a competitive disadvantage;
(e) make the conclusion of contracts subject to acceptance by the other parties of supplementary obligations which, by their nature or according to commercial usage, have no connection with the subject of such contracts.

It should be noted that this list of examples in Article 85(1) subparagraphs (a) to (e) is not exhaustive; other arrangements, not falling within one of these subparagraphs, may still come within the general prohibition of Article 85(1). However, the list does serve to warn traders and their legal advisers of the most obvious forms of arrangements likely to raise problems as far as compliance with EEC competition law is concerned.

Although the EEC competition rules may initially seem quite daunting because of their complexity, it is suggested that in order to decide whether any particular arrangement falls within the prohibition in Article 85(1), one should check for the presence of four factors—(i) the parties involved in the transaction, (ii) the form of the restrictive practice, (iii) the scope of the restrictive practice and (iv) the substantive nature of the transaction.[18] All

[16] S 3(1) of the European Communities Act 1972.

[17] For a useful summary see Plender, *A Practical Introduction to European Community Law* (1980) Ch 7; and for a detailed analysis Wyatt and Dashwood, *The Substantive Law of the EEC*, Ch 18.

[18] The remainder of this chapter follows the text of a lecture on "The Law of Competition of the EEC", delivered by the author to the Belfast Solicitors' Association on 24 April 1980.

four factors must be present for Article 85(1) to apply to the trading arrangement.

(i) Parties: As regards the parties, Article 85(1) governs arrangements between "undertakings" or "associations of undertakings". There is no definition of these terms in the Treaty itself but the term "undertaking" is understood to include various types of entities carrying on some economic activity. Thus it includes a company, a partnership or a sole trader but excludes non-profit making bodies. Most of the cases involving "associations of undertakings" have been trade associations, usually formed to protect the interests of their members. Note that Article 90 of the Treaty contains special provisions for public undertakings as regards the competition rules.

(ii) Form of the Restrictive Practice: The restrictive practice must take the form of either an agreement between undertakings or a decision of an association of undertakings or a concerted practice. "Agreements" refer to legally binding ones, whether between parties at the same trading level, known as "horizontal agreements", or between parties at different trading levels, the so-called "vertical agreements".[19]

"Decisions of associations of undertakings" will include actions taken on the joint decision of the members of the association or action which the members are obliged to abide by under the rules of the particular association.[20]

The term "concerted practice" is included in Article 85(1) to ensure that informal modes of co-operation between firms, that fall short of any formal agreement or decision, do not escape the application of the EEC Treaty. In the leading case of *ICI* v *Commission* the Court of Justice laid down the standard definition of what amounts to a concerted practice. The Court defined a "concerted practice" as:

> . . . a form of co-ordination between undertakings which, without going so far as to amount to an agreement properly so called, *knowingly* substitutes a practical co-operation between them for the risks of competition.[21]

In this particular case the Court held that there had been a concerted practice between Europe's largest chemical companies as regards three general and uniform price increases for certain dyestuffs over several years. Although there was no formal agreement between the companies, there was enough circumstantial evidence, like telex messages, for the Commission to prove that there had been a conscious effort towards co-operation between the parties. The Court further explained that purely innocent parallel conduct by companies would not be caught by Article 85(1) of the Treaty and must be distinguished from a concerted practice. The former normally occurs where there are few companies in a market so that when one firm

[19] See *La Technique Minière* v *Maschinenbau Ulm* [1966] ECR 235; [1966] CMLR 357.

[20] See *Vereeniging van Cementhandelaren* v *Commission* [1972] ECR 977; [1973] CMLR 7.

[21] *Op cit, supra,* n 5. [1972] CMLR 557, 622. Emphasis supplied.

steals a lead in that market others, without any collaboration, follow suit; whereas for a concerted practice there is direct or indirect co-operation between the parties.

At this juncture it should also be noted that whatever the form of the arrangement, be it an agreement or concerted practice, it must be between economically independent parties, otherwise their arrangements cannot restrict competition in the EEC within the meaning of Article 85(1). If, therefore, certain parties are economically dependent upon each other, they cannot be in competition with one another and so arrangements between them cannot be caught by Article 85(1). Thus, for example, an agreement between a parent company and its subsidiaries to fix prices charged in EEC countries will not fall within the prohibition of Article 85(1) if the subsidiaries are not economically autonomous.[22] The test, therefore, is whether the parent and its subsidiary form a single economic unit and the answer to that test will depend on the facts of each case. Similarly an agreement or trading practice between a firm acting as principal and its commercial agent will not be prohibited by Article 85(1). Such agency agreements do not restrict competition if the agent has only "an auxiliary function" in the market—finding buyers and sellers for his principal and acting on that principal's instructions. If, however, the agent takes upon himself financial risks, the EEC Commission is likely to regard him as an independent trader and restrictive arrangements with such independent traders may be caught by Article 85(1). One should have regard to the Commission's Notice giving guidelines as to what it regards as true commercial agents.[23]

(iii) Scope of the Restrictive Practice: In order for any agreement, decision or concerted practice by undertakings to come within the prohibition in Article 85(1) of the Treaty, it must "affect trade between member states". This is absolutely essential for Article 85(1) to apply. For instance, if a contract between two Northern Ireland firms to fix prices for certain goods only affects trade within the United Kingdom, that contract will escape the prohibitions in the EEC Treaty. Nevertheless, businesses and legal practitioners should be very cautious at this point because, as mentioned earlier, the Court of Justice has given the phrase "affect trade between member states" such a wide interpretation that it can be fulfilled in what may appear unlikely circumstances. In *Consten and Grundig* v *Commission* the Court of Justice, when considering whether an exclusive distribution agreement between a German manufacturer and a French distributor affected trade between member states, explained that:

[22] See *eg Re Christiani and Neilsen NV* [1969] CMLR D 36, especially pp D 38-39. See also *Re Kodak* [1970] CMLR D 19.

[23] See the "Commission's Announcement on Exclusive Agency Contracts made with Commercial Agents" of 24 December 1962 (JO 1962, 2921/62).

> . . . it is necessary in particular to know whether the agreement is capable of endangering, either directly or indirectly, in fact or potentially, freedom of trade between member states in a direction which could *harm the attainment of the objects of a single market between States.*[24]

Therefore, the crucial test for determining whether an arrangement "affects trade between member states" is whether it may contribute to the perpetuation of national markets and hinder the development of the Common Market. The Court has subsequently added that the arrangement must *appreciably* affect trade between member states thereby introducing what may be regarded as a *de minimis rule* before Article 85 (1) bites.[25]

Arrangements that affect trade between member states may arise in various ways. The most obvious is, as in *Consten and Grundig,* where the parties were in different EEC countries. Not so obvious though is the case where all the parties to the particular arrangement are situated within just one member state. In *Vereeniging van Cementhandelaren* v *Commission*[26] (the Dutch Cement Dealers Case) the Court of Justice held that an agreement, which extends through the whole of a member state, but not beyond it, has the effect of consolidating the national market, thereby hindering trade with other member states and thus "affects trade between member states". In this case the Dutch Cement Dealers' Association, whose members had 70% of the cement market, decided to operate a system of recommended prices for its members and also made it harder for cement dealers from other EEC countries to sell their cement in The Netherlands. Their decision was held to affect trade between member states and thus fell within Article 85(1). Finally, even if all or some of the parties to an arrangement are based outside the European Community, but carry on business within the Community, that arrangement may still affect trade between EEC member states. The Court of Justice has already declared that:

> The fact that one of the undertakings participating in the agreement is situated in a non-member country is no obstacle to the application of [Article 85 (1) of the Treaty] so long as the agreement produces *its effects* in the territory of the Common Market.[27]

In this particular case one of the parties to the exclusive distribution agreement was based in Japan while the other was in Belgium. The agreement would affect trade between member states if the distributor was prevented from re-exporting the products to other member states.

(iv) The Substantive Nature of the Restrictive Practice: The anti-competitive nature of the arrangement is the most important factor. It must

[24] *Op cit, supra,* n 8. [1966] CMLR 418, 472. Emphasis supplied. See also Wyatt and Dashwood, *The Substantive Law of the EEC,* 259-261.

[25] See *eg Béguelin Import Co* v *Import-Export SA* [1972] CMLR 81, 96.

[26] *Op cit, supra,* n 3. [1972] ECR 977; [1973] CMLR 7.

[27] *Op cit, supra,* n 4. [1974] CMLR 81, 95. Emphasis supplied.

be stressed that not only must the agreement, decision or concerted practice affect trade between member states but it must also have as its "object or effect the prevention, restriction or distortion of competition within the common market". As explained above, Article 85(1) does list in subparagraphs (a) to (e) examples of particular types of arrangements most likely to fall foul of the prohibition in Article 85. In an early decision in 1966, *La Technique Minière* v *Maschinenbau Ulm*[28], the Court of Justice first considered the tests to be applied in deciding whether an arrangement has as "its object or effect the prevention, restriction or distortion of competition" within the EEC.

In this case a small French company, LTM, entered into a contract with a West German company whereby LTM had the exclusive right to sell in France some thirty-seven levellers made by the German firm. LTM, later wanting to resile from the contract, asked a Parisian court to declare the contract void for infringing Article 85 of the EEC Treaty. The French court referred the case to the Court of Justice for a ruling on whether the contract was caught by Article 85(1). In deciding whether the contract had the "object or effect" of adversely affecting competition in the EEC, the Court explained that:

> The fact that these are not cumulative but alternative conditions, indicated by the conjunction "or" suggests first the need to consider the very object of the agreement, in the light of the economic context in which it is to be applied . . . Where . . . an analysis of the said clauses does not reveal a sufficient degree of harmfulness with regard to competition, examination should then be made of the effects of the agreement and, if it is to be subjected to the prohibition, the presence of those elements which establish that competition has in fact been prevented, restricted or distorted to a *noticeable extent* should be required. The competition in question should be understood within the actual context in which it would occur in the absence of the agreement in question.[29]

For the actual context of what competition would be like without the agreement, the Court will look at the size and number of parties involved in the agreement, the severity of its clauses, whether it is a sole agreement or part of a series of agreements and also the nature and quality of the products involved.

Here again the Court of Justice introduced a *de minimis rule*. Consequently, for an arrangement to fall foul of Article 85(1) it must appreciably affect trade between member states and also restrict or distort competition within the EEC to a noticeable extent.[30] For guidance as to whether a trading agreement, decision or practice is of *de minimis* importance and thus outside Article 85(1), one should refer to the Commission's Notice Concerning Minor Agreements. According to this

28 *Op cit, supra,* n 19. [1966] ECR 235; [1966] CMLR 357. This case serves as a useful example of how Article 85 is analysed by the Court of Justice.

29 [1966] CMLR 357, 375. Emphasis supplied.

30 See eg *Völk* v *Verwaecke* [1969] ECR 295; [1969] CMLR 273.

Notice, originally issued in 1970 and amended in 1977, it is the Commission's view that agreements between undertakings do not come within Article 85(1) if the products covered by them constitute less than five per cent of the amount of business done in identical or similar products *and* the total annual turnover of the undertakings involved is less than 50 million ECU (about £29 million).[31] It must be emphasised though that if advising a client, one should be cautious about relying upon such Commission Notices since they are not included as legally binding measures in Article 189 of the EEC Treaty. This Notice serves merely as a guideline for the Commission to distinguish agreements of *de minimis* importance but it does not bind the Court of Justice or national courts as to what they might consider *de minimis*. Consequently the exact position of small and medium sized firms which enter into contracts to fix prices, sources of supplies and so forth is uncertain. Therefore, it may be a wise precaution for them to notify the Commission of their agreements and ask for "Negative Clearance". "Negative Clearance" is a statement by the Commission that, on the basis of the facts in its possession, there are no grounds under Article 85(1) of the Treaty for action on its part in respect of the agreement, decision or practice.[32] The onus is upon the undertakings concerned to apply to the Commission for a "Negative Clearance". An undertaking should obtain Form A/B from the Directorate-General for Competition, The Commission of the European Communities, Rue de la Loi 200, Brussels. Part A of this form relates to an application for "Negative Clearance" while Part B deals with "Notification" of trading arrangements (considered below). Plender's warning should, however, be heeded:

> A negative clearance gives only precarious relief. It may be withdrawn at any time. Even if not withdrawn it may be superseded by events . . . Despite all this, a negative clearance is still a valuable document. The Commission seldom revives its investigations unless prompted to do so by a complainant; and at the minimum, a clearance helps its bearer to escape the Commission's fines, or at least to reduce their size.[33]

Fines may be imposed for intentionally or negligently supplying incorrect or misleading information to the Commission when applying for "Negative Clearance".[34]

CONSEQUENCES OF INFRINGING ARTICLE 85(1)

The primary responsibility for the enforcement of the EEC competition rules rests with the Commission. Article 89 of the EEC Treaty requires the Commission to investigate cases of suspected infringements of both Articles 85 and 86 and to take the appropriate measures to bring them to an end. As

[31] The Notice concerning Minor Agreements issued 27 May 1970 (JO 1970 C84/1) and revised on 19 December 1977 (OJ 1977 C 313/3). European Units of Account have since been replaced by European Currency Units.

[32] Art 2, Council Regulation 17/62 (OJ Sp Ed, 1959-62, p 87).

[33] Plender, *A Practical Introduction to European Community Law* (1980) 98.

[34] See Art 15(1)(a), Council Regulation 17/62.

the independent Community institution, whose general task it is to ensure the proper functioning and development of the Common Market, the Commission is well suited for enforcing these particular rules. It is Directorate-General IV within the Commission that deals with competition matters and it may be contacted directly in Brussels for advice and further information.

The detailed powers of the Commission to enforce the EEC competition rules are contained in Regulation 17/62, which came into force on 13 March 1962 and which remains the most important Regulation in this area.[35] (See Appendix V.)

To determine whether or not an infringement of the EEC competition rules has occurred, Regulation 17/62 gives the Commission extensive powers. Under Article 14 of this Regulation, for example, Commission officials are empowered to examine books and other business records, to take copies or extracts from them, to ask for oral explanations on the spot and enter any premises, land and transport of firms. In *National Panasonic (UK) Ltd* v *Commission*[36] the English subsidiary of a Japanese company sought to challenge the legality of these investigative powers of the Commission, on the ground, *inter alia,* that they were in breach of Article 8 of the European Convention on Human Rights, guaranteeing the right to respect for private correspondence. In this case Commission officials had arrived, without prior warning, at 10 am at the National Panasonic sales office in Slough and carried out on-the-spot investigations for seven hours, in the absence of the firm's solicitor for about half of that time. The Court of Justice held that Article 8 of the Convention had not been infringed as it itself permitted limitations "necessary in a democratic society". By analogy, the Court felt that the EEC Commission needed these investigative powers, including the element of surprise, in order to protect effective competition within the European Community.

Where undertakings intentionally or negligently supply the required books and other business records in an incomplete form during investigations under Article 14 of Regulation 17/62, or if they refuse to submit to such investigations where the Commission has decided to carry them out, the Commission may impose fines. In this context the recent decision of the Court of Justice in *A M & S Europe Ltd* v *Commission*[37] marks an important limitation on the investigative powers of the Commission under Article 14 of Regulation 17/62. Early in 1979 Commission officials had investigated the applicant firm's premises near Bristol to check if the EEC competition rules had been infringed. The

[35] Council Regulation 17/62, (OJ Sp Ed, 1959-62, p 87). The main provisions of this Regulation are reproduced by Rudden and Wyatt in *Basic Community Laws,* 251-262. See also Kerse, *EEC Anti-trust Procedure* (1981 with 1982 supplement).

[36] [1980] ECR 2033; [1980] 3 CMLR 169.

[37] [1983] 1 All ER 705; [1982] ECR 1575; [1982] 2 CMLR 264.

applicant, the English subsidiary of an Australian firm, had refused to hand over certain documents on the ground that they were protected by legal privilege. The documents comprised solicitors' advice to the applicant and most of this legal advice, given at the time of the United Kingdom's accession to the EEC, was concerned with how the applicant firm could avoid infringing the competition rules. The Commission rejected the applicant's offer to show parts of each document to prove that they were in fact privileged. The applicant applied to the Court of Justice arguing, *inter alia,* that the principle of legal privilege should be respected by the Commission when investigating a firm under Article 14 of Regulation 17/62. The Court of Justice declared that:

> Community law, which derives from not only the economic but also the legal interpenetration of the member states, must take into account the principles and concepts common to the laws of those states concerning the observance of confidentiality, in particular, as regards certain communications between lawyer and client. That confidentiality serves the requirement, the importance of which is recognised in all of the member states, that any person must be able, without constraint, to consult a lawyer whose profession entails the giving of independent legal advice to all those in need of it.[38]

Viewed in this context, Regulation 17/62 had to be interpreted as protecting the confidentiality of written communications for defence purposes between an independent lawyer, that is one not bound to the firm by a relationship of employment, and his client. The Court then outlined the procedures to be followed by Commission officials in observing this principle of legal privilege.

Obviously legal advisers and business undertakings should acquaint themselves with the provisions of Council Regulation 17/62 and be apprised of the serious consequences that may follow for infringing the EEC competition rules.

If the Commission finds that an arrangement falls foul of Article 85(1) of the EEC Treaty, then various consequences may follow:

(i) the parties may be fined; and

(ii) their agreement or decision may be automatically void under Article 85 paragraph 2, while in the case of a concerted practice, the parties will be ordered to cease and desist from their practice; or

(iii) despite their arrangement falling within the prohibition of Article 85(1), it may be exempted under Article 85 paragraph 3.

Each of these consequences—fines, nullity and exemptions—requires further comment.

Fines: The Commission may by Decision impose on undertakings or associations of undertakings fines ranging from 1000 to 1 million European

[38] *Ibid* [1983] 1 All ER 705, 742. See the very useful article by Joshua, "The Element of Surprise: EEC Competition Investigations under Art 14(3) of Regulation 17" (1983) 8 *EL Rev* 3.

Currency Units (1 ECU=58 pence approximately), or a greater sum of up to 10 per cent of the turnover in the preceding year of business of each of the undertakings participating in the infringement, where they have intentionally or negligently infringed Article 85(1) of the Treaty. In fixing the amount of the fine, the Commission must take into account both the gravity and the duration of the infringement by each party involved. To compel the parties to end their restrictive arrangement promptly, the Commission also has power to impose additional fines, known as periodic penalty payments, for every day they remain in breach of the competition rules. These payments may range from 50 to 1000 ECU per day, calculated from the date set in the Commission's Decision.[39] There is, however, a limitation period which bars the Commission from imposing fines for infringements that occurred more than five years before the start of "any action" by the Commission as long as such action has been notified to at least one of the parties.[40]

Any party which has been fined or required to pay a periodic penalty payment may apply to the Court of Justice to review the Decision of the Commission fixing the fine or payment. Under Article 17 of Regulation 17/62 the Court has unlimited jurisdiction to review penalties within the meaning of Article 172 of the EEC Treaty. Thus the Court may cancel, reduce or increase the fine or penalty imposed. The role of the Court of Justice in competition cases is essentially a supervisory one, checking to see that the facts relied upon by the Commission are correct and that the Commission has properly assessed those facts. In the past the Court of Justice has quite frequently annulled, wholly or partially, the Commission's Decisions and has reduced the fines imposed by it.[41] Clearly then the unlimited jurisdiction of the Court of Justice under Article 172 of the Treaty to review penalties imposed by the Commission should not be overlooked.

Nullity: As well as the risk of fines for infringing Article 85(1) of the Treaty, undertakings will be unable to enforce their particular arrangement since Article 85(2) states quite categorically that . . . "[a]ny agreements or decisions prohibited pursuant to this Article shall be automatically void".

In the case of a concerted practice, where there is no formal or informal agreement as such, the parties should cease and desist from the practice. Since Article 85(2) is directly effective, giving rise to immediate rights, it follows from the express wording of this paragraph that any agreement or decision prohibited by Article 85 is void *without* any prior decision to that effect being required. Nevertheless, it is far more likely that if a party to a

[39] See Arts 15(2) and 16 Council Regulation 17/62. See the useful article by Harding, "The Use of Fines as a Sanction in EEC Competition Law" (1979) 16 *CML Rev* 591.

[40] See Arts 1 and 2 of Council Regulation 2988/74, (OJ 1974 L 319/1).

[41] See Art 17 of Council Regulation 17/62. See also the article by Usher, "Exercise by the European Court of Justice of its Jurisdiction to Annul Competition Decisions" (1980) 5 *EL Rev* 287.

particular arrangement relies upon Article 85(2) to impugn the validity of that arrangement, the matter will end up being disputed in court to decide whether or not it is actually caught by the prohibition in Article 85(1).

As the consequences of nullity vary between the member states, much depends on where the litigation is pursued. In the United Kingdom, in the case of a contract which is void for illegality, property or money passed under it normally cannot be recovered because of the maxim *in pari delicto potior est conditio defendentis*.

To limit the far-reaching consequences of nullity, or perhaps to prevent an unscrupulous party resiling from all his contractual obligations by invoking Article 85(2), it is worth noting the possibility of severing the offending provisions from the rest of an agreement or decision. *In La Technique Minière* the Court of Justice held that the automatic nullity of Article 85(2):

> . . . applies only to those elements of the agreement which are subject to the prohibition of Article 85(1), or to the agreement as a whole if those elements do not appear severable from the agreement itself.[42]

Besides severance, there is the possibility that the arrangement may be given an exemption by the Commission under Article 85, paragraph 3 and so a national court may well prefer to stay its proceedings until the Commission has decided whether or not to exempt the agreement. (For further details on exemption, see below.) Otherwise, the unfortunate situation might arise where a United Kingdom court declares an agreement void for being in breach of Article 85(1) of the EEC Treaty whereas the Commission subsequently decides that there are in fact so many beneficial features about the particular agreement that it deserves an exemption. Although the Court of Justice has recognised that a national court has a duty not to hold parties to an allegedly void contract, it has advised national courts, when faced with such a quandary, either to make a reference to the Court of Justice itself for a preliminary ruling in the case or to adjourn the proceedings to allow the parties to apply to the Commission for an exemption *unless* the national court finds either that the agreement is not caught by Article 85(1) because it is of *de minimis* importance or that there can be *no doubt* that the agreement is incompatible with Article 85(1) and would not merit an exemption.[43]

Exemptions: It is very important to note that even if an agreement, decision or concerted practice comes within Article 85(1), it may nevertheless be granted a "declaration of inapplicability", or, as it is more generally known, "an exemption" by the Commission. By virtue of Article 9(1) of Council Regulation 17/62, it is the EEC Commission and it *alone* which has power to grant exemptions. The Commission may grant an "individual exemption" under Article 85, paragraph 3 of the Treaty provided that the particular arrangement satisfies the specific conditions

[42] [1966] CMLR 357, 376.

[43] See *Brasserie de Haecht* v *Wilkin (No. 2)* [1973] CMLR 287, 302.

listed therein. It may also grant "block exemptions" for certain categories of agreements which will be discussed below.

It must be emphasised that in the majority of cases the Commission can only grant an individual exemption if the arrangement is first notifed to it.[44] (There are only a few non-notifiable agreements listed in Article 4(2) of Regulation 17/62.) The onus is on the parties themselves to notify their agreement, decision or practice to the Commission and request an individual exemption; any one of the parties may notify the arrangement, without the consent of the other parties but the others should be informed. Notification of a trading arrangement is done by completing the B section of Form A/B, copies of which may be obtained free of charge from the Directorate-General for Competition, the Commission of the European Communities in Brussels. This form, together with the required supporting documents, must be forwarded in thirteen copies along with the proof, in triplicate, of any relevant agreement and one copy of other supporting documents. By notifying their agreement, decision or practice the parties may reap a double benefit in that their arrangement may eventually be exempted from the Article 85(1) prohibition by the Commission and in the interim period, between notification and the date when the Commission decides to grant or refuse an exemption, the parties escape being fined;[45] the fact that fines will not be imposed after notification is a "tender carrot" to encourage undertakings to inform the Commission of their trading arrangements within the Common Market. If, however, after a preliminary investigation, the Commission informs the parties concerned that it is of the opinion that the prohibition in Article 85(1) applies and that an exemption under Article 85(3) is not justified, the parties may be fined if, ignoring such a preliminary warning, they continue to operate their agreement, decision or practice.[46]

The Commission may only grant an "individual exemption" where the particular agreement, decision or practice satisfies all four conditions specified in Article 85(3) of the EEC Treaty.

The agreement, decision or practice must:

- contribute to improving the production or distribution of goods or to promoting technical or economic progress; and
- allow consumers a fair share of the resulting benefit; and
- not impose on the undertakings concerned restrictions which are not indispensable to the attainment of these objectives; and
- not afford such undertakings the possibility of eliminating competition in respect of a substantial part of the products in question.

[44] Arts 4-7 of Council Regulation 17/62.
[45] Art 15(5) Council Regulations 17/62.
[46] See Art 15(6) of Council Regulation 17/62.

Article 85(3) provides a gateway through which an agreement, decision or practice, that would otherwise be prohibited by Article 85(1), may be saved provided that all four conditions are met. Even if the conditions are met, the Commission still has a wide discretion in granting exemptions. The onus of proving that the two positive and two negative conditions in Article 85(3) are satisfied rests primarily upon the parties themselves. Nevertheless, the Court of Justice has urged the Commission, as a matter of good administration, to co-operate with the parties using its own resources to ascertain the relevant facts and circumstances.[47]

How these four conditions can be satisfied will inevitably vary from one case to another but a good illustration of what is needed for an individual exemption under Article 85(3) is *Re Omega Watches.*[48] In this case the Swiss company, Omega, wanted to introduce its watches on to the market of several European Community countries and so it organised a distribution network with a general agent in each of the then six member states. Each general agent was allowed to sell the watches to only a very limited number of retailers in main towns or cities, who were selected on the basis, *inter alia,* of having good after-sales service and well positioned shops. The Commission decided that these agreements fell within the prohibition of Article 85(1) of the EEC Treaty as the limited number of approved retailers in each member state restricted competition within the European Community. However, with some amendments to their agreements, the Commission granted an individual exemption under Article 85(3) because it found that all four conditions were met in this instance. The agreements did improve the distribution of the Swiss watches within the Common Market, and they gave consumers a new range of watches to choose from as well as offering good after-sales service, and the limited number of retailers was considered necessary as there were so few Omega watches initially for distribution and, moreover, the agreement did not eliminate competition with watch-makers as the retailers were free to sell other competing brands of watches.

When the Commission grants an individual exemption, Article 8(1) of Regulation 17/62 requires it to set a time-limit on that exemption and also allows it to attach conditions and obligations to it. In *Re Omega Watches,* for example, the exemption was for a ten year period and annual reports had to be submitted giving such details as the current number of approved retailers. An exemption may, on application, be renewed by the Commission if the conditions in Article 85(3) continue to be satisfied. Alternatively, the Commission may, under Article 8(3) of Regulation 17/62, revoke or amend an individual exemption or prohibit specific acts by the parties if:

[47] *Consten and Grundig* v *Commission* [1966] CMLR 418, 477.

[48] [1970] CMLR D 49. See also *Re Transocean Marine Paint* [1967] CMLR D 9.

(1) there is a change in the facts that were basic to the grant of the exemption; or
(2) it was based upon incorrect information or induced by deceit; or
(3) the parties abuse it; or
(4) the parties breach any conditions attached to it.

Any such revocation on grounds 2-4 may have retroactive effect.

In the case of individual exemptions it may take the Commission two or three years to carry out its investigations and decide whether or not an exemption should be granted. There seems to be some disagreement between commentators about the exact status of an agreement, decision or concerted practice in the interim period between the time of notification and the eventual Decision of the Commission granting or refusing an exemption. For "old agreements" (ones entered into before Regulation 17/62 came into force on 13 March 1962, or in the case of Ireland, Denmark and the United Kingdom, ones in force before their accession on 1 January 1973) the general consensus of opinion seems to be that during that interim period the arrangement should be regarded as "provisionally valid" since the Commission can retrospectively validate old agreements if the parties agree to modify any provisions that are contrary to Article 85(1).[49] However, in the case of "new agreements" (ones entered into after 13 March 1962 or, for the United Kingdom etc, after 1 January 1973), parties operate upon it at their own risk because it may ultimately be declared void *ab initio* if the Commission refuses an exemption and the Commission has no power to validate retrospectively new agreements.[50]

It is worth noting that as the result of a recent case, *Camera Care Ltd* v *Commission*[51] brought by a Belfast based company, the Court of Justice has established that, pending its investigations under Article 85 or 86 of the Treaty, the Commission has power to take interim measures under Article 3(1) of Regulation 17/62 to protect an undertaking from serious and irreparable damage.

As well as being able to grant individual exemptions under Article 85(3), the Commission has also been empowered by the Council of Ministers to make Regulations exempting certain categories of agreements *en bloc* from the application of Article 85(1). This enables the Commission to grant exemptions to certain groups of agreements that have beneficial effects on competition, like those set out in Article 85(3), and thus saves it time and labour examining every single agreement. For example, the Commission has, since 1972, granted block exemptions for certain categories of

[49] Art 7 of Council Regulation 17/62.

[50] See *Brasserie de Haecht* v *Wilkin (No. 2)* [1973] ECR 77; [1973] CMLR 287.

[51] [1980] ECR 119; [1980] 1 CMLR 334 and the subsequent Commission Notice, [1980] 2 CMLR 369. For further comment see Chapter 16 *post*.

specialisation agreements provided they satisfy specific criteria laid down by Regulation.[52]

In addition, the Commission, by Regulation 67/67[53], had for over fifteen years given a block exemption to categories of exclusive dealing agreements. That important Regulation expired on 30 June 1983 and has now been replaced by Commission Regulations 1983/83 and 1984/83,[54] granting block exemptions to categories of exclusive distribution agreements and exclusive purchasing agreements. (Appendices VI and VII.) The Commission has published a Notice concerning these two new Regulations, setting out the main considerations that will determine its view of whether or not an exclusive distribution or purchasing agreement is covered by the block exemption.[55] Again it should be stressed that since a Notice is not a legally binding measure, it is without prejudice to the jurisdiction of national courts to apply these Regulations, although it may well be of persuasive authority in proceedings before such courts. Similarly, this Notice does not bind the Court of Justice in its interpretation of the Regulations. These new Regulations contain important rules governing beer-supply and service-station agreements. So legal advisers with clients engaged in such activities should have regard to these particular Regulations. The publication by Valentine Korah in 1984 of *Exclusive Dealing Agreements in the EEC; Regulation 67/67 Replaced* provides a very useful commentary on these new Regulations and also reproduces them in full at the end of the text.

If an agreement satisfies the strict conditions laid down in the Regulations governing block exemptions, then it is valid and need not be individually notified to the Commission. However the Commission still retains the right to investigate an individual agreement where it believes the agreement is not having advantageous or beneficial effects on competition within the Common Market.

More recently the Commission has also adopted Regulations granting block exemptions for certain vehicle distribution and servicing agreements,[56] patent licensing agreements,[57] and also for certain research and development co-operation agreements.[58]

Even if an agreement does not come within the terms of the relevant block exemption, it may nevertheless be individually exempted by the

[52] Commission Regulation 2779/72 (OJ 1972 L 292/23). This Regulation is regularly renewed, most recently by Commission Regulation 417/85 (OJ 1985 L 53/5).

[53] (OJ Special ed, 1967 p 10).

[54] (OJ 1983 L 173/1) and (OJ 1983 L 173/5) respectively; Corrigenda to Regulations 1983/83 and 1984/83, (OJ 1983 L 281/24).

[55] (OJ 1983 C 355/7).

[56] Commission Regulation 123/85, (OJ 1985 L 15/16). See also Commission Notice 17/03, (OJ 1985 C 17/3) for further guidance.

[57] Commission Regulation 2349/84, (OJ 1984 L 219/15).

[58] Commission Regulation 418/85 (OJ 1985 L 53/1).

Commission under Article 85(3) provided, of course, that the arrangement is notified and meets the four conditions specified therein.

If legal advisers or businesses are in any doubt about whether the EEC competition rules apply to a particular trading arrangement they should contact the Directorate-General for Competition, at the Commission's headquarters in Brussels for advice. By completing both sections of Form A/B, the arrangement may receive a clean bill of health, in the form of a "Negative Clearance", under section A of the Form and section B may then be ignored. If, however, the arrangement does not merit a "Negative Clearance", then at least it has been notified to the Commission by the completion of Part B and the parties may avoid being fined for the period between notification and the time of the Commission's Decision to grant or refuse exemption.[59] Besides this, as Wyatt and Dashwood explain:

> Frequently the [procedure for establishing infringements, granting exemptions and imposing fines] is not gone through because the parties and the Commission are able to come to an amicable arrangement as regards the abandonment of offensive provisions or the cessation of an investigation. The Commission then usually publishes an announcement to that effect.[60]

The Commission has in recent years begun to issue what are called "comfort letters" where it intends to take no action and the main contents of these are now published in the Official Journal of the European Communities, "C" section.

[59] For the Commission's Notices on procedures about applications for Negative Clearance and Notification see [1984] 1 CMLR 38 and [1984] 1 CMLR 128. On amendments to Form A/B see Commission Regulation 2526/85 (OJ 1985 L 240/1).

[60] *The Substantive Law of the EEC,* p 281.

CHAPTER 16

THE EEC COMPETITION RULES: PROHIBITION OF ABUSES BY DOMINANT UNDERTAKINGS

While Article 85 of the EEC Treaty prohibits restrictive trade practices that affect trade between member states and distort competition within the European Community, Article 86 of the Treaty prohibits, as being incompatible with the Common Market, "[a]ny abuse by one or more undertakings of a dominant position within the common market or in a substantial part of it . . . in so far as it may affect trade between Member States". The full text of Article 86 can be found in Appendix IV. Again it is worth reminding readers that Article 86 is directly effective and is therefore, by virtue of section 2(1) of the European Communities Act 1972, part and parcel of the United Kingdom law. Article 86 gives rise, therefore, to immediate rights which parties may rely upon without the need for any United Kingdom implementing legislation. As observed recently by Lord Diplock in the House of Lords case, *Garden Cottage Foods Ltd* v *Milk Marketing Board,* where the appellant sought an injunction to prevent the MMB allegedly abusing its dominant position in the supply of bulk butter:

> A breach of duty imposed by art 86 not to abuse a dominant position in the Common Market or in a substantial part of it can thus be categorised in English law as a breach of statutory duty that is imposed not only for the purpose of promoting the general economic prosperity of the Common Market but also for the benefit of private individuals to whom loss or damage is caused by a breach of that duty.[1]

In this particular case, the majority felt that damages, rather than an injunction, was the proper remedy for a breach of Article 86. As part of the United Kingdom law, legal practitioners and traders in Northern Ireland should be aware of the implications of Article 86, especially if a business undertaking is suffering as the result of some form of abusive conduct carried out by a dominant undertaking. Already a Belfast-based firm, Camera Care Ltd, has sought to rely upon Articles 85 and 86 of the EEC Treaty in order to complain to the Commission about the refusal of a Swedish manufacturer of camera equipment and its subsidiaries to continue supplying Camera Care with equipment.[2]

It is really only in the past dozen years or so that the Commission and Court of Justice have resorted to using Article 86 to curb a wide variety of

[1] [1983] 2 All ER 770, 775. See also Davidson, "Enforcing Community Competition Law in National Courts" (1984) 35 *NILQ* 68.

[2] *Camera Care Ltd* v *Commission* [1980] ECR 119; [1980] 1 CMLR 334.

business activities regarded by them as abusive. During this time Article 86 has been used to control such activities as mergers, the charging of excessive or unfair prices for goods and services, the use of loyalty rebates, and the refusal to supply goods to former customers. Since the scope of the Article 86 prohibition is being expanded all the while by the Commission and the Court of Justice, then, rather like Negligence in the Law of Torts, the categories of abusive conduct by dominant undertakings are not closed. Consequently there is still uncertainty about precisely what forms of conduct may infringe Article 86. As well as this uncertainty for undertakings operating within the European Community, there is the additional sting in Article 86 in that, once caught by it, there is no provision for an exemption. Unlike Article 85(3) of the Treaty which allows the Commission to exempt an individual agreement, decision or concerted practice on account of its beneficial features, Article 86 contains no equivalent exemption clause. If an undertaking infringes Article 86, it faces fines imposed by the Commission, for an intentional or negligent infringement. Again firms may appeal to the Court of Justice against the imposition of such fines.[3]

In the light of these comments, are there any guidelines to warn legal advisers and their clients when Article 86 of the EEC Treaty is likely to apply? For the Article 86 prohibition to operate one should check for the presence of four factors namely, (i) one or more undertakings must have (ii) a dominant position in the EEC or a substantial part thereof and (iii) there must be an abuse of that position so that (iv) it affects trade between member states. Each of these factors now needs further examination.[4]

(i) Parties: Here again an "undertaking" means an entity carrying on some economic activity and includes a company, partnership or sole trader. If a parent company and its wholly-owned subsidiaries form one economic unit, together they will constitute an "undertaking" for the purposes of Article 86. This is a very important point as the dominance of the parent may be added to the abuse by its subsidiary.[5]

(ii) Dominant Position: Since the EEC Treaty does not define the term "dominant position", it has been left to the EEC Commission and the Court of Justice to interpret the term. The basic definition is that given by the Court of Justice in *United Brands Co* v *Commission* where a "dominant position" was described as:

[3] See Art 15, Council Regulation 17/62 and also the notes on Fines at p 169 *ante*.

[4] See Wyatt & Dashwood, *The Substantive Law of the EEC,* Ch 19; Plender, *A Practical Introduction to European Community Law,* Ch 8.

[5] See *eg Istituto and Commercial Solvents Corp* v *Commission* [1974] ECR 223; [1974] 1 CMLR 309.

> . . . a position of economic strength enjoyed by an undertaking which enables it to prevent effective competition being maintained in the *relevant market* by giving it the power to behave *to an appreciable extent independently* of its competitors, customers and ultimately of its consumers. In general a dominant position derives from a combination of several factors which, taken separately, are not necesarily determinative.[6]

In other words, an undertaking will have a dominant position where it has such overall power in a particular market as to enable it to influence normal competitive conditions in the market to an appreciable extent. Here again the Court applies a *de minimis* rule and so the activities of one large firm in Northern Ireland may not fall foul of Article 86. The sort of factors that may put a firm into a dominant position are its market share (obviously the most important factor) as well as capital resources, technical expertise and access to raw materials. Thus, for example, in the *United Brands* case, although the company's share of world banana exports in 1974 was only 40 per cent, the market shares of its competitors were small by comparison. As well as this share of the market, United Brands had large financial resources, advanced technology for developing good, disease-resistant bananas and had its own banana plantations in South America as well as ships to transport the fruit. All of these factors together gave the company a dominant position. As the Court of Justice summed up:

> An undertaking's economic strength is not measured by its profitability; a reduced profit margin or even losses for a time are not incompatible with a dominant position . . . The cumulative effect of all the advantages enjoyed by UBC . . . ensures that it has a dominant position on the relevant market.[7]

The dominant position held by an undertaking cannot exist in a vacuum. Rather it must exist in what the Court keeps referring to as "the relevant market", that is relevant in terms of the geographical market and the products market. As for the geographical market, Article 86 will only bite if an undertaking has a dominant position in the EEC or a substantial part of it. What amount of territory constitutes a "substantial part of the EEC" is determined by the Commission and the Court of Justice from case to case. In determining what amounts to a "substantial part" of the Community, the Court of Justice looks not only at the actual amount of territory in question but also at the economic importance of the market for the particular product there. In *Liptons' Cash Registers Ltd* v *Hugin Kassaregister AB and Hugin Cash Registers Ltd*[8] the Commission held that Great Britain alone constituted a substantial part of the EEC. In this case a Swedish manufacturer of cash registers, Hugin AB, controlled the supply of all Hugin-type spare parts in the world. It had a number of subsidiaries in the EEC, including one in the United Kingdom. For several years Liptons Cash Registers, a London firm, had traded in secondhand registers including

[6] [1979] 1 CMLR 429, 486. Emphasis supplied.

[7] *Ibid* p 491.

[8] [1978] 1 CMLR D19 (Comm.); [1979] ECR 1869; [1979] 3 CMLR 345 (ECJ).

Hugin ones. When Hugin refused to supply any more of its spare parts to Liptons, the latter firm complained to the EEC Commission about a breach of Article 86 of the Treaty. The Commission considered that Hugin AB had a dominant position through its English subsidiary as regards its spare parts in the United Kingdom. The Court of Justice agreed but nevertheless annulled the Commission's Decision because its conduct could not affect trade between member states.

In order to decide whether an undertaking has a dominant position in the relevant products market, the Court of Justice will consider if there is competition not only from identical products but also from any products that are readily interchangeable. It can indeed be hard to determine what exactly is the relevant products market because products may look the same in appearance but yet may not be in competition with each other because they are not easily interchangeable for reasons such as consumer preference, or the production costs are too high for other manufacturers to swop readily from making one product to another.

Alternatively, although products may be very different in appearance, they may still be in competition for a certain purpose as was the case in *Europemballage and Continental Can* v *Commission*[9] Here the applicant company, Continental Can Co, sought the annulment of a Commission Decision finding that CCC had abused its dominant position in metal containers within the Common Market by taking over a Dutch manufacturer of light metal containers. Continental Can Co of America, the world's largest producer of metal packages, had wanted to enter the European market and so in 1969 it had bought about 85 per cent of the capital in a West German firm making light metal containers. Then in 1970 Continental Can formed a wholly-owned subsidiary, Europemballage, based it in Brussels, and transferred to it all its European holdings, including its stake in the German company. Acting upon the instructions of its parent company, Europemballage bought up 91 per cent of a rival Dutch company, the biggest manufacturer of light metal containers in the Benelux countries. When the Commission investigated this merger, it held that Continental Can had already acquired a dominant position in the market for light metal containers for preserved meat and fish and metal tops for glass jars in a substantial part of the Common Market when it took over the West German company. CCC had then abused that position by the merger as it had eliminated a competitor. The Court of Justice, however, subsequently annulled the Commission's Decision on the ground that the Commission had not properly assessed the relevant products market. The Court concluded that producers of metal containers for other products such as tinned fruit, milk and so on could have been in competition with CCC and, moreover, glass and plastic containers might have been just as acceptable to consumers as metal ones. Since the Commission had failed to consider these alternatives, it had not defined the proper products market.

9 [1973] ECR 215; [1973] CMLR 199.

Obviously then, the delimitation of the relevant products market is absolutely crucial before Article 86 applies. The undertaking suspected of having a dominant position in a particular market will try to define the products market as widely as possible since it is then harder for the Commission to prove the undertaking's dominance. The Commission, on the other hand, will try to define the market as narrowly as possible. This is precisely what happened in the *United Brands* case. The company contended that the relevant products market was that of fresh fruit generally and not just that of bananas; in other words that United Brands did not have a dominant position in the general market for fruit. The Court of Justice, however, accepted the Commission's evidence that the banana market could be differentiated from that of other fruits by virtue of the banana's special features. As the Court explained:

> The banana has certain characteristics, appearance, taste, softness, seedlessness, easy handling, a constant level of production which enables it to satisfy the constant needs of an important section of the population consisting of the very young, the old and the sick.[10]

The specific qualities of bananas influenced consumer preference so that they would not readily accept other fruits as substitutes. Since bananas were not, therefore, regarded as readily interchangeable with other fresh fruits, the Commission was correct in deciding that the banana market alone was the relevant products market and United Brands certainly did dominate that particular products market within the European Community.

To summarise then, it is possible for a firm operating only in the United Kingdom in a specialised products market, where there is virtually no competition from other products, to have a dominant position within the meaning of Article 86 of the EEC Treaty. It is not just the large multinational companies that can have a dominant position within the European Community. Of course it must be remembered that having a dominant position in the EEC or a substantial part thereof is not *per se* an infringement of Article 86 of the Treaty. There has to be an abuse by an undertaking of its dominant position within the EEC and that abuse must affect trade between member states.

(iii) Abuse of a Dominant Position: There is no precise definition of "abuse" of a dominant position in the EEC Treaty although Article 86 does list certain examples. It provides that abuse may, in particular, consist of:

(a) directly or indirectly imposing unfair purchase or selling prices or unfair trading conditions;

(b) limiting production, markets or technical development to the prejudice of consumers;

(c) applying dissimilar conditions to equivalent transactions with other trading parties, thereby placing them at a competitive disadvantage;

[10] [1978] 1 CMLR 429, 483.

(d) making the conclusion of contracts subject to acceptance by the other parties of supplementary obligations which, by their nature or according to commercial usage, have no connection with the subject of such contracts.

These examples of abuse are in fact similar to the types of restrictive practices listed as prohibited by Article 85(1) of the Treaty and well illustrate the point that Article 86 and Article 85 share the same aim—that competition within the European Community should not be distorted either by the unilateral action of a dominant undertaking (Article 86) or by the joint agreement, practice or decision of several parties (Article 85). As the two Articles are not mutually exclusive, it means that if undertakings have gained a dominant position in a market by virtue of a restrictive agreement, decision, or practice and then abused that position, they may be ordered to terminate the agreement as well as to desist from the abuse.

The list of typical abuses in Article 86 of the Treaty is certainly not exhaustive. In fact the major cases involving Article 86 have concerned different forms of abuse by dominant undertakings. A brief look at several of these cases will serve to highlight the versatility of the term "abuse" of a dominant position. In the *Europemballage and Continental Can* case, it is worth noting that although the Court of Justice did annul the Commission's Decision on the ground that it had failed properly to assess the relevant products market, the Court nevertheless endorsed the Commission's view that mergers can in certain circumstances constitute an "abuse" within the meaning of Article 86 of the EEC Treaty. The Court stated that:

> There may be abusive behaviour if an undertaking in a dominant position strengthens that dominant position so that the degree of control achieved substantially obstructs competition, i.e. that the only undertakings left in the market are those which are dependent on the dominant undertaking with regard to their market behaviour.[11]

This judgment attracted considerable criticism because Article 86 seemed to many commentators a clumsy weapon to control mergers as it operated *ex post facto,* maybe three or four years after the merger had taken place.[12] Besides this, the Council of Ministers was at that time, and still is, trying to produce a Regulation on the Control of Concentrations between Undertakings, requiring in certain cases advance notice of mergers to be given to the Commission.[13]

A quite different form of "abuse" caught by Article 86 is the refusal of a dominant undertaking to supply goods to a customer. In *Istituto and Commercial Solvents* v *Commission*[14] the Commercial Solvents Company of

[11] [1973] ECR 215, 223.

[12] See *eg* Valentine Korah, "The Control of Mergers Under Article 86 of the Rome Treaty: Continental Can" (1973) *CLP* 82.

[13] See Merkin and Willams, *Competition Law: Antitrust Policy in the United Kingdom and the EEC* (1984) 284 *et seq*.

[14] [1974] ECR 223; [1974] 1 CMLR 309.

America, a major world producer of raw materials essential for the production of certain anti-tuberculosis drugs, acquired in 1962 a majority of shares in an Italian company, Istituto. Istituto then supplied the raw materials for the manufacture of anti-TB drugs to other companies, including another Italian company, Zoja. Early in 1970 CSC decided that instead of selling its raw materials, it would keep them and produce the anti-TB drugs itself. Its customers, including Zoja, were informed by Istituto that CSC would no longer supply them with these essential materials. Zoja complained to the Commission that this refusal to supply it with chemicals constituted a breach of Article 86 of the EEC Treaty. The Commission and, subsequently, the Court of Justice agreed that CSC had indeed abused its dominant position in the relevant market, namely, the market in raw materials for manufacturing anti-tuberculosis drugs. The Court declared that:

> . . . an undertaking which has a dominant position in the market in raw materials and which, with the object of reserving such raw materials for manufacturing its own derivatives, refuses to supply a customer, which is itself a manufacturer of these derivatives, and therefore risks eliminating all competition on the part of this customer, is abusing its dominant position within the meaning of Article 86.[15]

Accordingly, CSC was ordered to re-supply Zoja and, together with its subsidiary, CSC was fined for violating Article 86 of the Treaty.

In the subsequent case of *United Brands* v *Commission* the Court of Justice reiterated the general rule that an undertaking having a dominant position for marketing a particular product cannot stop supplying a long-standing customer, who abides by regular commercial practice, if the orders placed by that customer are in no way out of the ordinary. The Court of Justice did, however, accept that a dominant undertaking is entitled to protect its own commercial interests if they are attacked by a customer through, for example, an advertising campaign for a rival firm. The dominant firm may take such reasonable steps as it deems appropriate to protect its interests but such steps would not be permitted if their actual purpose was to strengthen the firm's dominant position and abuse it. The steps that a dominant firm could properly take to protect itself must be proportionate to the threat, taking into account the economic strength of the undertakings confronting each other. In this particular case United Brands had cut off supplies of its bananas to its long-standing Danish distributor, Olesen, because the latter had taken part in an advertising campaign for other bananas sold by UB's main rival. The Court of Justice regarded this sanction of the refusal by a dominant company to supply a former customer to be in excess of what might be regarded as a reasonable step to protect its own commercial interests. By cutting off supplies like this, UB deterred other small and medium sized banana distributors from advertising for other brand names, thus reinforcing UB's dominance in the banana market.

[15] *Ibid* [1974] 1 CMLR 309, 340.

Dominant firms must, therefore, be very careful when refusing to supply former customers.[16] The position as regards refusing to supply a new customer is still unresolved. The Court has at least recognised that a dominant undertaking may take reasonable steps that are proportionate to the threat to protect its own commercial interests but exactly what these steps are has not yet been enunciated by the Court.

A different form of "abuse" within the meaning of Article 86 is the charging of unfair prices for goods or services. In *General Motors Continental* v *Commission*[17], General Motors Continental, the European subsidiary of the major American car manufacturing company, was found by the Commission to have charged excessively high fees for providing a particular service, namely certifying that certain European-made Opel cars, imported privately into Belgium, satisfied the Belgian technical standards of road worthiness. When the company challenged this Decision, the Court of Justice held that there may be an abuse within the terms of Article 86 of the Treaty where a dominant undertaking charges a price that is excessive in relation to the economic value of the service provided and which has the effect of curbing cheaper parallel imports thereby leading to unfair trade within the meaning of Article 86(a). In this particular case, however, the Court, went on to take account of various mitigating factors—that General Motors Continental had suddenly had to provide this certification service for privately imported GM vehicles coming into Belgium when state-run testing stations stopped doing the inspection, had only over-charged in five cases before fixing lower fees for the service and had already paid rebates to the five people concerned. The Court accepted these factors as justifying the company's conduct and so annulled the Commission's Decision, declaring that the Commission had been over-zealous in this instance. It seems that while Article 86 contains no exemption clause like Article 85(3), the Court of Justice will take account of mitigating factors in cases of alleged breaches thereof.

Thus far the types of abuse considered have included mergers, refusal to deal and unfair prices. In *Hoffmann-La Roche* v *Commission*[18] yet another form of conduct, namely the use of fidelity or loyalty rebates, was regarded by the Court of Justice as constituting an "abuse" within the meaning of Article 86 of the Treaty. Roche, a Swiss company and the world's largest manufacturer of bulk vitamins, had concluded agreements with many companies producing and/or selling vitamins within the European

[16] See also *Camera Care Ltd* v *Commission* [1980] ECR 119; [1980] 1 CMLR 334 and *Garden Cottage Foods Ltd* v *Milk Marketing Board* [1983] 2 All ER 770.

[17] [1975] ECR 1367; [1976] 1 CMLR 95. See also *United Brands* v *Commission* [1978] ECR 207 where the Commission found unfair prices charged for bananas.

[18] [1979] ECR 461; [1979] 3 CMLR 211. *Roche versus Adams* (1984) by Richard Adams, a former director of Hoffman-La Roche, concerns his views about this case. He is currently seeking damages from the Commission for breaches of confidentiality in connection with this case. See *Adams* v *Commission, The Times,* 8 Nov 1985.

Community. The Commission decided that Roche had abused its dominant position in the vitamin market by including in these agreements exclusivity clauses or the offer of fidelity rebates as an incentive for customers to buy all or most of their requirements from Roche. The Court of Justice endorsed the Commission's view, declaring that an undertaking which is in a dominant position in a particular market "and ties purchasers—even if it does so at their request—by an obligation or promise on their part to obtain all or most of their requirements exclusively from the said undertaking abuses its dominant position within the meaning of Article 86 of the Treaty, whether the obligation in question is stipulated without further qualification or whether it is undertaken in consideration of the grant of a rebate." It was abusive because it restricted the choice of supply for customers and denied other producers access to the market. It follows that granting fidelity rebates, that is discounts conditional upon the customer taking all or most of its requirements from the grantor, no matter whether the actual quantity of its purchases be large or small, also constitutes an "abuse" within Article 86. Quantity rebates, as opposed to these fidelity rebates, are permissible since the price paid is directly related to the amount purchased and the rebates are not designed to prevent customers from obtaining their supplies from other producers.

From this sample of cases one can see how the scope of Article 86 has been widened by the Court of Justice and the Commission to cover a very wide range of commercial activities. In doing so the Court often refers to "the spirit of the Treaty" and, in the area of competition, this means that it looks at the general activities of the European Community as found in particular in Article 3(f) of the EEC Treaty, which requires "the institution of a system ensuring that competition in the common market is not distorted". The Court uses the generality of this phrase in order to interpret Article 86 and, judging by the cases mentioned above, it has done so in order to widen its scope.[19] Be aware, therefore, that the full content of Article 86 of the Treaty has yet to be fully worked out.

(iv) Affect Trade Between Member States: Article 86 of the EEC Treaty only prohibits an abuse by an undertaking of its dominant position within the European Community or a substantial part of it *in so far as* it may "affect trade between member states". Like Article 85 of the Treaty, Article 86 only applies if *intra-Community* trade is affected. This phrase serves as a jurisdictional test, intended to define the sphere of application of the EEC competition rules as opposed to national rules about monopolies. As explained in Chapter 15 *ante* the phrase "affect trade between member states" has been given a very wide interpretation by the Court of Justice (See p 164). Moreover, in cases involving Article 86 the Court seems to have given

[19] See *eg Europemballage and Continental Can* v *Commission* [1973] ECR 215; [1973] CMLR 199.

the phrase an even more flexible meaning, regarding this element of Article 86 as satisfied once it is established that the particular abuse by the dominant undertaking "will have repercussions on the competitive structure within the Common Market".[20]

CONSEQUENCES OF INFRINGING ARTICLE 86

Uncertainty about the full content of Article 86 is no defence in proceedings for infringing this provision.[21] If a firm has doubts about the application of Article 86 to its activities, then it should contact the Commission's Directorate-General for Competition in Brussels for advice. It may also seek a "Negative Clearance" by completing section A of Form A/B, obtainable free from the Commission. If given a "Negative Clearance", that simply means that, on the basis of the facts in its possession at that time, the Commission is of the opinion that the undertaking is not infringing Article 86 of the Treaty. It must be stressed though that a "Negative Clearance" is precarious since the Commission may later withdraw it if further incriminating information comes to its attention. Fines may be imposed under Article 15(2) of Council Regulation 17/62 for supplying incomplete or misleading information when seeking a "Negative Clearance".

If an undertaking does not bother to apply for "Negative Clearance" the Commission may investigate its operations of its own initiative or upon complaints from individuals and may impose substantial fines for any negligent or intentional infringement of Article 86 of the Treaty. In imposing fines the Commission must take account of the gravity and duration of the infringement by each of the parties involved in it. The Court of Justice has unlimited jurisdiction under Article 172 of the EEC Treaty to review such fines and so an undertaking that is fined by the Commission may apply to the Court seeking the annulment of the Commission's Decision imposing a fine. (For further details about Negative Clearance and fines, see pp 167 and 169-70 *ante*).

Again it is worth repeating the point that, unlike Article 85 of the Treaty, Article 86 admits of no possibility of an exemption for an undertaking abusing its dominant position. That said, it is nevertheless significant that the Court of Justice has taken into account certain mitigating factors whenever it is determining whether or not an undertaking has abused its position. The *General Motors* case mentioned above illustrates this point. The Court has on several occasions reduced fines or cancelled them because of mitigating factors or because the Commission's reasoning or evidence was defective in some respect.[22]

[20] See *Istituto and Commercial Solvents* v *Commission* [1974] 1 CMLR 309, 342.

[21] See *eg Hoffmann-La Roche* v *Commission* [1979] ECR 461; [1979] 3 CMLR 211.

[22] See Usher, "Exercise by the European Court of its Jurisdiction to Annul Competition Decisions" (1980) 5 *EL Rev* 287.

EEC COMMISSION'S POWERS IN COMPETITION CASES[23]

As explained earlier the Commission is the Community institution primarily responsible for ensuring that undertakings comply with the EEC competition rules. Any party found by the Commission to have infringed those rules may go to the Court of Justice seeking the annulment of the Commission's Decision finding an infringement and review of any fine which it imposed. The Commission's powers in respect of competition matters are contained in Council Regulation 17/62. (For further details of the Commission's powers under this Regulation, see pp 167-9 *ante.*) As the Commission's investigations into possible infringements of Article 85 and 86 of the Treaty may take several years it is important to remember that the Commission does have power to order interim measures until it completes its investigations. This power was first established in the case of *Camera Care Ltd* v *Commission*[24] when a Belfast-based company, Camera Care, involved in the repair and sale of professional photographic equipment, complained to the Commission in June 1979 that a Swedish company, Hasselblad, had infringed the EEC competition rules by refusing, together with its British subsidiary, to continue supplying the Belfast company with spare parts for Hasselblad cameras. Camera Care insisted that the prolonged withholding of these supplies would cause it substantial damage and loss of business. It therefore requested the Commission to take interim measures like ordering Hasselblad to recommence supplies. In August 1979 the Commission informed Camera Care that it would investigate its complaint but that it had no power to take interim measures because under Community law there was no legal basis for it to do so. Camera Care then brought an action before the Court of Justice seeking a declaration that the Commission had acted unlawfully in failing to order interim measures. The Court held that the Commission did in fact have power to adopt interim measures under Article 3(1) of Regulation 17/62 even though that provision does not say so expressly; the Court took the view that such powers had to be implied as there might be circumstances where the Commission needed to take interim measures, pending the final outcome of its investigations. The Court did stress though that:

> . . . it is essential that interim measures be taken only in cases proved to be urgent in order to avoid a situation likely to cause serious and irreparable damage to the party seeking their adoption, or which is intolerable for the public interest. A further requirement is that these measures be of a temporary and conservatory nature and restricted to what is required in the given situation . . . [and] the decisions must be made in such a form that any action may be brought upon them before the Court by any party which considers it has been injured.[25]

[23] See the excellent study by Kerse, *Antitrust Procedure* and supplements.

[24] *Op cit, supra,* n 2.

[25] [1980] 1 CMLR 334, 348.

Following this Court ruling, the Commission issued a "Practice Note" to the parties in which it stated the guidelines it would apply to applications made to it for interim measures under Article 3(1) of Regulation 17/62.[26] Instead of ordering interim measures the Commission subsequently decided that Hasselblad had infringed Article 85(1) and so had to re-supply its equipment to Camera Care. It was also fined for infringing the EEC competition rules. However, when Hasselblad later challenged the Commission's Decision, the Court of Justice found that the Commission had mistakenly taken account of a particular clause and so the Decision was partially annulled.[27] Nevertheless, this case demonstrates once again the relevance of Community law to the business community in Northern Ireland.

[26] See [1980] 2 CMLR 369. See also Farmiloe, "Obtaining Interlocutory Relief in EEC Competition Cases" (1980) *ECLR* 393. See *Re The Agreement of Ford Werke AG* [1982] 3 CMLR 267.

[27] See *Hasselblad GB Ltd* v *Commission* [1984] 1 CMLR 559.

CHAPTER 17

AGRICULTURE

Since Northern Ireland has a greater dependence upon farming than the rest of the United Kingdom, with some 20 per cent of the Province's workforce engaged directly or indirectly in agriculture, the EEC's Common Agricultural Policy (the "CAP") is obviously of considerable importance for people here. The current controversy over milk quotas imposed on Northern Ireland's dairy farmers, requiring them to decrease milk production, while their neighbours in the Republic of Ireland may increase their production, has merely added to the criticism already levelled at the CAP, which is regarded by many as inefficient and too costly. It is seen as encouraging surplus production of foodstuffs that are then bought and stored by EEC intervention agencies and which may eventually be sold off cheaply to Eastern European countries.

Apart from the economics of the EEC's agricultural policy, what are its legal implications and where might lawyers in Northern Ireland expect to encounter problems involving the Community's rules on agriculture?

PROBLEMS INVOLVING THE COMMON AGRICULTURAL POLICY

As the rules governing the CAP share the common and essential characteristic of all Community legislation, namely supremacy over all forms of national legislation of the EEC member states, it follows that problems will arise where there is a conflict between the agricultural legislation of the United Kingdom, or any other member state, and that of the European Community. The following cases serve to illustrate the range of problems that have involved aspects of the CAP:

- the most obvious case is *Pigs Marketing Board (NI)* v *Redmond*[1] where the Northern Ireland legislation applicable to the movement and marketing of bacon pigs in the Province was found to be incompatible with the EEC Regulation on the common organisation of the market in pigmeat and with other provisions of the EEC Treaty;
- The recovery of monetary compensatory amounts (MCAs) by a United Kingdom beef exporter from the British Intervention Board for Agricultural Produce by reliance upon the wording of the relevant EEC Regulations;[2]

[1] [1978] ECR 2347; [1979] 1 CMLR 177.

[2] *British Beef Co Ltd* v *Intervention Board for Agricultural Produce* [1978] ECR 1347; [1978] 3 CMLR 47.

— the incompatibility of a national licensing system for bulb growers with an EEC Regulation establishing a common organisation of the market in live plants and horticultural products;[3]
— the fixing of maximum prices for certain foodstuffs as part of a member state's (in this particular case, Italy's) policy for controlling national inflation was regarded as improper intervention by that country in the overall aims of the European Community's agricultural policy;[4]
— the operation by a member state (France) of a quota system for imports of a particular agricultural product (in this case, bananas) was contrary to the general provisions of the EEC Treaty even in the absence of a common organisation of the market for that product.[5]

These cases demonstrate how national legislation of member states concerning the movement of agricultural products, or licences, quotas and fixed prices for such products was challenged successfully by private litigants relying upon the superiority of Community law. Since the vast majority of the EEC's detailed rules about the CAP are laid down by Regulations which as explained in Article 189 of the Treaty (see p 34 *ante*) are directly applicable in all of the member states and are binding in their entirety, individual litigants may rely upon these EEC Regulations before their local courts in order to challenge the compatibility of national law. In a local example, *Pigs Marketing Board (NI)* v *Redmond,* the defendant was prosecuted under the Movement of Pigs Regulations (Northern Ireland) 1972 for transporting bacon pigs within Northern Ireland without the proper authorisation required by these regulations. The regulations in question reinforced the monopoly the Board had over the sale of bacon pigs as producers had to register with the Board and sell to it. The defendant faced a possible fine and/or imprisonment and/or forfeiture of the pigs in question. In his defence he argued that the local regulations were incompatible with European Community law, in particular with EEC Regulation 2759/75 which established a common organisation of the market in pigmeat. On an Article 177 reference to the Court of Justice for a preliminary ruling, the Court upheld his argument and declared the Northern Ireland regulations incompatible with Community law.

3 *Officier van Justitie* v *Van Haaster* [1974] ECR 1123; [1974] 2 CMLR 521.

4 See *Russo* v *Aima* [1976] ECR 45; and see also the cases of *Tasca* [1976] ECR 291; [1977] 2 CMLR 183 and *Sadam* [1976] ECR 323; [1977] 2 CMLR 183.

5 See *Charmasson* v *Minister for Economic Affairs (for France)* [1975] ECR 1383; [1975] 2 CMLR 208. But *cf The Irish Creamery Milk Suppliers' Association* v *The Government of Ireland* [1981] ECR 735; [1981] 2 CMLR 455.

The Court ruled that:

> . . . a marketing system on a national or regional scale set up by the legislation of a Member State and administered by a body which, by means of compulsory powers vested in it, is empowered to control the sector of the market in question or part of it by measures such as subjecting the marketing of the goods to a requirement that the producer shall be registered with that body, the prohibition of any sale otherwise than to that body or through its agency on conditions determined by it, and the prohibition of all transport of the goods in question otherwise than subject to the authorisation of the body in question are to be considered as incompatible with the requirements of Articles 30 and 34 of the EEC Treaty and of Regulation 2759/75.[6]

Consequently the case against Redmond was dismissed and the Pigs Marketing Board had to re-organise itself to end its monopoly on the purchase of bacon pigs. As this case well demonstrates, Community law may provide a defence to a criminal charge imposed by domestic legislation upon a person producing or trading in agricultural produce, and so it is obviously important for such persons and their legal advisers to know where to find the EEC rules on agriculture.[7]

MAIN EEC RULES ON AGRICULTURE

When the EEC Treaty was drawn up in the mid-1950s, memories of food-carrying ships being blown up at sea and of food rationing in Europe, resulting from the Second World War, were fresh in people's minds. Indeed some food rationing still existed when the Treaty was drafted in 1955. The drafters of the Treaty were therefore well aware of the need for the European Economic Community to have a common policy on agriculture which would ensure stable and sufficient supplies of food within the EEC, giving good incomes to its farmers and food to its citizens at reasonable prices. Consequently "the adoption of a common policy in the sphere of agriculture" features early in the list of the Community's activities in Article 3 of the Treaty. Just how this policy on agriculture was to be developed is to be found in Articles 38 to 47 of the EEC Treaty which contain details for its implementation.

Article 38 makes clear that the Common Market shall extend to "agriculture and trade in agricultural products"; in other words it is not just industrial products that benefit from the free movement of goods within the Community but also agricultural products. "Agricultural products" are defined by Article 38(1) to include ". . . products of the soil, of stock-farming and of fisheries and products of first-stage processing directly related to these products". The products subject to the provisions of the CAP were listed in Annex II of the EEC Treaty and include all the main agricultural

6 [1978] ECR 2347, 2372-3.

7 See Plender, *A Practical Introduction to European Community Law* (1980) ch 9; Wyatt and Dashwood, *The Substantive Law of the EEC* (1980), ch 16. See also Hill, *The CAP: Past, Present and Future* (1984); Snyder, *Law of the Common Agricultural Policy* (1985).

products such as cereals, beef and milk. Furthermore, the Council of Ministers was empowered by Article 38(3) of the Treaty to add products to this list within two years of the entry into force of the EEC Treaty, *ie* before 31 December 1959.

The Council did in fact exercise this option by making Regulation 7a/59, adding products like ethyl alcohol to the list, but the Council did not publish this Regulation until 30 January 1961. Consequently, the validity of Regulation 7a/59 was challenged on the ground of its belatedness in *Hauptzollamt Bielefeld* v *König*[8] but the Court of Justice upheld its validity because the contents of the Regulation had been settled before expiry of the two year deadline so that its late publication had no significance. In this case the Court of Justice was also required to interpret the concept of "products of first-stage processing directly related" to agricultural products in Article 38(1) of the Treaty. The plaintiff company contended that the Council's inclusion of ethyl alcohol in the list of agricultural products was wrong because after its distillation it had to be diluted with water. The Court interpreted the phrase to include as agricultural products those with:

> . . . a *clear economic interdependence* between basic products and products resulting from a productive process, irrespective of the number of operations involved therein. Processed products which have undergone a productive process, the cost of which is such that the price of the basic agricultural raw materials becomes a completely marginal cost, are therefore excluded.[9]

Since the number of operations necessary to obtain the processed product was not critical, the fact that ethyl alcohol had to be diluted with water after distillation did not affect its classification as an agricultural product. On the other hand, if the cost of processing a product was so high that it made the price of the basic agricultural product remote, then the end product would not be considered as an "agricultural product". The net result is that a whole range of products from beef and cereals, to sheepmeat, flower bulbs, bananas, potatoes and ethyl alochol are regarded as agricultural products.

The basic idea of the drafters of the Treaty was that the member states would develop and operate common organisations of the markets in these agricultural products to replace their national organisations. The operation and development of the Common Market for these products was to be guided by a Common Agricultural Policy which was to be established among the member states. The aims, or objectives, of this Common Agricultural Policy were laid out for the member states by Article 39(1) of the EEC Treaty. These five aims are as follows:

(a) to increase agricultural productivity by promoting technical progress and by ensuring the rational development of agricultural production and the optimum utilisation of the factors of production, in particular labour;

8 [1974] ECR 607.

9 *Ibid* pp 618-9. Emphasis supplied.

(b) thus to ensure a fair standard of living for the agricultural community, in particular by increasing the individual earnings of persons engaged in agriculture;
(c) to stabilise markets;
(d) to assure the availability of supplies;
(e) to ensure that supplies reach consumers at reasonable prices.

In developing the CAP these aims have to be balanced by the Commission and Council of Ministers. This is not an easy task, especially since it is so hard to balance the desire to give a fair return to farmers against that of making food available at reasonable prices to the consumers.[10] As well as stipulating these five aims of the CAP, the EEC Treaty also required the Commission to convene a conference of the member states immediately after the EEC Treaty came into force. At this conference in Stresa in 1958 the ministers from the then six member states compared their agricultural policies and agreed upon a plan, "the Mansholt Plan", for the development of the CAP. With some amendments this plan was accepted and it was agreed that the implementation of the CAP would be guided by three overriding principles—Community preference, financial solidarity and market unity. Each of these principles merits some further explanation.

The principle of "Community preference" means that producers within the European Community are protected from competition from cheaper agricultural goods from producers outside the Community.[11] By imposing import levies on agricultural goods imported from non-EEC countries, the prices paid to the Community's farmers are not undercut. Import levies charged on such imported agricultural goods make up part of the Community's own financial resources. When agricultural products are being exported from the European Community "export refunds" may be paid to the EEC producers to compensate for any difference between the Community market price and a lower world price. These import levies and export refunds seek to ensure that the Community's producers have a preference over those outside the Community.

As regards the principle of "financial solidarity", member states agreed that there should be common funding for the CAP, rather than leaving each individual member state to pay for the agricultural sector in its own country. In fact one of the first things the Council of Ministers did after approving the plans for the CAP was to set up a fund, the European Agriculture Guidance and Guarantee Fund (better known perhaps by its French acronym, FEOGA), to finance the policy. FEOGA is divided into two sections. First there is the Guidance Section, which only accounts for about 6 per cent of spending on agriculture and goes towards funding the re-structuring and modernising of agricultural holdings throughout the European Community.

[10] See *eg Beus* v *Hauptzollamt München* [1968] ECR 83; [1968] CMLR 131. See also Wyatt and Dashwood, *The Substantive Law of the EEC* pp 210 *et seq.*
[11] *Ibid.*

There are now many grants, loans and subsidies available from the Guidance Section of FEOGA such as subsidies to farmers in less-favoured areas, which now include about 70 per cent of the Province. These grants etc are provided for by EEC Regulations and Directives and are published in the Official Journal of the European Communities, "L section". The Northern Ireland Department of Agriculture should be contacted for details of entitlement to such funding. Again it should be emphasised that if a person is eligible to claim such monies under EEC legislation, any conflicting Northern Ireland legislation or the lack of local implementing measures should not deprive the claimant of them.[12]

The other, larger section of FEOGA is the Guarantee Section. It is, as its title suggests, spent on guaranteeing to farmers within the European Community prices for cereals, beef and other agricultural products. In April or May each year the Council of Ministers fixes what are called the "target prices" for various agricultural products. These prices represent the best price a farmer could get for his particular products within the European Community. For example, the target price for cereals is calculated on the basis of what producers would receive for their cereals if sold at Duisburg, a German industrial centre with the greatest deficit for all cereals. The actual price that farmers will obtain in the open market will normally be below the target price (unless there are exceptionally bad harvests and cereals are scarce while demand is high). However if the price falls to a certain level, known as the "intervention price" (which is also fixed annually by the Council), then the EEC's intervention agencies will buy cereals from the producers. The "intervention price" for cereals is calculated as at Ormes in France, where there is the greatest surplus for cereals, plus the cost of transport to Duisburg. Moreover, to ensure that the prices paid to EEC farmers are not undermined by cheap imports of grain from outside the Community, the Council of Ministers also fixes a "threshold price" for foreign cereals coming into the European Community. The threshold price equals the "target price" less the transport costs between Rotterdam and Duisburg. Therefore if cereals from America, for example, coming into the EEC free of charge would cost less than this "threshold price" an import duty is levied on them to increase the price of that foreign grain. This maintains the principle of Community preference, mentioned above. This particular operation has greatly annoyed pig and cattle farmers in Northern Ireland since the Province is far from self-sufficient in cereals and so imports a great deal of its cereals, especially from America. The import levies on these cereals make animal feedstuffs very expensive for livestock producers in Northern Ireland.

[12] See *eg Commission* v *Italy (Re Premiums for Slaughtering Cows)* [1973] ECR 101; [1973] CMLR 439.

As well as this particular local problem, the operation of intervention prices means that farmers are guaranteed minimum prices for their produce no matter how much they produce, with the net result that the infamous mountains of cereals, beef etc are built up in intervention centres throughout the Community. Both the United Kingdom and Ireland have one intervention agency for all commodities. In the United Kingdom it is a special agency—the British Intervention Board for Agricultural Produce—whereas in Ireland the Department of Agriculture itself acts as the intervention agency. Other member states, such as France, have several different intervention bodies. The recent introduction of milk quotas and super-levies is a serious attempt to reduce the Community's over-production in this particular sector. The cost of guaranteed prices plus storage costs for millions of tonnes of surplus food within the European Community mean that the Guarantee Section of FEOGA accounts for the vast majority of Community expenditure. Overall, about 65 per cent of the Community's budget is spent on funding the Common Agricultural Policy. This is seen by the United Kingdom Government as wasteful and has been used by it as a bargaining counter for agricultural reform in return for its acceptance of an increase in the British contribution to the European Community's resources. At present the Community's financial resources comprise agricultural levies and customs duties on other goods imported from non-EEC countries together with a small percentage of Value Added Tax contributed annually by each member state. The United Kingdom agreed to a rise in the VAT contribution, from 1 to 1·4 per cent on condition, *inter alia,* that agricultural reforms would follow to make the CAP more efficient and cost-effective.

Finally, the principle of "market unity" means in this context that there should be uniform prices for agricultural products and free movement of these products throughout the Community. When the Council fixes agricultural prices in April or May each year, it does so in European Currency Units (ECUs) which are then translated, by means of their "green" equivalents, into national currencies. The value of these representative green pounds (or lire or francs etc) is also periodically fixed by the Council so that each national currency is valued at different amounts of ECUs. Moreover, if a member state's currency appreciates, or alternatively depreciates, in value, monetary compensatory amounts (MCAs) are charged or awarded on imports of agricultural products to try to even out the prices farmers are receiving throughout the European Community. By the introduction of the European Monetary System (EMS) in 1979, whereby the currencies of the member states are tied to a central rate against the ECU and only allowed to fluctuate by 2.25 per cent (or in Italy's case by 6 per cent), it was hoped that monetary compensatory awards could be phased out. However, since the United Kingdom did not join the EMS these awards are still payable on certain products traded between Northern Ireland and the Republic of Ireland.[13]

[13] See Hill, *The CAP: Past, Present and Future* (1984) on MCAs.

It is against a background of these three overriding principles of Community preference, financial solidarity and market unity that the Common Agricultural Policy has been implemented. The member states were required by Article 40(1) of the EEC Treaty to develop the CAP gradually during the transitional period and to bring it into force by the end of that period. In order to attain the aims of the CAP as set out in Article 39(1) of the Treaty, common organisations of agricultural markets had to be established. From 1962 onwards the Council of Ministers, therefore, set about creating common organisations of the markets (COMs) for those agricultural products listed in Annex II of the EEC Treaty as extended by Regulation 7a/59. The main structure of any common organisation of the market is established by a Council Regulation and the details of its operation worked out in further Regulations made by the Commission. It is assisted by Management Committees, set up for each of the main agricultural products and comprised of expert representatives from each of the member states. A common organisation of the market established by Council Regulation for various agricultural products may by virtue of Article 40(3) of the Treaty:

> . . . include all measures required to attain the objectives set out in Art. 39, in particular regulation of prices, aids for the production and marketing of the various products, storage and carry-over arrangements and common machinery for stabilising imports or exports.

Consequently, individual COMs for cereals, beef or other agricultural products may contain a combination of such measures as the Council of Ministers considers suitable for a particular product, including a price support system with target, intervention and threshold prices (as in the case of cereals discussed on p 194 *ante*) together with storage facilities for surpluses, minimum quality controls etc. Most COMs include some form of price support system.

It is worth noting that EEC Regulations are used to establish these common organisations of the markets to replace individual national organisations. Since Regulations have the peculiar characteristics of being binding in their entirety, directly applicable and of general application in all the member states, they are ideally suitable for establishing uniform common organisations for agricultural products throughout the Community. As the Court of Justice stressed in *Variola* v *Italian Minister of Finance* where Italy had tried to alter the date of entry into force of a Council Regulation on cereals:

> The direct application of a Regulation means that its entry into force and its application in favour of or against those subject to it are independent of any measure of reception into national law . . . Member States are under a duty not to obstruct the direct applicability inherent in Regulations and other rules of Community law.
>
> Strict compliance with this obligation is an indispensable condition of simultaneous and uniform application of Community Regulations throughout the Community.[14]

[14] [1973] ECR 981, 990.

In this case the Court was also emphatic about the duty of member states not to repeat an EEC Regulation on its statute book as that only disguises its true nature as Community, not domestic, law and hides its peculiar characteristic, namely its primacy over all other forms of domestic legislation. Similarly in *Hauptzollamt Hamburg* v *Bollmann* (the Turkey Tail case) where the German authorities tried to redefine the types of goods covered by a Council Regulation, the Court of Justice declared that because Regulations are:

> . . . directly applicable in all Member States, the latter, unless otherwise expressly provided, are precluded from taking steps, for the purposes of applying the Regulation, which are intended to alter its scope or supplement its provisions.
>
> . . . moreover the common organisations of the markets in agriculture . . . can only achieve their objectives if the provisions adopted for their realisation are applied in a uniform manner in all Member States. The descriptions of goods covered by these organisations must therefore have exactly the same range in Member States.[15]

Therefore, the Court went on to rule that, in accordance with the relevant Council Regulation, turkey rumps should be classified as "edible poultry offals" rather than "poultry cuts" since they are most akin to edible offals ". . . on the basis not only of their physical characteristics but also their use and commercial value".[16]

Clearly then, the United Kingdom authorities are precluded by EEC Regulations from altering the scope and application of any of the common organisations of the market in agricultural products established by the Council of Ministers and supplemented by the Commission. In fact the establishment of these COMs by Regulations for all the main agricultural products means that the freedom of member states to take national measures in the sphere of agriculture has been considerably limited. If one is confronted with a problem of how far the United Kingdom authorities can, for example, impose criminal sanctions for breaches of EEC agricultural Regulations or fix retail prices for basic foodstuffs or even impose special taxes on farmers, then one should consider the case law of the Court of Justice in this area. The Court has, in a series of cases, developed certain tests for establishing the compatibility of national measures with the EEC's common market organisations for agricultural products.[17]

The type of problem that can arise in this area is well illustrated by the 1974 case of *Officier van Justitie* v *Van Haaster*[18] where a Dutch bulb grower faced prosecution for breaching certain Dutch regulations that prohibited the cultivation of hyacinth bulbs except under licence. Van Haaster had no licence but he contended that the Dutch legislation was incompatible with a

[15] [1970] ECR 69, 79-80.

[16] *Ibid* p 80.

[17] See Blumental, "Implementing the CAP: Aspects of the Limitations on the Powers of Member States" (1984) 35 *NILQ* 28.

[18] *Op cit supra* n 3.

Council Regulation of 1968 establishing a common organisation of the market in live plants and horticultural products. On an Article 177 reference to the Court of Justice, the Dutch authorities argued that their legislation operated at a different stage in the economic process, namely the production stage, from the Community legislation which regulated the marketing stage. Nevertheless, the Court of Justice ruled that the Community measures, concerning the introduction of common quality standards for bulbs, aimed at encouraging the improvement of the quality of the products and the organisation of their production. The Court considered that the Community's ". . . quality norms, even if they were to cover only the marketing of the products, would nevertheless have a restrictive repercussion on the production stage".[19] The Court, therefore, concluded that this EEC Regulation, interpreted in the context of all the provisions establishing a common organisation of the market in live plants and horticultural products, excluded the existence of any national system aimed at quantitatively restricting the cultivation of one of the products, hyacinths, coming under the COM. As a result of this ruling, Van Haaster could have a complete defence to a criminal charge.

In order to establish whether or not national measures are compatible with Community legislation, the Court of Justice applies what may be called the golden rule in that:

> . . . [f]rom the moment that the Community adopts regulations under Article 40 of the [EEC] Treaty establishing a common organisation of the market in a specific sector the Member States are under *a duty not to take any measure which might create exemptions from them or affect them adversely.*[20]

This was the rule enunciated by the Court of Justice in 1977 in *Amsterdam Bulb* v *Produktschap voor Siergewässen,* a very useful and instructive case indeed. To check if national measures create exemptions or adversely affect EEC Regulations establishing a common organisation of a particular agricultural product, the Court explained that one should first ask if the national measure conflicts with the express provisions of the relevant Regulation. Even if it is compatible with its express provisions, one should then ask whether the national measure is in conflict with the aims and objectives of the EEC Regulation establishing the COM. Applying these tests in the *Amsterdam Bulb* case, the Court of Justice found that certain provisions of Dutch legislation, which created exemptions from the EEC Regulations regulating the common organisation of the market in live trees, plants and bulbs, and which also imposed export prices for flower bulbs of a smaller size than those permitted by the Regulations, could not be regarded as compatible with Community law since the Dutch measures conflicted with the express provisions of the Regulations. In this same case however,

[19] *Officier van Justitie* v *Van Haaster* [1974] 2 CMLR 521, 535.

[20] *Amsterdam Bulb BV* v *Produktschap voor Siergewassen* [1977] ECR 137, 147. Emphasis added.

the Court did uphold other Dutch legislation, providing specific sanctions for breaches of these EEC Regulations and also fixing minimum export prices for types of bulbs other than those covered by the Regulations, because that legislation did not conflict with the express provisions of the Community system nor with its aims and objectives.

From the *Amsterdam Bulb* case one can see that the Court of Justice's approach by no means condemns every national measure in the sphere of agriculture but only those which create exemptions or adversely affect the EEC Regulations establishing a common organisation of the market. If, for instance, the relevant EEC Regulations are silent about the sanctions to be imposed for their infringement, the member states are competent to adopt such sanctions as appear to them to be appropriate, including criminal sanctions.[21] Furthermore, in *Pigs Marketing Board (NI)* v *Redmond,* the Court of Justice made it clear that not only must the compatibility of national measures be tested against the express provisions and aims of the EEC Regulation establishing the common organisation of the market for a particular agricultural product, but the national measures must also be tested against provisions of the EEC Treaty itself. This is because, as the Court explained, those provisions of the EEC Treaty on the free movement of goods that required the abolition of customs duties and quantitative restrictions were often repeated verbatim in the EEC Regulations establishing a COM although it had become current practice not to insert in the consolidated text of agricultural Regulations any provisions that merely re-enacted the provisions of the EEC Treaty itself. Therefore, the Court of Justice will test the compatibility of national agricultural measures against the relevant EEC Regulation setting up a common organisation of the market and also against:

> . . . the provisions of the Treaty relating to the abolition of tariff and commercial barriers to intra-Community trade and in particular Articles 30 and 34 on the abolition of quantitative restrictions and of all measures having equivalent effect on imports and exports [which] are to be regarded as an *integral part* of the common organisation of the market.[22]

As explained above, when the Court applied these tests, it found that the Northern Ireland Pigs Marketing Board's monopoly over the marketing of bacon pigs in the Province was incompatible with the requirements of Articles 30 and 34 of the EEC Treaty and of Regulation 2759/75 on the common organisation of the market in pigmeat.

From the *Redmond* and *Van Haaster* cases one can understand why it can be so useful for individual litigants, facing prosecution under domestic agricultural legislation, to be able to challenge the validity of that legislation on the ground of its incompatibility with EEC agricultural legislation. A rather interesting and novel development along these lines occurred in the

[21] *Ibid* [1977] ECR 137, 150; [1977] 2 CMLR 218, 243.

[22] *PMB (NI)* v *Redmond* [1978] ECR 2347, 2371. Emphasis added.

recent joined cases of *The Irish Creamery Milk Suppliers' Association* v *The Government of Ireland* and *Boyle* v *An Taoiseach*.[23] In 1979, the Irish Government decided, as part of the national incomes policy designed to share out the tax burden more equally amongst the population, to impose a temporary excise duty of 2 per cent on fresh milk, live cattle, cereals and sugar beet. Some producers affected by this tax argued that it was contrary to the EEC Treaty provisions on the CAP and also to the common organisations of the markets for each of these products. The duty was payable by the exporter or the processing undertaking (the creameries, slaughter-houses, sugar factories or mills). If the exporter or processing undertaking had bought the product, he could deduct the amount of the duty from the price payable. The Irish High Court decided to refer to the Court of Justice for a preliminary ruling under Article 177, the question of whether a national tax, like the one in issue here, was compatible with the EEC Treaty and the relevant Regulations establishing COMs for milk, cereals, sugar-beet and beef. In a rather general statement, the Court of Justice declared that:

> . . . [t]he Common Agricultural Policy is not intended . . . to shield those engaged in agriculture from the effects of a national incomes policy. Moreover, the fixing of common prices within the framework of the common organisations of markets does not serve to guarantee to agricultural producers a net price independently of any taxation imposed by the national authorities . . . It follows that a national tax such as that at issue in the present case is not, in itself, contrary to the Community rules on the common organisation of markets.[24]

Nevertheless, the Court went on to hold that the methods used to implement a national incomes policy, which affect farmers, would be incompatible with the EEC Treaty and with the Regulations establishing common organisations of markets if those methods interfered with the functioning of the machinery used by those market organisations to achieve their aims. Rather than rule on the sensitive point of a member state's right to impose internal taxation, the Court of Justice declared that it was for the national court to decide whether the tax had in fact had effects that obstructed the working of the machinery establishing the common organisations of the markets in beef, cereals, milk and sugar-beet. As guidance for the Irish High Court, the Court of Justice explained that the machinery of the COMs might be jeopardised by national measures that had "an appreciable influence, even if unintentionally, on price levels on the national market"[25] at the production or wholesale stages, which these particular common organisations tried to guarantee, or on supplies on the national market. To decide if the tax had an "appreciable influence", the national court should look at the rate of the tax, the length of time it was in force, and also how general or specific it was, because a short-term tax on a

23 [1981] ECR 735; [1981] 2 CMLR 455.

24 *Ibid* [1981] 2 CMLR 455, 474.

25 *Ibid* p 476.

large range of agricultural products might have a "neutral" effect in that it would not alter the structure of agricultural production. On the other hand, if it was a long-term tax on only specific types of product, then such a duty would be liable to distort agricultural markets as farmers would swop their production into products that did not attract the tax.

When the Irish High Court subsequently applied this ruling, it held that only the 2 per cent levy imposed on cattle exporters in 1979 operated as an export duty and was, therefore, contrary to the EEC Treaty.[26] As for the other products, namely milk, cereals and sugar-beet, it was held that the tax was so low and was imposed for so short a period that it did not have an "appreciable influence" on the operation of the common organisations of these particular markets.

It would appear from *The Irish Creamery Milk Suppliers* case that the power of member states specifically to tax agricultural produce may in certain circumstances be curtailed by the Community's rules on agriculture. Certainly the legislative competence of member states to take unilateral measures fixing maximum prices for foodstuffs to counter inflation has been limited by the EEC's rules. In a series of Italian cases such as *Galli*[27] in 1975, the Court of Justice ruled that where EEC Regulations established common organisations of the markets which guaranteed minimum prices for producers, then any Italian legislation that interfered with that price by freezing the prices Italian producers could obtain for their produce would be incompatible with the COM.

From the case-law of the Court of Justice, it is clear that the existence of an EEC Regulation establishing a common organisation of the market for a particular agricultural product severely limits the scope for unilateral action by member states in that area. It seems that national agricultural measures will only be allowed to stand provided they are not in conflict with the express provisions of the Regulation nor its aims and objectives, nor in conflict with the EEC Treaty provisions on the free movement of goods. Therefore, if one is dealing with a problem concerning a particular agricultural product, one should always check the Official Journal of the European Communities, "L" section, for the relevant EEC Regulations establishing a COM for that product and also remember to consider the Articles of the Treaty on the free movement of goods.

Finally, it should be noted that there are now very few agricultural products for which a common organisation of the market has not yet been established by the Council of Ministers. Potatoes, bananas and ethyl alcohol are amongst the few not yet covered by a COM. Even in the case of these products, the member states are not free to regulate them irrespective of the Community's rules. It was established in 1974 in the important case of

26 Reported in *The Irish Times*, 27 April 1983.

27 [1975] ECR 47; [1975] 1 CMLR 211. See also the cases mentioned in n 4 *supra*.

Charmasson v *Minister for Economic Affairs and Finance*[28] that if, at the end of the transitional period, there was no common organisation of the market for a particular product then for trade in that product the member states must comply with the general provisions of the EEC Treaty on the free movement of goods. It followed that in this case, the imposition by the French authorities of import quotas for bananas, a product for which no COM had been established, was contrary to the Treaty provisions prohibiting such quotas.

[28] [1974] ECR 1383; [1975] 2 CMLR 208. See also *Commission* v *France (Re: Lamb Imports) Nos 1 and 2* [1979] ECR 2729: [1980] 1 CMLR 418 and; [1981] 3 CMLR 25 [1980] ECR 1 319.

CHAPTER 18

PROTECTION OF HUMAN RIGHTS BY COMMUNITY LAW

Judging by media reports and by comments of various individuals in Northern Ireland, there is still a great deal of confusion about the different roles of the European Community and the European human rights organisations based in Strasbourg. For instance, when the homosexual laws in Northern Ireland were changed in December 1982, following the decision of the European Court of Human Rights in *Dudgeon* v *United Kingdom,*[1] the EEC was the organisation mistakenly regarded by many as responsible for bringing about changes in the laws of this Province. The EEC and its European Court of Justice in Luxembourg had nothing whatever to do with the *Dudgeon* case. That case concerned a violation of the European Convention on Human Rights and was decided by the European Court of Human Rights in Strasbourg. In the light of such confusion it would be useful first to distinguish between the EEC Treaty and the European Convention on Human Rights and then to consider if and how European Community law protects fundamental human rights.

As mentioned in Chapter 1 *ante,* the European Convention for the Protection of Human Rights and Fundamental Freedoms (often referred to as the ECHR) was drawn up in 1950 (some years before the EEC Treaty of 1957) under the auspices of the Council of Europe, an international organisation now comprising twenty-one Western European countries including all the EEC countries plus others such as Iceland, Cyprus, Sweden and Turkey. All of the member states of the European Community have signed and ratified the Convention; the United Kingdom ratified it as long ago as 1951. It guarantees certain baisc fundamental human rights and is enforced by the European Commission of Human Rights, the European Court of Human Rights and a Committee of Ministers, all of which are based in Strasbourg.[2] Despite the similarity of their names, it must be emphasized that these human rights institutions are wholly distinct from those of the European Community.

Under British constitutional law, before an international treaty, like the European Convention on Human Rights, becomes part and parcel of the domestic law of the United Kingdom, it must be incorporated by an Act of

1 *Dudgeon* v *UK* [1982] 4 EHRR 149.

2 For further details see Beddard, *Human Rights in Europe* (2nd ed, 1983).

Parliament. Although the United Kingdom Government ratified the Convention in 1951 and is therefore bound by it at international level, there has been no statute passed by the Westminster Parliament making the Convention an integral part of the United Kingdom's domestic law. Consequently, in the United Kingdom the Convention does not give rise to direct rights that may be enforced before United Kingdom courts and none of those courts would give precedence to the Convention in case of conflict with British statutes. Instead, an individual within the jurisdiction of the United Kingdom must bring proceedings before the European Commission and, if his complaint is admissible, eventually before the European Court of Human Rights in Strasbourg if he considers himself a victim of a violation of rights guaranteed to him by the Convention. All applications, whether brought by states party to the Convention or by individuals, must first go to the European Commission of Human Rights, which decides if the application is admissible. If it is, and the Commission finds that there is a violation, it must first seek a friendly settlement between the parties. Failing this, it may then refer the case to the Court within three months, if the state involved accepts the right of individual petition to the Court, or else to the Committee of Ministers for a decision. If the European Court of Human Rights gives judgment against the United Kingdom, as in the *Dudgeon* case, the United Kingdom Government is bound by Article 53 of the Convention to comply with that judgment. The Government may comply in various ways such as introducing new legislation like that introduced after the *Dudgeon* decision, the Homosexual Offences (Northern Ireland) Order 1982, or by changing domestic administrative procedures found to be in breach of the Convention. Although the Convention has not been incorporated into United Kingdom domestic law, some British courts have, nevertheless, used the Convention as an aid to statutory interpretation as there is a *prima facie* presumption that the Westminster Parliament does not intend to act in breach of international obligations.[3]

By comparison with the European Convention on Human Rights, the EEC Treaty has a very different status in the United Kingdom for the EEC Treaty has been incorporated into the internal law of the country by the European Communities Act 1972. As part and parcel of the law of the United Kingdom, European Community law can therefore give rise to direct rights that may be enforced before the local courts and tribunals. This is a most important point as it means that United Kingdom courts may be faced with arguments about fundamental human rights[4] because the European

[3] See for example *Ahmad* v *ILEA* [1978] 1 All ER 574 and in N. Ireland see the statement by Lowry LCJ in *R* v *Deery* [1977] NI 164, 167. But *cf* the attitude of the Scottish courts in *Surjit Kaur* v *The Lord Advocate* [1981] SLT 322; [1980] 3 CMLR 79.

[4] See an article by Karpenstein & Crossick, "Pleading Human Rights in British Courts—the Impact of EEC Law" *The Law Society's Gazette* 28 January 1981, p 90.

Court of Justice in Luxembourg (not to be confused with the European Court of Human Rights) has declared that fundamental human rights are part of the general principles of Community law and are protected by it.

Initially it may seem surprising to find that the European Economic Community, concerned essentially with economic matters, should be involved in the protection of fundamental human rights. This view is strengthened when one looks at the EEC Treaty itself because in fact it contains very few provisions guaranteeing such rights.[5] Moreover, the Treaty has no general provision to the effect that in carrying out its activities the EEC should act in ways least likely to conflict with fundamental rights. Consequently, in the late 1950s and 1960s when the European Court of Justice was confronted with cases involving arguments about violations of fundamental rights, the Court rejected such cases as being outside the scope of its jurisdiction. This is, however, an area where the Court of Justice, not being bound by precedent, has changed its views.

In 1969 the Court of Justice, for the first time, was prepared to admit that fundamental rights were protected by Community law. The case, *Stauder* v *City of Ulm*,[6] involved a West German pensioner, who challenged the validity of an EEC Commission Decision which compelled him to disclose his name in order to obtain a voucher entitling him to cheap butter. He claimed that the Decision infringed his human dignity, which is protected as a fundamental right in West Germany. On an Article 177 reference, the Court of Justice ruled that the problem had arisen because the German translation of the Decision was much stricter than that of the other official translations and so could be resolved if the German authorities gave it a more liberal construction that did not involve identification of the claimant by name. Although that resolved the case, the Court of Justice, nevertheless, concluded its ruling by declaring that:

> . . . fundamental human rights [are] enshrined in the general principles of Community law and protected by the Court.[7]

The inclusion of this concluding statement reflects a certain amount of sympathy in the Court for the views expressed in the case.

This decision was followed in 1970 by the landmark case of *Internationale Handelsgesellschaft* v *EVST*[8] where the Court of Justice reiterated the point that:

> . . . respect for fundamental rights forms an integral part of the general principles of law protected by the Court of Justice. The protection of such rights whilst inspired by the constitutional traditions common to the Member States must be ensured within the framework of the Community's structure and objectives.[9]

[5] See *eg*, Arts 7, 48, 52 and 119 of the EEC Treaty.

[6] [1969] ECR 419; [1970] CMLR 112.

[7] *Ibid* [1969] ECR 419, 425.

[8] [1970] ECR 1125; [1972] CMLR 255.

[9] *Ibid* [1972] CMLR 255, 283.

In other words, while the level of protection given to fundamental rights by the Court was inspired by the standards common to the member states, the Court would, nevertheless, measure the protection Community law offers such rights against the overall best interests of the European Community. Thus, for example, in this particular case where a German exporter of cereals complained that two EEC Regulations, providing for the forfeiture of deposits if export licences were not fully used up, were invalid as they infringed certain fundamental rights guaranteed by the German constitution, the Court of Justice concluded that the deposit system was necessary to regulate the cereal market within the European Community. Therefore the Regulations in question did not, in the Court's opinion, infringe any fundamental rights. This ruling did in fact give rise to considerable unease and criticism in the West German courts, including the Federal Constitutional Court which subsequently called, *inter alia,* for a catalogue of fundamental rights to be adopted by the EEC.

Since the *Internationale* case the Court of Justice has gone on to state that it would annul a Community measure if it conflicted with the fundamental rights protected by the Court.[10] Therefore, amongst the four grounds for annulment of an act of the Council of Ministers or EEC Commission specified in Article 173 of the EEC Treaty (discussed in Chapter 8 *ante*), the violation of fundamental rights is included in the third ground, namely infringement of the EEC Treaty or of any rule of law relating to its application.

As regards the determination of the particular kinds of fundamental rights protected by the Court of Justice, subsequent cases show that the Court draws not only upon the constitutional traditions common to the member states but also upon:

> . . . international treaties for the protection of human rights on which the Member States have collaborated or of which they are signatories, [as they] can supply guidelines which should be followed within the framework of Community law.[11]

Since all member states of the European Community have signed and ratified the European Convention on Human Rights, it is hardly surprising that the Convention is the international treaty which has subsequently given the Court of Justice particular guidelines. For instance, in *Rutili* v *Minister for the Interior for France*[12] the Court of Justice referred specifically to Article 11 of the European Convention on Human Rights, guaranteeing the right to join trade unions and participate in their activities. In this case an Italian national, resident and working in France and a trade union activist, had challenged residence restrictions imposed upon him, excluding him from certain departments of France. He argued that they conflicted with his rights under EEC law as a migrant Community worker. The Court

[10] See *Nold* v *Commission* [1974] ECR 491; [1974] 2 CMLR 338.

[11] *Ibid* [1974] ECR 491, 507.

[12] [1975] ECR 1219; [1976] 1 CMLR 140.

concluded from the Convention that since rights guaranteed therein were not always absolute (as limitations could be imposed by a country if necessary) then similarly restrictions were also permissible under Community law in certain very limited circumstances.

Since the Court of Justice has begun to use the ECHR for guidance, applicants have increasingly relied upon it to impugn EEC measures. For example, in *Prais* v *Council*[13] Article 9 of the European Convention on Human Rights, guaranteeing freedom of religion, was invoked before the Court of Justice by a Jewish woman in order to challenge the validity of a Council Decision refusing to change the date of an examination as it coincided with a Jewish religious holiday. She felt it discriminated against her on religious grounds. More recently in a German case, *Hauer* v *Land Rheinland—Pfalz*[14] and in the English case of *National Panasonic (UK) Ltd* v *Commission*[15] various Articles of the European Convention have been pleaded before the Court of Justice to impugn the validity of certain provisions of Community law. In the *Hauer* case the applicant complained that certain EEC Regulations infringed Article 1 of the First Protocol to the European Convention, guaranteeing the peaceful enjoyment of one's possessions. Hauer had been prevented from planting new vines on her property by EEC Regulations, which were part of the Community's effort to reduce the "wine lake". The *National Panasonic* case concerned the powers of the EEC Commission officials to investigate the books and records of a business without giving it prior notice. The company felt that this action was contrary to Article 8 of the European Convention on Human Rights, protecting the right to privacy of one's correspondence.

In all these cases the Court of Justice upheld the validity of the individual Community measure that was being challenged. The Court felt that the overall objectives of the European Community justified certain limitations upon the fundamental freedoms of the individual. To date the Court of Justice has never annulled a Community measure on the ground that it infringes fundamental rights. This has given rise to some scepticism and so other methods have been mooted to try to improve upon the present level of protection of fundamental rights by Community law. One method would be the adoption by the EEC of its own written code of fundamental rights. This is not a new idea as it was called for by the European Parliament in 1975 and, as mentioned above, by the Federal Constitutional Court in 1974 following the *Internationale* ruling by the Court of Justice.[16] Such a code would have many advantages in that it would be more up-to-date than the European Convention on Human Rights, reflecting the importance of social and economic rights within an essentially economic Community. Moreover, as part of Community law, the code would be enforced directly by individuals

[13] [1975] ECR 1589; [1976] 2 CMLR 708.

[14] [1979] ECR 3727; [1980] 3 CMLR 42.

[15] [1980] ECR 2033; [1980] 3 CMLR 169; [1981] 2 All ER 1. See p 168 *ante* for details.

[16] [1974] 2 CMLR 540.

before the national courts of member states or the Court of Justice as appropriate.[17] However desirable, realistically it must be said that agreement between the member states upon the content of such a code would take a considerable amount of time and may not even be politically acceptable to some of the countries.

Consequently, the most-favoured method of protecting human rights within the EEC context now seems to be by the accession of the European Community itself to the European Convention on Human Rights. In a Memorandum of 4 April 1979[18] the EEC Commission recommended the accession of the Community to the European Convention as being:

> . . . the best way of replying to the need to reinforce the protection of fundamental rights at Community level at the present stage.[19]

It should be noted that although all of the member states of the EEC are parties to the Convention, it does not follow that the European Community itself is a party to the Convention. As may be recalled from *Costa* v *ENEL,*[20] the Court of Justice has stressed that the EEC has its own personality and its own legal capacity, and so is capable of entering into international agreements in its own right and has done so in international trading agreements like the Lomé Convention with developing countries. Since the European Community is not at present a party to the Convention, the European Commission and the European Court of Human Rights in Strasbourg have apparently no jurisdiction to hear applications about alleged breaches of fundamental rights by Community institutions.[21]

Discussions about the EEC Commission's Memorandum have already begun in the member states. Within the United Kingdom the House of Lords' Select Committee on the European Communities has considered the reasons for and against the proposed accession by the European Community to the European Convention on Human Rights. In the Committee's report of 21 October 1980, it concluded that such accession would present many technical difficulties and be largely symbolic rather than afford any real protection and that fundamental rights would best be protected by supporting the jurisprudence of the Court of Justice at Luxembourg and by increasing the resources of the human rights organisations in Strasbourg.[22]

[17] For a more detailed analysis see Paisley, "A Stitch in Time to Save the Nine: A Code of Fundamental Rights for the EEC" (1980) 31 *NILQ* 267.

[18] See Bulletin of the European Communities (1979), Supp 2/79.

[19] *Ibid* p 5.

[20] [1964] ECR 585; [1964] CMLR 425. See also Art 210, EEC Treaty.

[21] See *eg CFDT* v *The European Communities* [1979] 2 CMLR 229 where a complaint brought by a French trade union was declared inadmissible by the European Commission of Human Rights in respect of the Community itself, individual member states of the Community and the Council of Ministers. In the complaint it was alleged that the Council of Ministers had violated certain provisions of the European Convention on Human Rights.

[22] 71st Report, Session 1979-80, HL 362.

Subsequent debate of this report in the House of Lords showed little support for the Commission's proposal[23] and the United Kingdom Government has not yet expressed enthusiasm for accession by the EEC to the Convention.[24]

For the foreseeable future, therefore, fundamental rights will remain protected within the general principles of Community law by the Court of Justice. Moreover, in a Joint Declaration of 5 April 1977 the other Community institutions, the European Parliament, the Commission and the Council of Ministers, stressed:

> . . . the prime importance they attach to the protection of fundamental rights as derived in particular from the constitutions of the Member States and the European Convention for the Protection of Human Rights and Fundamental Freedoms. In the exercise of their powers and in pursuance of the aims of the European Communities they respect and will continue to respect these rights.[25]

While this Joint Declaration is not a legally binding act, it is nevertheless very significant as it was the first public acceptance by all the other institutions of the European Community of their desire to respect fundamental rights, especially those contained in the European Convention on Human Rights.

At present it seems that someone in Northern Ireland, aggrieved by a particular measure of Community law—like a farmer, who feels that the EEC Regulations, imposing a milk quota on him, have interfered with the use he makes of his property—could challenge the validity of those Regulations before a Northern Ireland court on the ground that they infringe his fundamental rights, in this instance Article 1 of the First Protocol to the European Convention on Human Rights. Since national courts have no power to determine the validity of a Community measure and the Court of Justice alone has jurisdiction to decide if an act of a Community institution is void, an Article 177 reference would be appropriate. The Court of Justice would have to rule upon the compatibility of the Regulations with the relevant provisions of the European Convention on Human Rights. This important aspect of the jurisprudence of the Court of Justice should not be overlooked. As well as human rights, other rights included within the "general principles of Community law" protected by the Court include the principle of proportionality, *audi alteram partem,* non-discrimination, equality and *nulla poena sine lege.*[26]

23 Session 1981-82, HL, 1348.

24 For a discussion of the advantages and disadvantages of accession by the EEC to the ECHR see Schermers, "The Communities under the European Convention on Human Rights" (1978) 1*LIEI* 1. See also an article by Ehlermann in Campbell (ed) *Do we Need a Bill of Rights?* (1980).

25 (OJ 1977 C 103/1).

26 See p 42 *ante* on "General principles of Community Law". See also Wyatt and Dashwood, *The Substantive Law of the EEC* (1980) pp 48-52.

APPENDIX I

THE RULES OF THE SUPREME COURT (NORTHERN IRELAND) 1980

Order 114

REFERENCES TO THE EUROPEAN COURT

Interpretation

1. In this Order—

"the Court" means the court by which an order is made and includes the Court of Appeal;

"the European Court" means the Court of Justice of the European Communities; and "order" means an order referring a question to the European Court for a preliminary ruling under Article 177 of the Treaty establishing the European Economic Community, Article 150 of the Treaty establishing the European Atomic Energy Community or Article 41 of the Treaty establishing the European Coal and Steel Community.

Making of order

2. (1) An order may be made by the Court of its own motion at any stage in a cause or matter, or on application by a party before or at the trial or hearing thereof.

(2) Where an application is made before the trial or hearing, it shall be made by motion.

(3) In the High Court no order shall be made except by a judge in person.

Schedule to order to set out request for ruling

3. An order shall set out in a schedule the request for the preliminary ruling of the European Court, and the Court may give directions as to the manner and form in which the schedule is to be prepared.

Stay of proceedings pending ruling

4. The proceedings in which an order is made shall, unless the Court otherwise orders, be stayed until the European Court has given a preliminary ruling on the question referred to it.

Transition of order to the European Court

5. When an order has been made, the Master (Queen's Bench and Appeals) shall send a copy thereof to the Registrar of the European Court: but in the case of an order made by the High Court, he shall not do so, unless the Court otherwise orders, until the time for appealing against the order has expired or, if an appeal is entered within that time, until the appeal has been determined or otherwise disposed of.

Appeals from orders made by High Court

6. An order made by the High Court shall be deemed to be a final decision and accordingly an appeal against it shall be to the Court of Appeal without leave; but the period within which a notice of appeal must be served under Order 59, rule 4(1) shall be 21 days.

APPENDIX II

COUNTY COURT RULES (NORTHERN IRELAND) 1981

Order 23

REFERENCES TO THE EUROPEAN COURT

Interpretation

1. "the European Court" means the Court of Justice of the European Communities; and

"order" means an order referring to the European Court for a preliminary ruling under Article 177 of the Treaty establishing the European Economic Community, Article 150 of the Treaty establishing the European Atomic Energy Community or Article 41 of the Treaty establishing the European Coal and Steel Community.

Making an order

2. (1) The Court may make the order at any stage in the course of action or matter whether of its own motion or on application by a party before or at the hearing thereof.

(2) Where an application for an order is made before the hearing nothing in Rule 1 of Order 14 shall be construed as authorising the hearing of the application other than by the judge in person and that Rule shall apply accordingly.

Schedule to order to set out request for ruling

3. An order shall be in Form 109 and shall set out in a schedule the request for the preliminary ruling of the European Court and the Court may give directions as to the manner and form in which the schedule is to be prepared.

Stay of proceedings pending ruling

4. The proceedings in which an order is made shall, unless the court otherwise orders, be stayed until the European Court has given a preliminary ruling on the question referred to it.

Transmission of order to the European Court

5. When an order has been made the chief clerk shall send a copy thereof to the parties and to the Registrar of the European Court; but, where there is a right of appeal against the order he shall not do so, unless the court otherwise orders, until the time for appealing has expired or, as the case may be, until any appeal has been decided or disposed of.

APPENDIX III

ARTICLE 85 OF THE EEC TREATY

(1) The following shall be prohibited as incompatible with the common market: all agreements between undertakings, decisions by associations of undertakings and concerted practices which may affect trade between Member States and which have as their object or effect the prevention, restriction or distortion of competition within the common market, and in particular those which:

(a) directly or indirectly fix purchase or selling prices or any other trading conditions;

(b) limit or control production, markets, technical development, or investment;

(c) share markets or sources of supply;

(d) apply dissimilar conditions to equivalent transactions with other trading parties, thereby placing them at a competitive disadvantage;

(e) make the conclusion of contracts subject to acceptance by the other parties of supplementary obligations which, by their nature or according to commercial usage, have no connection with the subject of such contracts.

(2) Any agreements or decisions prohibited pursuant to this Article shall be automatically void.

(3) The provisions of paragraph (1) may, however, be declared inapplicable in the case of:

— any agreement or category of agreements between undertakings;

— any decision or category of decisions by associations of undertakings;

— any concerted practice or category of concerted practices;

which contributes to improving the production or distribution of goods or to promoting technical or economic progress, while allowing consumers a fair share of the resulting benefit, and which does not:

(a) impose on the undertakings concerned restrictions which are not indispensable to the attainment of these objectives;

(b) afford such undertakings the possibility of eliminating competition in respect of a substantial part of the products in question.

APPENDIX IV

ARTICLE 86 OF THE EEC TREATY

Any abuse by one or more undertakings of a dominant position within the common market or in a substantial part of it shall be prohibited as incompatible with the common market in so far as it may affect trade between Member States. Such abuse may, in particular, consist in:

(a) directly or indirectly imposing unfair purchase or selling prices or unfair trading conditions;

(b) limiting production, markets or technical development to the prejudice of consumers;

(c) applying dissimilar conditions to equivalent transactions with other trading parties, thereby placing them at a competitive disadvantage;

(d) making the conclusion of contracts subject to acceptance by the other parties of supplementary obligations which, by their nature or according to commercial usage, have no connection with the subject of such contracts.

APPENDIX V

COMPETITION

Regulation No 17[1]

First Regulation implementing Arts. 85 and 86 of the Treaty

The Council of the European Economic Community,

Having regard to the Treaty establishing the European Economic Community, and in particular Art. 87 thereof;

Having regard to the proposal from the Commission;

Having regard to the Opinion of the Economic and Social Committee;

Having regard to the Opinion of the European Parliament;

Whereas, in order to establish a system ensuring that competition shall not be distorted in the common market, it is necessary to provide for balanced application of Arts. 85 and 86 in a uniform manner in the Member States;

Whereas in establishing the rules for applying Art. 85 (3) account must be taken of the need to ensure effective supervision and to simplify administration to the greatest possible extent;

Whereas it is accordingly necessary to make it obligatory, as a general principle, for undertakings which seek application of Art. 85 (3) to notify to the Commission their agreements, decisions and concerted practices;

Whereas, on the one hand, such agreements, decisions and concerted practices are probably very numerous and cannot therefore all be examined at the same time and, on the other hand, some of them have special features which may make them less prejudicial to the development of the common market;

Whereas there is consequently a need to make more flexible arrangements for the time being in respect of certain categories of agreement, decision and concerted practice without prejudging their validity under Art. 85;

Whereas it may be in the interest of undertakings to know whether any agreements, decisions or practices to which they are party, or propose to become party, may lead to action on the part of the Commission pursuant to Art. 85 (1) or Art. 86;

Whereas, in order to secure uniform application of Arts. 85 and 86 in the common market, rules must be made under which the Commission, acting in close and constant liaison with the competent authorities of the Member States, may take the requisite measures for applying those Articles;

Whereas for this purpose the Commission must have the co-operation of the competent authorities of the Member States and be empowered, throughout the common market, to require such information to be supplied and to undertake such investigations as are necessary to bring to light any agreement, decision or concerted practice prohibited by Art. 85 (1) or any abuse of a dominant position prohibited by Art. 86;

Whereas, in order to carry out its duty of ensuring that the provisions of the Treaty are applied, the commission must be empowered to address to undertakings or associations of undertakings recommendations and decisions for the purpose of bringing to an end infringements of Arts. 85 and 86;

Whereas compliance with Arts. 85 and 86 and the fulfilment of obligations imposed on undertakings and associations of undertakings under this Regulation must be enforceable by means of fines and periodic penalty payments;

Whereas undertakings concerned must be accorded the right to be heard by the Commission, third parties whose interests may be affected by a decision must be given the opportunity of submitting their comments beforehand, and it must be ensured that wide publicity is given to decisions taken;

Whereas all decisions taken by the Commission under this Regulation are subject to review by the Court of Justice under the conditions specified in the Treaty; whereas it is moreover desirable to confer upon the Court of Justice, pursuant to Art. 172, unlimited jurisdiction in respect of decisions under which the Commission imposes fines or periodic penalty payments;

Whereas this Regulation may enter into force without prejudice to any other provisions that may hereafter be adopted pursuant to Art. 87;

Has adopted this Regulation:

ART. 1. Basic provision

Without prejudice to Arts. 6, 7 and 23 of this Regulation, agreements, decisions and concerted practices of the kind described in Art. 85 (1) of the Treaty and the abuse of a dominant position in the market, within the meaning of Art. 86 of the Treaty, shall be prohibited, no prior decision to that effect being required.

ART. 2. Negative clearance

Upon application by the undertakings or associations of undertakings concerned, the Commission may certify that, on the basis of the facts in its possession, there are no grounds under Art. 85 (1) or Art. 86 of the Treaty for action on its part in respect of an agreement, decision or practice.

ART. 3. Termination of infringements

1. Where the Commission, upon application or upon its own initiative, finds that there is infringement of Art. 85 or Art. 86 of the Treaty, it may by decision require the undertakings or associations of undertakings concerned to bring such infringement to an end.

2. Those entitled to make application are:

(a) Member States;

(b) natural or legal persons who claim a legitimate interest.

3. Without prejudice to the other provisions of this Regulation, the Commission may, before taking a decision under paragraph 1, address to the undertakings or associations of undertakings concerned recommendations for termination of the infringement.

ART. 4. Notification of new agreements, decisions and practices

1. Agreements, decisions and concerted practices of the kind described in Art. 85 (1) of the Treaty which come into existence after the entry into force of this Regulation and in respect of which the parties seek application of Art. 85 (3) must be notified to the Commission. Until they have been notified, no decision in application of Art. 85 (3) may be taken.

2. Paragraph 1 shall not apply to agreements, decisions or concerted practices where:

(1) the only parties thereto are undertakings from one Member State and the agreements, decisions or practices do not relate either to imports or to exports between Member States;

(2) not more than two undertakings are party thereto, and the agreements only:

  (a) restrict the freedom of one party to the contract in determining the prices or conditions of business upon which the goods which he has obtained from the other party to the contract may be resold; or

  (b) impose restrictions on the exercise of the rights of the assignee or user of industrial property rights—in particular patents, utility models, designs or trade marks—or of the person entitled under a contract to the assignment, or grant, of the right to use a method of manufacture or knowledge relating to the use and to the application of industrial processes;

(3) they have as their sole object:
   (a) the development or uniform application of standards or types; or
   (b) joint research and development;
   (c) specialisation in the manufacture of products, including agreements necessary for achieving this,
      — where the products which are the subject of specialisation do not, in a substantial part of the common market, represent more than 15% of the volume of business done in identical products or those considered by consumers to be similar by reason of their characteristics, price and use,
      and
      — where the total annual turnover of the participating undertakings does not exceed 200 million units of account.

These agreements, decisions and practices may be notified to the Commission.

ART. 5. Notification of existing agreements, decisions and practices

1. Agreements, decisions and concerted practices of the kind described in Art. 85 (1) of the Treaty which are in existence at the date of entry into force of this Regulation and in respect of which the parties seek application of Art. 85 (3) shall be notified to the Commission before 1 November 1962. However, notwithstanding the foregoing provisions, any agreements, decisions and concerted practices to which not more than two undertakings are party shall be notified before 1 February 1963.

2. Paragraph 1 shall not apply to agreements, decisions or concerted practices falling within Art. 4 (2); these may be notified to the Commission.

ART. 6. Decisions pursuant to Art. 85 (3)

1. Whenever the Commission takes a decision pursuant to Art. 85 (3) of the Treaty, it shall specify therein the date from which the decision shall take effect. Such date shall not be earlier than the date of notification.

2. The second sentence of paragraph 1 shall not apply to agreements, decisions or concerted practices falling within Art. 4 (2) and Art. 5 (2), nor to those falling within Art. 5 (1) which have been notified within the time limit specified in Art. 5 (1).

ART. 7. Special provisions for existing agreements, decisions and practices

1. Where agreements, decisions and concerted practices in existence at the date of entry into force of this Regulation and notified within the time limits specified in Art. 5 (1) do not satisfy the requirements of Art. 85 (3) of the Treaty and the undertakings or associations of undertakings concerned cease to give effect to them or modify them in such manner that they no longer fall within the prohibition contained in Art. 85 (1) or that they satisfy the requirements of Art. 85 (3), the prohibition contained in Art. 85 (1) shall apply only for a period fixed by the Commission. A decision by the Commission pursuant to the foregoing sentence shall not apply as against undertakings and associations of undertakings which did not expressly consent to the notification.

2. Paragraph 1 shall apply to agreements, decisions and concerted practices falling within Art. 4 (2) which are in existence at the date of entry into force of this Regulation if they are notified before 1 January 1967.

ART. 8. Duration and revocation of decisions under Art. 85 (3)

1. A decision in application of Art. 85 (3) of the Treaty shall be issued for a specified period and conditions and obligations may be attached thereto.

2. A decision may on application be renewed if the requirements of Art. 85 (3) of the Treaty continue to be satisfied.

3. The Commission may revoke or amend its decision or prohibit specified acts by the parties:

(a) where there has been a change in any of the facts which were basic to the making of the decision;

(b) where the parties commit a breach of any obligation attached to the decision;

(c) where the decision is based on incorrect information or was induced by deceit;

(d) where the parties abuse the exemption from the provisions of Art. 85 (1) of the Treaty granted to them by the decision.

In cases to which subparagraphs (b), (c) or (d) apply, the decision may be revoked with retroactive effect.

ART. 9. Powers

1. Subject to review of its decision by the Court of Justice, the Commission shall have sole power to declare Art. 85 (1) inapplicable pursuant to Art. 85 (3) of the Treaty.

2. The Commission shall have power to apply Art. 85 (1) and Art. 86 of the Treaty; this power may be exercised notwithstanding that the time limits specified in Art. 5 (1) and in Art. 7 (2) relating to notification have not expired.

3. As long as the Commission has not initiated any procedure under Arts. 2, 3 or 6, the authorities of the Member States shall remain competent to apply Art. 85 (1) and Art. 86 in accordance with Art. 88 of the Treaty; they shall remain competent in this respect notwithstanding that the time limits specified in Art. 5 (1) and in Art. 7 (2) relating to notification have not expired.

ART. 10. Liaison with the authorities of the Member States

1. The Commission shall forthwith transmit to the competent authorities of the Member States a copy of the application and notifications together with copies of the most important documents lodged with the Commission for the purpose of establishing the existence of infringements of Arts. 85 or 86 of the Treaty or of obtaining negative clearance or a decision in application of Art. 85 (3).

2. The Commission shall carry out the procedure set out in paragraph 1 in close and constant liaison with the competent authorities of the Member States; such authorities shall have the right to express their views upon that procedure.

3. An Advisory Committee on Restrictive Practices and Monopolies shall be consulted prior to the taking of any decision following upon a procedure under paragraph 1, and of any decision concerning the renewal, amendment or revocation of a decision pursuant to Art. 85 (3) of the Treaty.

4. The Advisory Committee shall be composed of officials competent in the matter of restrictive practices and monopolies. Each Member State shall appoint an official to represent it who, if prevented from attending, may be replaced by another official.

5. The consultation shall take place at a joint meeting convened by the Commission; such meeting shall be held not earlier than fourteen days after dispatch of the notice convening it. The notice shall, in respect of each case to be examined, be accompanied by a summary of the case together with an indication of the most important documents, and a preliminary draft decision.

6. The Advisory Committee may deliver an opinion notwithstanding that some of its members or their alternates are not present. A report of the outcome of the consultative proceedings shall be annexed to the draft decision. It shall not be made public.

ART. 11. Request for information

1. In carrying out the duties assigned to it by Art. 89 and by provisions adopted under Art. 87 of the Treaty, the Commission may obtain all necessary information from the Governments

and competent authorities of the Member States and from undertakings and associations of undertakings.

2. When sending a request for information to an undertaking or association of undertakings, the Commission shall at the same time forward a copy of the request to the competent authority of the Member State in whose territory the seat of the undertaking or association of undertakings is situated.

3. In its request the Commission shall state the legal basis and the purpose of the request and also the penalties provided for in Art. 15 (1) (b) for supplying incorrect information.

4. The owners of the undertakings or their representatives and, in the case of legal persons, companies or firms, or of associations having no legal personality, the persons authorised to represent them by law or by their constitution shall supply the information requested.

5. Where an undertaking or association of undertakings does not supply the information requested within the time limit fixed by the Commission, or supplies incomplete information, the Commission shall by decision require the information to be supplied. The decision shall specify what information is required, fix an appropriate time limit within which it is to be supplied and indicate the penalties provided for in Art. 15 (1) (b) and Art. 16 (1) (c) and the right to have the decision reviewed by the Court of Justice.

6. The Commission shall at the same time forward a copy of its decision to the competent authority of the Member State in whose territory the seat of the undertaking or association of undertakings is situated.

ART. 12. Inquiry into sectors of the economy

1. If in any sector of the economy the trend of trade between Member States, price movements, inflexibility of prices or other circumstances suggest that in the economic sector concerned competition is being restricted or distorted within the common market, the Commission may decide to conduct a general inquiry into that economic sector and in the course thereof may request undertakings in the sector concerned to supply the information necessary for giving effect to the principles formulated in Arts. 85 and 86 of the Treaty and for carrying out the duties entrusted to the Commission.

2. The Commission may in particular request every undertaking or association of undertakings in the economic sector concerned to communicate to it all agreements, decisions and concerted practices which are exempt from notification by virtue of Art. 4 (2) and Art. 5 (2).

3. When making inquiries pursuant to paragraph 2, the Commission shall also request undertakings or groups of undertakings whose size suggests that they occupy a dominant position within the common market or a substantial part thereof to supply to the Commission such particulars of the structure of the undertakings and of their behaviour as are requisite to an appraisal of their position in the light of Art. 86 of the Treaty.

4. Art. 10 (3) to (6) and Arts. 11, 13 and 14 shall apply correspondingly.

ART. 13. Investigations by the authorities of the Member States

1. At the request of the Commission, the competent authorities of the Member States shall undertake the investigations which the Commission considers to be necessary under Art. 14 (1), or which it has ordered by decision pursuant to Art. 14 (3). The officials of the competent authorities of the Member States responsible for conducting these investigations shall exercise their powers upon production of an authorisation in writing issued by the competent authority of the Member State in whose territory the investigation is to be made. Such authorisation shall specify the subject matter and purpose of the investigation.

2. If so requested by the Commission or by the competent authority of the Member State in whose territory the investigation is to be made, the officials of the Commission may assist the officials of such authorities in carrying out their duties.

ART. 14. Investigating powers of the Commission

1. In carrying out the duties assigned to it by Art. 89 and by provisions adopted under Art. 87 of the Treaty, the Commission may undertake all necessary investigations into undertakings and associations of undertakings. To this end the officials authorised by the Commission are empowered:

(a) to examine the books and other business records;

(b) to take copies of or extracts from the books and business records;

(c) to ask for oral explanations on the spot;

(d) to enter any premises land and means of transport of undertakings.

2. The officials of the Commission authorised for the purpose of these investigations shall exercise their powers upon production of an authorisation in writing specifying the subject matter and purpose of the investigation and the penalties provided for in Art. 15 (1) (c) in cases where production of the required books or other business records is incomplete. In good time before the investigation, the Commission shall inform the competent authority of the Member State in whose territory the same is to be made of the investigation and of the identity of the authorised officials.

3. Undertakings and associations of undertakings shall submit to investigations ordered by decision of the Commission. The decision shall specify the subject matter and purpose of the investigation, appoint the date on which it is to begin and indicate the penalties provided for in Art. 15 (1) (c) and Art. 16 (1) (d) and the right to have the decision reviewed by the Court of Justice.

4. The Commission shall take decisions referred to in paragraph 3 after consultation with the competent authority of the Member State in whose territory the investigation is to be made.

5. Officials of the competent authority of the Member State in whose territory the investigation is to be made may, at the request of such authority or of the Commission, assist the officials of the Commission in carrying out their duties.

6. Where an undertaking opposes an investigation ordered pursuant to this Article, the Member State concerned shall afford the necessary assistance to the officials authorised by the Commission to enable them to make their investigation. Member States shall, after consultation with the Commission, take the necessary measures to this end before 1 October 1962.

ART. 15. Fines

1. The Commission may by decision impose on undertakings or associations of undertakings fines of from 100 to 5000 units of account where, intentionally or negligently:

(a) they supply incorrect or misleading information in an application pursuant to Art. 2 or in a notification pursuant to Arts. 4 or 5; or

(b) they supply incorrect information in response to a request made pursuant to Art. 11 (3) or (5) or to Art. 12, or do not supply information within the time limit fixed by a decision taken under Art. 11 (5); or

(c) they produce the required books or other business records in incomplete form during investigations under Arts. 13 or 14, or refuse to submit to an investigation ordered by decision issued in implementation of Art. 14 (3).

2. The Commission may by decision impose on undertakings or associations of undertakings fines of from 1000 to 1 000 000 units of account, or a sum in excess thereof but not exceeding 10% of the turnover in the preceding business year of each of the undertakings participating in the infringement where, either intentionally or negligently:

(a) they infringe Art. 85 (1) or Art. 86 of the Treaty; or

(b) they commit a breach of any obligation imposed pursuant to Art. 8 (1).

In fixing the amount of the fine, regard shall be had both to the gravity and to the duration of the infringement.

3. Art. 10 (3) to (6) shall apply.

4. Decisions taken pursuant to paragraphs 1 and 2 shall not be of a criminal law nature.

5. The fines provided for in paragraph 2 (a) shall not be imposed in respect of acts taking place:

(a) after notification to the Commission and before its decision in application of Art. 85 (3) of the Treaty, provided they fall within the limits of the activity described in the notification;

(b) before notification and in the course of agreements, decisions or concerted practices in existence at the date of entry into force of this Regulation, provided that notification was effected within the time limits specified in Art. 5 (1) and Art. 7 (2).

6. Paragraph 5 shall not have effect where the Commission has informed the undertakings concerned that after preliminary examination it is of opinion that Art. 85 (1) of the Treaty applies and that application of Art. 85 (3) is not justified.

ART. 16. Periodic penalty payments

1. The Commission may by decision impose on undertakings or associations of undertakings periodic penalty payments of from 50 to 1000 units of account per day, calculated from the date appointed by the decision, in order to compel them:

(a) to put an end to an infringement of Arts. 85 or 86 of the Treaty, in accordance with a decision taken pursuant to Art. 3 of this Regulation;

(b) to refrain from any act prohibited under Art. 8 (3);

(c) to supply complete and correct information which it has requested by decision taken pursuant to Art. 11 (5);

(d) to submit to an investigation which it has ordered by decision taken pursuant to Art. 14 (3).

2. Where the undertakings or associations of undertakings have satisfied the obligation which it was the purpose of the periodic penalty payment to enforce, the commission may fix the total amount of the periodic penalty payment at a lower figure than that which would arise under the original decision.

3. Art. 10 (3) to (6) shall apply.

ART. 17. Review by the Court of Justice

The Court of Justice shall have unlimited jurisdiction within the meaning of Art. 172 of the Treaty to review decisions whereby the Commission has fixed a fine or periodic penalty payment; it may cancel, reduce or increase the fine or periodic penalty payment imposed.

ART. 18. Unit of account

For the purposes of applying Arts. 15 to 17 the unit of account shall be that adopted in drawing up the budget of the Community in accordance with Arts. 207 and 209 of the Treaty.

ART. 19. Hearing of the parties and of third persons

1. Before taking decisions as provided for in Arts. 2, 3, 6, 7, 8, 15 and 16, the Commission shall give the undertakings or associations of undertakings concerned the opportunity of being heard on the matters to which the Commission has taken objection.

2. If the Commission or the competent authorities of the Member States consider it necessary, they may also hear other natural or legal persons. Applications to be heard on the part of such persons shall, where they show a sufficient interest, be granted.

3. Where the Commission intends to give negative clearance pursuant to Art. 2 or take a decision in application of Art. 85 (3) of the Treaty, it shall publish a summary of the relevant application or notification and invite all interested third parties to submit their observations within a time limit which it shall fix being not less than one month. Publication shall have regard to the legitimate interest of undertakings in the protection of their business secrets.

ART. 20. Professional secrecy

1. Information acquired as a result of the application of Arts. 11, 12, 13 and 14 shall be used only for the purpose of the relevant request or investigation.

2. Without prejudice to the provisions of Arts. 19 and 21, the Commission and the competent authorities of the Member States, their officials and other servants shall not disclose information acquired by them as a result of the application of this Regulation and of the kind covered by the obligation of professional secrecy.

3. The provisions of paragraphs 1 and 2 shall not prevent publication of general information or surveys which do not contain information relating to particular undertakings or associations of undertakings.

ART. 21. Publication of decisions

1. The Commission shall publish the decisions which it takes pursuant to Arts. 2, 3, 6, 7 and 8.

2. The publication shall state the names of the parties and the main content of the decision; it shall have regard to the legitimate interest of undertakings in the protection of their business secrets.

ART. 22. Special provisions

1. The Commission shall submit to the Council proposals for making certain categories of agreement, decision and concerted practice falling within Art. 4 (2) or Art. 5 (2) compulsorily notifiable under Art. 4 or 5.

2. Within one year from the date of entry into force of this Regulation, the Council shall examine, on a proposal from the Commission, what special provisions might be made for exempting from the provisions of this Regulation agreements, decisions and concerted practices falling within Art. 4 (2) or Art. 5 (2).

ART. 23. Transitional provisions applicable to decisions of authorities of the Member States

1. Agreements, decisions and concerted practices of the kind described in Art. 85 (1) of the Treaty to which, before the entry into force of this Regulation, the competent authority of a Member State has declared Art. 85 (1) to be inapplicable pursuant to Art. 85 (3) shall not be subject to compulsory notification under Art. 5. The decision of the competent authority of the Member State shall be deemed to be a decision within the meaning of Art. 6; it shall cease to be valid upon expiration of the period fixed by such authority but in any event not more than three years after the entry into force of this Regulation. Art. 8 (3) shall apply.

2. Applications for renewal of decisions of the kind described in paragraph 1 shall be decided upon by the Commission in accordance with Art. 8 (2).

ART. 24. Implementing provisions

The Commission shall have power to adopt implementing provisions concerning the form, content and other details of applications pursuant to Arts. 2 and 3 and of notifications pursuant to Arts. 4 and 5, and concerning hearings pursuant to Art. 19 (1) and (2).

ART. 25. 1. As regards agreements, decisions and concerted practices to which Art. 85 of the Treaty applies by virtue of accession, the date of accession shall be substituted for the date of entry into force of this Regulation in every place where reference is made in this Regulation to this latter date.

2. Agreements, decisions and concerted practices existing at the date of accession to which Art. 85 of the Treaty applies by virtue of accession shall be notified pursuant to Art. 5 (1) or Art. 7 (1) and (2) within six months from the date of accession.

3. Fines under Art. 15 (2) (a) shall not be imposed in respect of any act prior to notification of the agreements, decisions and practices to which paragraph 2 applies and which have been notified within the period therein specified.

4. New Member States shall take the measures referred to in Art. 14 (6) within six months from the date of accession after consulting the Commission.

[Final provisions omitted.]

[1] (OJ Sp Ed, 1959–62, 87). This text has been reproduced, with permission, from the Official Journal.

APPENDIX VI

EXCLUSIVE DISTRIBUTION REGULATIONS 1983/83

Commission Regulation (EEC) 1983/83[1] of 22 June 1983 on the application of Article 85 (3) of the Treaty to categories of exclusive distribution agreements.

Having regard—

to the Treaty establishing the European Economic Community,

to Council Regulation 19/65 of 2 March 1965 on the application of Article 85 (3) of the Treaty to certain categories of agreements and concerted practices, as last amended by the Act of Accession of Greece, and in particular article 1 thereof,

Having—

1. Published a draft of this Regulation,
2. Consulted the Advisory Committee on Restrictive Practices and Dominant Positions,

Whereas—

1. Regulation 19/65 empowers the Commission to apply Article 85 (3) of the Treaty by regulation to certain categories of bilateral exclusive distribution agreements and analogous concerted practices falling within Article 85 (1).

2. Experience to date makes it possible to define a category of agreements and concerted practices which can be regarded as normally satisfying the conditions laid down in Article 85 (3).

3. Exclusive distribution agreements of the category defined in Article 1 of this Regulation may fall within the prohibition contained in Article 85 (1) of the Treaty. This will apply only in exceptional cases to exclusive agreements of this kind to which only undertakings from one Member State are party and which concern the resale of goods within that Member State. However, to the extent that such agreements may affect trade between Member States and also satisfy all the requirements set out on this Regulation there is no reason to withhold from them the benefit of the exemption by category.

4. It is not necessary expressly to exclude from the defined category those agreements which do not fulfil the conditions of Article 85 (1) of the Treaty.

5. Exclusive distribution agreements lead in general to an improvement in distribution because the undertaking is able to concentrate its sales activities, does not need to maintain numerous business relations with a larger number of dealers and is able, by dealing with only one dealer, to overcome more easily distribution difficulties in international trade resulting from linguistic, legal and other differences.

6. Exclusive distribution agreements facilitate the promotion of sales of a product and lead to intensive marketing and to continuity of supplies while at the same time rationalising distribution; they stimulate competition between the products of different manufacturers. The appointment of an exclusive distributor who will take over sales promotion, customer services and carrying of stocks is often the most effective way, and sometimes indeed the only way, for the manufacturer to enter a market and compete with other manufacturers already present; this is particularly so in the case of small and medium-sized undertakings. It must be left to the contracting parties to decide whether and to what extent they consider it desirable to incorporate in the agreements terms providing for the promotion of sales.

7. As a rule, such exclusive distribution agreements also allow consumers a fair share of the resulting benefit as they gain directly from the improvement in distribution, and their economic and supply position is improved as they can obtain products manufactured in particular in other countries more quickly and more easily.

8. This Regulation must define the obligations restricting competition which may be included in exclusive distribution agreements. The other restrictions on competition allowed under this Regulation in addition to the exclusive supply obligation produce a clear division of functions between the parties and compel the exclusive distributor to concentrate his sales efforts on the contract goods and the contract territory; they are, where they are agreed only for the duration of the agreement, generally necessary in order to attain the improvement in the distribution of goods sought through exclusive distribution. It may be left to the contracting parties to decide which of these obligations they include in their agreements. Further restrictive obligations and in particular those which limit the exclusive distributor's choice of customers or his freedom to determine his prices and conditions of sale cannot be exempted under this Regulation.

9. The exemption by category should be reserved for agreements for which it can be assumed with sufficient certainty that they satisfy the conditions of Article 85 (3) of the Treaty.

10. It is not possible, in the absence of a case-by-case examination, to consider that adequate improvements in distribution occur where a manufacturer entrusts the distribution of his goods to another manufacturer with whom he is in competition. Such agreements should, therefore, be excluded from the exemption by category. Certain derogations from this rule in favour of small and medium-sized undertakings can be allowed.

11. Consumers will be assured of a fair share of the benefits resulting from exclusive distribution only if parallel imports remain possible. Agreements relating to goods which the user can obtain only from the exclusive distributor should therefore be excluded from the exemption by category.

The party cannot be allowed to abuse industrial property rights or other rights in order to create absolute territorial protection. This does not prejudice the relationship between competition law and industrial property rights, since the sole object here is to determine the conditions for exemption by category.

12. Since competition at the distribution stage is ensured by the possibility of parallel imports, the exclusive distribution agreements covered by this Regulation will not normally afford any possiblity of eliminating competition in respect of a substantial part of the products in question. This is also true of agreements that allot to the exclusive distributor a contract territory covering the whole of the Common Market.

13. In particular cases in which agreements for concerted practices satisfying the requirements of this Regulation nevertheless have effects incompatible with Article 85 (3) of the Treaty, the Commission may withdraw the benefit of the exemption by category from the undertakings party to them.

14. Agreements and concerted practices which satisfy the conditions set out in this Regulation need not be notified. An undertaking may nonetheless in a particular case where real doubt exists, request the Commission to declare whether its agreements comply with this Regulation.

15. This Regulation does not affect the applicability of Commission Regulation (EEC) 3604/82 of 23 December 1982 on the application of Article 85 (3) of the Treaty to categories of specialisation agreements[2]; it does not exclude the application of Article 86 of the Treaty.

THE COMMISSION OF THE EUROPEAN COMMUNITIES HAS ADOPTED THIS REGULATION:

Article 1

Pursuant to Article 85 (3) of the Treaty and subject to the provisions of this Regulation, it is hereby declared that Article 85 (1) of the Treaty shall not apply to agreements to which only two undertakings are party and whereby one party agrees with the other to supply certain goods for resale within the whole or a defined area of the Common Market only to that other.

Article 2

1. Apart from the obligation referred to in Article 1 no restriction on competition shall be imposed on the supplier other than the obligation not to supply the contract goods to users in the contract territory.

2. No restriction on competition shall be imposed on the exclusive distributor other than:

(a) the obligation not to manufacture or distribute goods which compete with the contract goods;

(b) the obligation to obtain the contract goods for resale only from the other party;

(c) the obligation to refrain, outside the contract territory and in relation to the contract goods, from seeking customers, from establishing any branch and from maintaining any distribution depot.

3. Article 1 shall apply notwithstanding that the exclusive distributor undertakes all or any of the following obligations:

(a) to purchase complete ranges of goods or minimum quantities;

(b) to sell the contract goods under trade marks, or packed and presented as specified by the other party;

(c) to take measures for promotion of sales, in particular:

— to advertise,

— to maintain a sales network or stock of goods,

— to provide customer and guarantee services,

— to employ staff having specialised or technical training.

Article 3

Article 1 shall not apply where:

(a) manufacturers of identical goods or of goods which are considered by users as equivalent in view of their characteristics, price and intended use enter into reciprocal exclusive distribution agreements between themselves in respect of such goods;

(b) manufacturers of identical goods or of goods which are considered by users as equivalent in view of their characteristics, price and intended use enter into a non-reciprocal exclusive distribution agreement between themselves in respect of such goods unless at least one of them has a total annual turnover of no more than 100 million ECU;

(c) users can obtain the contract goods in the contract territory only from the exclusive distributor and have no alternative source of supply outside the contract territory;

(d) one or both of the parties makes it difficult for intermediaries or users to obtain the contract goods from other dealers inside the Common Market or, in so far as no alternative source of supply is available there, from outside the Common Market, in particular where one or both of them:

1. exercises industrial property rights so as to prevent dealers or users from obtaining outside, or from selling in, the contract territory properly marked or otherwise properly marketed contract goods;

2. exercises other rights or takes other measures so as to prevent dealers or users from obtaining outside, or from selling in, the contract territory contract goods.

Article 4

1. Article 3(a) and (b) shall also apply where the goods there referred to are manufactured by an undertaking connected with a party to the agreement.

2. Connected undertakings are:

(a) undertakings in which a party to the agreement, directly or indirectly:

— owns more than half the capital or business assets, or

— has the power to exercise more than half the voting rights, or

— has the power to appoint more than half the members of the supervisory board, board of directors or bodies legally representing the undertaking, or

— has the right to manage the affairs;

(b) undertakings which directly or indirectly have in or over a party to the agreement the rights or powers listed in (a);

(c) undertakings in which an undertaking referred to in (b) directly or indirectly has the rights or powers listed in (a);

3. Undertakings in which the parties to the agreement or undertakings connected with them jointly have the rights or powers set out in paragraph 2(a) shall be considered to be connected with each of the parties to the agreement.

Article 5

1. For the purpose of Article 3 (b), the ECU is the unit of account used for drawing up the budget of the Community pursuant to Articles 207 and 209 of the Treaty.

2. Article 1 shall remain applicable where during any period of two consecutive financial years the total turnover referred to in Article 3 (b) is exceeded by no more than 10 per cent.

3. For the purpose of calculating total turnover within the meaning of Article 3 (b), the turnovers achieved during the last financial year by the party to the agreement and connected undertakings in respect of all goods and services, excluding all taxes and other duties, shall be added together. For this purpose no account shall be taken of dealings between the party to the agreement and its connected undertakings or between its connected undertakings.

Article 6

The Commission may withdraw the benefit of this Regulation, pursuant to Article 7 of Regulation 19/65/EEC, when it finds in a particular case that an agreement which is exempted by this Regulation nevertheless has certain effects which are incompatible with the conditions set out in Article 85 (3) of the Treaty, and in particular where:

(a) the contract goods are not subject, in the contract territory, to effective competition from identical goods or goods considered by users as equivalent in view of their characteristics, price and intended use;

(b) access by other suppliers to the different stages of distribution within the contract territory is made difficult to a significant extent;

(c) for reasons other than those referred to in Article 3(c) and (d) it is not possible for intermediaries or users to obtain supplies of the contract goods from dealers outside the contract territory on the terms there customary;

(d) the exclusive distributor:

1. without any objectively justified reason refuses to supply in the contract territory categories of purchasers who cannot obtain contract goods elsewhere on suitable terms or applies to them differing prices or conditions of sale;
2. sells the contract goods at excessively high prices.

Article 7

In the period 1 July 1983 to 31 December 1986, the prohibition in Article 85 (1) of the Treaty shall not apply to agreements which were in force on 1 July 1983 or entered into force between 1 July and 31 December 1983 and which satisfy the exemption conditions of Regulation 67/67/EEC.

Article 8

This Regulation shall not apply to agreements entered into for the resale of drinks in premises used for the sale and consumption of drinks for the resale of petroleum products in service stations.

Article 9

This Regulation shall apply *mutatis mutandis* to concerted practices of the type defined in Article 1.

1 (OJ 1983, 173/1). This text incorporates the corrigenda published in (OJ 1983, 281/24) and has been reproduced, with permission from the Official Journal.

APPENDIX VII

EXCLUSIVE PURCHASING REGULATIONS 1984/83

Commission Regulation (EEC) 1984/83[1] of 22 June 1983 on the application of Article 85 (3) of the Treaty to categories of exclusive purchasing agreements.

Having regard—

to the Treaty establishing the European Economic Community,

to Council Regulation 19/65 of 2 March 1965 on the application of Article 85 (3) of the Treaty to certain categories of agreements and concerted practices, as last amended by the Act of Accession of Greece, and in particular Article 1 thereof,

Having—

1. Published a draft of this Regulation,

2. Consulted the Advisory Committee on Restrictive Practices and Dominant Positions,

Whereas—

1. Regulation 19/65 empowers the Commission to apply Article 85 (3) of the Treaty by regulation to certain categories of bilateral exclusive purchasing agreements entered into for the purpose of the resale of goods and corresponding concerted practices falling within Article 85 (1).

2. Experience to date makes it possible to define three categories of agreements and concerted practices which can be regarded as normally satisfying the conditions laid down in Article 85 (3): the first category comprises exclusive purchasing agreements of short and medium duration in all sectors of the economy; the other two categories comprise long-term exclusive purchasing agreements entered into for the resale of beer in premises used for the sale and consumption of drinks (beer supply agreements) and of petroleum products in service stations (service station agreements).

3. Exclusive purchasing agreements of the categories defined in this Regulation may fall within the prohibition contained in Article 85 (1) of the Treaty. This will often be the case with agreements concluded between undertakings from different Member States. An exclusive purchasing agreement to which undertakings from only one Member State are party and which concerns the resale of goods within that Member State may also be caught by the prohibition. This is in particular the case where it is one of a number of similar agreements which together may affect trade between Member States.

4. It is not necessary expressly to exclude from the defined categories those agreements which do not fulfil the conditions of Article 85 (1) of the Treaty.

5. The exclusive purchasing agreements defined in this Regulation lead in general to an improvement in distribution. They enable the supplier to plan the sales of his goods with greater precision and for a longer period and ensure that the reseller's requirements will be met on a regular basis for the duration of the agreement; this allows the parties to limit the risk to them of variations in market conditions and to lower distribution costs.

6. Such agreements also facilitate the promotion of the sales of a product and lead to intensive marketing because the supplier, in consideration for the exclusive purchasing obligation, is as a rule under an obligation to contribute to the improvement of the structure of the distribution network, the quality of the promotional effort or the sales success. At the same time, they stimulate competition between the products of different manufacturers. The appointment of several resellers, who are bound to purchase exclusively from the manufacturer and who take over sales promotion, customer services and carrying of stock, is often the most effective way, and sometimes the only way, for the manufacturer to penetrate a market and compete with other manufacturers already present; this is particularly so in the case of small and medium-sized undertakings. It must be left to the contracting parties to decide whether and to what extent they consider it desirable to incorporate in their agreements terms concerning the promotion of sales.

7. As a rule, exclusive purchasing agreements between suppliers and resellers also allow consumers a fair share of the resulting benefit as they gain the advantages of regular supply and are able to obtain the contract goods more quickly and more easily.

8. This Regulation must define the obligations restricting competition which may be included in an exclusive purchasing agreement. The other restrictions of competition allowed under this Regulation in addition to the exclusive purchasing obligation lead to a clear division of functions between the parties and compel the reseller to concentrate his sales efforts on the contract goods; they are, where they are agreed only for the duration of the agreement, generally necessary in order to attain the improvement in the distribution of goods sought through exclusive purchasing. Further restrictive obligations and in particular those which limit the reseller's choice of customers or his freedom to determine his prices and conditions of sale cannot be exempted under this Regulation.

9. The exemption by categories should be reserved for agreements for which it can be assumed with sufficient certainty that they satisfy the conditions of Article 85 (3) of the Treaty.

10. It is not possible, in the absence of a case-by-case examination, to consider that adequate improvements in distribution occur where a manufacturer imposes an exclusive purchasing obligation with respect to his goods on a manufacturer with whom he is in competition. Such agreements should, therefore, be excluded from the exemption by categories. Certain derogations from this rule in favour of small and medium-sized undertakings can be allowed.

11. Certain conditions must be attached to the exemption by categories so that access by other undertakings to the different stages of distribution can be ensured. To this end, limits must be set to the scope and to the duration of the exclusive purchasing obligation. It appears appropriate as a general rule to grant the benefit of a general exemption from the prohibition on restrictive agreements only to exclusive purchasing agreements which are concluded for a specified product or range of products and for not more than five years.

12. In the case of beer supply agreements and service-station agreements, different rules should be laid down which take account of the particularities of the markets in question.

13. These agreements are generally distinguished by the fact that, on the one hand, the supplier confers on the reseller special commercial or financial advantages by contributing to his financing, granting him or obtaining for him a loan on favourable terms, equipping him with a site or premises for conducting his business, providing him with equipment or fittings, or undertaking other investments for his benefit and that, on the other hand, the reseller enters into a long-term exclusive purchasing obligation which in most cases is accompanied by a ban on dealing in competing products.

14. Beer supply and service-station agreements, like the other exclusive purchasing agreements dealt with in this Regulation, normally produce an appreciable improvement in distribution in which consumers are allowed a fair share of the resulting benefit.

15. The commercial and financial advantages conferred by the supplier on the reseller make it significantly easier to establish, modernise, maintain and operate premises used for the sale and consumption of drinks and service stations: the exclusive purchasing obligation and the ban on dealing in competing products imposed on the reseller incite the reseller to devote all the resources at his disposal to the sale of the contract goods. Such agreements lead to durable co-operation between the parties allowing them to improve or maintain the quality of the contract goods and of the services to the customer and sales efforts of the reseller; they allow long-term planning of sales and consequently a cost effective organisation of production and distribution. The pressure of competition between products of different makes obliges the undertakings involved to determine the number and character of premises used for the sale and consumption of drinks and service stations, in accordance with the wishes of customers.

16. Consumers benefit from the improvements described, in particular because they are ensured supplies of goods of satisfactory quality at fair prices and conditions while being able to choose between the products of different manufacturers.

17. The advantages produced by beer supply agreements and service-station agreements cannot otherwise be secured to the same extent and with the same degree of certainty. The exclusive purchasing obligation on the reseller and the non-competition clause imposed on him are essential components of such agreements and thus usually indispensable for the attainment of these advantages. However, this is true only as long as the reseller's obligation to purchase from the supplier is confined in the case of premises used for the sale and consumption of drinks to beers and other drinks of the types offered by the supplier, and in the case of service stations to petroleum-based fuel for motor vehicles and other petroleum-based fuels. The exclusive purchasing obligation for lubricants and related petroleum-based products can be accepted only on condition that the supplier provides for the reseller or finances the procurement of specific equipment for the carrying out of lubrication work. This obligation should only relate to products intended for use within the service station.

18. In order to maintain the reseller's commercial freedom and to ensure access to the retail level of distribution on the part of other suppliers, not only the scope but also the duration of the exclusive purchasing obligation must be limited. It appears appropriate to allow drinks suppliers a choice between a medium-term exclusive purchasing agreement covering a range of drinks and a long-term exclusive purchasing agreement for beer. It is necessary to provide special rules for those premises used for the sale and consumption of drinks which the supplier lets to the reseller. In this case, the reseller must have the right to obtain from other undertakings, under the conditions specified in this Regulation, other drinks, except beer, supplied under the agreement or of the same type but bearing a different trade mark. A uniform maximum duration should be provided for service-station agreements, with the exception of tenancy agreements between the supplier and the reseller, which takes account of the long-term character of the relationship between the parties.

19. To the extent that Member States provide, by law or administrative measures, for the same upper limit of duration for the exclusive purchasing obligation upon the reseller in service-station agreements as laid down in this Regulation but provide for a permissible duration which varies in proportion to the consideration provided by the supplier or generally provide for a shorter duration than that permitted by this Regulation, such laws or measures are not contrary to the objectives of this Regulation which, in this respect, merely sets an upper limit to the duration of service-station agreements. The application and enforcement of such national laws or measures must therefore be regarded as compatible with the provisions of this Regulation.

20. The limitations and conditions provided for in this Regulation are such as to guarantee effective competition on the markets in question. Therefore, the agreements to which the exemption by category applies do not normally enable the participating undertakings to eliminate competition for a substantial part of the products in question.

21. In particular cases in which agreements or concerted practices satisfying the conditions of this Regulation nevertheless have effects incompatible with Article 85 (3) of the Treaty, the Commission may withdraw the benefit of the exemption by category from the undertakings party thereto.

22. Agreements and concerted practices which satisfy the conditions set out in this Regulation need not be notifed. An undertaking may nonetheless, in a particular case where real doubt exists, request the Commission to declare whether its agreements comply with this Regulation.

23. This Regulation does not affect the applicability of Commission Regulation (EEC) 3604/82 of 23 December 1982 on the application of Article 85 (3) of the Treaty to categories of specialisation agreements. It does not exclude the application of Article 86 of the Treaty.

THE COMMISSION OF THE EUROPEAN COMMUNITIES HAS ADOPTED THIS REGULATION:

TITLE I

General provisions

Article 1

Pursuant to Article 85 (3) of the Treaty, and subject to the conditions set out in Articles 2 to 5 of this Regulation, it is hereby declared that Article 85 (1) of the Treaty shall not apply to agreements to which only two undertakings are party and whereby one party, the reseller, agrees with the other, the supplier, to purchase certain goods specified in the agreement for resale only from the supplier or from a connected undertaking or from another undertaking which the supplier has entrusted with the sale of his goods.

Article 2

1. No other restriction of competition shall be imposed on the supplier than the obligation not to distribute the contract goods or goods which compete with the contract goods in the reseller's principal sales area and at the reseller's level of distribution.

2. Apart from the obligation described in Article 1, no other restriction of competition shall be imposed on the reseller than the obligation not to manufacture or distribute goods which compete with the contract goods.

3. Article 1 shall apply notwithstanding that the reseller undertakes any or all of the following obligations:

(a) to purchase complete ranges of goods;

(b) to purchase maximum quantities of goods which are subject to the exclusive purchasing obligation;

(c) to sell the contract goods under trade marks, or packed and presented as specified by the supplier;

(d) to take measures for the promotion of sales, in particular:

— to advertise,

— to maintain a sales network or stock of goods,

— to provide customer and guarantee services,

— to employ staff having specialised or technical training.

Article 3

Article 1 shall not apply where:

(a) manufacturers of identical goods or of goods which are considered by users as equivalent in view of their characteristics, price and intended use enter into reciprocal exclusive purchasing agreements between themselves in respect of such goods;

(b) manufacturers of identical goods or of goods which are considered by users as equivalent in view of their characteristics, price and intended use enter into a non-reciprocal exclusive purchasing agreement between themselves in respect of such goods, unless at least one of them has a total annual turnover of no more than 100 million ECU;

(c) the exclusive purchasing obligation is agreed for more than one type of goods where these are neither by their nature nor acccording to commercial usage connected to each other;

(d) the agreement is concluded for an indefinite duration or for a period of more than five years.

Article 4

1. Article 3(a) and (b) shall also apply where the goods there referred to are manufactured by an undertaking connected with a party to the agreement.

2. Connected undertakings are:

(a) undertakings in which a party to the agreement, directly or indirectly:
- owns more than half the capital or business assets, or
- has the power to exercise more than half the voting rights, or
- has the power to appoint more than half the members of the supervisory board, board of directors or bodies legally representing the undertaking, or
- has the right to manage the affairs;

(b) undertakings which directly or indirectly have in or over a party to the agreement the rights or powers listed in (a);

(c) undertakings in which an undertaking referred to in (b) directly or indirectly has the rights or powers listed in (a).

3. Undertakings in which the parties to the agreement or undertakings connected with them jointly have the rights or powers set out in paragraph 2(a) shall be considered to be connected with each of the parties to the agreement.

Article 5

1. For the purpose of Article 3(b), the ECU is the unit of account used for drawing up the budget of the Community pursuant to Articles 207 and 209 of the Treaty.

2. Article 1 shall remain applicable where during any period of two consecutive financial years the total turnover referred to in Article 3(b) is exceeded by no more than 10 per cent.

3. For the purpose of calculating total turnover within the meaning of Article 3(b), the turnovers achieved during the last financial year by the party to the agreement and connected undertakings in respect of all goods and services, excluding all taxes and other duties, shall be added together. For this purpose no account shall be taken of dealings between the party to the agreement and its connected undertakings or between its connected undertakings.

TITLE II

Special provisions for beer supply agreements

Article 6

1. Pursuant to Article 85 (3) of the Treaty, and subject to Articles 7 to 9 of this Regulation, it is hereby declared that Article 85 (1) of the Treaty shall not apply to agreements to which only two undertakings are party and whereby one party, the reseller, agrees with the other, the supplier, in consideration for the according of special commercial or financial advantages, to purchase only from the supplier, an undertaking connected with the supplier or another

undertaking entrusted by the supplier with the distribution of his goods, certain beers, or certain beers and certain other drinks, specified in the agreement for resale in premises used for the sale and consumption of drinks and designated in the agreement.

2. The declaration in paragraph 1 shall also apply where exclusive purchasing obligations of the kind described in paragraph 1 are imposed on the reseller in favour of the supplier by another undertaking which is itself not a supplier.

Article 7

1. Apart from the obligation referred to in Article 6, no restriction on competition shall be imposed on the reseller other than:

(a) the obligation not to sell beers and other drinks which are supplied by other undertakings and which are of the same type as the beers or other drinks supplied under the agreement in the premises designated in the agreement;

(b) the obligation, in the event that the reseller sells in the premises designated in the agreement beers which are supplied by other undertakings and which are of a different type from the beers supplied under the agreement, to sell such beers only in bottles, cans or other small packages, unless the sale of such beers in draught form is customary or is necessary to satisfy a sufficient demand from consumers;

(c) the obligation to advertise goods supplied by other undertakings within or outside the premises designated in the agreement only in proportion to the share of these goods in the total turnover realised in the premises.

2. Beers or other drinks are of different types where they are clearly distinguishable by their composition, appearance or taste.

Article 8

1. Article 6 shall not apply where:

(a) the supplier or a connected undertaking imposes on the reseller exclusive purchasing obligations for goods other than drinks or for services;

(b) the supplier restricts the freedom of the reseller to obtain from an undertaking of his choice either services or goods for which neither an exclusive purchasing obligation nor a ban on dealing in competing products may be imposed;

(c) the agreement is concluded for an indefinite duration or for a period of more than five years and the exclusive purchasing obligation relates to specified beers and other drinks;

(d) the agreement is concluded for an indefinite duration or for a period of more than 10 years and the exclusive purchasing obligation relates only to specified beers;

(e) the supplier obliges the reseller to impose the exclusive purchasing obligation on his successor for a longer period than the reseller would himself remain tied to the supplier.

2. Where the agreement relates to premises which the supplier lets to the reseller or allows the reseller to occupy on some other basis in law or in fact, the following provisions shall also apply:

(a) notwithstanding paragraphs (1)(c) and (d), the exclusive purchasing obligations and bans on dealing in competing products specified in this Title may be imposed on the reseller for the whole period for which the reseller in fact operates the premises;

(b) the agreement must provide for the reseller to have the right to obtain:

— drinks, except beer, supplied under the agreement from other undertakings where these undertakings offer them on more favourable conditions which the supplier does not meet,

— drinks, except beer, which are of the same type as those supplied under the agreement but which bear different trade marks, from other undertakings where the supplier does not offer them.

Article 9

Articles 2(1) and (3), 3(a) and (b), 4 and 5 shall apply *mutatis mutandis*.

TITLE III

Special provisions for service-station agreements

Article 10

Pursuant to Article 85 (3) of the Treaty and subject to Articles 11 to 13 of this Regulation, it is hereby declared that Article 85 (1) of the Treaty shall not apply to agreements to which only two undertakings are party and whereby one party, the reseller, agrees with the other, the supplier, in consideration for the according of special commercial or financial advantages, to purchase only from the supplier, an undertaking connected with the supplier or another undertaking entrusted by the supplier with the distribution of his goods, certain petroleum-based motor-vehicle fuels or certain petroleum-based motor-vehicle and other fuels specified in the agreement for resale in a service station designated in the agreement.

Article 11

Apart from the obligation referred to in Article 10, no restriction on competition shall be imposed on the reseller other than:

(a) the obligation not to sell motor-vehicle fuel and other fuels which are supplied by other undertakings in the service station designated in the agreement;

(b) the obligation not to use lubricants or related petroleum-based products which are supplied by other undertakings within the service station designated in the agreement where the supplier or a connected undertaking has made available to the reseller, or financed, a lubrication bay or other motor-vehicle lubrication equipment;

(c) the obligation to advertise goods supplied by other undertakings within or outside the service station designated in the agreement only in proportion to the share of these goods in the total turnover realised in the service station;

(d) the obligation to have equipment owned by the supplier or a connected undertaking or financed by the supplier or a connected undertaking serviced by the supplier or an undertaking designated by him.

Article 12

1. Article 10 shall not apply where:

(a) the supplier or a connected undertaking imposes on the reseller exclusive purchasing obligations for goods other than motor-vehicle and other fuels or for services, except in the case of the obligations referred to in Article 11(b) and (d);

(b) the supplier restricts the freedom of the reseller to obtain from an undertaking of his choice goods or services for which under the provisions of this Title neither an exclusive purchasing obligation nor a ban on dealing in competing products may be imposed;

(c) the agreement is concluded for an indefinite duration or for a period of more than 10 years;

(d) the supplier obliges the reseller to impose the exclusive purchasing obligation on his successor for a longer period than the reseller would himself remain tied to the supplier.

2. Where the agreement relates to a service station which the supplier lets to the reseller, or allows the reseller to occupy on some other basis, in law or in fact, exclusive purchasing obligations or bans on dealing in competing products specified in this Title may, notwithstanding paragraph 1(c), be imposed on the reseller for the whole period for which the reseller in fact operates the premises.

Article 13

Articles 2(1) and (3), 3(a) and (b), 4 and 5 of this Regulation shall apply *mutatis mutandis*.

TITLE IV

Miscellaneous provisions

Article 14

The Commission may withdraw the benefit of this Regulation, pursuant to Article 7 of Regulation 19/65, when it finds in a particular case that an agreement which is exempted by this Regulation nevertheless has certain effects which are incompatible with the conditions set out in Article 85 (3) of the Treaty, and in particular where:

(a) the contract goods are not subject, in a substantial part of the Common Market, to effective competition from identical goods or goods considered by users as equivalent in view of their characteristics, price and intended use;

(b) access by other suppliers to the different stages of distribution in a substantial part of the Common Market is made difficult to a significant extent;

(c) the supplier without any objectively justified reason:

1. refuses to supply categories of resellers who cannot obtain the contract goods elsewhere on suitable terms or applies to them differing prices or conditions of sale;
2. applies less favourable prices or conditions of sale to resellers bound by an exclusive purchasing obligation as compared with other resellers at the same level of distribution.

Article 15

1. In the period 1 July 1983 to 31 December 1986, the prohibition in Article 85 (1) of the Treaty shall not apply to agreements of the kind described in Article 1 which either were in force on 1 July 1983 or entered into force between 1 July and 31 December 1983 and which satisfy the exemption conditions of Regulation 67/67/EEC.

2. In the period 1 July 1983 to 31 December 1988, the prohibition in Article 85 (1) of the Treaty shall not apply to agreements of the kinds described in Articles 6 and 10 which either were in force on 1 July 1983 or entered into force between 1 July and 31 December 1983 and which satisfy the exemption conditions of Regulation 67/67/EEC.

3. In the case of agreements of the kinds described in Articles 6 and 10, which were in force on 1 July 1983 and which expire after 31 December 1988, the prohibition in Article 85 (1) of the Treaty shall not apply in the period from 1 January 1989 to the expiry of the agreement but at the latest to the expiry of this Regulation to the extent that the supplier releases the reseller, before 1 January 1989, from all obligations which would prevent the application of the exemption under Titles II and III.

Article 16

This Regulation shall not apply to agreements by which the supplier undertakes with the reseller to supply only to the reseller certain goods for resale, in the whole or in a defined part of the Community, and the reseller undertakes with the supplier to purchase these goods only from the supplier.

Article 17

This Regulation shall not apply where the parties or connected undertakings, for the purpose of resale in one and the same premises used for the sale and consumption of drinks or service station, enter into agreements both of the kind referred to in Title I and of a kind referred to in Title II or III.

Article 18

This Regulation shall apply *mutatis mutandis* to the categories of concerted practices defined in Articles 1, 6 and 10.

Article 19

This Regulation shall enter into force on 1 July 1983. It shall expire on 31 December 1997.

This Regulation shall be binding in its entirety and directly applicable in all Member States.

[1] (OJ 1983, 173/5). This text incorporates the corrigenda published in (OJ 1983, 281/24) and has been reproduced, with permission, from the Official Journal.

BIBLIOGRAPHY

Adams, *Roche versus Adams* (1984) (Jonathan Cape)
Beddard, *Human Rights in Europe* (2nd ed, 1983) (Sweet & Maxwell)
Bellamy & Child, *Common Market Law of Competition* (2nd ed, 1978) (Sweet & Maxwell)
Brown and Jacobs, *The Court of Justice of the European Communities* (2nd ed, 1983) (Sweet & Maxwell)
Collins, *European Community Law in the UK* (3rd ed, 1984) (Butterworths)
de Smith, *Constitutional & Administrative Law* (5th ed, 1985) (Pelican Books)
Evans, *Immigration Law* (2nd ed, 1983) (Sweet & Maxwell)
Hartley, *The Foundations of European Community Law* (1981) (Clarendon Press)
Hill, *The Common Agricultural Policy: Past, Present & Future* (1984) (Methuen)
Hunnings, *Gazetteer of European Law* (1984) (European Law Centre)
Jacobs & Durand, *References to the European Court: Practice & Procedure* (1975) (Butterworths)
Kerse, *EEC Anti-Trust Procedure* with *Supplement* (1982 and 1984) (European Law Centre)
Korah, *Exclusive Dealing Agreements in the EEC; Regulation 67/67 Replaced* (1984) (European Law Centre)
Lasok & Bridge, *Introduction to the Law & Institutions of the European Communities* (3rd ed, 1982) (Butterworths)
Merkin & Williams, *Competition Law: Antitrust Policy in the United Kingdom and the EEC* (1984) (Sweet & Maxwell)
Ogus & Barendt, *The Law of Social Security* (2nd ed, 1982) (Butterworths)
Oliver, *Free Movement of Goods in the EEC Under Articles 30 to 36 of the Rome Treaty* (1982) (European Law Centre)
Palmer, Lambert, Forsyth, Morris & Wohlgemuth, *European Unity: A Survey of the European Organisations* (1968) (Allen & Unwin)
Parry & Dinnage, Parry and Hardy: *EEC Law* (2nd ed, 1981) (Sweet & Maxwell)
Plender, *A Practical Introduction to European Community Law* (1980) (Sweet & Maxwell)
Rudden & Wyatt, *Basic Community Law* (1980) (Oxford University Press)
Snyder, *Law of the Common Agricultural Policy* (1985) (Sweet & Maxwell)
Swann, *Competition & Industrial Policy in the European Community* (1983) (Methuen)
Sweet & Maxwell's, *European Community Treaties* (4th ed, 1980) (Sweet & Maxwell)
Usher, *European Court Practice* (1983) (Sweet & Maxwell)
Watson, *Social Security Law of the European Communities* (1980) (Mansell)
Whish, *Competition Law* (1985) (Butterworths)
Wyatt & Dashwood, *The Substantive Law of the EEC* (1980) (Sweet & Maxwell)

INDEX

Abuse of Dominant Position (see also **Competition and Dominant Position**) 177-188
abuse 181-185
discriminatory prices 160
loyalty rebates 184-185
mergers 180, 182
refusal to supply 182-184
unfair prices 184
de minimis 179
direct effect 161-162, 177
dominant position 178-181
fines 178, 186
Form A/B 186
mitigating factors 184, 186
negative clearance 186
role of
Commission 167-169, 178, 187-188
Court of Justice 75, 79, 170, 178, 180, 184, 187
scope 185-186
undertakings 187
UK remedy 177
Accession
Ireland 1, 6, 7
unanimity of Council of Ministers 6, 13
UK 1, 6, 7, 32
Accountants 138, 139, 143
Acte clair 70
Action for Annulment 75-79
challengeable acts 36, 75, 83
consequences 79
grounds 37, 78, 82, 206
locus standi requirements 36, 76-77, 83
partial annulment 79
time-limits 78, 83
Action for Damages (see **Non-Contractual Liability**)
Action for Inactivity 80-82
challengeable omissions 80
consequences 82
locus standi requirements 80-81
procedure 81-82
time-limits 81-82
Actions Against Member States
Commission 17, 28, 34, 99
jurisdiction of Court of Justice 17, 28, 157
Member States 17, 28
Acts of Community Institutions
annulment 36, 37, 75, 78, 79
citation 40-41
Communications 18, 35, 40, 99
Decisions (See **Decisions**)
Directives (See **Directives**)
entry into force 39-40
General Programme 124, 125, 128, 129
information 35
interpretation 8, 60, 63
judicial review 22, 28, 36, 37, 40, 60, 63
legislative process 38-39
modifications 23
Notices 18, 35, 164, 166-167, 175, 176
Opinions 18, 22, 33, 35, 37, 38, 75, 78, 80
publication and notification 35,39, 40, 78
reasoned opinion 17
reasons 36
Recommendations 18, 33, 35, 75, 80
Regulations (See **Regulations**)
Reports 22
Resolutions 22
sui generis 63
Advocate-General (see also **European Court of Justice**)
appointment 25
reasoned submission 26, 41, 42
role 26
Aggregation, Principle of (see also **Social Security**), 141, 142, 143, 148-149
Agreements
agency 164
association 63
beer-supply 175
exclusive dealing 175
exclusive distribution 175, Appendix VI
exclusive purchasing 175, Appendix VII
horizontal 163
minor 166-167
new 174
non-notifiable 172
old 174
patent-licensing 175
research and development co-operation 175
service-station 175
specialisation 175
vehicle distribution and servicing 175
vertical 163

Agricultural Products (see also **Common Agricultural Policy**) 191-192, 196
Agriculture (see also **Common Agricultural Policy**) 189-202
Appeal against Fines 75, 170
Associations of Undertakings 163, 165
Audi alteram partem 42, 209

Brussels Treaty Organisation 3, 5
Budget of the European Community
  compulsory expenditure 13, 23
  non-compulsory expenditure 23
  preparation 23-24
  resources 23, 195
  UK contribution 53, 58,195
Bulletins of the European Communities 42

Capital (see **Free Movement of Capital**)
CEEC (see **Committee of European Economic Co-operation**)
Cereals (See also **Common Agricultural Policy**)
  common organisation of market 194, 200-201, 206
  intervention price 194, 196
  target price 194, 196
  threshold price 194, 196
Churchill 2, 3
Coins (see also **Legal Tender**) 92, 104
Congress of Europe 3
Commission
  Annual General Report 24, 42
  attendance at Council meetings 12, 39
  composition 15-16
  Directorates-General 16, 17
  dismissal 16, 28
  functions 17-19, 167, 168, 187, 188
  motions of censure 24
  powers in competition cases 167-169, 187, 188,
  preparation of budget 23
  reasoned opinion 17
Committee of European Economic Co-Operation (CEEC) 3
Committee of Permanent Representatives (See **COREPER**)
Common Agricultural Policy 189-202
  agricultural products 191-192, 196
  aims and objectives 192-193
  cereals 192, 194, 196
  common organisation of markets 192, 194, 196, 197, 198, 199, 200, 201, 202
  Community preference, principle of 193, 196
  compulsory expenditure 23
  effect on national marketing systems 191, 196-202
  financial solidarity, principle of 193, 196
  free movement of goods, relationship with 191, 195, 199, 201-202
  "green" currencies 195
  guarantee section of FEOGA 193-194, 195
  guidance section of FEOGA 193-194
  intervention agencies 194, 195
  less-favoured areas 194
  Management Committees 196
  Mansholt Plan 193
  market unity, principle of 193-195, 196
  monetary compensatory amounts 189, 195
  prices 194, 195, 196
Community Customs Tariff 91, 92, 93-94
Common Customs Union 91, 92, 94
Common Market (see **European Economic Community**)
Common Organisation of Markets (see also **Common Agricultural Policy**) 192, 194, 196, 197
  absence 201-202
  bulbs and live plants 198-199
  cereals 194, 200-201, 206
  pigmeat 152, 190, 199
Communications 18, 35, 40, 99
Community Law (see also **Acts of Community Institutions**)
  acte clair 70
  autonomous 44
  decisions on and proof of in UK courts 57-59
  direct applicability 46-50
  direct effect 46-50, 51
  general application 50
  general principles 41, 42, 50
  interpretation 8, 60
  impact on criminal process (see **Criminal Process**)
  legislative process 13-15, 38-39
  nature 27, 44-51
  protection of human rights 27, 79, 203-209
  relationship with UK law 52-58
  sources 1, 32-43
  supremacy 27, 41, 45-46, 48, 50-51
Community Preference, Principle of 193, 196

Companies (See also **Freedom to Provide Services** and **Right of Establishment**) 137-139
  Convention on Mutual Competition Recognition 138
  definition 137
  Directives 138-139
Competition (see also **Abuse of Dominant Position** and **Restrictive Trade Practices**) 159-188
  agreements (see **Agreements**)
  comfort letters 176
  concerted practices 163-164
  de minimis 165, 166-167, 171, 179
  Directorate-General 159, 167, 168, 172, 176, 186
  dominant position 178-181
  dumping 161
  exemptions 171-176, 178
    block 174-175
    individual 171, 172-174, 175
  fines 75, 79, 160, 167, 168, 169-170, 172, 176, 186
  Form A/B 167, 172, 176, 186
  interim measures 187-188
  national courts 161-162, 171
  negative clearance 167, 176, 186
  parent/ subsidiary company 164, 178
  public undertakings 163
  role of
    Commission 167-169, 171, 173, 175, 187-188, 207
    Court of Justice 75, 79, 170, 187
  scope 159, 161, 164-165, 185-186
  state aids 161
  undertakings 161, 178
Congress of Europe 3
Consolidated Fund of the UK 58
Contractual Liability of EEC 84-85
COREPER 15, 38
Council of Europe 3, 203
Council of Ministers
  composition 12
  control over budget 23-24
  functions 13-15
  relationship with European Parliament 22, 23, 37, 78
  residual powers 36
  voting procedures 13-15, 39
Court of Justice (see **European Court of Justice**)
Criminal Convictions 119, 120, 154
Criminal Process, Effect of Community law 151-158, 199
  complete defence 133-134, 152-153, 158 190-191, 198, 199
  mitigation of sentence 48, 120, 154-157
  non-application 103, 109, 156-157
  source of new offence 157-158
Customs Duties (see also **Free Movement of Goods**) 92-93, 96
  measures having equivalent effect 93

Decisions (see also **Acts of Community Institutions**)
  action for inactivity 80-82
  annulment 76-77, 79, 83
  characteristics 35
  citation 41
  direct effect 48
  distinguished from Regulations 35
  publication 35, 39, 40
  reasons 36, 38
Defence of Inapplicability (see **Plea of Illegality**)
Deportation 118, 120-121, 133, 135, 154-157
Depository Libraries 24, 43
Diplomas and Certificates, Mutual Recognition of (see also **Freedom to Provide Services** and **Right of Establishment**)
  lawyers 122, 127, 130
  nurses 127
  veterinary surgeons 127
Direct Applicability 46-50
  direct effect, distinction between 46-47
  meaning 46-47
  Regulations 34, 47, 49
Direct Effect 46-50
  conditions 48
  Decisions 48
  development by ECJ 27
  direct applicability, distinction between 46-47
  Directives 35, 48, 49, 119, 130
  EEC Treaty provisions 47, 48, 51, 92, 99, 108, 119, 125, 129, 161-2, 170-1, 177
  meaning 47
  Regulations 48
Directives (see also **Acts of Community Institutions**)
  annulment 76
  characteristics 34-35
  citation 41
  companies 138-139
  direct effect 35, 48, 49, 119, 130
  freedom to provide services 129, 130
  harmonisation 34, 98, 100
  implementation within UK 54-55

liberalisation 101-102,103
publication 35, 39, 40
reasons 36, 38
right of establishment 125, 126, 127

Documentation Centres 43

Dominant Position (see also **Abuse of Dominant Position** and **Competition**) 178-181

Dumping 161

Dunkirk Treaty 3

Economic and Social Committee 30, 36, 37, 38

ECHR (see **European Convention on Human Rights**)

ECJ (see **European Court of Justice**)

ECSC (see **European Coal and Steel Community**)

EDC (see **European Defence Community**)

Education (see also **Free Movement of Workers**)
children of migrant workers 116
equal access to vocational training 114-115

EEC (see **European Economic Community**)

EEC Law (see **Community Law**)

EFTA (see **European Free Trade Association**)

Equal Treatment for Men and Women
access to employment, vocational training 34, 36, 49
equal pay 35, 51
social security 34, 36

Equality, Principle of 87, 209

Elections to European Parliament 19, 20, 80

Employees of Community Institutions
liability 85
staff cases 28, 84-85

EMS (see **European Monetary System**)

Enforcement of Member State Obligations (see **Actions against Member States**)

EURATOM (see **European Atomic Energy Community**)

European Agricultural Guidance and Guarantee Fund (FEOGA) 193-194, 195

European Assembly (see **European Parliament**)

European Atomic Energy Community (EURATOM) 1, 2, 6, 11

European Coal and Steel Community (ECSC)
activities 4, 5
history 4
institutions 4, 11

European Community Law (see **Community Law**)

European Court of Justice
advocate-general 25, 26
aids to interpretation 8, 48, 161, 185
annual synopsis of cases 27, 42
composition 25-26
costs 71
form of judgments 26
functions 27-29
judicial review 28, 36, 37, 40, 60, 61, 63, 74-88, 170
jurisdiction 28-29, 60, 74, 83, 84, 85, 170, 205
legal aid 71
precedent 27, 41, 205
preliminary rulings 27-28, 60-72
publications 26, 27, 41-42
revision of judgments 26, 27
source of Community law 41
staff cases 28, 84-85

European Convention on Human Rights (see also **Fundamental Human Rights**) 4, 12, 29, 168, 203-204, 206, 207, 208, 209

European Council 29

European Currency Unit 103, 104, 167, 170

European Defence Community 5

European Documentation Centres 24, 43

European Economic Community
activities 1, 8-9, 191
budget 23, 24
contractual liability 84-85
Commission 15-19
Council of Ministers 12-15
Economic and Social Committee 30
European Council 29
European Court of Justice 25-29
European Parliament (Assembly) 19-24
history 5-7
non-contractual liability 85-88
own resources 23-24
task 8

European Free Trade Association (EFTA) 6, 92

European Monetary System (See also **Free Movement of Capital**) 103-104, 195

European Parliament
Bureau 21, 37
composition 19-22, 30-31
control over budget 23-24
consultation on legislation 22, 37, 38
elections 19, 20, 80
functions 22-24
location 20-21

motions of censure 24
political groups 21
specialised committees 21, 22, 38, 42
Exclusive Dealing Agreements 175
Exclusive Distribution Agreements 175, Appendix V1
Exclusive Purchasing Agreements 175, Appendix VII

Failure to Act (see **Action for Inactivity**)
FEOGA (see European Agricultural Guidance and Guarantee Fund)
Financial Resources of the Community (see **Budget of the European Community**)
Free Movement of Capital 101-104
Free Movement of Goods 90-100
agricultural products 191, 195, 199, 201-202
arbitrary discrimination 95, 96, 97
Common Customs Tariff 91, 92, 93-94
Community Customs Union 91, 92, 93
customs duties 92-93, 96
derogations 95-100, 153
protection of health or life of animals 95, 97, 98
public morality 94, 96
public policy 96, 97, 104, 153
public security 97, 153
direct effect 92, 99
disguised restriction on trade 95, 96, 97
goods 91-92, 104
import licences 95, 97, 98
internal taxation 100
marketing restrictions 98
measures having equivalent effect
customs duties 93
quantitative restrictions 95, 98-99
non-tariff barriers 98-100
quantitative restrictions 94, 95, 96, 97, 104, 153
timetable for abolition 93
Free Movement of Payments (see also **Free Movement of Capital**) 104-105
Free Movement of Self-Employed Persons (see also **Right of Establishment** and **Freedom to provide Services**) 122-139
Free Movement of Workers 106-121
access to vocational training 114-115
deportation 118, 120-121
direct effect 108, 119
entry formalities 111
equality of treatment 113-116
housing 107, 115
limitations 117-121, 154
public health 118, 121
public policy 118, 119, 120, 154-155
public security 118, 119, 156-157
public service 114, 117-118
members of family 110, 111, 115-116, 117
non-discrimination on grounds of nationality 108, 113, 114
persons seeking work 112, 133, 141, 149
residence permit 111, 112, 113, 155
right of entry 110
right of residence 111
right to remain 116-117
social security entitlement 107, 112, 141-150
social and tax advantages 107, 114, 148
terms and conditions of employment 113-114
trade union rights 107, 206
wholly internal situation 108-109, 156-157
work permits 110
Freedom of Establishment (see **Right of Establishment**)
Freedom to Provide Services (see also **Right of Establishment**) 122-129
companies 137-139
definition 123-124, 128
deportation 133, 135
direct effect 129
General Programme 128-129
lawyers 127, 130-131
limitations 132, 135-137, 154
official authority 136-137
public health 132, 135
public policy 132, 133, 135, 136
public security 132, 135
mutual recognition of diplomas etc 122, 127, 130
right of abode 133
right of entry 132
right to remain 134
social security entitlement 134, 144, 145
wholly internal situation 126-127
Frontier Workers 112
Fundamental Freedoms of the EEC (see also **Free Movement of Capital, Free Movement of Goods, Free Movement of Payments, Free Movement of Workers, Freedom to Provide Services** and **Right of Establishment**) 90
Fundamental Human Rights (see also **European Convention on Human Rights**)
accession to ECHR by European Communities 208-209
Council of Europe 3, 203

influence of ECHR 206-207, 208, 209
Joint Declaration 209
protection by Community law 27, 41, 79, 203-209

General Principles of Community Law (see also **Community Law**) 41, 42, 50, 78
audi alteram partem 42, 209
equality 87, 209
legal certainty 42
natural justice 42
non-discrimination 100, 113, 114, 125, 153, 209
nulla poena sine lege 42, 209
proportionality 42, 155, 156, 183, 209
protection of human rights 41, 205, 209
General Programme
freedom to provide services 128-129
right of establishment 124-125
Goods (see also **Free Movement of Goods**) 91-92, 104
"Green" Currencies 195

Haagerup Report 22
Harmonisation 34, 98, 100
High Authority 4, 11
Historical Development 1-7
ECSC 4
EEC 5-7
EURATOM 5-6
House of Lords 94, 95, 177, 209
Housing 107, 115
Human Rights (see **Fundamental Human Rights**)

Import Licences (see also **Free Movement of Goods**) 95, 97, 98
Information Offices
Commission 43
Court of Justice 27, 42
Information Retrieval 43
Institutions of the Community (see also **Commission, Council of Ministers, European Court of Justice, Economic and Social Committee, European Council** and **European Parliament**) 11-31
Interim Measures
Commission 174, 187-188
Ireland, Republic of
accession 1, 6, 7
Commissioner 16
Council Voting 14
EMS 103-104, 195
lawyers 131
MEPs 20
non-NATO 3
taxation 200-201
Internal Taxation 100
International Law 28, 44
Intervention Agencies 194, 195

Judicial Review (see also **Action for Annulment, Action for Damages, Action for Inactivity, Defence of Inapplicability, Liability of the Community, Preliminary Rulings** and **Review of Fines**) 74-89

Legal Aid 71
Legal Certainty, Principle of 42
Legal Personality of EEC 15, 208
Legal Privilege
competition cases 168-169
Legal Profession
freedom to provide services 122, 127-128, 130-131, 136-137
mutual recognition of qualifications 127, 131
right of establishment 127, 131, 136-137
Legal Tender 91, 104
Legislation (see **Acts of Community Institutions**)
Liability of the Community (see also **Contractual Liability** and **Non-Contractual Liability**) 83-88
Locus Standi
action for annulment 36, 76-77
action for inactivity 80-81
non-contractual liability 85
Luxembourg Accords 14, 15, 39

Management Committees 196
Mansholt Plan 193
Marshall Plan 2
Means of Payment (see also **Free Movement of Payments**) 92
Measures of the Community Insitutions (see **Acts of Community Institutions**)
Measures Having Equivalent Effect (see also **Free Movement of Goods**)
customs duties 93
quantitative restrictions 95, 98-99
Members of the Family
definition
migrant workers 100
self-employed 132
education 116
entry 110, 116
employment 115-116
right to remain 117
right of residence 110, 111

Mergers (see also **Abuse of Dominant Position**) 180, 182
Migrant Community Workers (see **Free Movement of Workers**)
Monetary Compensatory Amounts 189, 195

National Courts and Tribunals
preliminary references,
definition of 64-65
discretion to refer 67-70
duty to refer 68-70
role in
competition cases 161-162, 171
contractual liability of EEC 84
non-contractual liability of EEC 86-88
National Market Organisations (see **Common Agricultural Policy**)
NATO (see **North Atlantic Treaty Organisation**)
Negative Clearance (see also **Competition**) 167, 176, 186
Non-contractual Liability of EEC 85-88
apportionment of liability 88
concurrent liability 88
conditions 86
damages 87-88
jurisdiction of Court of Justice 85, 86
locus standi 85
time limits 85-86
Non-discrimination, Principle of 100, 113, 114, 125, 153, 209
North Atlantic Treaty Organisation (NATO) 3
Non-tariff Barriers (see also **Free Movement of Goods**) 98-100
Northern Ireland
agriculture 189-190, 194, 195
companies 138
elections to European Parliament 20
Haagerup Report 22
MEPs 20
poultry imports 97-98
social security 145-150
Notices 18, 35, 164, 166-167, 175, 176
Notification (See also **Competition**) 167, 172
***Nulla poena sine lege,* principle of** 42, 209
OECD (see **Organisation for Economic Co-operation and Development**)
OEEC (see **Organisation for European Economic Co-operation**)
Official Journal 38, 40, 78
judicial notice of, by UK courts 57, 59
sections
C 18, 24, 30, 35, 39-40, 176
L 19, 34, 35, 39-40, 127, 130, 194, 201
S 40
Special Edition 40
Opinions 17, 18, 22, 33, 35, 37, 38, 75, 78, 80
Organisation for European Co-operation and Development (OECD) 3
Organisation for European Economic Co-operation (OEEC) 3

Payments (see also **Free Movement of Payments**) 92, 104
Plea of Illegality (or **Defence of Inapplicability**) 82-83
consequences 83
grounds 82
procedure 82-83
Pleven Plan 5
Preliminary rulings
acte clair 70
aim 61-62, 86-87
costs 71
development of Community law 27, 62
effect 71-72
jurisdiction of ECJ 27-28, 61
legal aid, availability of 71
national courts 64-65
discretion to refer 67-70
duty to refer 68-70
procedure 70-71
questions 63-64
timing 65-67
Publications 42-43
Proportionality, Principle of 42, 155, 156, 183, 209
Protection of Human Rights (see **Fundamental Human Rights**)
Protection of Health of Humans or Animals
exception, on ground of free movement of goods 95, 97, 98
Public Health
exception on ground of
free movement of workers 118, 121
freedom to provide services 132, 135
right of establishment 132, 135
Public morality
exception, on ground of
free movement of goods 94, 96
Public Policy
exception on ground of
free movement of goods 96, 97, 104

free movement of workers 118, 119, 120, 154, 155
freedom to provide services 132, 133, 135, 136
right of establishment 132, 133, 135, 136
Public Security
exception, on ground of
free movement of goods 97
free movement of workers 118, 119, 156-157
freedom to provide services 132, 135
right of establishment 132, 135
Public Service
exception, on ground of
free movement of workers 114, 117-118
Public Undertakings 163

Quantitative Restrictions (see also **Free Movement of Goods**) 94, 95, 96, 97, 104, 153
measures having equivalent effect 95, 98-99

Reasoned Opinion (see **Commission**)
Reasoned Submission (see **Advocate-General**)
Recommendations (see also **Acts of Community Institutions**) 18, 33, 35, 75, 80
Regional Policy 23
Regulations (see also **Acts of Community Institutions**)
agriculture 190, 196-197
annulment 22, 28, 29, 37, 76, 79
characteristics 34, 35
citation 40
direct application 34, 47, 49, 50
directly effective 48, 49
inapplicable 82-83
publication 34, 35, 40
reasons 36, 38
tachograph 33, 47, 49, 151, 157, 158
uniformity 50
Republic of Ireland (see **Ireland, Republic of**)
Residence Permit 111, 112, 113, 133, 155
Resolutions (see **Acts of Community Institutions**)
Restrictive Trade Practices
agreements (see also **Agreements**) 163-164
associations of undertakings 163
comfort letters 176
concerted practices 163-164
de minimis 165, 166-167
decisions of associations 163, 165
direct effect 161-162, 170-171
effect on competition 165-167
exemptions 171-176
block 174-175
individual 171, 172-174, 175
fines 167, 168, 169-170, 172, 176
Form A/B 167, 172, 176
interim measures 174
negative clearance 167, 176
notification 167, 172
nullity 170-171, 174
role of
Commission 167-169, 171, 173, 174, 175, 187, 188
Court of Justice 75, 79, 170, 187
scope 159, 164-165
severance 171
state aids 161
undertakings 163
Right of Establishment (see also **Freedom to Provide Services**) 124-128, 131, 139
companies 137-139
definition 123-124
deporatation 133, 135
direct effect 125
General Programme 124-125
limitations 132, 135-137, 154
official authority 136-137
public health 132, 135
public policy 132, 133, 135, 136
public security 132, 135
members of family 132, 134
mutual recognition of diplomas etc 125, 126, 127
right of entry 132
right of residence 132-133
right to remain 134
residence permits 133
social security entitlement 134, 144-145
wholly internal situation 126-127

Schuman Plan 4
Secondary Community Law (see **Acts of Community Institutions**)
Seasonal Workers 112-113
Social Assistance (see also **Social Security**) 146-148
Social Policy 23
Social and Tax Advantages for Migrant Workers 107, 114, 148
Social Security 140-150
aggregation, principle of 141, 142, 143, 148-149

social assistance 146-148
social security 146-148
unemployment benefits 148-149
Spaak Committee 5
Staff Cases 28, 84, 85
State Aids 161
Supplementary Benefits (see also **Social Security**) 146-148

Taxation 100, 200-201
Trade (see **Free Movement of Goods**)

United Kingdom
accession 1, 6-7
advocate-general 25
Commissioners 15-16
companies 138
ECJ judge 25
EMS 103-4, 195
documentation centres 43
elections to European Parliament 19, 20
human rights 203-205, 207, 208-209
Lawyers Services Directive 130-131
referendum 7
relationship with Community law 52-58
social security 146-150
taxation 100

Vocational Training (see also **Free Movement of Workers** and **Equal Treatment for Men and Women**) 34, 36, 49, 114-115

Western European Union (WEU) 5
Work Permits (see also **Free Movement of Workers**) 110